MUSIC IN KENYAN CHRISTIANITY

Ethnomusicology Multimedia

Ethnomusicology Multimedia (EM) is a collaborative publishing program, developed with funding from the Andrew W. Mellon Foundation, to identify and publish first books in ethnomusicology, accompanied by supplemental audiovisual materials online at www.ethnomultimedia.org

A collaboration of the presses at Indiana, Kent State, and Temple universities, EM is an innovative, entrepreneurial, and cooperative effort to expand publishing opportunities for emerging scholars in ethnomusicology and to increase audience reach by using common resources available to the three presses through support from the Andrew W. Mellon Foundation. Each press acquires and develops EM books according to its own profile and editorial criteria.

EM's most innovative features are its dual web-based components, the first of which is a password-protected Annotation Management System (AMS) where authors can upload peer-reviewed audio, video, and static image content for editing and annotation and key the selections to corresponding references in their texts. Second is a public site for viewing the web content, www.ethnomultimedia.org, with links to publishers' websites for information about the accompanying books. The AMS and website were designed and built by the Institute for Digital Arts and Humanities at Indiana University. The Indiana University Digital Library Program (DLP) hosts the website and the Indiana University Archives of Traditional Music (ATM) provides archiving and preservation services for the EM online content.

MUSIC IN KENYAN CHRISTIANITY

LOGOOLI RELIGIOUS SONG

Jean Ngoya Kidula

INDIANA UNIVERSITY PRESS
Bloomington and Indianapolis

Indiana University Press
Office of Scholarly Publishing
Herman B Wells Library 350
1320 East 10th Street
Bloomington, Indiana 47405 USA

iupress.indiana.edu

Telephone orders   800-842-6796
Fax orders   812-855-7931

© 2013 by Jean Ngoya Kidula
All rights reserved

No part of this book may be reproduced or utilized in any form or by any means, electronic or mechanical, including photocopying and recording, or by any information storage and retrieval system, without permission in writing from the publisher. The Association of American University Presses' Resolution on Permissions constitutes the only exception to this prohibition.

∞ The paper used in this publication meets the minimum requirements of the American National Standard for Information Sciences—Permanence of Paper for Printed Library Materials, ANSI Z39.48-1992.

Manufactured in the United States of America

Library of Congress Cataloging-in-Publication Data

Kidula, Jean Ngoya.
  Music in Kenyan Christianity : Logooli religious song / Jean Ngoya Kidula.
    pages ; cm. — (Ethnomusicology multimedia)
  Includes bibliographical references and index.
ISBN 978-0-253-00667-7 (cloth : alkaline paper) — ISBN 978-0-253-00668-4 (paperback : alkaline paper) — ISBN 978-0-253-00702-5 (ebook)
1. Church music—Kenya. 2. Logooli (African people)—Music—History and criticism.
3. Songs, Logooli—History and criticism—20th century. I. Title. II. Series: Ethnomusicology multimedia.

ML2951.K455 K53   2013
782.25096762—dc23   2012036069

1 2 3 4 5 18 17 16 15 14 13

WITH MUCH GRATITUDE TO MY PARENTS,
WHO AGAINST ALL ODDS ALLOWED ME TO BE

Mark Edwin Kidula (1926–1993) and Emmy Angose

Until then, my heart will go on singing with joy.

CONTENTS

PREFACE *xi*

ACKNOWLEDGMENTS *xvii*

NOTE ON SPELLING AND ORTHOGRAPHY *xxi*

LIST OF ABBREVIATIONS *xxiii*

1 Prelude   1
2 Assembly: Logooli Historical, Cultural, and Musical Background   14
3 Encounter: Avalogooli and Euro-American Religion, Culture, and Music   37
4 Consolidation: Christian Religious Genres in Logooli-Land   71
5 Accommodation: Logooli Adoption and Use of 'Book' Music   96
6 Syncretism: Logooli Christian Songs of the Spirit   153
7 Invocation: Logooli Christian Songs in Contemporary Education and Media   183
8 Epilogue   228

APPENDIX 1. Archival and Media House Records   235

APPENDIX 2. Song Text and Hymn Tune Sources   239

GLOSSARY OF TERMS   243

NOTES   249

BIBLIOGRAPHY   267

INDEX   281

PREFACE

Each of the audio, video, or still image media examples listed below is associated with specific passages in this book, and each example has been assigned a unique persistent uniform resource identifier, or PURL. The PURL points to the location of a specific audio, video, or still image media example on the Ethnomusicology Multimedia website, www.ethnomultimedia.org. Within the running text of the book, a "PURL number" in parentheses functions like a citation and immediately follows the text to which it refers, for example, (PURL 3.1). The numbers following the word "PURL" relate to the chapter in which the media example is found and the number of PURLs contained in that chapter. For example, PURL 3.1 refers to the first media example found in chapter 3, PURL 3.2 refers to the second media example found in chapter 3, and so on.

There are two ways to access and play back a specific audio, video, or still image media example. When readers enter into a web browser the full address of the PURL associated with a specific media example, they will be taken to a web page containing that media example as well as a playlist of all of the media examples related to this book. Information about the book and the author is also available through this web page. Once readers have navigated to the Ethnomusicology Multimedia website they may also access media examples by entering into the "Media Segment ID" search field the unique six-digit PURL identifier located at the end of the full PURL address. Readers will be required to electronically sign an end-user license agreement the first time they attempt to access a media example on the Ethnomusicology Multimedia project website.

CHAPTER 1

PURL 1.1 | Women of Goibei PAG church, "Vali no vugasu" (Blessed are they)
http://purl.dlib.indiana.edu/idl/em/Kidula/910190

CHAPTER 2

PURL 2.1 | Jean Kidula, "Si walinda ndeya" (You did not wait for me to clean up the house)
http://purl.dlib.indiana.edu/iudl/em/Kidula/910183
PURL 2.2 | Jean Kidula, "Lelo kunyoye idimbidi" (We have now acquired one who is deaf and dumb)
http://purl.dlib.indiana.edu/iudl/em/Kidula/910184
PURL 2.3 | Jean Kidula, "Long'oli."
http://purl.dlib.indiana.edu/iudl/em/Kidula/910186
PURL 2.4 | Jean Kidula, "Tula ichova" (Come on out)
http://purl.dlib.indiana.edu/iudl/em/Kidula/910187
PURL 2.5 | Jean Kidula, "Lufweye kulanga baba" (Calling him dad is over).
http://purl.dlib.indiana.edu/iudl/em/Kidula/910204
PURL 2.6 | Jean Kidula, "Mwilwadze kuli Petero Yilwadza" (Preach as Peter did)
http://purl.dlib.indiana.edu/iudl/em/Kidula/910179

CHAPTER 3

PURL 3.1 | Women of Goibei PAG church, "Kwenya kulola vamuyanza" (We want to see those who love the [person])
http://purl.dlib.indiana.edu/iudl/em/Kidula/910188
PURL 3.2 | Jean Kidula, "Sisi was Goibei" (We, of Goibei)
http://purl.dlib.indiana.edu/iudl/em/Kidula/910170
PURL 3.3 | Jean Kidula, "Kwinye vaana va Goibei"(We, the children of Goibei)
http://purl.dlib.indiana.edu/iudl/em/Kidula/910185
PURL 3.4 | Jean Kidula, "Elori" (A lorry)
http://purl.dlib.indiana.edu/iudl/em/Kidula/910169
PURL 3.5 | Focus group of Goibei Women, Set beginning with "Mulikhayira yambonyia" (He lifted me up)
http://purl.dlib.indiana.edu/iudl/em/Kidula/910181

PREFACE   xiii

CHAPTER 4

PURL 4.1 | Focus group of Goibei Women, "Ni ngusaalilanga" (While I am praying for you)
http://purl.dlib.indiana.edu/iudl/em/Kidula/910174
PURL 4.2 | Jean Kidula, "A tonde."
http://purl.dlib.indiana.edu/iudl/em/Kidula/910168

CHAPTER 5

PURL 5.1 | Women of Goibei PAG church, "Kale mmadiku yago" (In those long ago days)
http://purl.dlib.indiana.edu/iudl/em/Kidula/910167
PURL 5.2 | Focus group of Goibei Women, "Yesu oveye lwanda" (Jesus you are a rock)
http://purl.dlib.indiana.edu/iudl/em/Kidula/910166
PURL 5.3 | Focus group of Goibei Women, "Njereranga" (I am returning [home])
http://purl.dlib.indiana.edu/iudl/em/Kidula/910202
PURL 5.4 | Focus group of Goibei Women, "Lwa inze ndola" (When I see/survey)
http://purl.dlib.indiana.edu/iudl/em/Kidula/910165
PURL 5.5 | Women of Goibei PAG church, "O Yesu nguyanza" (Oh Jesus, I love you)
http://purl.dlib.indiana.edu/iudl/em/Kidula/910164
PURL 5.6 | Visukulu va Zakayo, "Si gali masahi" (It was not the blood of beasts) and "O Yesu nguyanza" (Oh Jesus I love you)
http://purl.dlib.indiana.edu/iudl/em/Kidula/910163
PURL 5.7 | Focus group of Goibei Women, "Lwa avayi vali ni valinda" (While shepherds watched)
http://purl.dlib.indiana.edu/iudl/em/Kidula/910173
PURL 5.8 | Jean Kidula, "Mu mugera gwe liluva" (In the fishing river)
http://purl.dlib.indiana.edu/iudl/em/Kidula/910172
PURL 5.9 | Women of Goibei PAG Church, "Mukonyi ali himbi" (The great physician)
http://purl.dlib.indiana.edu/iudl/em/Kidula/910203

PURL 5.10 | Focus group of Goibei Women, "Ya kudzera" (He died [The solid rock])
http://purl.dlib.indiana.edu/iudl/em/Kidula/910201
PURL 5.11 | Avisukulu va Zakayo Imbukule, "Kwake Yesu" (On Jesus [The solid rock])
http://purl.dlib.indiana.edu/iudl/em/Kidula/910200
PURL 5.12 | Quaker women's group, "Ndilonda ku inzila" (I will take the road)
http://purl.dlib.indiana.edu/iudl/em/Kidula/910182

CHAPTER 6

PURL 6.1 | Focus group of Goibei Women, "Ligulu lili ihale" (The heavens are yonder)
http://purl.dlib.indiana.edu/iudl/em/Kidula/910199
PURL 6.2 | Jean Kidula, "Ingata yange ufwale" (Vest me with my crown)
http://purl.dlib.indiana.edu/iudl/em/Kidula/910198
PURL 6.3 | Focus group of Goibei Women, "Kidaho kyo mwigulu" (The river of heaven)
http://purl.dlib.indiana.edu/iudl/em/Kidula/910197
PURL 6.4 | Focus group of Goibei Women, Song set beginning with "Yesu yasaala" (Jesus prayed)
http://purl.dlib.indiana.edu/iudl/em/Kidula/910176

CHAPTER 7

PURL 7.1 | Kariokor Friends Choir, "Gendi kwilwadze" (Let us preach)
http://purl.dlib.indiana.edu/iudl/em/Kidula/910196
PURL 7.2 | Kariokor Friends Choir, "Valimu vayuda" (Traitors are in [our] midst)
http://purl.dlib.indiana.edu/iudl/em/Kidula/910171
PURL 7.3 | Kariokor Friends Choir, "Lisuvira, Kwinye kogende" (Faith, let us walk)
http://purl.dlib.indiana.edu/iudl/em/Kidula/910195
PURL 7.4 | Focus group of Goibei women, "Musalaba" (The cross)
http://purl.dlib.indiana.edu/iudl/em/Kidula/910194

PURL 7.5 | Kenyatta University Choir, "Musalaba." (Kemoli Arrangement) (The cross)
http://purl.dlib.indiana.edu/iudl/em/Kidula/910193
PURL 7.6 | Francis and Keren Illavadza, "Ulivolela." (1992 version) (What will you say)
http://purl.dlib.indiana.edu/iudl/em/Kidula/910192
PURL 7.7 | Francis and Keren Illavadza, "Ulivolela." (2008 version) (What will you say)
http://purl.dlib.indiana.edu/iudl/em/Kidula/910191

CHAPTER 8

PURL 8.1 | Focus group of Goibei Women, Women introduce themselves and sing set beginning with "Valoji valalila" (Sorcerers will cry)
http://purl.dlib.indiana.edu/iudl/em/Kidula/910175
PURL 8.2 | Focus group of Goibei Women, Set featuring "Heri Kuwa na Yesu"
http://purl.dlib.indiana.edu/iudl/em/Kidula/910180

ACKNOWLEDGMENTS

When I first began this project in 1983, I collected Christian songs from women in Goibei village in Western Kenya for ear training, sight-reading, and music theory exercises at Kenyatta University College. In 1986, the research resulted in a musicological treatise on Arthur Kemoli's invocation of Logooli melodies for academic and civic discourse. That work at East Carolina University, funded by the International Student Exchange Program, was supervised by Dr. Otto Henry. In the 1990s, the investigation included Logooli musicians I interviewed as part of my PhD document of religious popular music in Kenya. I studied at the University of California, Los Angeles, on a Fulbright Fellowship.

I am hugely indebted to many people for their encouragement, support, and assistance. My teacher (since high school), friend, and mentor Luzili Mulindi-King not only documented one of the first studies on Logooli music; she has consistently availed resources and insights. Her work investigates places in Maragoli, Nairobi, and among Quakers that I did not access. I gained further insights from Dr. Julie Ojango and her mother, who is a Quaker pastor. Mary Oyer, my teacher, senior mentor, and friend, started me on the journey to transcribe African repertoire as a resource for teaching theory and composition. She encouraged me to initiate music education by drawing on resources familiar to students. This work is an outgrowth of that counsel. Dr. Jacqueline Djedje has mentored, challenged, and encouraged my scholarly growth. Most significantly, my friend Maud Andersson has provided spiritual, academic, and financial support throughout the course of this project.

In 1986 and from 1995–2011, I interviewed Dr. Arthur Kemoli and other known Logooli musicians such as Gideon Mwelesa, Francis Ilavadza, and Reuben Kigame for this and related projects. Mwelesa and Kemoli, older and well-respected personalities, 'tested' me before 'permitting' me into their creative minds. Dr. Kemoli and his wife, Patroba (who edited some of the Lulogooli texts), granted me interviews, conversations, and discussions from 1986 to 2011. They also shared handwritten music score copies and unpublished recordings. I encountered Kemoli and performed his arrangements as an undergraduate at Kenyatta University from 1978 to 1981. Kemoli has since then shared his knowledge, expertise, and experiences as a master musician. His pieces analyzed in this manuscript are from his private collection. Sadly, Dr. Kemoli passed away in September 2012 while this work was in press. He will be sorely missed.

Many thanks to Gideon Mwelesa for interviews in 2005, 2007, and 2011. He is an amazing repository of cultural, social, and political knowledge of Avalogooli. Special thanks also to Francis Jumba Ilavadza for interviews in 1995 and 2011, and for his 'popular' cassette recordings of Logooli spirit songs. Reuben and Mercy Kigame and Douglas and Gladys Jiveti granted me interviews in 1995. The encounters led to ongoing collaborative work. Mercy passed away in 2006, but her input was invaluable.

Women from Goibei village have nurtured and performed for and with me with patience and humor over the years. Of special mention are veterans (over 75 years old) Hanah Ivayo, Dorah Monyi, Ezina Vita, and Sarah Begisen (died 2006) and the mature ones like Eside Kidake (died 2011), Agnetta Sikina, Jane Muhonja Likomba, Rose Luganiro Mugatsia, Violet Kenyani, and Jessica Kihung'ani (died 2006).

Marylyn Stroud of the Pentecostal Assemblies of Canada (PAOC) Archives in Mississauga, Ontario, graciously allowed archival access to letters and reports of missionary work in Kenya from the 1920s to the 1970s. I have also benefited from the archives at Swarthmore College that house Deborah Rees's original correspondence on Quaker work in Maragoli from 1904 to the early 1920s. The Friends archival holdings at Guilford College, Earlham College's holdings of Quaker involvement in Kenya, and Haverford College provided additional materials. I thank the librarians, curators, and archivists: Christopher Densmore, Gwen Erickson, Thomas Hamm, and Ann Upton.

Iris Scheel, a Canadian missionary, lived in Goibei village from 1954 to 2005. Before returning to Canada, she graciously provided some photo slides of her work. Through them, I glimpsed Goibei and Avalogooli through the missionary lens. Her view corroborates or contrast with other Kenyan and missionary narratives and memoirs. For other figures/photos, texts, and music, permission was granted by Dr. Kemoli, Mr. Mwelesa, Mr. and Mrs Ilavadza, and Evangel Publishing House editor Paul Kimani.

I am indebted to my siblings, Peter, Bilha, Roselyn, Iris, Nancy, James, John, and Charles. They helped to gather data, connected dots, and provided insights. My cousins Mmbone, Inyangala, Katumika, and Mwandihi also refreshed my cultural memory.

I am most grateful to my parents, Mark Kidula (1926–1993) and Emmy Angose, who worked in administration and music with the Pentecostal Assemblies of God (PAG) at all levels, from children to youth work to central government. They interviewed their fellow Pentecostal and Quaker administrators and provided data from church records for my initial research until my father passed away. My mother has continued to provide insights and support. She most recently facilitated the 2007 and 2011 encounters with Gideon Mwelesa.

I am also grateful for the input of several readers. Lois Anderson and Mellonee Burnim provided invaluable insights to the text. My colleagues David Schiller, Helen Rees, Kevin Kelly, and Susan Thomas, as well as my student Elizabeth Ozment, provided insightful comments.

I owe a great debt of gratitude to professor Ruth Stone, who encouraged me in more ways than she knows. Special thanks also to Dee Mortensen of Indiana University Press for not just great help but the positive energy that emanated from her. In addition, I thank Angela Burton, Mollie K. Ables, Sarah Jacobi, and others at the press for their input and encouragement during this book process.

An undertaking of this sort has its challenges and moments of reflexivity. The kinetics of cultural politics and beliefs has to be consciously navigated. As a female Mlogooli, I really should not be so interested in things Logooli, as I could very easily 'become' some other culture through marriage. I was cautioned by one of the people I interviewed about this position. The man then justified me by noting that regardless of my possible defection, I am Mlogooli by birth and therefore by heritage. At another time during casual conversation with a Logooli musician and church leader, I was questioned about this type of documentation of Logooli history. Logooli have other ways of re-enacting and reinvigorating history—whether through rites and rituals, through naming, or through other visual or audio media. Translating this history into a different medium constitutes challenging 'indigenous' repositories of knowledge and is an undesirable legacy of Euro-American education and systems of thought. I argued that I was not merely working on Logooli historical fact but on dynamic cultural and musical heritage, both of which were invoked and reworked regularly in rites of passage and were 'different' from traditional static historiographies. I also contended with the fact that lack of documentation in contemporary society tended to lead to marginalization as well as social, political, and cultural disempowerment. So I wrote.

Translations from Lulogooli to English or Kiswahili, and from Kiswahili or English to Lulogooli are by the author unless otherwise indicated. I apologize for any inadequate translations. However, I hope the translations enable multiple readings of the rich text provided by singers, poets, and other interpreters. The music transcriptions are all mine unless otherwise indicated. In 'folk' situations, several versions, variations, and readings of a given tune or text may exist. I transcribed the versions I was either most familiar with or those from the private collections and public records that I was able to access.

NOTE ON SPELLING AND ORTHOGRAPHY

All vowels in Lulogooli are pure, pronounced as in Latin vowels. With diphthongs, the affected vowels are spelled out. Some consonants have various spellings related to tongue and teeth placement. For example, "z" is spelled as "z," "dz," or "ts." The spelling for a lapped "l" is either "l" or "r." These spellings are ignored when I directly quote poems from hymnals. I tried to leave the spelling of the poetry as intact as possible. Thus the word for peace is spelled "mirembe" or "milembe" depending on the hymnal source. "G" is pronounced either soft—close to a "j"—or hard—as in the English word "give." In most cases, if it is followed by an "i" it will be soft. An apostrophe after a "g" indicates that it is nasalized as in the English word "sing."

ABBREVIATIONS

ADC: African Divine Church
AFBFM: American Friends Board of Foreign Missions
AIC: African Inland Church
AICN: African Israel Church Nineveh
C.A.: Christ's Ambassadors
CMS: Church Missionary Society
FAIM: Friends Africa Industrial Mission
FAM: Friends African Mission
GB: Golden Bells (hymnal)
KNA: Kenya National Archives
NZI: Nyimbo za Injili (hymnal)
OAU: Organization of African Unity
PAG: Pentecostal Assemblies of God
PAOC: Pentecostal Assemblies of Canada
RS: Redemption Songs (hymnal)
SATB: soprano, alto, tenor, bass
SSS: Sunday School Songs (hymnal)
TH: Tabernacle Hymns (hymnal)
TTN: Tsinyimbu tsya Nyasaye (hymnal)

MUSIC IN KENYAN CHRISTIANITY

ONE

PRELUDE

Music and religion are both incarnational processes and archival resources. As processes, they narrate themselves in lived experiences as dynamic forms; as resources, they inscribe, crystallize, and document social identity. Starting in the nineteenth century, music practices in Africa have been transformed by contact with modern Christianity. These practices are as diverse as the religious, ethnic, and national groups found in Africa. The individuality of the musics might be concealed under a historical association arising from an overarching 'Christian' umbrella. However, the varieties of Christianity and African ethnic groups underscore distinctive musical identities. These musics have struggled for recognition in music studies given that European church music is, and was, recognized as a category of European art and folk music, whereas African church musics neither fit indigenous molds nor gained acceptance in the canon of European church, popular, or art musics. Nonetheless, the musics are vibrant religious, artistic, and popular expressions on the continent and in other spaces.

Musics of African Christianity have historically garnered a variety of responses from different interested parties. Some missionaries questioned the legitimacy of an African Christian music and banned its use in public arenas;[1] others advocated for Africanizing Western songs.[2] Several promoted the idea of an African-style church music to mitigate the foreignness of Western hymns,[3] leading to compositions in African forms.[4] Researchers commented on the appropriation of Euro-American hymn styles[5] and on the use of indigenous music among independent Africanist church groups.[6] Meanwhile, different musics embracing African concepts, traits, and aesthetics have adjudicated the continent's identity starting in the nineteenth century and to date.

At the same time, religious, historical, and anthropological studies in and of Africa recognized the indigenization of European hymns and songs and the creation of afro-centric repertoire that essentially presenced an 'African Christianity.' Research in these disciplines had little musicological analysis, although music's enormous role was implied or described.[7] Meantime, musicologists and ethnomusicologists were slow to acknowledge a Christian music considered indigenous African, different from that of the missionary or the American (European or African American). The African music academy was also so overpowered by European ideologies that it had few avenues to display African works on the world stage. In addition there were concerns in the appropriate disciplines about what constitutes African music, who should study it, and how it should be (re)presented outside the continent.

Given the (post)colonial and denigrating readings of Christianity in Africa, there was little academic tolerance of Christian musics as bona fide African expressions. Meanwhile, Christian musics were many and diverse. Some had become African traditions and were practiced by different groups as indigenous to their understanding, practice, and interpretation of Christianity.[8] Others had grown out of grassroots Christian movements in Africa. The route to dissect indigenous African Christian musics began to be justified when studies in popular music recognized and analyzed African continental forms[9] and due to interest in the work of music in identity construction.[10] Missionaries and missiologists also documented African Christians' musical expressions and promoted these processes in Christian communication.[11] Such interests helped to legitimize studies of Christian popular music in the African urban or urbanizing space.[12] Since then, an explosive interest has developed in Christian musics as a historical, current, and indigenous continental African practice.

This text therefore sets out to explore contemporary African music through one ethnic group's engagement of Christianity as a unifying ideology in the historical tide of modernity, nationalism, and globalization. The group, Avalogooli, mostly located in Kenya, was evangelized from the early 1900s. As with other colonized or marginalized cultures, Avalogooli learned Eurogenic musics to express their adoption of Christianity processed through a European hermeneutic. They also summoned indigenous musical resources to articulate their understanding and interpretation of biblical Christianity. Avalogooli therefore adopted, appropriated, and developed Euro-American hymn and gospel traditions. They also embraced and composed 'songs of the spirit' birthed in the religious movements of the late nineteenth century in North America and the twentieth century in Africa for theological and musical agency. The dynamic outcome is a compound historical and contemporary repertoire that is at once local, national, and global.

From the 1920s, Christianization and colonialism led to a reconfiguration of Logooli political identity amidst the superstructures of the emerging Kenyan nation. By the 1940s, Christianity had been integrated into local worldviews. In the 1960s, it became a vehicle for national assimilation and distinction. Since then, local, national, pan-African, and global processes have continued to reconstitute the layer of ancient, revised, novel, and contemporary music practices. Therefore, a study of the Avalogooli's historical and current invocation of Christian song may offer some understanding of the intricate dynamics of modern Africa's religious activities and also explicate the agency of music in the formation of contemporary identity.

AVALOGOOLI

Avalogooli (sing. mulogooli) are classified under the broad linguistic group known as Abaluyia,[13] a Bantu people found in many parts of Eastern, Central, and Southern Africa. The prefix *aba/ava* means 'people of,' 'descendants of,' or 'belonging to.' Thus Abaluyia are people of Luyia descent or Luyia lineage. The root 'Luyia' without the prefix is also an index for the group. Abaluyia are further identified as a set of language groups with cultural similarities, living in contiguity with each other, resident mostly north of Lake Victoria in Kenya. These subgroups include, among others, the Bukusu (Avabukusu), Idakho (Avidakho), Tsotso (Avatsotso), Isukha (Avisukha), Tiriki (Avadirichi), and Logooli (Avalogooli). Abaluyia generally adhere to similar customs, varied due to migratory paths and contact with non-Abaluyia. Abaluyia's neighbors are the non-Bantu Luo, Teso, and Kalenjin groups and Elgoń Maasai (see fig. 1.1). To distinguish them from other lacustrine ethnic groups, the British colonial government initially referred to Abaluyia as the Bantu of North Kavirondo, Kavirondo being the name given to the Lake Victoria region (Wagner 1949, 3). Avalogooli reside at the southernmost part of Luyia land, known as Ivulogooli. Their immediate Luyia neighbors are Avadirichi, Avanyore, and Avidakho. In Luluyia (language of Abaluyia), Lulogooli is placed at one extreme, almost unintelligible to Lubukusu at the other end.

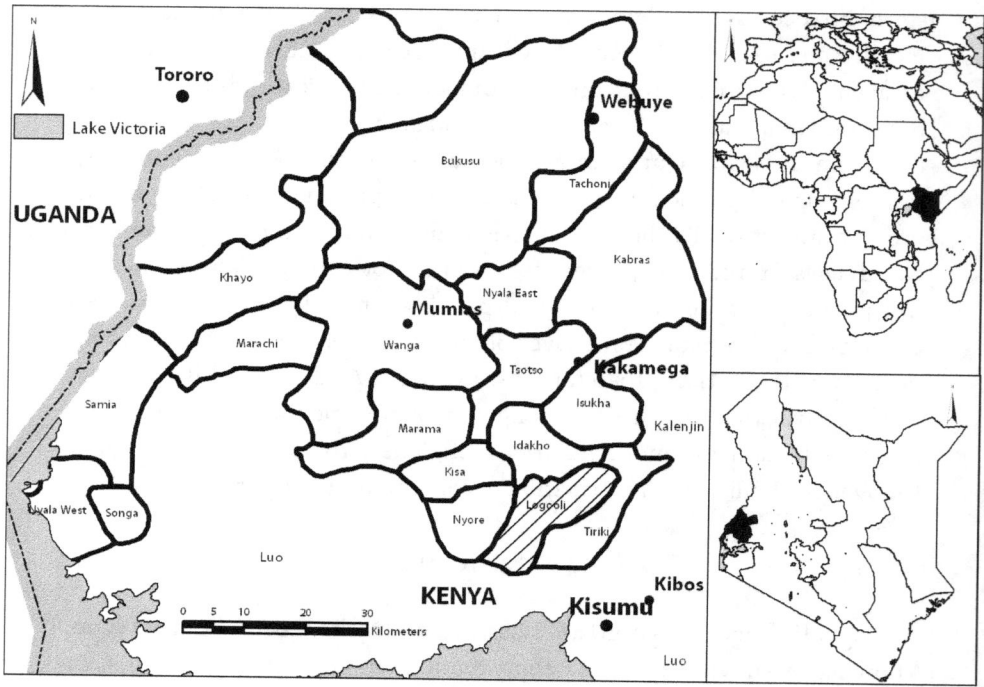

FIGURE 1.1. Map of Logooli locale within the Luyia complex.

The history, migration, location, and social systems of Avalogooli support interaction with other Luyia and African culture groups and the incorporation of their ideas into Logooli worldviews. More so, because of mutual intelligibility with other Luyia languages, Logooli music repertoire includes texts and styles from these groups, borrowed, adapted, assimilated, and appropriated due to resident proximity. Further, according to Osogo's pioneering studies (1966), as was the case with other Luyia groups, Avalogooli maintained a history of relocation due to family or other conflict, broken taboos, overpopulation, and exogamous marriage preferences. Consequently any given village sustained cultural diversity from voluntary or obligatory movement.[14] To compound the identity structures extant in Logooli locales and worldviews, diverse Christianities were introduced to the Luyia complex. The result was a rich palate of religious beliefs and rites with their concomitant musical and other artifacts.

In order to provide a backdrop for this dynamic junction, I will narrate part of my Logooli background as an expositional exemplar. My story resonates with that of others born and raised in the 1950s and 1960s, a period of marked political angst, change, and independence in many African nations. This was an era of realignment, of ideological and religious liminality, a regrouping for both the elders and the children of these times. The population nurtured in that epoch navigated the potent effects of colonialism and the stirrings of African self-governance. This generation, with deep ties to their parents' ethnic heritage, also embraced the political and socially sensational processes of nationalism, pan-Africanism, and globalism.

GOIBEI HERITAGE

I grew up in the 1960s in Goibei village in Western Kenya, a place of mixed heritage, diverse ethnicity, and plural nationalities (see fig. 1.2). I spent my first ten years in Goibei before leaving to study in other parts of Kenya for primary, secondary, and university education. Until I graduated with my first degree, I lived in Goibei for at least three months a year. I was (and still am) recognized in this village as mulogooli by language and culture. Goibei's initial inhabitants were Nandi peoples.[15] From the 1920s, migrants from different Luyia groups, particularly Avalogooli and Avadirichi, relocated to the region. These patrilineal, patrilocal, and exogamous societies suggest the presence of more culture groups in the village through wives.[16]

Goibei was also trespassed by the Luo, a non-Bantu ethnic group that passed through the village at least twice a week on their way to the nearest market, Serem, to sell fish and buy commodities. Several Luo words became part of village rhetoric. Some families in Goibei therefore spoke various languages although they recognized themselves as belonging principally to a specific cultural lineage. Thus Goibei, while initially habited by the Nandi, was in the 1960s a village of immigrants with cultural and ethnic diversity. Each group in Goibei and the vicinity retained its language or dialect even if individuals learned other tongues. Community meetings required a translator, or English and Kiswahili were employed.

Beyond culture and language, Goibei had religious diversity. Each culture and language group maintained its indigenous belief systems. Additionally, each group had been Christianized by different denominations such as Pentecostals, Quakers, Salvation Army, Roman Catholics, or African inde-

FIGURE 1.2. A view of the Goibei landscape.

pendent churches. Most Logooli of my paternal grandfather's generation began as Quakers. While some stayed Quaker, others became Pentecostals, Salvation Armists, or members of indigenous Christian movements such as the African Israel Church Nineveh (AICN). Not all villagers embraced Christianity; 'pagans' continued to frequent ancestral shrines associated with their respective groups. There also existed such a gap between the practice of missionary Christianity and African life that most people embraced varying syncretic levels of cultural, social, religious, and denominational beliefs.

Little effort was made to create seamless order or homogeny from the worlds of villagers and any other. The other was more than just the colonist and missionary; it included other African and Kenyan cultures that informed the -scapes of our existence. One required a strong sense of self or a clear cultural affinity more than a social or political alliance. Apart from religious and ethnic affiliations, we negotiated possibilities brought about by increased population, changing landscapes, European-style formal education, and urban migration. We had relatively stable cultural and linguistic roots and great tolerance for different church groups. Thus we were tacitly affiliated with one Christian denomination in the face of the evolving socio-political order. Even if a kinsman changed Christian affiliation, we all assembled at rites of passage. At these rites we conducted some affairs according to our cultural heritage and others in line with religious association. Things had and still have their place so much so that when I return to the village, I embrace its ambiance in mannerisms.

Growing up in Goibei therefore introduced me to things Logooli and to things of other cultures. I have elsewhere discussed circumcision rites of Avadirichi (Kidula 1999b). When I turned 5, I went to grade school. I was the youngest member of my class. By fourth grade, only two of my original girl classmates from first grade were still in school. Most others either got married or dropped out to earn a living. Since many of my classmates were essentially approaching puberty by the time we were in third grade, I did not fully appreciate what I learned from them through work and play until I was grown.

Social and cultural education was conducted in public and private through stories, songs, and by example. For instance, when I was 4, my maternal grandmother explained male-female relationships to me through story and song. Such was village life. Other elements of cultural education included those sanctioned by the school or church. For example, most village children within 5–7 years of my age were familiar with solfège whether or not they went to school. Children who attended the Pentecostal church and/or school participated in choral activities. They learned hymns and other Euro-American social songs initially through solfège. They traveled to other villages, schools, and churches to perform or compete against other choirs. We were familiar with brass bands through the activities of the Salvation Army. We were introduced to the guitar and popular Logooli, Kenyan, Tanzanian, Congolese, and South African songs on radio. The radio playlist also included popular contemporary repertoire of Europe (Britain) and the Americas (North, South, and the Caribbean). Thus musical resources in the village were varied. They included the indigenous cultural works of different ethnic groups, mediated and live popular songs, the repertoire of various Christian groups, and music learned in schools with a colonial British curriculum.

Goibei residents were not only familiar with European, North American, and African cultures; the British colonial system that encouraged the migration of South Asians to their colonies enabled an acquaintance with certain aspects such as food, clothing, music, and beliefs. Further, Arab Muslims, who were guides for early explorers and colonists, proselytized local populations. Goibei was particularly dynamic because it had a Pentecostal mission station and a resident Canadian missionary, Iris Scheel, who lived there for more than fifty years (1954–2005). Goibei also boasted day and boarding schools since the 1930s. In the 1970s, a center for national religious education was built. Such institutions ensured that Goibei catered to more than just local villagers.

My village life can well be a metaphor for Logooli identity in conflux with Christianity and its music. Kesby (1977, 90) concedes that Luyia people (amongst whom Avalogooli are grouped linguistically) "recognized a diversity of groups among themselves." Avalogooli also acknowledge separate migratory routes for the various clans that are the basis of their communal identity. Diversity and migration were therefore inherent in Logooli selfhood. Two distinct Christian groups, Quakers and Pentecostals, were the initial proselytizers. These groups' mission stations were first located in no-man's-lands bordering Logooli country. Avalogooli initially commuted to listen to missionaries. Beyond these two denominations, missionaries associated and worked with Anglicans, the African Inland Church (AIC), the Salvation Army, and other entities, including British colonial officials. 'Christian villages' were created in the 1920s (Strayer 1978), where Christianized Logooli relocated without cutting ties with non-Christian family and clan members.

Missionaries initially employed a trade language, Kiswahili, in early efforts to introduce Christianity and literacy. The missionaries soon realized that Christianity could only be indigenized if it spoke, was spoken, sang, and was sung in the language of the proselytized (Rees, E. 1905).[17] Missionaries also collaborated with colonists whose educational agenda shaped, positively and otherwise, missionary efforts. British colonial ideas were therefore imparted to Avalogooli as part of a religio-political complex. Muslims also sought Logooli converts. It was indeed a confluence of political and religious cultures into which the Logooli Christian struggled consciously or otherwise to find a "place to feel at home" (Ogot and Welbourn 1966). Goibei village and Christianity amongst Avalogooli posit an aporia on the process and affirmation of identity. I will propose the aporia in Goibei and extend the discussion to Avalogooli.

APORIA

How then was and is a sense of particular identity or ethnic affiliation maintained, reinforced, and even obliterated in such an environment as Goibei? Is it possible to isolate differentials in the multiplicity and blend of historical, religious, political, and ethnic configurations that make up not just invented nations but also rural communities such as Goibei? How does a 'foreign' religion and musical style become the basis for consensus amongst disparate local communities? How does or can music articulate and distinguish individual, social, and artistic identity? How can or does a music rooted in a foreign or new belief system become symbolic of ethnic unity and difference?

Goibei village probably exemplifies, typically and otherwise, how diversity and multiculturalism engender individuality at the personal, communal, and national level. Christianity, much more than education, became, and may still be, the most integrative factor and space in the village. That may partly be because the varieties of Christianity enable individuals, families, clans, and social groups to cohere by becoming affiliated with one or the other by choice rather than force. Thus there is room for distinctiveness and community, for conformity and preference. But perhaps the most stable Christian artifact is the music with its range of genres and styles, its possibilities for mutation and use, and also its accessibility and lack of particular ownership. It belongs to some, to everybody, and to nobody. It is adopted, appropriated, transformed, and produced in multifarious ways. The texts, tunes, and functions are static and dynamic, specific and ambiguous, fixed and mutable ad infinitum. One can assert that Christianity and its music constitute a part of Goibei, Logooli, and national Kenyan identity.

Goibei village can well be a metaphor for the larger Luyia nation. Abaluyia are a collection of culture groups. Their various migratory routes led to settlement in villages. A village consists of more than just those of patrilineal lineage; wives are acquired from elsewhere. The village may house more than one ethnic group. Apart from travel by villagers, novelty is introduced by physical visitors and by those who traverse the space through the media or the national educational system. The radio and the modern school are ubiquitous. How then does a village or an ethnic group distinguish itself or posit a unique character? Music as a cultural marker provides an avenue for the articulation of a distinctive character. There are broad distinctions in Luyia musicking expressed in specific features associated with the group. However, musicians illuminate the work of individuals in the construction of an archetypical tradition. The collective Luyia identity is thus collated through individuals' creativity.

Luyia individuality and diversity are typical of the configuration of most African nations: an assembly of numerous cultures. The aporia therefore applies to modern African nations whose distinct selfhood is located in the collection of diverse culture groups that inhabit the countries' borders. These groups were consolidated by colonial resolve and also internally fragmented by various factions of Islam and Christianity. The nations, framed by external politics, offer a complex intersection of music and religion as archival, historical, and incarnational processes. This study attempts to unwrap the aporia inherent in homogenizing identity while advancing a distinctive quality, particularly if the bases of consensus and distinction are what initially dismantled the group's core identity. Christian religious song is a possible avenue for uncovering the work of music in both fragmenting and consolidating local, national, and global identity. My approach to dissecting the aporia is outlined below.

BACKDROP

In 1983, I gathered Luyia women from Goibei to sing Christian religious songs they perceived as classics and representative of their Pentecostal denomination. In reality, I sought to confirm whether or not the tunes arranged by Arthur Kemoli (a prolific composer/arranger of Logooli descent) were considered archetypes by the group whose music he appropriated, given that he was a Quaker. The women performed what I knew were Luyia Pentecostal 'spirit' songs, having grown up in the tradition myself. They also performed translated hymns, gospel songs, and choruses as part of the set they assembled. When I called them up on their appropriation of translated songs as core indigenous Christian repertoire, their various explanations were "Kwimba kebende" (We are singing in a Pentecostal style, manner, or attitude), "Ni ulwimbu lwa amakono" (It is a song of hands—a song where hand clapping is imperative to the style), or "Ni ulwimbu lwa Mwelesa" (It is a song composed by Mwelesa [a known Logooli Quaker composer, translator, and singer whose hymns had been incorporated into Logooli Christian and ritual practice]), and "Ni ulwimbu lwa imiluka" (It is a song normally used in Logooli rites/

functions). I transcribed the tunes that were not translated hymns, and those by Mwelesa and others, as part of exercises in musicianship for my students at Kenyatta University. I assumed I could also teach basic concepts in common practice procedures from Kemoli's pieces. The experiments yielded mixed results (PURL 1.1).[18]

In 1986, I expanded the study. My primary aim was to analyze Kemoli's musical style. By assuming a musicological stance, I deliberately examined the material and the person not as 'other,' as was the standard vantage of music and anthropology scholars regarding non-Western musicians, but as key, focal, central, and mainstream, with a history rooted in a dynamic culture, representing a particular space and time. Kemoli was after all exploring structures emanating from Western academic music parameters. The project gained an ethnomusicological vein as I purposefully interviewed people and participated in events in the culture that nurtured and informed Kemoli. That multifaceted complex included indigenous Logooli rural and urban cultures, Logooli Quakerism, and the contemporary Kenyan educational system and music academy. Apart from observing and participating in church services, music festivals, and choir rehearsals, I researched the histories and musical practices of Pentecostal and Africanist Christian movements amongst Avalogooli since Kemoli's core tunes for adaptation and arrangement were derived from these groups. Here, I observed and participated in cultural events, held discussions with select focus groups, and drew on my outstanding heritage as a Logooli culture bearer, a Kenyan nurtured in the education system, and one brought up in Pentecostal Christianity, to question, negate, and confirm practices in the culture, in the two denominations, and in the education system. I concluded that regardless of denominational affiliation, Avalogooli considered the music sung by the women and arranged by Kemoli and others as Logooli Christian repertoire.

From 1988, I studied gospel performers in Kenya, including some of Logooli ethnicity and heritage. The core repertoire for difference in the gospel market by Logooli artists was pieces rooted in Pentecostal and Africanist church aesthetics. I interviewed musicians, observed and participated in their churches and concerts, analyzed their works between 1988 and 1997, and arranged their songs for the church choir that I directed at that time, the Nairobi Pentecostal church choir. The study was revived in 2001–2002 with students and faculty at Kenyatta University. In discussing the history and trends of contemporary Kenyan musical and related identity, we searched for appropriate theories for our data. During this period I interviewed Arthur Kemoli as well as some members of his family and choirs with a view of highlighting his contributions at conferences organized by Akin Euba on interculturalism and on composition in Africa and the diaspora (Kidula 2008). I also revisited some of my earlier work in order to problematize the music history of Logooli Pentecostals and Quakers in rural space and in urban dispersion.

My analyses led me to posit that contemporary music identity is an amorphous but essential construct in the tide of political, social, and economic motion for Africans. This identity is informed, consolidated, and transformed in dialogue with the African indigenous cultural past and the intra-African (continental and diasporic) contact over time. It is further complicated by historical and contemporary encounters with non-Africans that resulted in the reconstruction of indigenous social, political, and religious values; the adoption of new religious and political convictions; and the integration or restructuring of local and global music cultures. One of the broad objectives of this work is to dissect tensions of resilience and transformation in the music, its practitioners, and its audiences. This process engenders an aporia transversing music, identity, tradition and, in this work, religion.

OUTLOOK

Avalogooli provide a case from which to consider the intersection of music, religion, and identity in Africa since the end of the nineteenth century. Specifically, I dissect the musico-cultural interaction of Avalogooli with the Christianity initially introduced by Euro-Americans but appropriated by the group. With Christianity and colonial politics, Avalogooli acquired new layers of repertoire as well as alternative approaches to musicking. The addition of a layer presupposes the existence of an a priori Logooli musical tradition. Avalogooli as a people recognize particular fabrics that they consider traditional or indigenous to their core identity. They historically invoke certain fundamental cultural and musical features in alignment to, and differentiation from, others within linguistic, cultural, and national proximity. Identifying and deconstructing musical aspects and structures considered Logooli provides a window in the development of Logooli music history, theory, and practice. Avalogooli as a people have historically also been known to absorb otherness and yet also retain distinctiveness. Thus is it possible to imagine a distinctive Christian religious Logooli song tradition.

While Avalogooli are a specific language and culture group, the clan, the family, and the individual are essential to social continuity, cultural preservation, and ethnic distinction in time and place. In this work, I will highlight reports and analyses that privilege the collective Logooli identity in order to document the general or fluid parameters of music. I will also outline the agency of specific genres, small groups, and individuals. The text will begin with the collective voice asserted as historically Logooli in rites of inclusion and exclusion, belief systems, social structures, and cultural arts. I specifically highlight music's ubiquity in identity affirmation. Subsequent chapters will examine Logooli adoption of Christianity and its music, with the resultant impact on indigenous social, political, and musical structures. New music traditions birthed in the encounter with Christianity will then be introduced. The heart of the project is a detailed examination of the most significant musical directions, their characteristics, and their embodiment of Logooli identity in time and space. The document closes with historical summaries and a reflexive ethnographic homage to the archived musical heritage and the perpetual translation of the arts in time.

TWO

ASSEMBLY

Logooli Historical, Cultural, and Musical Background

CULTURAL HISTORY AND IDENTITY

The Logooli call themselves *Avalogooli* (sing. mulogooli). They refer to their land as *Ivulogooli*. According to oral tradition, Avalogooli descended from the man from whom they derive their name, Mulogooli, said to have settled very close to present-day Ivulogooli. His sons, Saali, Kizungu, Kilima, and Maavi, founded the four main clans: Avasaali, Avakizungu, Avakilima, and Avamaavi.[1] The names of other clans and subclans are derived from Mulogooli's grandsons and from dissident clansmen. More clans were created as neighboring groups were absorbed.[2] Avalogooli are called *Maragoli* by non-Luyia.[3] It has become the accepted national reference to the group. Maragoli is also the official Kenyan government name for Logooli country. It is currently subdivided into several counties with different names. Avalogooli have also migrated to other parts of Kenya and abroad.

Prior to the demarcation of land by British colonists, each Logooli clan or subclan had territorial boundaries owned by and distributed amongst the men. Clans were/are the political nucleus of the subgroup. They originally had a central authority administered by a council of elders (*luhya*), each presided over and moderated by the wealthiest landowner or the medicine man.[4] Individual families, made up of parents and their unmarried children, are the hearthstones of the clan. In the past, elders settled disputes between families, attended to ceremonial gatherings involving clan members, and also sanctioned interclan alliances through marriages, friendship, and other avenues. Interclan meetings strengthened Logooli solidarity. With colonial rule, Avalogooli were restricted to reside in the North Kavirondo Native Reserve, essentially referred to as Ivulogooli by the locals, and in the process, historical, political, and social

FIGURE 2.1. A Logooli house decorated for the Christmas season.

patterns of migration were altered (Verma 2001, 82). With nationalism, even Avalogooli who had migrated elsewhere were often returned to this land.

Due to a high population and with few industrial outlets, Avalogooli subsist on small-scale farming. The typical landscape is hilly and rocky but fertile and therefore arable. The patrilineal hereditary system subdivides a man's ancestral land amongst his sons. A homestead has one house if the male has only one wife. More houses are built as sons approach puberty and are circumcised. In some homes, a separate hut houses domestic animals and serves as a kitchen. The farm has maize (corn), beans, sweet potatoes, green vegetables, and bananas in the backyard (see fig. 2.1). Cattle are kept for meat, milk, and dowry. Sheep and goats are also raised for meat, to keep the lawn properly 'mowed,' and as part of dowry exchange.

In order to discuss the nature of being mulogooli, it is perhaps necessary to examine indigenous notions regarding an individual (*mundu*). Such a discussion might facilitate an understanding of what informed Logooli views of the natural and other worlds. In essence, a person was imaged with the terms *ombili* (*omuvili*), *umwoyo* (*mwoyo*), and *ekilili* (Wagner 1949, 159–167). Ombili is the physical body, the visible core that is the flesh and bones of a being. The physical body can cease to exist but the being once formed lives on. Umwoyo refers to the heart as a physical organ, as well as to the seat of emotions, feelings, and mental sensibilities. Derivative constructions refer to these processes as predicative, active, or dynamic; for example, *kuva mwoyo* (lit. to have a heart) means to be alive. Umwoyo also signifies consciousness beyond the physical to dream, and spirit worlds. The term umwoyo further translates as 'voice' or voicing, and sounding. It is the term for vocal organs and is invoked to reference the sounding of a pitch—*kuhana mwoyo* (to provide the pitch/key/tonality/timbre; the phrase also means to encourage). Ideas contained in such concepts as aesthetics and artistry, philosophy, reflection and mindset, as well as personality and attitude are imagined, perceived, acknowledged, or enacted with umwoyo. An individual's makeup also includes ekilili (lit. shadow). Ekilili relates to notions recognized as the attributes, traits, or unique characteristics of the said being. When the physical body dies, the shadow continues to frame the being's essence. To distinguish one being from another, the individual is named.[5]

It is essential for a mulogooli to be named. A name personifies and identifies the being. It roots and characterizes a person. A name facilitates and explains behaviors and relationships. It is a way to distinguish ancestry and kinship. Clan names are inherited. Others are based on, among other things, natural or other occurrences at the child's birth, a child's personality, or an action the child seems to delight in.[6] Nicknames are adopted and even passed on to acquire familial or clan status. A name may therefore not intimate close kin. Beyond the name, individuals identify with the father's clan and reference the mother's clan-stranger relationship with the term *mwifwa*.[7] The word mwifwa connotes a 'dying to' and a 'pulling out of,' a metaphoric cutting or severing of roots by the woman when she relocates to live with her husband's people. The word is also related to the term for 'thorn,' with implications of being pricked to bleed out or transfuse. Thus one always recognizes the mother's fate—one that died to, was pulled out, was pricked, and was grafted onto, transplanted, or bled into another.[8] The importance of names and naming is evinced and reinforced in song texts.

Music is a persistent marker of continuity, change, and transformation amongst Avalogooli. According to Mulindi (1983), music was pervasive in indigenous society as a pedagogical tool; as functional in play, work, ritual, and religion; and as entertainment. It not only accompanied every significant occasion; it was a constituent of daily life. This view is deduced partly from the existence of songs spanning a person's life. Children had a body of repertoire, *Tsinyimbu tsia avaana* (children's songs), that included lullabies, play songs, and story songs (Mulindi 1983, 137). There were well-known lullabies and particular song styles associated with babysitting. One could compose a song or improvise new texts to known tunes and in appropriate styles while babysitting. Some texts revealed the feelings of children and adults about their situations, conditions, and expectations. This lullaby, "Ndolo,"[9] teaches a child what to do if a baby refuses food.

Lulogooli	English Translation
Ndolo mbombela[10] mwana	Slumber, I am soothing the child
Libwoni sambe	[With] a roasted sweet potato
Mbombela mwana ala lila	I am soothing the child—lest he/she cry
Mbombela mwana ala gona	I am soothing the child—so he'll/she'll sleep
Mbombela mwana	I am soothing the child
Libwoni sambe	A roasted sweet potato
Kohe mwana	Let's give the child
Mwana ni asuyi	If the child refuses (to eat it)
Kohe baba	We'll give daddy
Baba ni asuyi	If daddy refuses (to eat it)
Kohe mama	We'll give mommy
Mama ni asuyi	If mommy refuses (to eat it)
Kohe senge	We'll give aunty
Senge ni asuyi	If aunty refuses (to eat it)
Kohe koza	We'll give uncle
Koza nasuyi	If uncle refuses (to eat it)
Lihevwe muleli	It will be given to the babysitter

From the song, the hierarchy of those closest to the baby was recounted. The babysitter also learned not to eat the child's food at first refusal. Only after repeated pleas and help from these other adults could the food be given to the sitter. Mulindi (1983, 152) maintains that lullabies and other cradlesongs "express some of the fundamental principles of Logooli society ... the songs dwell on themes of nature ... relationships between man and his environment

... values about work ... [and] human relationships." Thus this category of songs was not intended only for the individual baby's comfort; it also laid the foundation for expressing and imparting broader social and musical values, structures, and practices. Beyond lullabies, play and story songs inculcated Logooli concepts, morals, ethics, and aesthetics (Akaranga 1996).

Adults sang during work. Children, working alongside parents, had their repertoire and knowledge expanded in a seemingly informal manner. Music not only instilled values; it entertained and provided professional development. Talented composers, singers, instrumentalists, and dancers were displayed, critiqued, and encouraged at social and other events. Singing conveyed sentiments and relieved pent-up emotions in circumcision, wedding, and funeral rites. Music extended to the nonphysical world. At communal ceremonies, songs were used to implore ancestral benediction. Most repertoire was acquired by participation, which was the right of every individual (Mulindi 2000). It was not just a right; it was expected that every individual not only perform but perform "correctly." Mulindi recounts that

> during a recording session at Ivudidi, some children rose to chase a boy across the field because he made a mistake in performance ... Kezia Migaliza an elder woman from Elosengeri had the following to say concerning her experiences at the dormitory (Edis) for unmarried girls: "We used to take it in turn to tell stories or to sing. If you were unable to tell a story, you would be beaten. Yes! Whose music will you be listening to (i.e. without performing your own)? You were forced to go back home and say, 'I want to learn something to tell others.'" (Mulindi 1983, 148)

Mulindi further observed that a song leader often refused to lead if the response was unsatisfactory. A chorus responded half-heartedly or not at all if the soloist's vocals or lyrics were substandard or inaccurate. The point was not that everyone should excel, but that all should be aware of musical standards of excellence. Thus music skills, suitable performance practices, and proper aesthetics were learned and critiqued in public. In fact, public performance was so ingeniously integrated into life's routine, it was often inconspicuous except when it was staged for rituals or social events.

To underline the worth of music in Logooli identity and its subsequent translation with the adoption of Christianity, I will reconstruct pertinent religio-cultural history from colonial, anthropological, missionary, and other archival documents; from postcolonial works of Kenyan and other scholars in religion, music, and culture; and from personal observation, participation, conversations, and interviews with groups and individuals from 1983 to 2011.

LOGOOLI RELIGIOUS AND CULTURAL SYSTEMS

According to early anthropologists and missionaries (e.g., Wagner 1949, Rees, E. 1918), religion was an important constituent in the overall cycle and daily life of mulogooli. It was so intertwined in day-to-day affairs and beliefs that when Christianity was presented and adopted, it both layered onto and saturated local ideas, values, and practices. Wagner, the first Western ethnographer to research Avalogooli in the 1930s, comments on the difficulty he encountered in his search for precolonial Logooli weddings because the 'Christian' rite seemed to be the approbated version (Wagner 1936, 319).[11] Some scholars argue that Christianity did not necessarily alter Logooli basic beliefs but rather it found a way to be "both catholic and local, both universal and vernacular" (Ogot and Welbourn 1966, 133). Since the early twentieth century, Logooli religious and cultural systems have been maintained, abandoned, or altered to reflect stability and contact and to service indigenous and foreign concerns.[12]

In indigenous practice, offerings, sacrifices, and prayers were presented not just at major turning points in the life of an individual; they were part of everyday life. Egara (2005, 33–36) posits that invocations were prevalent because of the desire to procure fertility of people and land, for life and continuity, and for health and prosperity. Normal occurrences were attributed empirical and supernatural causes, assigning a dual determinant to any one event. Supernatural agents were invoked for blessing or to counter misfortunes. Arbiters included a Supreme God the originator of all things, ancestral spirits with benevolent or malevolent intentions, and human agents with learned or inherent ability to affect others.[13]

Avalogooli believed in the existence of a Supreme Being referred to as *Esai (Isahi)* or *Emungu* and said to be the origin of all things.[14] Legend has it that the first man to offer sacrifices to Isahi was Ang'oma. Some sources state that Ang'oma was another name for Isahi. Others contend that he may have been the brother or father of Mulogooli, the founder of the Logooli nation (Mulindi 1983, 47). Ang'oma lived before Mulogooli and is perceived as an ancestor. The venue where people gathered to offer national semiannual sacrifices was known as *Mwing'oma*, etymologically identified as the place of Ang'oma. Ang'oma was and is viewed as an intermediary between Avalogooli and God. Prayers were at times addressed to him. His role as an intermediary ushered all other ancestors into this role (Wagner 1949, 168, 293).[15]

Avalogooli further acknowledged ancestral spirits. Ancestral spirits, said to have a subterranean abode, were believed to have a life similar to the one on earth including owning cattle and other material goods. Ancestors visited their kinsmen through dreams. They could cause harm or good. Ancestors manifested their interference and disapproval in ways such as sicknesses with no apparent cause, repeated misfortunes in a family, or, in the case of naming a child, continuous crying for no apparent reason. Although the Supreme Being was held in high esteem, he was too far removed from regular people to have immediate and proper contact with them. Ancestors were therefore intermediaries. It was always important to maintain proper relationships with them to secure goodwill and avert misfortunes.

Human beings were capable of willingly causing harm (by profession or request) or could unwittingly bring misfortune when they were 'impure.' One could also be a carrier of mystical power with the potential to curse and bless. Some individuals were known paranormal specialists, as was the case with medicine men, herbalists, sorcerers, and witches. Anyone considered an agent of mystical power was either avoided or had to be ceremonially sanctioned in order to participate in social gatherings or ritual events.

MUSIC IN THE CONSOLIDATION OF COLLECTIVE RELIGIO-CULTURAL IDENTITY

While the hand of God appeared to permeate daily life as evinced in the prayers of individual families, Avalogooli met as a group in (pre) colonial times twice a year to specifically address the Supreme Being. The agricultural calendar dictated the timing. Sacrifices were held in March or April and in September or October after planting and weeding crops. The purpose of these sacrifices was to invoke divine help to secure ample harvest, to avert crop failure, and to petition for success in war. Invocations were also addressed to the ancestors and to oracles (Wagner 1949, 167, 225–229, 290–294). Clan heads usually fixed a date for the ceremony. Messengers blowing horns informed the clans of the event on the eve of the ceremony. On that day everyone was to abstain from farming and other work. All clans had to be present, otherwise any subsequent disaster was ascribed to displeasure by the Supreme Being or ancestors for nonattendance, or else it was believed that the clan that abstained wished ill on the collective group.

The ceremony was called *Ovwali*, also the name for an altar of sacrifice that involves fire. The sacrifice was offered in a sacred cave. Only two priests, *avasaalisi*, were permitted inside and only during the ceremony. The interior of the cave was cleansed by avasaalisi before they could offer sacrifices, as nobody had used it since the last rite.[16] Avasaalisi came from one particular clan, therefore the position was hereditary. The chief *musaalisi* (sing.) was called *Mfwani wa Ovwali* (He who lights the sacrificial fire). He performed all the essential rites associated with the sacrifice, including the killing of the sacrificial animal, while the other musaalisi acted as his acolyte. It was imperative that the priests and the people be pure, otherwise the exercise would result in harm rather than good. Purity was observed particularly in the selection of the human and animal participants. The sacrificial animal (a white hen or a white goat) was supplied by an old man who, like the priest, was without blemish (*dzimbala*). A second old man from whose hut the firebrand for kindling the fire was procured also had to be 'untainted.' The chief priest selected two young girls (virgins) to fetch firewood, grind the eleusine flour, and carry it to the front of the sacrificial space (Wagner 1949, 292).

Music was an important part of the rite. This may be because among Avalogooli, music making "fostered meaningful relationships" amongst the participants and with the invisible collective, with an "emphasis ... on communication and on self expression" (Mulindi 1983, 90).[17] Musicking had already begun on the eve of the rite when messengers were sent to inform the people of the upcoming event. On the morning of the ceremony, each clan arrived led by a singing group.[18] Wagner's informant, a priest, stated: "as soon as the sacrificial priest had kindled the fire, he sings a song addressed to Isahi or to Ang'oma in which all the people join" (Wagner 1949, 193). The song attributed the first fire ever kindled to Ang'oma and invoked Ango'ma's favor on Logooli progeny. The song, begun by the priest and his acolyte, was continued by the gathered crowd while musaalisi repaired to the sacrificial grove. War songs and victory songs were raised throughout the ceremony. The chief object of ritual importance was the drum (*Ing'oma*), said to have been kept in the cave for many generations (ibid.).

Clans also held sacrifices during rites of passage and after harvest. Offerings to ancestors were extended to the familial level in the form of daily food libations offered to the recently departed to sustain them as they settled in their new abode.[19] All significant family occasions and sicknesses necessitated sacrificial offerings. The sacrifices were intended to appease antagonistic spirits and to invoke blessing and sympathy. Every notable man (*mundu mudukilu*) had a sacrificial shrine in the front yard. It consisted of a set of three or more stones arranged in a triangular shape, resembling hearthstones. The offerings, pieces of meat from the slaughtered animal, as well as blood, were sprinkled on the stones. The center post of the hut in homes (*itiru*) was also deemed a shrine, as all objects to be blessed were placed here. Thus the notion of luhya was embodied not just in gatherings; it was also memorialized in outdoor and indoor shrines.[20]

Certain rites certified clan and ethnic membership. For example, circumcision was a principal male rite of passage. A son could not be circumcised unless and until his father acknowledged him, not just for reasons of manhood but also for inheritance (Kidula 2005b, 2–4). In circumcision, a boy's clan membership and Logooli paternity was certified. Neither could a woman be buried just anywhere if she had children. Her marital status was ascertained before she was interred, including whether or not she was dowered by the father of her first child.[21] Rites of passage were therefore important institutions of identity and belonging. These rites became locales for negotiating change and continuity. The place and function of music in these sites are detailed in the ensuing discussion.

RITES OF PASSAGE

Rituals are recognized as occasions where a group collectively acts out its norms and values within given parameters of time and space—set apart from normal life—in condensed and exaggerated forms. These community events may be shells, signifiers, symbols, and codes of complex and private knowledge or actions. Ritual events, as public productions of continuous rites, process "new ways of being in relation" (Foucault 1978, 82) or provide spaces for the struggle for identity and power (Argyrou 1996, 2).

Rites of passage confirmed belonging to and membership of Logooli ancestry for both male and female children.[22] They further reiterated gender roles and expectations of the father's progeny. However, these rites also signified inclusion into the Logooli complex through marriage and other alliances.[23] While belief systems provided moral and social standards for accountability and kinship management, visible and physical emblems and behaviors served to consolidate membership and relationships to clan, family, age, and gender groups.

Sacrifices were the most sacred or binding symbolic activities. They were held at transitional rites of birth, circumcision for males, weddings, and funerals. That sacrifices were intimately enshrined in daily life was enacted at the central pole (*itiru*) in a house where food for ancestors, spirits, and the newly dead was left or scattered. Awareness of spirit life was nowhere more evident than in funerals and burial rites. Food in particular was placed in the attic (*lilungu*) for the newly deceased. This 'attic,' usually in the kitchen/cowshed, was frequented daily for firewood stored there to dry. Hence there was a ubiquitous awareness of the dead among the living: an acknowledgement of death as inevitable in life. Music and song in particular were used to educate, symbolize, or entertain regarding and during these rites.

BIRTH RITES

The birth of a child had the double duty of bringing a new individual into the community as well as ushering two people into the role of parenthood, thus assigning them a new social status. The birth of a child also cemented the relationship between the two families and the various clans involved. Apart from food taboos by the community and a mother's preference, hardly any preparation was made to anticipate a birth. In any case, preparation was considered a bad omen. The actual delivery was not accompanied by any ceremony. Both the new mother and her baby were quarantined and isolated from the general public for a while to guard against potential carriers of danger and bad luck. The first child had to be acknowledged by both families through a ritual ceremony.[24]

The first ancestral rite offered on behalf of the first born, the *liswakila* ceremony, occurred two to three months after birth. Its purpose was to induce the spirits to adopt a benevolent attitude toward the child and refrain from interfering with its health. A goat without blemish was killed by suffocation on this occasion. An invited priest blessed the child and the home. The elaborate ceremony (Wagner 1949, 311–313) culminated in the eating of the goat by all present. By partaking of the food, the relatives bound themselves to care for the child. An ancestral name was also given at this time, if the family had not already done so. Ancestors visited the family through dreams if they desired to be named. The family normally complied with requests not only to avert conflict but also to affirm clan names and for continuity. In some cases, a diviner was consulted to find an appropriate name.

Ceremonies were also performed for weak and sickly children to determine the causes of the disease and present ways to combat the forces behind the illness. The most famous of these rites was the *mbumbelee* ceremony. In this instance, several old women were invited to coax health into the child. The child's ear was pierced and a small iron plug inserted as a visible sign of the preventive measure against the disease or spirits plaguing the child (Mulindi 1983, 11–12; Wagner 1949, 332–334). A song, "Mbumbelee," was performed during the ritual. The refrain, usually sung by the chorus, posited the idea of inducing health in the way one fans cinders to blaze. It stated, *Mbumbeele ndole ni gwaka*, translated as "Let me gently fan it to see if it will blaze." Other lyrics enumerated what was considered of worth, virtuous, or desirable, such as a child, a gentle person, being helpful, good food, being healthy. A few of the lyrics are outlined below.[25]

Lulogooli	English Translation
Akana nikyo kindu	A child has worth (is precious)
Vokonyi nikyo kindu	To offer help (being helpful) is a noble thing
Mugosi nikyo kindu	To be gentle is wholesome
Isudzi niyo inyama	Fish is proper meat
Uvulamu nivwo kindu	Good health is a desirable thing
Likere nigwo muyaga	A frog is fever (With fever one looks like a frog)
Avavila vivwo vulasi	Sorcerers, yours are stings/irritants

On the other hand, a frog with its pimpled look was synonymous with things unworthy to pursue or to behold. These were carriers of dis-ease. Sorcerers with the potential for evil and harm were also denigrated. However, things of worth were mentioned more than those that brought pain, sickness, or disharmony. From the lyrics, belief systems were reinforced, such as disease emanating from more than natural causes, or healing resulting from more than natural resources. There were natural, social, psychological, and supernatural causes and cures for illnesses.

CIRCUMCISION RITES

Circumcision was the most important rite in a boy's life. The ideal age for the event was 18 years, but anyone between age 13 and 30 could participate if he was uncircumcised. The ceremony was performed every 6–8 years, usually in the month of August at a date determined by clan elders. August was an ideal month, as it was near the end of the harvest season (Adede 1982, 6–9). The month was between the cultivating seasons, and women were in between farming tasks. Music marked the rite's various stages. The candidates slept in the open for three nights before circumcision. Usually the preferred location was near a stream, in a valley. During the day, the boys sang songs designed to boost their morale and encourage themselves to be brave. In the evening, they were instructed in the conventions of the rite. It was also here that boys confessed their transgressions in order to exonerate themselves before moving on to the next phase of their lives. These confessions to their peers and elders engendered a clan, male, and family bonding that continued throughout the life of the participants, as these were the people entrusted with each other's darkest secrets. The experience strengthened male belonging to and ownership of the clan.

A small cylindrical high-pitched hand drum, *mudindi* or *kidindi*, announced the impending arrival of the surgeon. The man "ran from one end of the village to the other calling the boys and beating his drum. As he passed by the homesteads, he would shout a catchword and the boys, already instructed by their fathers, would follow him" (Adede 1982, 7–8). Usually boys were circumcised in an open field close to a stream. The surgeon moved from one group to another. A boy's father had to be present to acknowledge paternity, to grant permission for the boy to undergo the rite, and to encourage his son to be brave. Women and children watched from a distance until all the boys in the groups were circumcised. They sang and danced in praise of the initiates for their courage (Wagner 1949, 345–348; Adede 1982, 6–9; Kidula 1999b, 90–97).

The boys were thereafter kept in seclusion in a widower's hut (*itumbi*) or in a hut constructed for that purpose. While in itumbi, the boys were instructed on how to behave as adult men, as well as in practical skills such as hunting, building houses, and other jobs considered male domain. The boys wove masks to wear in public until the coming-out or graduation ceremony (*lyaluku*) (see fig. 2.2). These masks were also used in outdoor dances. In the evenings, they learned songs in praise of their "new status of manhood" (Adede 1982, 8). Egression from itumbi was marked by a variety of activities including burning the hut and all items used by the boys during the isolation period. The new adults sang songs learned during seclusion, accompanied

EXAMPLE 2.1. "Nandio kwalange"

by ceremonial dancing in competition amongst *tsitumbi* (pl.). There were classic songs that spoke of the bond that tied the clansmen and the ethnic group together. The most famous of these songs was "Nandio kwalange vana vitu" (That is the way we were my children/my brethren/my clansmen; see music ex. 2.1).[26]

Since every age-set had a name, other songs enumerated the circumcision lineages. Some classic songs were in languages other than Lulogooli, speaking to the larger Luyia collective or the sharing of the rite with neighboring groups. Others were drawn from story and play songs that expounded on social and moral values. The most popular songs were new compositions in the dance styles of the day, usually about girls, sex, romance, and related topics. The donor of the ceremonial cow whose meat was sacrificed to the ancestors gave the new men a valedictory address. Only the initiates and older men ate the meat. The ceremony promoted loyalty within the clan and the culture group, instituting men to continue Logooli progeny (Wagner 1949, 363–371; Kidula 2005b).

Missionary resistance to the circumcision rite met with an interesting settlement. As documented by Sangree (1966, 88), the neighboring Avadirichi opted for two ceremonies in 1940: one for the Christianized population, *Vasoomi* (those who were learned), and another for the nonconverts, *Vadirichi* (those true to Tiriki rites). Vadirichi wore masks in public during the seclusion period, observed indigenous customs associated with the rite (public and private), and performed not just classic circumcision and social songs but music with overt sexual lyrics on how to seduce, please, and keep a woman and wife. Thus women, girls, and the general public were forewarned of the intentions of the men when they would emerge from isolation.

Those who had adopted Christianity (Vasoomi) neither wore masks nor appeared in public. They also avoided practices such as learning the best way

FIGURE 2.2. Circumcised masked Vadirichi.

to hold alcohol. For music, they sang classic circumcision songs, middle-of-the-road social songs, and Christian hymns. Thus all the initiates learned clan and family history through song. This music was heard nightly echoing in the hilly countryside during seclusion.

Avalogooli, on the other hand, choose a different route. By 1910, some boys who had converted to Christianity but wanted to observe circumcision were cared for at the Maragoli mission station (Africa Record 1910, 7). Thereafter Avalogooli opted to behave as if the whole ceremony had been Christianized. The rite was conducted so publicly that when Joy Adamson (1967), a renowned wildlife conservationist, was looking for Logooli models for her portrait of Kenyan people project in the 1940s, she was informed by missionary teachers at Madira Girls School (the first girls' boarding school in Maragoli) that the practice had been eradicated, although it was still being conducted under their very eyes. Boys were publicly led to the grove to the sound of Christian songs and were afterward secluded in agreed-on backyards. Wearing of masks was also discontinued. The night sings consisted of Christian middle-of-the-road social songs and some classic repertoire including "Nandio kwalange." The practice was still vibrant at the time of this research, with younger boys initiated each time and with sanctioned options such as circumcision in hospitals instead of in ancestral groves.

MARRIAGE CEREMONIES

While circumcision established male belonging, marriage was most traumatic for the woman. In an exogamous society with agnatic ties, a girl left her parents to join a group of strangers. In proper matrimony, one neither married from the same clan nor for up to two generations of the maternal grandmother's clan. Any deviation invoked the wrath of ancestors manifested by such misfortunes as barrenness, ectopic pregnancies, deformed children, general physical disasters, or calamities that compelled the offering of sacrifices. Girls were usually betrothed at 18–20 years of age, but often girls of 15 or 16 years secretly eloped.[27] Otherwise, a betrothal was confirmed by bride wealth given to the girl's parents after negotiations between the two families and clan elders. Weddings normally took place in October and November when food was still plentiful. A visit by either the bride's or groom's parents to the other's home required feasting and the exchange of food products (Wagner 1949, 396–433).

The beginning of the wedding process was marked by two celebrations held simultaneously at both the bride's and groom's homes. Neither party invited the other. The chief attraction at the bride's home was killing a bullock during the first two feast days. No specific rituals were observed. The party at the groom's homestead culminated in the first visit of the bride. She was escorted by a bevy of unmarried girls and a few young men. En route, the group sang, extolling the virtues of the bride and ridiculing the groom. A few miles from their destination, a singing party from the groom's village, countering the claims of the bride's escort, met the group. A song and dance contest ensued. Below (music ex. 2.2) is a sample text of a song by the bride's party popular in the 1960s–1970s:

EXAMPLE 2.2. "Si walinda ndeya" (PURL 2.1)

Call	Response
Si walinda ndeya	Ee
Ondeva si walinda ndeya	Hamuliango yaho
Gwasimbidza dzing'ombe	Ee
Ondeva gwasimbidza dzing'ombe	Hamuliango yaho

English translation:

Couldn't you wait for me to sweep	Eee
Ondeva couldn't you wait for me to sweep	that doorway (door entrance)?
You persistently (aggravatingly) sent cows	Ee
Ondeva persistently sent cows	to that doorway

The text complains that the groom is impatient. While the girl was doing her normal duties, learning to be a good housewife, the anxious man sent cows (symbols of dowry or agreement with the parents), although he had not established his intentions. Or else he was impatient because he had never seen a girl who, although young, already seemed to possess qualities of a mature woman. This type of song reinforced held values that a fine woman is "industrious, modest, and physically strong so that she can stand up under the strain of heavy work that is expected of a wife" (Wagner 1949, 395).

The use of the prefix *gwa* in the word *gwasimbidza* denigrates the man, presenting him as an ogre or as beastly instead of human by using the prefix *ya* (*yasimbidza*). The word suggests that the man was resolutely insistent rather than patiently persistent. Other readings of the text imply that just because the woman finally folded does not necessarily mean that the man won. Rather, he should be grateful that he is getting a good model for his erstwhile incapable clan. If his people had been better custodians, he would not have been so eager to marry. What is implied is the man is beholden to the woman's people for the good education and proper instruction of his bride. Such a basis for a stable relationship problematizes an essential cultural axiom of male arrogance and female subservience.

A soloist's knowledge of the groom led to other improvised texts. For instance, if the groom had been to school and wanted to impress the girl, he may have written her letters, in which case the soloist faulted the man for frequently writing letters to the girl ("Gwasimbidza zibarua"—You relentlessly sent letters). The girl may have shared the information with her friends and family and they turned it into a vice rather than a virtue. Why would a girl agree to marry such a man? Possibly her father had already accepted dowry, or maybe she was sacrificing herself for her brothers' sake, or else she had

EXAMPLE 2.3. "Lelo kunyoye idimbidi" (PURL 2.2)

economic, socio-political, or romantic reasons. Otherwise, the song was an opportunity for rejected or jealous girls to get back at the man, in which case it might be translated that the man was getting a girl who was inexperienced—who was still sweeping the doorway, who was untried. Thus a girl's jealous friends hid their feelings in double-edged song lyrics.[28]

The groom's party countered with songs of their own, lauding the virtues of the groom and belittling the bride. The following (music ex. 2.3) is an example of such a song, popularized in the late 1960s and still sung occasionally:

Lulogooli
Lelo kunyoye idimbidi isietsanga masia
Ae ae aea umwana wa mama

English translation:
Now we have found a deaf and dumb person who grinds coarse flour
Ae ae aea (exclamation of resignation or pity) poor baby (mother's crybaby)

The groom's supporters' response is that the girl is deaf and dumb (*idimbidi*) and that she has yet to master the fundamentals of housewifery, specifically how to grind flour finely. Consequently, she will be incapable of preparing good food. Clearly, the lyrics insulted the bride's relatives by suggesting that the girl was neither a good listener nor a skilled communicator. Deaf and dumb and its qualifying prefix *i*, *isietsanga*, further classify the girl as subhuman, possibly in the category of an animal or thing. The second line can be read as sympathy for the man that he is getting a 'child' that still clings to her mother or that the man, poor baby, is to be pitied for the untrained woman. In this context where a bride was prohibited from smiling, talking, or showing any positive demeanor, the groom's party taunted the bride's entourage not just with lyrics; they even resorted to pinching the bride to provoke angst or as physical displays of emotional turmoil. I was told that on occasion, some jealous girls or boys saw it as an opportunity to vent without repercussions. These mock-abuse songs lauded each candidate's attributes by their constituents while disparaging their challengers. In essence, each group was positing that their candidate was the better person, thereby initiating grounds for defense if marital dissent occurred.

Music was such an integral part of weddings that early missionaries commented on its ubiquity. Deborah Rees, one of the first missionaries to Avalogooli, wrote about her experience of it in 1906:

> A wedding party went by this morning taking the bride to the home of the groom. As it was only a short distance away, we went too. We were there in time for the wedding breakfast, which was prepared only for the bride and her companions. It consisted of green bananas boiled with their skins on. The people . . . took the skins off and rolled the banana into a ball. This, with the dancing before breakfast occupied so much time that we could not stay to see the ceremony of putting on the sen-sen. (Africa Record 1907a, 8)

The wedding process held over several days/weeks incorporated diverse songs and song styles due to the variety of peoples, activities, and venues involved. The rite was probably the most musicked communal ceremony that incorporated different generations, all the gender groups, and outsiders. The musics were resourced from classic pieces such as "Mwana wa mberi,"[29] to appropriate songs drawn from children's repertoire and work songs, to popular styles, to songs from the broader Luyia complex or other languages (PURL 2.3; PURL 2.4).

From my participation in and analysis of the musics, weddings and circumcision rites were the most legitimate spaces to introduce new songs. At initiation rites, boys of each itumbi learned new songs to display their ingenuity. Circumcisions, however, also reinforced known repertoire to articulate clan, ethnic, and male identity. At weddings, two music groups competed to demonstrate their superior and socially elitist stance and knowledge of current affairs and styles. The music was the equivalent of popular repertoire of the time, with old favorites and classic songs. The group with the most entertaining lyrics, tunes, dances, and novel styles was commended. It was inevitable that new music was introduced at weddings since the bride was an outsider. She figuratively and literally brought novelty to the groom's people. Music as song, dance, drama, and entertainment was the audible and visual cultural signifier of innovation. Meanwhile, the groom's supporters presented new songs to demonstrate they were equally creative and fashionable as well as to impress the bride's entourage. In addition to popular songs, ritual classic songs were performed because they held historical significance, they were representative expressions of emotional angst associated with the rites, or they were "axiomatic statements of Logooli values" (Mulindi 1983, 130).

FUNERAL RITES

Avalogooli venerated ancestors. Rituals and taboos were meticulously observed to avoid ancestral malcontent. Precautions were taken to safeguard and protect the living as well as to prevent any kind of retribution from the ancestors and the newly deceased. It was from the proper observance of mortuary rites that the dead, as intermediaries and agents of the living, were benevolent or malevolent.

The funeral rite was the last important ceremony performed for/on an individual. Death was perceived as a translation from a physical into a spirit realm. The bonds between the living and the deceased were transformed, rather than severed. The mystery surrounding the fate of individuals after death necessitated sacrifices to absolve the living from having caused the death, since death was attributed to mystical sources including human beings. When death was imminent for an old and prominent man, all the relatives assembled at the deathbed. The nearly dead's last sacrifice involved killing an ox and dividing the meat amongst the kindred present. Ancestors were perforce invited to participate. The patient, if still strong, summoned all his sons and distributed his wealth among them. The family then waited for the man's demise (Wagner 1949, 449–451).

Ritual and actual mourning included chanting and singing classic dirges in vocables and in regular text during daytime vigils and at all-night wakes. The repertoire as well as the manner of music performance at the rite signified the importance and worth of the deceased to the immediate family and relatives and to the general public.[30] Even before a patient was certified dead, women began to wail aloud while men cried silently. Wailing usually began at the site where a person died, which was not necessarily at the person's home. A fire was then kindled in the homestead of the deceased. New arrivals came wailing and mourning. Whether or not the wailing was ritual, it helped relieve pent-up emotions and announced the death. When the body was laid in the front porch (*lusimbu*), mourners sang dirges over the corpse, some wordless, others verbally expressing their feelings. Some compositions were in ritual poetry and rhetoric, while others were improvised chants. These dirges, called *ezinzikuulu*[31] and *elyimbu*,[32] were sung only at funerals and nowhere else.

One well-known contemporary dirge was adopted from a Christian exhortation song. The text below, sung at the demise of a male, noted the termination of normal earthbound relationships:

Lulogooli	English Translation
Lufweye kulanga "Baba," lufweye	Calling him "Dad" is ended. It is over
Lufweye, lufweye	It is over, it is over
Lufweye kulanga "Baba," lufweye	Calling him "Dad" is ended. It is over
Lufweye, Nyasaye amulinde	It is over. May God watch over you

The totalistic nature of the event is encapsulated in the reiteration of the word *lufweye*, translated variously as "it has ended," "it's all over," "it has come to a close/end," "it is no longer possible." Logooli fatalistic worldview in the line

EXAMPLE 2.4a. "Lufweye kulanga" (PURL 2.5)

"May God watch over you" implies that since no one else can embody that familial role, the most prudent recourse is to look to God. (See music ex. 2.4a).

The church song from which the tune was sourced urged believers to engage in aggressive evangelism to avoid regret should the end-times arrive before everyone was converted (see music ex. 2.4b). The last line was about closure, a conclusion, a finality. It was not unusual to adapt a song whose lyrics were associated with finality for those issues such as death, for which the clock cannot be turned back. The original lyrics read:

Lulogooli	English Translation
Mwilwadze kuli Petero yilwadza	Preach just as Peter [the apostle] preached
Mwilwadze, mwilwadze	Preach, preach
Mwilwadze kuli Petero yilwadza	Preach just as Peter preached
Mwilwadze tsinyinga tsifweye[33]	Preach, the seasons/times are over/ended

Here, the public was urged to preach, but they were provided with model preachers. Archetypical New Testament biblical personalities were enumerated to demonstrate the breadth of characters who were motivated by cataclysmic events in their world. Given that humans everywhere and in every generation are fated to die, it was not unusual that the tune was adopted. Perhaps the clincher was the last phrase, "tsinyinga tsifweye," translated as "the seasons/times are over/ended." The word *tsifweye* (are over, have come to an end) became the key emphasis in the adapted funeral song. The original tune was retained, but the meter and rhythm were altered to accommodate the new text and to infer the related event. The funeral adaptation was set in $^6_8$ meter. In the original exhortation song, the $^{12}_8$ meter was adjusted in the second and

EXAMPLE 2.4b. "Mwilwadze kuli Petero yilwadza" (PURL 2.6)

fourth phrase into $^6_4$, perhaps to 'confuse' the mortuary connotations evoked by the funeral style.

Death marked the end of a type of season; of a type of conceptualization of time and space. One had to be prepared for a new time, season, and place whose transition was mostly arbitrary. Music announced, emoted, commemorated, marked, and remarked on the transition as a process and product as it was understood in the physical realm.

On the death of a prominent wealthy man, a cattle drive was staged in his honor, accompanied by singing and dancing. The living mimed and re-enacted the heroic deeds of the deceased because it was believed he was in the vicinity to see that the rites were properly observed. It was not unusual for people to be possessed by spirits and to pass out at cattle drives, for here, the world of spirits and humans converged. For this man, songs at his death

> told of the dead man's doings, and the cause of his death ... Cattle were driven in the open space before the hut where the man will be buried. This was done that

> the spirit of the dead man might not trouble the cattle or the herders. The cattle were driven away and the men filed into the space and began a rhythmic step. Round and round they whirled until one was almost dizzy watching them. The women and girls had their turn dancing and singing... The men were charging imaginary enemies with spear and shield... At length, after hours of dancing, waiting and singing, the grave, shallow and small was finished... In three minutes, the earth had been returned, a mound heaped, and the scene closed with the feeble old mother weirdly singing and dancing on the fresh earth of her son's grave. (Rees, E. 1908b, 6–7)

Burials usually occurred early in the morning or late at night.[34] Before the corpse was interred, a short speech was addressed to the deceased, imploring him or her not to bear any grudge against the living. For months following the burial, offerings in the form of food were left in convenient places such as attics, underneath particular trees, near the fireplace at night, or around the center post of the house. The smell was believed to satisfy the ghost until he or she got used to the new environment.

The living abstained from serious work in the period between the demise and the burial. Digging, planting in particular, was prohibited, as it connoted the idea of turning the earth—unearthing or putting into the earth—burying. Anyone found digging was believed to have either wished for or participated in the demise of the person, or else he or she presaged death of family, kin, or villager. Three days after the burial, a hair-shaving ceremony (*luvego*) was performed for ritual purification of the kin of the deceased and others present at the passing. The real purpose of the ceremony was to examine the probable cause of the death, to discuss the debts and loans of the deceased, and to distribute his or her property. The newly dead, unsettled in their new abode, were assisted by the living through proper rituals to accept their lot.[35] Funeral rites were therefore for the benefit of the living as much as for the dead.[36]

Funerals had a classic repertoire of songs associated with death due to lyrical and stylistic features related to activities such as wailing, ritual mourning, and funeral processionals. These associations were so strong that a rendition of a song or music style associated with death (such as a $\frac{2}{4}$ fast song relayed in a slow $\frac{6}{8}$ without drumming) was perceived as a wish for or premonition about death. It is also at funerals that one finds some of the earliest Christian songs associated with death alongside a few newer ones. In my experience, there were few Logooli funeral songs without Christian association. However, moans and chants continued in Logooli modes, rhythmic structures, and vocables. Music was a definite symbol, marker, and facilitator in funerals. Music in these events was also educational and entertaining.

OBSERVATIONS

Since daily life was closely intertwined with religion, and religion served to reinforce cultural values, norms, and practices, the introduction of a radical and new religion was bound to affect Logooli life. Certain Christian philosophical, religious, and social values resonated with Logooli views and were quickly customized into Logooli practice. However, an assessment of the translation or interpretation of these changes as surface layers or as deeply transformational could perhaps be gauged by analyzing cultural markers such as music. Inevitably the place and practice of indigenous Logooli music was reinforced, acculturated, or eliminated with alternative beliefs. In fact, in the 1930s, Wagner (1939) reported that 'Christian' music had replaced indigenous songs. Mwelesa's (2005) explanation, corroborated by Emory Rees (1907), was that replacement was partly instigated consciously by clan leaders, who recognized that cultural invigoration and substitution were safer than dearth and abandonment.

With colonialism, and the subsequent nationalization of Avalogooli as Kenyans, there have been shifts, changes, and accommodation of other systems. The principal vector for change was the introduction of European Christianity with attendant political and educational systems leading to an evaluation and reinvention of worldviews. These developments set Logooli music history onto new tracts. After a little more than a century, Logooli music demonstrates stable and pliable elements. Music documents and archives the past, negotiates contact, facilitates change, and comments on the resilience and transformation of culture. Music archived through written, audio, and video recordings, as well as ethnographic research, provides a transcript on a people's choices in encounters with new systems. The pathways of these transcripts will be analyzed in the next chapters.

THREE

ENCOUNTER

Avalogooli and Euro-American
Religion, Culture, and Music

BEGINNINGS

The introduction of Euro-American Christian music into Logooli society was a direct result of missionary activity in Kenya. Kenya's first enduring encounter with European Christianity was through Portuguese explorers at the close of the fifteenth century (Were and Wilson 1971, 26; Ogot and Kieran 1968 Barrett et al. 1973 21, 29; Hildebrandt 1981, 63–65). These Catholic Christian attempts, concentrated on Kenya's coast, were abandoned when the Portuguese withdrew in the mid-eighteenth century due to strong Arab and Muslim opposition and political domination. Neither the Arabs nor the Portuguese ventured inland. Islam was therefore also concentrated along the coast.

Christianity's modern proliferation in Kenya began with the efforts of John Ludwig Krapf, a German Lutheran initially employed by the Church Missionary Society (CMS) of England.[1] Krapf believed that by evangelizing the greatly feared Galla people of Ethiopia, the rest of Eastern Africa would be Christianized. He was denied access into Ethiopia through Egypt; instead he arrived on the east coast of Africa in 1844, hoping to reach the Galla from a new direction. His preliminary efforts on the coast yielded one convert. He returned to England following the death of his wife and son in Africa. While in England he traveled extensively, creating awareness of the need for missionaries through speeches. He returned to Kenya and was joined by German Johann Rebmann. They established a mission station on Kenya's coast. The inhabitants of the coastal plains, already Islamized, resisted the adoption of yet another new religion. With few converts at the coast, Krapf, Rebmann, and other CMS and British United Methodist missionaries then began the trek to

Kenya's interior. Missionary efforts to penetrate the interior were thwarted by diseases resulting in the death of key members. Additional opposition came from wars and raids by Masai and Somali groups who inhabited the stretches of desert land separating the coast from Kenya's central highlands. Ideological and personal differences amongst the missionaries resulted in schisms that further decelerated the process of Christianizing Kenya's interior (Anderson, W. 1977, 1–8).

Christianity began to make practical sense when missionaries became involved in the pressing issues of the day, especially when they opposed the slave trade. In fact, Christianity began to flourish from about 1873 when a treaty to suppress slave trade was signed between the British and Zanzibar, the seat of the Islamic sultanate and center for Arab slave trade. Freed slaves were placed in designated townships since it was unclear from whence they had been captured (Nwulia 1975, 125–137).[2] The missionaries, seeking to facilitate adjustment into the new world order, introduced with Christianity the skills of reading, writing, and vocational training. Most of the first converts were therefore former slaves who had been resettled at Kenya's coast. The first African evangelists, martyrs, and teachers emerged from these resettlements (Barrett et al. 1973, 22). Thus, from its inception, Christianity in Kenya was associated with Western education.

Kenya's interior was opened to colonial settlement and missionary penetration with the completion of the Kenya-Uganda railway in 1902. Prior to this time, Arab slave caravans and European explorer expeditions had established trade routes into Uganda mainly through Tanzania, and only occasionally through Kenya. Western Kenya where Avalogooli live was initially a bypass to Uganda for both Arabs and Europeans. In 1874, the British government took over the administration of the Uganda protectorate, which included Luyia country. The first European recorded to have passed in the vicinity of the Abaluyia was Henry M. Stanley in 1875, in his search for the headwaters of the Nile (Osogo 1966, 118). There is little evidence that Avalogooli saw him. While traders and explorers stopped to replenish food supplies, little suggests that other aspects of the lives of Abaluyia were influenced by these contacts except when Arab traders or European explorers engaged in slavery or in military skirmishes. In 1876, British subcommissioner Charles W. Hobley traveled through Luyialand and met with clan leaders as part of British imperial subjugation of local resistance. After the railway was completed in 1902, Luyia country was annexed to Kenya from Uganda, to facilitate jurisdiction of railway property in a transaction completed in 1918. British protection and improved transport facilities may, unwittingly, have been the strongest incentives for missionary expansion. They were guaranteed safety and protection to the interior by powerful European political agency (Lonsdale 1977; Maxon 2002).

A policy of comity was established by the various Christian missionary societies, which encouraged the notion of spheres of influence.[3] According to this policy, if an organization established work within an ethnic group or locale, a different agency was encouraged to labor elsewhere. Protestant missions adhered to this policy. The CMS set up a mission compound in Logooli country as a stopgap en route to the Baganda in the late nineteenth century.[4] Although they proselytized other Abaluyia, the CMS barely touched Avalogooli. In fact, until 1902, no mission had instituted itself amongst Avalogooli (Stafford 1973, 78–82). The Friends African Mission (FAM; formerly the Friends Africa Industrial Mission [FAIM]), a society based in the United States, became the first group to claim Ivulogooli. Avalogooli were very soon after introduced to a different mode of Christianity through a fortuitous encounter with Pentecostalism.

THE FRIENDS/QUAKERS

The FAM (Quakers, or Friends) was the first missionary group to significantly impact Avalogooli (Barrett et al. 1973, 29–39; Stafford 1973, 72–103; Kasiera 1981, 82–208; Rasmussen 1995, 39–66). Other groups that had contact with Avalogooli at the beginning of the twentieth century included the CMS and the South African Compound and Interior Mission. The Quakers soon assumed responsibility of Ivulogooli. To understand the impact and subsequent effect of Quaker doctrines and devotional styles on Avalogooli, I will briefly trace the development of Quakerism in order to provide some perspective on the musics and performance practices considered appropriate in Christian worship.

Stafford (1973, 46–66) and Rasmussen (1995, 1–25) outline the beginnings of Quakerism to justify subsequent interest and approach to missionary endeavor in Africa. George Fox founded the Quaker movement in England in 1647. Fox, a former Calvinist, deviated from the idea of limited atonement and a view of man as totally doomed. He, instead, sought to portray Christianity as love and redemption for all mankind. Fox advocated for a personal salvation and viewed Christ as a living spirit working in man toward a moral transformation. Man had to find God's will for his life. The Bible was not the final authority on God's will. It was treated as a segment of God's purpose for an individual. To determine God's will, Fox and his friends meditated and searched for an 'Inner Light.' They then formed a Society of Friends, made up of "a small group of believers meeting together without a formal program of worship, waiting in silence for the spirit to speak to individuals, sharing the word with all and then seeking a corporate judgment as to what was actually the will of God" (Stafford 1973, 47). The movement, as it grew in numbers, was institutionalized, having not just weekly, monthly, and quarterly meetings but a Yearly Meeting whose function was to project annual events. These practices and beliefs were carried to mission fields.

The Quakers arrived in the United States around 1656, bringing from England administrative and liturgical practices. The nineteenth-century growth of evangelical Protestantism in Great Britain and in the United States, compounded by revival meetings, led to schisms in doctrine, resulting in the formation of three camps outlined by Stafford (1973, 52–59) as:

a) The fundamentals and elders who clung to the 'Inner Light' tradition,
b) The evangelicals who advocated for the Bible as the final authority on God's will and opposed the 'Inner Light' doctrine, and
c) The moderates who accepted both positions.

The Evangelicals transformed the silent and restrained Quaker meetings into services characterized by exuberant testimonies, emotional conversions, and fervent prayers. Their four main theological emphases of justification, sanctification, the second coming of Christ, and faith healing were reflected in their hymn texts. Music, especially singing, and Bible readings became fixed items of the worship rites. With a new view of Christianity, the Evangelicals determined to reach the world with the Christian message. It was from the fervor of Evangelicals that foreign mission societies were formed (Rasmussen 1995, 19).

Kasiera (1981, 112–141) also discusses the social and religious climate in the United States that motivated the types of approaches propagated by Quaker missionaries that in effect posited a kind of North American Christianity in philosophy, doctrine, and practice. According to Kasiera's analysis, proponents of the social gospel advocated for moral change and social justice, founded on what was understood to be Christian ethics, as imperative for humanity worldwide. These philosophical and doctrinal bases provided a frame of reference for evangelism, matters of what sin was and was not, consequently delineating what was acceptable or undesirable. The social aspect provided service emphases, such as medical ministry, industrial work, formal education, and tolerance for religious factionalism.

The link between the Friends in the United States and Kenya was established through Willis Hotchkiss, a Quaker graduate of Cleveland Bible Institute (Stafford 1973, 60–66; Kasiera 1981, 90–96). Hotchkiss had, in 1895, served the Kamba people of Kenya under the auspices of the African Inland Mission. A combination of factors culminating in the death of most of his companions eventuated his return to the United States. Hotchkiss, undeterred, determined more than ever to return to Kenya but with a new emphasis to his ministry (Stafford 1973, 83–89; Hotchkiss 1937). His earlier experience had impressed on him the idea of integrating Christianity with 'civilization.' He believed an industrial mission station would enable Africans to learn practical skills while being evangelized. The mission would profit from the sale of goods produced by a trained Christian labor force that would also maintain the station. He prevailed on the foreign missions board to send out workers to embark on a fourfold ministry. The branches were evangelistic, medical, educational, and industrial. Arthur Chilson, with industrial skills, and Edgar T. Hole, a business manager, were appointed to accompany Hotchkiss. The board was comprised of both Evangelical and Fundamentalist Quakers. Hole was of the Fundamental persuasion, while the other two were Evangelicals. The trio arrived in Kenya in 1902 (Hoskins 1945, 11–20; Spencer 1975, 266; Kasiera 1981, 90–96).

A chance campsite at Kaimosi in Tiriki territory in August of 1902 became the permanent location for the first and most important Friends' mission station (Hoyt and Hawthorne n.d., 5–6). This no-man's-land strip between the pastoral Nandi and the agricultural Logooli and Tiriki was strategic in that once the British subdued the warring Nandi in 1906, Avalogooli migrated into the area and became the Quakers' main adherents.[5] Nandi resistance had led to the evacuation of missionaries from Kaimosi to a station then called Maragoli (now Vihiga) that was previously owned by the CMS (Hoskins 1945, 20). Maragoli became the second venue for Quaker activity from 1906 (Hole 1907, 365) and the primary residence of missionary Emory Rees, who broke ground by translating the Bible and European/American hymns into Lulogooli. A third Quaker mission station was started at Lirhanda among

Avidakho, who neighbor Avalogooli. The first readers and primary hymnbook for all the converts were in Lulogooli (Hoskins 1945, 23; Adede 1986, 19–33). By the end of the first decade of the twentieth century, Quakers held monthly meetings at these stations. The most active locale, Maragoli, was the first to host a quarterly meeting (Records of Friends African Mission 1904–1907; Africa Record 1906–1916).[6]

Early missionaries experienced setbacks due to disease and internal disagreements that resulted in the retirement of Hotchkiss, along with a lack of adequate personnel to supervise their projects. Resistance was also experienced from Avadirichi, who refused to abandon traditional practices and rites frowned upon by missionaries. Thus Avalogooli became the target group for the Quaker enterprise. Missionaries initially had few adult converts. Consequently, some of the initial prayer meetings by Avalogooli on their own were conducted by children, "the oldest not being more than ten years old, ... singing hymns, praying, and talking to those assembled" (E. Rees 1910b, 544).[7] These meetings were upheld despite parental opposition. Famine endeared the missionaries to the adults, many of whom went to the station for food. Missionaries gained further acceptance through their medical work when Avalogooli profited from services provided during outbreaks of diseases such as smallpox and malaria. There was a marked turnaround when Logooli leaders and adults endorsed mission work. Elisha Blackburn of the Kaimosi station reported:

> The chief Mugera, urges his people to leave their work on the First-day and come to the service. One Sabbath, recently, he employed a rather unique method to compel their obedience. After service, he inquired about Makona and his people who live in a settlement apart from others. His people replied that they were in their gardens digging. Mugera thereupon commanded some of his headmen to go and take away their hoes from them, so that they could not work on the Sabbath. They did so, and we notice that the following Sabbath, Makona and his people were present for service. So the lesson is effectual. (Blackburn, E. 1908, 560)

Missionary efforts, especially in education, were rewarded only after World War I when socio-economic demands by the colonial government motivated many Avalogooli to learn to read and write in order to acquire employment. Avalogooli were enticed to the stations when they observed the economic mobility of those with missionary education. The high Logooli population rate also forced some to seek alternative sources of income at the mission station or from the colonial government. Access to missionary education bolstered the acquisition of a different type of job away from home (Wagner 1936).

Quaker missionaries emphasized evangelism followed by basic education. The prevailing attitude of racial superiority of the white man was part of the missionary worldview. The African was to acquire enough literacy to read the Bible and the hymnbook. This education was supplemented by vocational skills to enable the African to be a low-paid employee of the missionary enterprise, the settlers, or the colonial government (Rowe 1958, 2–4). Avalogooli initially learned to read and write in Kiswahili, the primary trade language (Hole 1905; Rees, E. 1905, 1907; Wendte 1904).[8] When the missionaries realized that Kiswahili was foreign to Avalogooli, they translated into Lulogooli select scriptures beginning with the Gospel of Mark, as well as hymn texts. Emory Rees, who replaced Hotchkiss in 1904, noted:

> Natives who had never heard the gospel in their own tongue and who heard all prayer and all singing in a foreign tongue very naturally concluded that Swahili was an essential part of religious exercises. With the introduction of hymns and prayers and testimonies in their own tongue the new religion ceased to be a foreign thing and began to come closer to home to their lives and those who heard it. (Emerson 1958, 15)

Rees wrote readers to induct Avalogooli into literacy. The orthography was based on that in Kiswahili readers, thus rules had to be invented to accommodate Logooli consonants without equivalency in Kiswahili. For example, the letter 'l' could be sounded as in English or rolled/lapped. Written, sometimes the letter 'r' was used for the rolled 'l.' One learned that relative to the preceding or ensuing consonants, the sound was spelled as an 'l' or as an 'r.' The first reader was printed by the CMS Press in Uganda in 1907. More copies were made in the United States.[9] By the end of 1907, the Maragoli mission acquired a printing press (White 1907). Readers and translations of the Gospels in Lulogooli gave Avalogooli literary and subsequent economic advantage over their neighbors. Thus, although mission stations existed in Kaimosi (Nandi/Tiriki country), Maragoli (Logooli country), Lirhanda (Idakho country), and Kitoshi (Bukusu country), only Lulogooli orthography was created to serve these groups. Thus Lulogooli speakers and readers gained literary and subsequent educational leverage over other Luyia.

Quakers are regarded as the pioneers of Christian work amongst Avalogooli. They not only sought Christian converts; they intended to introduce a new way of life. Missionary social impact was felt in vocational training, in medical work, and in the introduction of literacy. These developments transformed the lifestyle of Avalogooli, providing alternative means of survival besides farming. The Quakers further introduced new musics aimed at replacing 'pagan' and 'uncivilized' Logooli practices. Kasiera (1981, 204) reiterates the unworthiness of Logooli musical styles, stating: "Traditional dancing and singing was considered sin." Avalogooli had to learn the acceptable music styles and performance practices commensurate with the new belief system.

According to Rees's reports, a few hymns were printed and new ones gradually added until a complete hymnal was eventually standardized. By 1916, the book had forty songs and other matter such as the Lord's Prayer, the Ten Commandments, and some psalms (Friends Missionary Advocate 1916, 40). By 1918, a sizeable hymnal with the other matter was published.[10] The compilation, *Tsinyimbu tsyo Kwidzominya Nyasaye* (Songs of praise to God), was gradually expanded (see FAIM 1920). It was used in schools and in church gatherings. Near the end of World War I, Avalogooli demanded more schools. Kaimosi mission graduates were employed as teachers. These teachers, carrying the legacy of missionary hymnody, disseminated the songs to a wider audience. The hymns were usually sung a cappella. Canadian Pentecostals (begun in 1910 but registered in 1924; Barrett et al. 1973, 279) evangelized the same ethnic groups almost concurrently with the Quakers but from a different doctrinal and musical perspective. They incorporated hand clapping and drumming as distinctive features of the music of 'spirit' and Africanist groups. Thus, two mission groups taught similar hymns but performed using different practices.

THE PENTECOSTALS

The Pentecostal movement grew out of the Great American Awakening of the nineteenth century (Hollenweger 1997; Synan 1997). Like Evangelical Quakers, Pentecostals believed in a personal salvation (conversion), faith healing, Christ's second coming, and the Bible as the sole authority on God's will. Further, Pentecostals propagated for an additional religious experience after initial conversion, referred to as the 'Baptism in the Holy Spirit,' physically evidenced by speaking in 'an unknown tongue.' The movement, said to have begun in Kansas, spread rapidly to Canada at the beginning of the twentieth century. As the number of believers and congregations grew, a need arose for a central organization to coordinate planning and provide a basis for doctrinal agreement amongst pastors. The governing body was also to endorse and support missionaries. The first concrete organizational unit in Canada was achieved in 1917, with the official name, Pentecostal Assemblies of Canada, adopted in 1922 (http://www.paoc.org/, accessed March 22, 2004).

The Pentecostal Assemblies of Canada (PAOC) formally affiliated themselves with missionary work in Kenya in 1924 when they began to support Otto C. Keller and his wife, Marian.[11] Keller, a young American businessman, had arrived in Kenya in 1914 to continue the work begun in Tanganyika by his friend Rev. Karl Wittich, Marian's first husband. However, Keller was denied permission to enter Tanganyika. Using his personal funds, he purchased land in Kenya at Nyang'ori, located about seven miles north of Kisumu, the railway terminus. His no-man's-land separated four ethnic groups with different languages and cultures: the Bantu Logooli, the Nilotic Luo, the Highland Nilotic Terik (who are closely related to the Nandi), and some Somali (Cushites), who were originally part of Arab slave caravans (Keller, M. 1933, 22–23). The land had initially been given to an English subject, Percival H. Clarke, by the British colonial government as a gift for helping put down Nandi resistance in 1905 (Kasiera 1981, 215). Clyde Miller bought the land from Clarke in 1910. Miller was an American affiliated with the Apostolic Faith Mission of Iowa. His 'Pentecostal experience' inspired him to become a missionary. He and his wife arrived in Kenya around 1907. The policy of comity placed Quakers among Avalogooli and the South African Compound and Interior Mission with the neighboring Banyore. The CMS and a Nilotic Interior Missions group targeted the Luo. The region around Nyang'ori, inhabited by the unclaimed Terik, was a free sphere of influence. Miller purchased Clarke's no-man's-land to evangelize the Terik. Several factors including desertion by his wife, hostility from other missionaries, and differences with his U.S. supporters forced Miller to sell out to Keller, a fellow North American and Pentecostal (Kasiera 1981, 239). Keller's Canadian wife, Marian, was the eventual link between Nyang'ori and Canada.

The Kellers formally began work as independent missionaries in 1920 (Keller, M. 1946). Their Pentecostal backgrounds dictated the emphasis of their work be evangelical rather than educational. Although their station was located amidst various ethnic groups, "Only the Marigoli [sic] came in search of work [at the mission station] ... They saw in the white man's employment a path to the coveted European prestige" (Keller, M. 1933, 38). Keller, working on his own, built a large church at the station. He constructed a school with workshops to train Africans (mostly Logooli) in manual labor. Children were removed from their homes and housed in dormitories. As the Kellers' work expanded and branch schools were opened, the colonial government advised them to acquire backing by a chartered organization. The Kellers applied and were accepted as PAOC missionaries in 1924 (PAOC Archives).

Between 1926 and 1928, the Pentecostal mission was suddenly expanded when a revival, instigated by Quaker Arthur Chilson, broke out in Kaimosi, the Friends main station (Kasiera 1981, 338–468; Rasmusen 1995, 58–66). Fundamentalist Quakers felt that meetings were getting out of hand when the services were 'disturbed' by the 'ecstatic experiences' displayed and recounted by those who claimed to be filled with the Holy Spirit. These missionaries imposed restrictions, forcing the departure of some converts. While some dissidents formed independent movements such as *Dini ya Roho* (The religion of the Spirit), a large majority, including prominent members, joined the PAOC Nyang'ori station that embraced the 'Baptism in the Holy Spirit' doctrine (Ogot and Welbourn 1966, 74–75). In effect, Avalogooli were now officially proselytized by two different missionary societies. Quakers were known as *Vafurenzi*, a pluralized Lulogooli intonation of the word 'Friends' (sing. *mfurenzi*). Pentecostals were referred to as *Vabende* in Lulogooli (sing. *Mubende*).[12]

It may be that Pentecostalism brought Christianity closer to Logooli beliefs in spirits and how the supernatural is physically manifested amongst the living.[13] Christian spirit possession was not about convincing Avalogooli about spirit visitation and abode; it was regarding "the proper manner in which to receive The Spirit, conduct everything in an orderly way" (Kasiera 1981, 345), and to persuade Avalogooli that the Christian Holy Spirit would empower those who accessed 'it.' The spirit was perceived as a mediator, an enabler to transcend the physical and reach the otherworld, similar to roles of spirits in indigenous lore. It was from the spirit's manifestation and faculty that Logooli hymnody and 'Christian' performance practices were formed and sanctioned. In services, Africans sang European hymns with "no more enthusiasm than an English village church" (Ogot and Welbourn 1966, 99). There was a marked difference when they broke into their own hymns. An African Israel Church Nineveh[14] member remarked on the origin of indigenous hymnody: "In high moment with God, I would find myself singing new songs . . . Sometimes I just awoke to find myself singing. Many of the peculiarly African Israel Nineveh hymns have started this way before being communicated to the congregation. So have some of our distinctive practices" (Ogot and Welbourne 1966, 96).

Pentecostals embraced a Logooli aesthetic to singing/music performance particularly at prayer meetings. These meetings were held in homes for more intimate community fellowship (Ogot and Welbourne 1966, 81; Keller letters in PAOC Archives; Kasiera 1981, 532–536). Here, African Christians assumed musical mannerisms restrained in missionary presence. Drumming and hand clapping had initially been encouraged to help maintain the tempo of hymns, as missionaries complained about Logooli tendency to slow the speed.[15] The slow tempo might have been adopted because missionaries sang their hymns in ways that resembled solemn Logooli sacred ritual songs. Hand clapping at home prayer meetings engendered a different ethos. A close analysis reveals a Logooli music performance theory and practice. Here, the clap was a metronome against which one constructed cross-/polyrhythms and imaged and improvised in hemiola. It was a way of realizing or interpreting a song relative to personal or group preference but in a manner that was musically appropriate, correct, and pleasant according to Logooli aesthetics.[16] Euro-American hymns were altered not only in structure and performance practice; they were also assigned function and use in the larger Logooli life. As they gained functional value in ritual and social events, they were performed in styles dictated by those occasions.

Songs, hymns, and refrains emanating from Evangelical Quakers and Pentecostal missionaries became basic Christian repertoire. Compositions by Logooli Christians in these styles and from encounters with the Holy Spirit expanded musical resources, practices, and choices. The Salvation Army (first introduced in 1921 and registered in 1936—Barrett et al. 1973, 188), with their colorful parades, white uniforms, instruments, and style of presentation, added to the reservoir of choices adopted by Pentecostal and African Initiated and Separatist churches (see fig 3.1).[17]

EFFECTS OF CHRISTIANITY AND THE USE OF ITS MUSIC

The primary objective of Christianity was to completely revolutionize Logooli philosophy and worldview. Every aspect of African life was perceived as primitive or pagan and in need of reformation. Christianity was the vector for the 'civilization' of the African. Christianization was usually equated with Westernization. Missionaries used schools to propagate their dress, their mu-

FIGURE 3.1. Salvation Army processional.

sics, and their ideals and lifestyle. Avalogooli viewed some aspects of Western modernity as progressive. Others were rejected, ignored, or transformed when perceived as antagonistic to local values and resources. New ideas accepted by Avalogooli and integrated in daily life included the concept of a Supreme God who was directly accessible and the notion of a mediator or intercessor who had experienced physical life before becoming a spirit. These beliefs resonated with Logooli understandings of a supernatural being interested in human affairs with ancestors as possible intermediaries. Other foreign beliefs were blended with Logooli ideas to achieve a workable compromise. New practices and rites were integrated into the daily life and life cycle of Avalogooli, some wholesale, while others were adapted and/or adopted as alternatives. Avalogooli needed to find a vantage from which to embrace Christianity, at a pace they could handle and with resources they could manage. They became Logooli Christians and/or made Christianity Logooli.

The most significant effect of Christianity was a convert's decision to identify in a new way. Being mulogooli by birth was a set heritage. Becoming a Christian was a conscious choice. The choice may have been based on persuasive arguments presented by missionaries and converts. Other decisions were dictated by circumstances such as the need for food during hun-

FIGURE 3.2. Gathering for water baptism at a river in Ivojo village.

ger, medical treatment when sick or hurt, housing when displaced, a job for economic survival, education for social and economic mobility, and other pragmatic reasons. While Quakers claimed the 'right' to Avalogooli divvied to them by the policy of comity, the presence of other denominations provided options.

One chose to become a Quaker or a Pentecostal. On declaring his or her desire, an individual underwent 'classes' for up to two years to learn the basic tenets of the faith and to confirm the seriousness of intent to denominational and church leaders. He or she also made a public confession of faith and maintained regular and mandatory attendance at meetings. If the person 'sinned,' he or she could repent and start over (Hole 1911;[18] Keller letters in PAOC Archives). Quakers officially received new members into fellowship. For Pentecostals a member was confirmed by water baptism in ponds or rivers (see fig. 3.2). The immersion was witnessed by the general public and typically accompanied with singing as the people went to the pond or river, as the converts were dipped in the water, and when they returned to church or went home.

With the intent to be baptized or to be accepted into the fellowship, converts chose or were given a 'Christian' name of European or Biblical origin that was officially conferred when they were immersed or received into membership. Initially this designation set apart Christians from nonconverts or Muslims. It also aligned the convert with a particular type of Christian persuasion or colonizing agency.[19] Thus, at a fundamental level, conversion, signified by water baptism or being officially received into membership and affirmed by the adoption of a new name (different from a clan name), was commensurate with Logooli practice at the birth of a child.

Church members were hereafter required to adhere to new religious practices, observe alternative rituals, or change the ways in which they conducted or approached indigenous rites considered immutable (Rees D., private letters in *African Papers*; Keller letters in PAOC Archives). Members who failed to adhere to the rules were excommunicated. If they repented, they were monitored for a while before being accepted back into the fellowship. In time converts gave their children a 'Christian' and clan name at birth and added a family surname as required by the British colonial government. A child was essentially grandfathered into Christianity once the parents embraced the religion. But the said child eventually chose to become a member of a church and was baptized or received into the fellowship. In this instance, a new name was not conferred. Rather, the new member was officially entered into the church registry. With registration, new rights and responsibilities were embraced alongside and/or in opposition to those of the clan.

NEW RELIGIOUS PRACTICES
The Sunday Service

Pentecostals and Quakers set aside Sunday as a day of worship. Sunday was referred to as First-day or Sabbath. Avalogooli observed the day by abstaining from work and attending church. When this practice was first introduced, some who were not party to the new system decided to work in their farms. Among other things, these people are said to have encountered misfortunes. One old man is reported to have hurt his head with the hoe he was using to cultivate his land. The story was often recounted to warn the public about the consequences of desecrating Sunday (Kasiera 1981, 183). Chiefs sympathetic to the missionary enterprise also promoted the observance.

The most important Christian gathering for both Quakers and Pentecostals has been the Sunday service. In many cases, this service used to last from 9 A.M. to 2 P.M. In spite of idiosyncratic styles of worship, both groups observed singing, prayers, a sermon, and offertory in their services. A Pentecostal service was typically characterized by more exuberant singing than a Quaker one. The singing was often accompanied by clapping of hands. Drums and idiophones, such as a hoe, kept a metronomic tempo and a timeline. Most hymns included some call and response with the song leader regulating the mood, dynamics, tempo, and organization of the stanzas for religious and aesthetic fulfillment.

Singing in a Pentecostal gathering punctuated service items and articulated worship through praise and prayers. Until the 1980s, Pentecostal services always began with individual prayers as a call to participants to personally sanctify themselves (*kwitakasa*). The worshippers as they arrived in church each began by addressing God quietly or audibly in praise or in confession of sins. All the members prayed at the same time as individual expressions within a collective gathering. This practice further placed on individuals the onus for the success or failure of the collective service. The call for unity was signaled either by a prayer from the service leader or by someone beginning a song that was taken up by others in agreement with its appropriateness in the moment. Within the service different items were surrounded and punctuated by functional music such as songs to open a service, to pray, to invite visitors, to take up offering, and to reinforce a greeting, a teaching, a sermon, and so forth. Songs were even raised as an alternative to a testimony. Thus song was thoroughly integrated into the service.

Singing in Quaker services was perceived as slower or less emotional compared to that in Pentecostal services. Song items were also generally fewer. Amongst Fundamentalist Quakers and in general, songs were not usually accompanied by clapping of hands or any other type of instrument. The practice of silent meetings (waiting for 'Inner Light') was even eventually abandoned by many rural congregations. Instead, a pastor or an elder led the service. Visitors were invited to greet the congregation often after the sermon as part of social business. A constant feature of a Friends Sunday service in rural areas was to end with the Lord's Prayer, a practice that was introduced by missionaries in the early 1900s (Wendte 1904).[20]

Amongst both Quakers and Pentecostals, prayers were interspersed with congregational responses (*kufuminya*: rooted in a word denoting 'to cover protectively'), a practice carried over from ethnic sacrificial gatherings (Mulindi 1983, 79). In this way the congregation endorsed and agreed with the leader, becoming active participants in prayer. If the public was uncomfortable or disagreed with the content of a prayer, there was silence. Most prayers focused on protection, blessing, and praise. Special prayers were also said for the sick and disabled. In addition to the main service, children and adolescents attended Sunday school often before the main service or on being dismissed at some point from the main service.

Until the late 1960s, Sunday morning prayer meetings were an integral part of rural Pentecostal adherents' lives. Often these prayers were held as early as 5:00 A.M. The service included singing apart from prayer and a short exhortation designed to spotlight the focus of the prayer service. These meetings were well attended because here, the needs of the community that had perforce become the church's problems were presented and prayed over collectively and individually in a space considered safe (Kasiera 1981, 550–558). Afterward, members returned home to perform necessary morning chores before returning for the main service. Meetings for youth (originally called Christian Endeavor by Quakers, and Christ's Ambassadors by Pentecostals) often took place on Sunday afternoon.

Other Christian Meetings

On weekdays and on Saturdays, other services held by Pentecostals and Quakers included prayer meetings, women's gatherings, and youth programs. The general format of the meetings was the same as that of the Sunday service, but the sermons were directly related to the concerns of the participants.[21] The Quaker church calendar has, for example, a meeting named after a date in the month. The meeting held at the end of the month is called *Isalasini*, directly translated as 'of the 30th,' which refers to the last Sunday of the month. On this day, members bring in their tithes. Pentecostals and Africanist churches appropriated the word 'Isalasini' and used the day for similar practices.

The Quaker idea of meetings is much broader than just a religious gathering. It incorporates social and administrative dimensions. From an administrative perspective, a local congregation is referred to as a 'monthly' meeting, Isalasini. Isalasini is made up of two to twelve smaller meetings (Smuck 1985, 165). Several monthly meetings are administered as a 'quarterly' meeting under a central organizing body called the Yearly Meeting. Until 1973, Kenyans had only one Yearly Meeting. Internal squabbles led to two meetings, the East Africa Yearly Meeting and the Elgon Religious Society of Friends (Bukusu/

North), each autonomously administered. A further split occurred, birthing an entity called the East Africa Yearly Meeting—South (ibid., 169–170). By 2005, Kenya had fifteen Yearly Meetings, six of which comprised a Logooli majority.[22] The groups cooperated under an umbrella body known as Friends Church in Kenya.

From the onset, Quakers were encouraged to proselytize in their neighborhoods. Pentecostals also arranged for evangelistic campaigns. These services, held on weekday mornings and evenings, featured items designed to proselytize the public. Peculiar to advertising the meeting was a processional accompanied by drums within the assembly[23] location, an idea appropriated from the Salvation Army. The procession, known as *vushuhuda* (borrowed from the Kiswahili word *ushuhuda,* meaning testimony, witness), complete with a flag bearer, advertised the upcoming event (see fig. 3.3). The group paraded through the neighborhood, marching in double file with the song leader either at the front or walking up and down the file with a megaphone. Although the basic movement was a march, the tempo and style of their stride ranged from dignified military to spectacular jogging. They eventually congregated at church for a service. Vushuhuda was also conducted in market places and other public venues. A group marched from their church to the venue. They pitched their flag, around which members sang to attract a crowd. More songs, testimonies, prayers, exhortations, and sermons were delivered.[24] Afterward, members processed back to church, dropping along the route at their homesteads.

Vushuhuda in rural spaces had a few differences from that in urban centers. In the latter, meetings were held primarily on Sunday afternoons. After a church service, members processed to an open public arena; for example, a shopping center or an open-air market. They pitched their flag, continued singing, prayed, and gave testimonies and exhortations interspersed with songs. A group member preached and invited an audience response. After the meeting, members left individually or dropped along the processional route upon arriving at their homes.

Afrogenic 'spirit' churches, such as the African Divine Church (ADC) or the AICN, whose members traveled long distances on foot for their monthly gatherings expanded the idea of a vushuhuda processional. Dressed in colorful uniforms for distinction, they half-jogged in double file to a public space while singing. At the head or side of the group, a flag carrier identified the denomination and assembly, followed by drummers and a song leader with

FIGURE 3.3. African Divine Church vushuhuda.

a megaphone. The leader ran up and down the file to motivate the singers. Members of the public attracted to the procession joined the file. Those who were not appropriately attired brought up the rear. The procession became a little humorous in cities like Nairobi, when members boarded a bus and instead of sitting, continued to jog on the spot in the aisle until the bus driver either stopped them or the vehicle threatened to overturn because of the motion. Even when they sat down, they continued to sing, sway, and stamp their feet. Once the procession arrived at the venue designated for a meeting, the service was conducted in much the same manner as that of the Pentecostals but with music and other 'ritual' behavior styled as was appropriate for the denomination.

Other Christian Religious Ceremonies

Christianity introduced new religious festivals like Christmas (*Siguuku*, derived from the Kiswahili phrase *siku kuu*, meaning a great, important, or high day), Easter, and New Year's celebrations. Until the 1980s, Christmas was heralded at least two weeks in advance by caroling. This practice, although it may appear similar to what happens in Europe or the Americas, was easy to adopt because Avalogooli anticipated important events/rites with evening sings dubbed *kuhihiza* (related to the word *kuhia*, to warm, to heat, to burn).[25] Here, young people and children sung as they walked along the main road to arouse public interest. The music included social and religious songs performed in call-and-response style. If the group decided to visit, for example, the pastor's home, they sang a set of social/praise songs, carols, and hymns outside the house for 15–30 minutes until the pastor or an adult emerged and provided them with a treat (such as candy, ripe bananas, etc.). They then returned to the road and sang until they tired out and retired to their homes. It was also an occasion for courtship and fun. This practice gradually died out except for events on Christmas Day, originally the climax of the caroling (PURL 3.1).

On Christmas Day, each village church and assembly customarily participated in a music festival and competition, which also included group recitation of Bible passages (*malago*) relating to the birth of Christ. The competition event itself, including songs, recitations, and drama, is also called malago.[26] The contest typically took place outdoors because church buildings were too small to cater to the crowds gathered for the celebration. While most songs were carols, the occasion had, since its inception by missionaries, been used for evangelism, or to introduce new songs or 'Christian' ideas (Keller letters in PAOC Archives). Thus more than Christmas carols formed the body of repertoire. Competitors were classified by age group: Sunday school children (preteens), youth (teens–30-year-olds), adult church members (mixed gender), women's groups, and assemblies (mixed gender). Few men participated in the singing.

Carols sung at malago were in Lulogooli, Kiswahili, and English. Lulogooli carols were translations and Lulogooli versions of songs and carols initiated by missionaries, songs heard on radio or other media, or songs learned from elsewhere. Kiswahili carols could be translated missionary carols or compositions in *kwaya* (choir-music style), gospel numbers, and school songs. Other than drums, instruments were rarely used. Youth groups sang in English or Kiswahili and in four-part harmony to demonstrate participation in life beyond the village and acquisition of 'elite' culture. Children also sang in a several languages. Formerly, each ensemble selected its carol, but the assemblies' councils of elders prescribed malago scriptures. Recently, partly due to a lack of new repertoire by rural churches, a set piece is stipulated for different age groups.

Apart from the youth, all other groups announced their arrival with a processional song. While that of adults was staid and marchlike, children

Example 3.1. "Sisi wa Goibei" (PURL 3.2; PURL 3.3)

displayed creative dance moves learned specifically for show (see fig. 3.4). The song in Lulogooli or Kiswahili was not limited to religious content. Music ex. 3.1, a song commonly performed in the 1980s for entering the stage area, is in Kiswahili. The singers identified themselves by the name of their village church (Goibei) and declared that they were taking the stage: "Sisi wa Goibei, tunaingia" (We [the children] of Goibei are coming in/arriving). The entire song is based on a short melodic fragment, in call-and-response practice. The response has the character of a chant (PURL 3.3).

The leader varied the text by naming different ways of belonging, such as to a parent, to a school; identifying themselves as humble, beautiful, smart, well behaved, and so forth. Against the refrain line "tunaingia," other 'calls' included:

Lulogooli	**English Translation**
Sisi wana wa mama	We, the children of mothers/ladies
Sisi wana wapole	We, the humble children
Sisi wana wa shule	We, the schoolchildren, etc.

Performers thereafter arranged themselves in two to three lines and proceeded to sing. They faced the dais where honored guests and adjudicators were seated. The rest of the audience usually sat behind the performers (see fig. 3.5). The choir was always 'tuned' first. Here the conductor set the pitch by singing the first line or a portion thereof and asking the choir to sing it back to be sure they had the right pitch, prompted by the question "Tune?" The choir sang the set pitch. The conductor, to verify the pitch, said "again" and the choir tuned again. The conductor then set the tempo by either saying in time "Moja, Mbili, Tatu" (one, two, three—ready, steady, go), or "Three, Four." Then the choir sang to demonstrative 'conducting' by the leader. After singing, the group recited scriptures in English, Kiswahili, or Lulogooli. The conductor declared the scriptural basis of the recitation and then loudly prompted the group to recite in this manner:

FIGURE 3.4. A children's malago procession.

> Leader: Luka kaviri luvaso ishirini na sita kuduka sarasini livola ndi?
> (What does Luke [chapter] 2 verses 26–30 state?)

Or the leader stated the context, then prompted the group recitation:

> Leader: Luka kaviri luvaso ishirini na sita kuduka sarasini. Moja! Mbili! Tatu!
> (Luke [chapter] 2 verses 26–30. One! Two! Three! [Ready, steady, go])

The group then recited while the leader conducted syllabically or using gestures intended to both bring out the best in the group in terms of volume and expression and to entertain the crowd. This part of malago was often more entertaining to watch than the singing. An ensemble could also dramatize the recitation and the carol.

A Christmas Day celebration (malago) lasted about five to six hours. Pentecostal missionaries initiated this mode of celebrating Christmas in the 1920s (PAOC Archives video 1948; Keller letters in PAOC Archives).[27] Initially, Christmas was the most important service of the year. At first, all the assemblies met in Nyang'ori for a Christmas service that was more evangelistic than celebratory.

As the denomination expanded, various regional assemblies congregated at a central location for an outdoors festival that included singing, Bible reading, and a re-enactment of the Christmas story as the centerpiece of the ceremony. The re-enactment was usually in the form of a theatrical or dramatic piece. Songs at the event included translated Christmas carols, evangelistic songs, and songs with Bible teachings (Kasiera 1981, 474). In 1928, the Kellers recounted how students who were studying the book of Revelation were required to memorize portions of the book, which they recited at the Christmas celebrations interspersed with relevant songs:

> About our Xmas program. It is quite a problem to think out a new program, yet we must say that the Lord has sweetly inspired and helped each year. During the year 1928, there were about 75 girls, women and boys who were studying the Book of Revelations. To each one of these I gave a portion of this wonderful book to memorize, starting at the First chapter and going through to the end. To make it more interesting, I taught them five different hymns suitable to the verses that were memorized. For instance, when they got to the portion where it says "Behold I stand at the door and knock" they all joined in singing "There's a Saviour standing at the door."... It was very inspiring and encouraging to hear these Natives memorize the Living Word. This part of the program took an hour. There were about 12 more items and our Christmas service continued about three hours. (Keller, O. and M. 1929, 12)

Although malago began as a thanksgiving celebration, it soon turned into a song and scripture recitation competition. Since the exhibition staged a novel performance that included different song types, presentations acquired sophisticated theatrical work. In addition to singing and verse recitation, performers incorporated props to make their presentation more effective. Prizes were awarded for the best malago, adjudicated by missionaries and local teachers. In the year following, winners sought to retain their superi-

EXAMPLE 3.2. "Ni isiguku lero"

FIGURE 3.5. Malago performance.

ority or to transcend their previous ideas. For example, new repertoire by a choir rendered them progressive. If they won, they presented another new song the following year or an improved version of the previous year's song. Meanwhile, other choirs also presented the 'winning' song from the previous year. In this way, new songs were sought and learned, but by the same virtue, these songs were standardized when other ensembles adopted them. Malago was strangely reminiscent of singing contests at wedding rites and at annual collective cultural sacrifices, Mwing'oma.

By 2010, Christmas celebrations were more entertainment than education. The celebration began with singing the classic hymn "Ni isiguku lero" (It is Christmas today) in solemn fashion (slowly, without hand clapping or drumming; see music ex. 3.2).[28] After prayers and a short sermon, malago commenced. The celebration ended after results were announced and winners were presented with awards.

Since malago took up most of the day, participants snacked on sugarcane, juice, or other 'nibbles.' Vendors of foods such as ripe bananas or mandazi (deep-fried sweetened dough) set up mats. There was no communal feasting as happens in indigenous ceremonial gatherings. Instead, soft drinks such as Coca-Cola were served only to pastors, elders, adjudicators, and other recognized guests such as white people, community socialites, and political leaders. The absence of free food for the community is significant because in Logooli ceremonial gatherings, food is always provided for everybody present. Malago was therefore considered a Christian event with a purpose different from those rooted in a Logooli worldview. It was/is also recognized as a Kenyan national holiday. Christmas, therefore, is a Christian and public holiday.

Easter was a more subdued event. At Easter, Christians held services on both Good Friday and Easter Sunday. Good Friday services were usually solemn. Easter Sunday or Monday was initially marked by exuberant and high praise with church members dressed in white conducting vushuhuda on Easter Monday. Until the early 1980s, Easter Monday, a church and civic holiday, was observed by abstaining from work and holding a church service. Since then some churches hold a sunrise service on Easter Sunday and a regular indoor service later in the day that excludes the outdoor vushuhuda. While Christmas has traces of Logooli social music, Easter was/is celebrated with Christian songs of missionary and indigenous origin.

The beginning of a new calendar year was sometimes heralded by a watch-night service. Before the watch-night idea became fashionable in the late 1970s, church members gathered at 4:30–5 A.M. for song, testimony, and prayer. Later that day, a New Year's Day service was conducted. With the advent of a watch-night service, some churches discontinued holding a service on New Year's Day. A watch-night service comprised of singing, prayers, testimonies, and exhortative rhetoric was conducted on New Year's Eve. Testimonies reminisced about the passing year. As soon as the New Year was announced (at 12 midnight or soon after), members broke into prayers of praise and thanksgiving, which led to singing. The people left soon after, singing all the way home. In this way, the whole village was alerted that a new year had begun. In towns and big cities, congregations observed New Year's Eve vigils in church. Congregants stayed all night due to security and transportation concerns; thus it turned into an 'all-night prayer' service, *kukesha* (Kiswahili word for overnight vigil), a concept that easily became popular in many churches in both rural and urban areas.[29] Music was an integral element of these vigils.

NEW SOCIAL INSTITUTIONS

Christianity has created new social institutions based on church membership. The most important affiliation for any mulogooli is still the clan or marriage relationship. While kinship by birth and rite are fundamental, certain rituals acquired through Christian association provide strong bonds with nonclan or nonlanguage-group members. With the new birth doctrine, Pentecostals invoke a spiritual consanguinity through being 'born again' in the Christian family by 'the blood of Jesus' and confirmed through rites such as water and Holy Spirit baptisms. New authority figures and alternative community leaders include schoolteachers, church elders and pastors, or national, regional, and local denominational and political figures.

Teachers were included in clan activities as church and state representatives. Missionaries trained the first teachers for their schools. The classroom was initially used for evangelism and 'civilization.' The British government, through the Phelps-Stokes report, required missionaries to move beyond basic literacy to prepare Africans for the changing society (Stafford 1973, 146–188). A new social class emerged with young leaders mandated to administrate village affairs on behalf of the government. This layer confounded clan, age, and gender roles and further complicated authority structures based on economy and religion. While most Kenyan schools are now under government jurisdiction, religious groups still act as school sponsors. A sponsoring church dictates the order for the schools' religious services, the hymnals used, and the performance practices of the music in official school functions. Boarding school was and still is the preferred academic institution by parents. Students from parts of the country missionized by a different denomination brought new practices or introduced new songs. Students passed the repertoire to their respective villages.

The village also acquired a new hierarchy of leadership through the church. Beginning with the village church elders, congregations expressed accountability to denominational administrators, who could be members of other ethnic groups. Village elders and pastors settled disputes among church members who may or may not have belonged to the same clan as the pastor. The Pentecostal leadership included other Luyia groups as well as the Luo and Kisii, ethnic groups that nurtured different administrative and hierarchical systems. Students in theological colleges were taught by a variety of people, many of whom were not Avalogooli.[30] After graduation, the pastors then passed these ideas to their flock. Church leaders therefore became alternative authority figures.

A pastor currently officiates at the most important functions involving his church members, including transition rites such as weddings and funerals. Here, the pastor conducts the funeral and burial services while clan leaders deal with inheritance and other legal matters. New social groups have emerged based on denominational affiliation. Families and clans are divided along these new religious and economic associations. This adds to the layers of relationships that any one individual navigates depending on one's station.[31] These situations call for an intricate balance of diplomatic negotiation.

Education also generated new patterns of familial dependence. The father was the mainstay of the family, providing the land that the family (mainly the wife) tilled or managed. With the patriarchal worldview of British colonialism and Euro-American Christianity, it was not strange that male dominance was reinforced. The society is still patrilocal and patrilineal with a strong attachment to ancestral land. However, with education, economic dependence has shifted toward that family member with a job for support. This member may be the youngest male, or even a female with the financial wherewithal. Further, the Kenya government has recently (2010) provided a mandate that allows daughters to inherit ancestral land or a portion thereof alongside male siblings or relatives. Power dynamics in the household are contingent on a family's adherence to and interpretation of these new developments.

Other indigenous social and learning programs have either been altered or abandoned altogether. Take the case of the women's cooperative movement *Isilika*. Isilika was a women's solidarity group that provided economic and social support. Women, basically outsiders in male-owned villages, interacted both for survival and to enhance their economic and social status. A group organized itself to rotationally cultivate each other's farms; to dig wells; to share ideas about household duties, expectations, crafts, and pottery; and for other activities. Isilika provided a forum where women could voice dissatisfaction or approval.

When an Isilika worked a farm, they arrived in the morning at around 8:00 A.M., having fed their families and performed their own household chores. Each woman came with a hoe. They worked as a group on the farm. They sang in call and response as they worked, the rhythm of digging set to the speed of the song, with singing breaks as rest periods for their backs. After about two hours, they took a snack break for fifteen to twenty minutes. They discussed news not implied in the singing or elaborated on gossip and other reports. They then resumed their work until about 1:00 P.M. They went to the farm owner's homestead and ate together. If the owner had some gift, like extra bananas or maize, she shared it with the group. They then dispersed. Working on the farm was only one dimension of the impact of Isilika as described below by Febe and Salome in 1988 in their responses to Abwunza (1997):

> Where the goodness was in the older days was this: Women were helping each other... leaving one household to the next... they would eat plenty and then go to the next yard. Or we told the old stories: we sang and danced... We young girls went to our house and we sang the songs of the ancients... We used to plant vegetables and then they dried. And then an old lady would die; the vegetables would feed the people... we said we will go and sing for that one... Or a woman would be sick or give birth, we would care for and feed... When there was a wedding, we cooked bananas... And then the little girls who were born, did as we did when we were young. (Abwunza 1997, 161–163)

Isilika therefore provided opportunity for communal solidarity, instruction, and development of relationships.

With new education systems and the introduction of Christianity, changes were inevitable. Women organized themselves into choirs to raise funds to build schools and churches and cater for other community needs. Others began to work in the new education and mission institutions. By the 1950s, irregularities began to manifest in the Isilika movement resulting in the reorganization and even breakup of most groups. Women working outside the home as teachers or nurses but still needing their farms to be tended abetted the disintegration of Isilika. They employed and paid other village women since they could not participate in the rotational work themselves (ibid., 157–176). Today, individual women hire themselves out to work other people's farms for money. While they can develop relationships with their buddies, and while education and counseling still take place, it is more as individuals than as an organized community. Singing while working has virtually been abandoned.

NEW EDUCATIONAL INSTITUTIONS

Enlightenment philosophies and Eurocentric theories ranked African ideals as primitive or pagan. The modern school became the second most important agent to consolidate and communicate new values, essentially a culture new to the colonized. As agents of the colonial government and enjoying the protection of the same, missionaries were often requested or required to start schools (Rasmussen 1995; minutes in PAOC Archives). In some instances they were forced to expand the curriculum to promote the 'colonial agenda' over the missionary one. This requirement justified the teaching of European folk tunes and dances to Avalogooli, not just 'Christian' songs. Schoolchildren began to participate in music festivals organized by the colonial music and drama officers (Hyslop 1958b).

The school reorganized political, social, and gender constructs and roles. For example, a chief replaced the council of elders. He negotiated on behalf of individuals, families, and clans at the political level, although there was resistance (subtle and overt) at the social level (Mwelesa 2005). European-type education became the way to economic leverage. In many instances it created a malaise in clan and family social hierarchies. For example, people looked up to the most educated or most economically mobile person rather than the village elders (unless the elder was both wealthy and politically powerful). Song texts reflected the changing views and discussed markers of economic and social prestige. Additionally, the church was viewed as an educational institution in that it inculcated a new worldview as well as an alternative philosophy using Western European tools and methods.

Further education came from radio broadcasts. The media, employed as an agent of nationalizing in Europe, was also used in the colonies. Radio was first set up in Kenya in 1928 to cater for white colonists' needs for news about the rest of the world. It became a valuable tool during the Second World War to spread propaganda and for conscripted Kenyan and African soldiers to communicate with their families. News and greetings from soldiers or their families were always punctuated with music, such as American country music, Cuban rumba, or emergent African urban popular styles (Heath 1986; Wesonga and Ward 1973, 86–87). After World War II, portable radios became increasingly available. Christians became involved in radio production from the 1950s for the purposes of evangelism (Wesonga and Ward 1973, 88). The productions put in place and promoted the kinds of sounds and arrangements considered Christian, solidifying the practice of four-part harmony and the art of Bible storytelling through song. One of the earliest radio programmers, Sophia Kitts, who began in 1958, was affiliated with PAOC (Anderson, D. 1994, 227–229; minutes in PAOC Archives). These new information routes competed against rather than complementing Logooli systems. Let me provide some examples.

In indigenous Logooli society, education was incorporated in daily work and entertainment. For example, older siblings were required to look after younger ones and in the process learned how to care for a baby and watched the growth process. A 4-year-old was expected to lull younger siblings to sleep, thereby learning how to correctly hold the baby, what may ail a crying baby, to differentiate between deep sleep and a nap, kinship relationships, and Logooli values. Singing lullabies was a communal activity with other children performing the same chore, or a solo act. Lullabies are still sung with new ones composed in different styles. Some lyrics allude to contemporary possessions and values. In 1985, a 7-year-old sang a lullaby in which an adult female was wearing high heels and carrying a handbag. Lullabies, their values, and their compositional techniques are, however, not associated with modern schooling.

Young boys and girls exchanged ideas during play and while performing chores. Young boy herders made whistles from grass/bamboo. They also constructed a ground bow, *indovondovo*, to accompany the latest popular songs and dance moves. By the time they underwent circumcision rites, most boys had already bonded with their kinsmen. Today, young boys go to school and herders, some of whom are grown men, are hired. Young girls also formed attachments during play, as they fetched water from the river, or when they collected firewood from the surrounding forests. Bonding further occurred in sleeping quarters, usually in a grandmother's house with evening story/song sessions. Today these social spaces have been transformed. Informal music making has diminished. It is now facilitated in schools, at transition rites, and by media houses rather than in regular village or urban play and chore spaces.

CHRISTIANITY AND THE RITES OF PASSAGE

Logooli rites of passage consist of particular ceremonial conventions with music almost always as a requisite component. Kasiera (1981, 343) observes six major developments that impacted Logooli ritual life when Christian ideas were accommodated. They include (a) the abandonment of liswakila, sacrifices usually made on behalf of a child at 2–3 months old; (b) the adjustment of circumcision rite by 1910; (c) the adjustment of the wedding; (d) the abandonment of cattle drives; (e) the cessation of annual communal sacrifices; and (f) the abandonment of traditional dancing troupes. Five of these shifts relate to transitional rites or community identity rituals.

The birth of a child still helps to cement the relationship between a woman and her husband's clan. A child is still given a clan name. The child also acquires a biblical or other name designated by the national government as a Christian or first name. The maternal grandmother still officially visits following the birth of the first child. If one or both parents are church members, the pastor and church leader(s) are invited to pray for the child (*kusaalila mwana*); therefore the newborn is nominally grandfathered into church. The prayer ceremony will include singing Christian songs. Alternatively, the child is taken to church for prayers during a regular service that includes music.

Circumcision ceremonies have also acquired Christian overtones. A younger age group, as young as 4 years, now undergo the rite. This in itself downplays the significance of the ceremony for sexual and fraternal education, although it symbolically burdens males with maintaining the cultural mantle. As alternative methods of acquiring knowledge and skills in contemporary schools have given rise to economic resources outside farming, some of the purposes of the rite have been replaced. Mothers and siblings still escort the boys to the circumcision venue. If the group is Christian, Christian hymns and middle-of-the-road social songs accompany the process. In cases where boys undergo the surgery at a hospital, there are no singing escorts. After the operation the boys are still separated from their family during the healing period. A major difference lies also in what children learn during seclusion and in the fact that children in urban spaces do not sing in the evenings.

The graduation ceremony has been adjusted. The items associated with isolation are either destroyed or given to grandparents. Instead of a traditional music festival, the new graduates stage a 'Christian' one. Few indigenous songs celebrate the rite. Rather, Christian texts preponderate. The songs can be in Kiswahili. The ceremony also includes prayers and Bible readings. A valediction is given by a pastor chosen from the several denominations represented by the church affiliations of the graduates' parents. The pastor replaces the elder who traditionally donated a cow and therefore gave the final words of advice. Instead of a donation by the pastor, he is given an honorarium. The whole rite has to be complete in four to six weeks so the boys can go to school. Postinitiation visits to relatives are therefore kept at a minimum.

The wedding is the most important and transformative rite for the female. It is not a prerequisite for marriage. However, in marriage proceedings, pre-betrothal activities are carried out but not as elaborately as in the past. Two wedding ceremonies are still held on separate days. The first, held by the bride, introduces the groom's family to her relatives. Mock and insult songs are sung by supporters and relatives before and after a church service. The service has a processional, singing, prayers, speeches by family representatives, and a sermon. Most speeches by the bride's people laud her worth and achievements. The groom's family introduces clan members and key persons.

The second ceremony, held at the groom's village, is the real wedding in the eyes of the couple and the state. Modern means of travel have facilitated transportation of the bride's escort party that includes her family, clanspeople, and church members. Modern innovations have impacted song texts. For instance, the song (see music ex. 3.3) performed by the bride's party compliments the groom for renting vehicles to pick up his bride and yet bemoans modern means that escort her to the new home faster than in former days. The lyrics contain several double entendres. Lori (also spelled loli, or rori) is a short form of 'Elori,' a lorry. Elori can also mean "it has seen" with the idea that there is enlightenment. The word 'Lori' can also mean "behold, look, pay attention, can you see?" The word also references being proud or arrogant.

Call	Response
Lori, erori	Erori
Erori iginji aviha	Erori yambira mlukali

English translation:

A lorry [Look people, pay attention, there is a lorry]	A lorry [look at it]
A lorry [look at it] is carrying the bridal party	A lorry that [look at it] is taking me into marriage/wifehood

EXAMPLE 3.3. "Elori" (PURL 3.4)

Elori was also the name of a hairstyle made by creating a hair line/part on the left side of the head. The style was a fashion and elitist icon of the 1960s, adopted from entertainers and prominent Euro-American celebrities. The song's lyrics suggest that the girl was attracted to the trendy and progressive man sporting a contemporary hairstyle. The girl therefore boasts about her groom's looks rather than faulting him.

Wedding vows are exchanged at the groom's church in a ceremony officiated by a government-licensed clergyman. The ceremony includes a processional, songs/hymns, prayers, speeches, a sermon, and the exchange of vows. The processional incorporates elements of traditional culture and modernity. The bride, in white, should not look happy. Her party uses fancy footwork to show ingenuity and also to process the girl into the church in as slow a pace as possible. The groom's entourage, who usually does not know the steps, watches the procession closely to learn the movements for the recession. The bride's escort includes maids and flower girls. Often flower girls scattering flower petals precede the bride. Others carry objects such as paper balls to pictorially and symbolically announce the bride's arrival. A cassette/LP/CD player carried by a bridesmaid renders the processional/recessional music. Where available or as desired, a live ensemble or choir might precede or follow the bridal procession/recession. The music may be religious or popular love songs in English, Kiswahili, or Lulogooli. A girl from the bride's party bringing up the rear carries the bride's luggage. The practice provides entertainment and drama and affords cousins or aunties 'bride wealth' from the groom. He has to appease them monetarily to retrieve the bags.

In rural Pentecostal services, "Oh Happy Day" is sung after the party arrives at the altar. After the speeches, songs, and a sermon, the couple exchanges vows. The couple recesses using the bride's processional footwork. Outside the church, mock-abuse songs are exchanged in contest and to celebrate the occasion. After eating, the bride is left at the groom's home. An urban wedding often includes a processional, hymn singing, a sermon, an exchange of vows, and a recessional. Speeches are made at the reception. The couple's relatives may sing mock-abuse songs, but often a choir is hired to entertain guests and to evoke indigenous Logooli wedding ethos. The choir replaces rival music groups. Guests join in the song and dance, often invoking classic and current popular Logooli wedding repertoire.

Funerals are the distinguishing mark of a person's membership to a clan and to a Christian group. When a person dies, his or her denomination performs funeral and burial rites. The clan and family provide details on the obituary, gravesite, and other matters. Pronouncement of death is still greeted

Sia mu-ndu m-ku - bwa

RHYTHM 3.1. Sia

with wailing to announce the end of a life; to express grief, shock, or sorrow; to comfort the bereaved; and to exonerate anyone who so wishes from any blame relative to the demise of the deceased. A fire is still lit at the homestead. New mourners are still announced by wailing and the singing of elyimbu. They are met and escorted to the porch (lusimbu) where the corpse is laid out. The group then sings funeral hymns. After prayers, the mourners are led into the house to calm down (kuhuluka) and drink tea.

The corpse is laid in state for two to three days at the home. The deceased's relatives and fellow villagers spend the night at the homestead (kugona mu maliga; lit. to sleep in tears, to sleep at the place of tears, at the bereaved's home). In the evenings, mourners sing around the homestead, walk about the village, and visit nearby homes of the deceased's relatives while singing. To keep the public awake, various drumming, singing, and music styles from traditional culture, popular media, and different church groups are explored for entertainment.[32] A specific drum pattern is associated with a death. It is a carryover from indigenous practices. The text of the pattern is intoned on a church drum (Indumba) during periods of silence (see rhythm ex. 3.1) (PURL 3.5).

Most funerals services occur from midmorning with the burial in the afternoon. The funeral service resembles a church one except for eulogies, the song choices, and the manner of their performance. For the graveside service, pallbearers carry the casket. In this double file processional, family members follow the pallbearers. Behind them a group of women, dressed in white, march while singing. Other mourners process or scatter around to observe the interment. The processional *igwalide* (from the Kiswahili word *gwalide*, a filed procession of soldiers) songs are styled in a slow march. After prayers, the corpse is interred while the mourners continue to sing until the grave is completely covered with soil. The family is led into the house for prayers. Igwalide songs are slow in rhythm and tempo, a type of funereal speed. These songs have mortuary function or are regular songs styled to the occasion.[33] The discussion of the assets of a notable man, known as *Lidzulidza* in Lulogooli (*Makumbusho* in Kiswahili), is held days, weeks, or months later.

The ceremony is conducted like a church service with its attendant musics but without 'funeral' songs or songs in funeral styles.

In indigenous Logooli belief, the dead acted as intermediaries between the living and the Supreme Being. It was not surprising that Avalogooli embraced the idea of a mediator between God and man in Jesus Christ and other spirits or saints. Further in death, ancestors continued to live a life similar to what they had on earth. The Christian idea of life after death and of mansions in heaven resonated with Logooli worldview. Christian songs on living well on earth to prepare for the hereafter were therefore accepted and composed by Logooli adherents.

Christianity and its music have infiltrated almost every aspect of Logooli life. In some cases, 'Christian' music and manners have replaced indigenous practices. In other situations, 'Christian' music has been assimilated into rites and rituals. Christianity has also created new functions and ceremonies that until recently only incorporated Christian music but lately accommodate other contemporary musics including indigenous and contemporary folk and popular musics. In essence, Christianity and its music have become not just functional but are vibrant aspects of Logooli life.

FOUR

CONSOLIDATION

Christian Religious Genres in Logooli-Land

The musics accompanying Euro-American Christianity and cultures have been part of Logooli lore since the first decade of the twentieth century. In addition to translated and missionary styled songs, new musics have been composed in Logooli and Kenyan idioms. These songs are conceptualized as Logooli music and form part of the custodial corpus preserving and vitalizing Logooli repertoire. I will first discuss how Christian musics were introduced to Avalogooli and how these styles were appropriated. I will then catalogue and define the prevalent music varieties that were embraced by Logooli Christians and also by the broader Luyia and Kenyan population amongst whom Avalogooli are integrated.

HOW CHRISTIAN HYMNS WERE INTRODUCED

Christianity and its accompanying musics and cultures from Europe and the Americas were introduced simultaneously. Initially Kiswahili hymns were taught to workers at the mission station or to new converts. After 1905, missionaries began to translate hymns into Lulogooli. Quakers began printing these hymns in 1907 together with the first Lulogooli readers in order to introduce literacy. The readers contained everyday Lulogooli conversation mixed with teachings from the Bible.

Kasiera (1981, 178) records one early attempt made by Quakers to expose the general Logooli population to Western hymns. In 1906, Emory Rees held open-air evangelistic meetings in Mbale, South Maragoli. Initially, he camped at Mbale for several weeks at a time. Eventually, he enlisted the collaboration of a chief and came only on the weekends. Rees usually arrived on a Saturday evening. Before dawn on Sunday morning, he began to sing amplified by a megaphone, accompanying himself on an accordion.¹ At this time, the chief played ling'ala to inform the public that it was Sunday.² Ling'ala familiarized people with a seven-day week instead of the customary four and set Sunday apart as a day of worship and rest. At first people arrived dancing, generally perceiving Rees's display as a new form of entertainment. Groups of other Abaluyia came to participate in the music extravaganza. Meanwhile at the Friends headquarters in Kaimosi, another missionary, Arthur Chilson, attracted large crowds with a gramophone that rendered such hymns as "All Hail the Power of Jesus's Name." Chilson records: "They [the Africans] all came dancing and singing, blowing horns and making a great noise. Some were extravagantly decorated with ornaments, and red and white clay" (ibid., 180).³ The event turned into a musical spectacle pitting indigenous entertainment repertoire against missionary hymns.

Attempts were also made to introduce Avalogooli to hymn singing. Hole (1905, 132) records that local workers and converts at Kaimosi were "taught singing twice a week, the Tonic solfa system being used."⁴ Deborah Rees states that singing was in Kiswahili and she accompanied them on organ during Sunday morning services. She and her husband, Emory, arrived in Kaimosi for the first time on June 13, 1904. She played the organ on June 27 of that year. She documents further that missionaries held a service every morning at 7 A.M. to teach new songs or revise learned songs (Deborah Rees, *African Papers*, 1904).

The first song translated into Lulogooli by Emory Rees was "Come to Jesus." Rees undertook this translation of an English song into Lulogooli while on ten-day trip in the region surrounding the Kaimosi mission station:

> For the first, we made a free translation of the song "Come to Jesus." This we sang at various points and always found that it was very well understood. The boys with us were delighted with it, and soon had other members of our mission community singing it. The morning after our return home one boy was told to bring some eggs. He started on his errand singing in his own tongue "Bring the eggs" to the tune of "Come to Jesus." A few minutes later another boy was told to beat the drum to call the people to prayers. He started singing to the same tune "Beat the drum, beat the drum, beat the drum now." Both the hymn and tune of this first translation given to the people promise to be popular. (Rees, E. 1905 643)

Kasiera believes the song's popularity was due to the lyric's symbolism. The translation did not state "Come to Jesus"; rather, it read "Jesus is calling you right now." "Given the African setting where calling out someone's name was limited only by the distance to which such a loud call would reach, the urgency of such a call ... registered well with the hearers" (Kasiera 1981, 180). The translation implied that Jesus knew their names. He was close enough to be heard, making the imperative urgent. The song aroused curiosity about Jesus. As they mastered the language, missionaries translated hymns into Luluyia assisted by workers and students at the mission stations (Kasiera 1981, 226).

According to Mrs. Rees (*African Papers,* July 2 1905, July 10 1905), new songs in Lulogooli were systematically translated starting mid-July in 1905. Missionaries first met and learned the songs, then taught them to the natives, most of whom were men. In January 1906, Mrs. Rees states that they held a service where "women sang just as much as men ... many of them have good voices if they were properly trained" (ibid., January 12, 1906). In August, Mrs. Rees installed a singing service for girls and another for boys. By that time twelve hymns had been translated. They were played and sung every morning and twice on Sunday. "I am getting tired of them [the hymns] ... but it is much better than hearing their heathen singing" (ibid., August 12, 1906). Emory Rees notes that "We felt we set a milestone when the first native hymns were sung and the first services conducted in the native tongue" (Emerson 1958, 23). Boys sang the hymns while they were attending to their evening chores. Women were heard singing the songs while they did their work at home (Deborah Rees, *African Papers,* January 27, February 3, 1907). These songs replaced indigenous work songs. By 1908, up to eighteen songs had been translated (Rees, E. and Rees, D. 1908a, 2). An African adherent Mango also composed hymns "with sound doctrine sentiment in use on the station" by 1910 (Hole 1911). The missionary report in 1918 had described Logooli music, dance, culture, and people as "weird songs ... rhythmic motions ... vile gestures ... people strangers to righteousness but all too familiar with sin" (AFBFM 1918, 9). Kasiera (1981, 204) reiterates the unworthiness of Logooli musical styles, observing, "Traditional dancing and singing was considered sin." Therefore, the community learned the music styles and performance practices deemed appropriate for the new belief system.

Pentecostals discouraged participation in any 'heathen' practices by converts. They aimed particularly at children who had not yet been inculcated into traditional rites and practices. These children were employed and housed in dormitories at Keller's station. In place of African songs, children were taught Western European hymns and folk songs. In her biography *Twenty Years in Africa, 1913–1933,* Mrs. Keller reports:

FIGURE 4.1. Children's rhythm band.

> About six months ago, I organized a rhythm band. I selected thirty little boys and girls not over twelve years old who were in the second grade in school and gave them such instruments to play that would not require the knowledge of notes such as cymbals, drums, castanets, bells, triangles, tambourines and blocks. It has been such a huge success and it is remarkable how well they do in keeping time . . . and they all enjoy it very much. Now it is not so difficult to keep their voices together in singing as it was before. I lead them with the piano while the big bass drum and cymbals start with me, followed by the smaller instruments in rhythm time . . . If we take their enjoyment from them, the heathen dances and various worldly pleasures when we present the Gospel to them, we must give them something that will take their place. They do love all kinds of music and sing the songs of Zion with great fervor and vim. The Gospel hymns can be heard resounding in the air . . . these take the place of heathen dancing. (Keller 1933, 56–57)

The Kellers did not include the use of any African instruments in the children's band. The children's rhythm band concept was gradually expanded until a full-fledged Sunday school program was set up in the 1950s with instruments donated from Kitchener Pentecostal Church in Ontario, Canada. The band members were children from around Goibei (see fig. 4.1), where a mission station, established in 1932, administrated the denominational Sunday school department until the 1970s (PAOC Archives). The band travelled with the missionaries and local Sunday school workers to different churches in the region to teach translated songs and choruses to other children.

Pentecostal missionaries did not appreciate Africans singing Christian hymns as they performed menial tasks. However, Africans could not sing indigenous work songs, as they were considered heathen or obscene. Translated European folk tunes (e.g., "Yankee Doodle") were substituted for African ones. These innovations were introduced to children and youth. Adult converts, probably feeling left out, used idiophones and membranophones in the absence of missionaries, at home prayer meetings away from mission stations. Some gatherings were set up or encouraged by Keller in his zeal to attract adherents from outside his sphere of influence, to the chagrin of other mission groups (Keller letters in PAOC Archives). These services were less formal than those held in the presence of missionaries. It is from these meetings that African independent groups such as African Israel Church Nineveh emerged. These churches emphasized Old Testament scriptures, which identified with the local people's plight under colonial and missionary domination (Ogot and Welbourn 1966, 82–84).

A Logooli song style emerged during the informal prayer meetings, a 'spirit' song that became a permanent feature in Pentecostal services and the hallmark of breakaway denominations. However, the missionary hymn was not abandoned. Quakers continued to sing and compose in missionary hymn styles. Pentecostals provided such choices as singing the hymn in its original style; singing the hymn with drumming, hand clapping, or both; adjusting the style to the accompaniment or context; and using indigenous song styles. Missionaries had also introduced short songs known as 'choruses' drawn from the Great Awakenings and the Pentecostal explosion of the nineteenth and early twentieth century (Richardson 1998, 109; Massarelli 1998; Guthrie 1992). Lulogooli songs were composed in this style as well. Consequently, Logooli Christian circles embraced diverse music types whose core forms were Euro-American, Swahili, Logooli, and other Luyia.

MUSIC TYPES IN LOGOOLI CHRISTIANITY

Avalogooli recognize and identify several song categories used in Christian events and gatherings.[5] These categories were reiterated in the ways the women who performed songs for my taping sessions referenced them (1983, 1986, 2004, 2005). Leaders in church services and community gatherings also requested song types using these terms. Categories are recognized most often by the names of styles/genres introduced by missionaries; where the songs are documented; how the songs are/were 'received'; how, when, and where songs are performed; and who performs the songs. One type based on Lulogooli intonation of an English word is *Tsikorasi* (lit. many choruses, sing. *Ikorasi*), a direct appropriation of the word 'chorus.' Songs identified by documentation are called *Tsinyimbu tsya Ikitabu* (Songs of the book). Songs 'received' from the Holy Spirit are called *Tsinyimbu tsya Roho* (Songs of/from the spirit). *Tsinyimbu tsya Amakono* (Songs of the hands) are performed with clapping of hands.

Songs may be categorized by their function or context, or a song may be performed in a style that is associated with a particular event. Songs performed for Christmas celebrations and competitions are known as malago. *Tsinyimbu tsya igwalide* references songs styled for funeral processionals. Other musics are identified by the type of performing group. The most common types of performing ensembles and their subgenre types are tsikwaya (lit. choirs) performances by a mixed choir, *tsinyimbu tsya avakeere* (songs by/for women), and *tsinyimbu tsya avaana* (songs by/for children). It is a complex task to group songs using one criterion since any piece's performance practice can also be transformed based on context or ensemble type. I will therefore sort the general types using the most dominant stylistic features but still maintain consonance with Logooli categories.

Corbitt (1985), in discussing church music among the Baptist Taita of coastal Kenya, identified four prevalent church music styles:

a) 'Book' music to reference translated songs compiled in hymnals.
b) 'Body' music as music composed by Africans that involves body motion.
c) Indigenous choruses, composed by Africans in African languages.
d) Choir music as special choral music of academic music education or church anthems.

Corbitt credited the first two categories respectively to Anglicans and Pentecostals who preceded the Baptists in Kenya (American Baptists set up churches on the Kenyan coast from 1957). Corbitt summarizes extant musical practices and styles amongst Baptists in Kenya and also delineates frames for sorting musics embraced by Kenyan Christians.

Avalogooli have styles that variably correspond with Corbitt's categories. Rural and diasporic Logooli congregations employ all these types in musical, religious, and social contexts. Other genres, such as gospel music, incorporate elements of Logooli rural, Kenyan urban, and global popular styles. I categorize Logooli Christian music types relative to the most preponderant labels as follows:

a) Tsinyimbu tsya Ikitabu (Songs of the book) can also be referenced as 'book' music. 'Book' music is a song in missionary hymn style, whether it is a translated hymn/song or a composition by local musicians in structures associated with missionary music. It includes liturgical hymns, gospel hymns and songs, and other styles of European or American origin or form. These pieces are compiled into booklets or hymnals. The term also refers to a manner of performance, a stance of singing reminiscent of the way missionaries performed songs.

b) Tsinyimbu tsya Roho (Songs of/from the spirit) are compositions that first began with the revival movements in Kaimosi and coincided with the stabilization of the Pentecostal Assemblies of God mission station in Nyang'ori in the mid-1920s. These 'spirit' songs are intended for congregational performance. They are rarely printed in hymnals. They are also known as indigenous hymns.

c) Tsikorasi is appropriated from the word 'chorus' that refers to choruses and refrains. Chorus refers to an independent refrain, while refrain usually is the so-named section in a stanza/refrain form. This label effectively separates songs and hymns from choruses. Tsikorasi are of both local and missionary origin.

d) Tsikwaya is a term appropriated from the word 'choir.' A choir is distinguished from a congregational song by its purpose, arrangement, source, and performance practice. Thus the choir might sing a congregational song but the manner of performance, harmony, size of the group, and even the language used will set it apart. A choir is usually made up of at least twelve people, but a quartet singing a special number is often referred to as a choir (Ikwaya). Avalogooli reference the pieces, the events at which these pieces dominate, and the performing groups as Tsikwaya (sing. Ikwaya).

e) 'Gospel' is recognized by its instrumentation, contemporaneous stylistics, and intention for mass distribution. It draws from all the previously mentioned genres as well as contemporary trends and popular styles. It operates in a manner similar to the gospel music industry globally. Gospel is performed in English, Kiswahili, Lulogooli, and other languages by soloists, small ensembles, and choirs; and it is invoked by the mass media as an expression of Christian music. The public distinguishes performers not by a Lulogooli term but by the Kiswahili word *mwimbaji*, which translates as 'singer.'

Of these categories, 'book' music and 'songs of the spirit' are the foundational resources for the other stylistic types.

'BOOK' MUSIC

Tsinyimbu tsya Ikitabu (Songs of the book) is a Logooli term for pieces written in hymnals and songbooks. The idea of 'book' music is elitist, perceived as 'civilizing,' first used by missionaries but taken over by locals. It distinguished one as having 'been to school'—*musoomi*—one who was learned, literate, had 'book' knowledge. The genre includes translated songs and new compositions by Logooli lyricists. Hymn lyrics are in Lulogooli and Kiswahili. Both Quakers and Pentecostals use the Lulogooli hymnal, *Tsinyimbu tsyo Kwidzominya Nyasaye* (Songs of praise to God), also shortened as *Tsinyimbu tsya Nyasaye* (God's songs), and the Kiswahili hymnal *Nyimbo za Injili* (Songs of the Gospel).[6]

Translated hymns were derived from hymnals put out by different Christian traditions of Europe and the Americas, and from Sunday school songs and the gospel traditions of the Great Awakening of the eighteenth and nineteenth century.[7] Hymns were distinct from gospel songs more by the time and place of origin and by textual emphasis on worship or doctrine. Apart from worship, gospel lyrics focused on personal testimony, invitation to convert, and the afterlife. Gospel styles thus defined purportedly jelled in the music of North American singer/composer Ira Sankey in the nineteenth century (Sallee 1978, 9–67; also source hymnals listed in appendix 2), from whence they continued to transform in interaction with contemporary folk and popular traditions. Gospel repertoire, as congregational song, aspired to express the thoughts, experiences, and testimonies of the singers. The tuneful and simple melodies were designed to attract the general public to revival meetings and motivate them to be converted. Missionaries went out inspired by these meetings that stressed concern for non-Christians.

From the 1970s, Logooli Christian composers and translators like Gideon Wesley S. Mwelesa compiled new hymnals or book supplements. Mwelesa, born in 1934, is a prolific composer, performer, and translator of songs.[8] He marketed his songs and those of his colleagues through self-printed booklets. He later compiled the collection into the hymnal *Nditsominya Yahova ne Tsinyimbu* (Mwelesa 1988). At the top of each entry, he includes the title and the scriptures that inspired the song, a practice borrowed from *Nyimbo za Injili*. At the bottom, he provides dates when it was first sung to the public. If commissioned, he includes the name of the group or Quaker meeting that ordered it. By 2011, Mwelesa had recorded two cassettes of the repertoire. The songs have also been performed by gospel music artists and been arranged for choral groups. The songs, however, best function as congregational songs and for social use.

Mwelesa began his singing career as a political activist in Nairobi in the early 1950s. In this period of upheaval in Kenya with agitation for African self-rule, Mwelesa, a new immigrant to Nairobi, joined others to mobilize support for political independence through song. After being rounded up and escaping from a police truck on its way to a detention center, Mwelesa moved back to his Logooli birth village in 1958. He was invited to a Friends youth convention. While there, still politically at odds with white missionaries, he incited other participants against the leaders. At that time of political dissidence, he opined to the public on the role of missionaries in the colonial enterprise. The rebellion was not just in word but also in song. He gathered a following to protest what he understood as missionary political and religious dominance. He later reconciled with the missionaries and in his encounter with the Christian faith (Mwelesa 2005).

While this turnaround marked the conscious beginning of extensive composition for church, Mwelesa already had dabbled with writing Christian songs from around 1952. Starting in 1959, with renewed fervor he composed, translated or retranslated songs, and introduced new musics to congregations. Since ownership of books signified 'elitism,' Mwelesa collated the songs into pamphlets that he sold to recover printing costs. Despite falling out with some organizers, Mwelesa continued to sell due to public demand. When invited to speak, his address included a song, which he advertised as available in print. He was eventually commissioned to write for Quaker meetings. The leaders provided themes and scriptures. Mwelesa quoted directly from the Bible, paraphrased the texts, or interpreted the verses according to his understanding of Christian doctrine or theology and the local situation. He documented where and when he first performed a piece (Mwelesa 2005, 2007).

Mwelesa's songs on migration have been some of his best beloved. Avalogooli were familiar with the migratory theme and with land ownership by a powerful patron. Given the hard times, overpopulation, and other malaises, moving to a better place resonated with Logooli cosmology and practice. I read in Logooli migratory songs a longing, a yearning for a distinctive place to establish progeny, a notion that was curtailed by colonial containment in specific native 'reserves.' Transferring this desire for physical migration into heavenly space may have provided emotional and spiritual catharsis. Kasiera's analysis of themes in Logooli songs posits that heaven was "localized . . . in the light of the migration motif, which was a local phenomenon" (Kasiera 1981, 598). It was imagined as a vast, fertile, new land whose 'owner' was an impartial God. Migration to heaven was consolidated in Logooli worldview through musical and poetic text. A new song form, the hymn, provided expression that was commensurate with a new land, heaven, to fulfill Logooli desire for property and posterity.

The covers of Mwelesa's booklets and hymn supplements picture him holding a Logooli one-stringed fiddle—*kiriri*—(also spelled *kilili*, fig. 4.2). This was revolutionary since African melody instruments are rarely played in church. It is, however, symbolic of Mwelesa's ideology of independence from colonial and missionary micromanagement while still being modern. Most kiriri players at the time wore what was construed as indigenous regalia, with animal skin attire and distinctive headgear. Mwelesa wears the 'elite' person's suit, a mulogooli artist, cognizant of his heritage but embracing new options. The choice of kiriri can be read variously. The instrument, a bowed lute, takes its name from sound it makes. Kiriri 'speaks' or 'sings' the text in heterophony with a singer. It sometimes punctuates or responds to the singer. It can be performed solo or in ensemble with other instruments. Hymns are also perceived this way, as a text or melody, complementing a sermon or testimony. They punctuate or respond to a speech, emotion, or decision. Hymns can be performed alone or appended to other songs, accompanied or a cappella, sounded by an individual or in ensemble. The hermeneutic can be extended to how Christianity is perceived as a personal decision, yet lived in fellowship with others; as a spiritual decision, yet translates into physical manifestations. The Christian imagery on Mwelesa's hymnal cover is completed by the title: *Nditsominya Yahova ne Tsinyimbu* (I will praise Jehova with songs). The title

Figure 4.2. Cover of Mwelesa's booklets and hymnal.

is a play on the main hymnal of translated songs *Tsinyimbu tsyo Kwidzominya Nyasaye* (Songs of praise to God), but with a dynamic personalized and accessible dimension.

Mwelesa's compositions are fashioned after the missionary hymn with a few written in Logooli 'spirit' song styles. The missionary hymn stylings testify to his Quaker background and practice of almost exclusive use of 'book' music in services. Mwelesa's compilations incorporate translations of contemporary Christian songs that include ritual and popular numbers by such musicians as country singer Jim Reeves. Mwelesa said that he translated Reeves's version of

"Long Time Ago in Bethlehem"[9] that was popularly played on Kenyan radio during the late 1960s Christmas seasons. The song, "Mihiga tsimilioni javita" (Millions of years have passed), became an instant hit with Logooli congregations and was often performed in Christmas malago. In fact it was such a standard that younger people I talked to assumed it was a local composition.[10]

In the English original, the first verse is the first stanza. The second and third verses form the refrain. The same tune is used in the two refrain verses. In Mwelesa's version, only the second verse is the refrain. The third verse becomes the second stanza (Mwelesa 1988, 216). Below is an English translation of Mwelesa's text:

Mihiga tsimilioni javita	A million years had passed
Gamanywa mulilaga lia kale	It had been foretold in the Old Testament
Yesu Kristo mwana wa Nyasaye	Jesus Christ the Son of God
Yivulwa na Maria	Was born of Mary
Hulira lero tsingerosi vimbanga	Listen today/now, angels are singing
Livulwa lio Mwami Yesu	(about) the birth of the Lord/King Jesus
Livamwoyo lilava mu vandu	Life will be amongst the people
Kigira lidiku yili	Because of this day
Lwanga lukubanga lwe visiliva	The signal is being sounded by trumpets
Tsingerosi vimbanga	Angels are singing
Hulira kuli tsivolanga	Listen to what they say
Livamwoyo liveye mu vandu	Life is amongst the people

Mwelesa records that he first sang the piece in Kaimosi in August 1970 (Mwelesa 1988, 216), a time when the English version was extremely popular. His translation at a time of peak national popularity of the English original brought modern culture to the village, but styled in a way that resonated theologically and appealed musically to Avalogooli. The song remains a classic Logooli Christmas carol.

Mwelesa, commissioned by different Quaker meetings at local, regional, and national levels, reworked his Lulogooli songs into Kiswahili to reach a wider audience. He also translated classic Kiswahili kwaya songs into Lulogooli. Even so, he did not necessarily work alone. He collaborated with other composers and singers. The biggest advantage to cooperative work, according to Mwelesa (2007), was the possibility of critiquing a piece. The small ensemble first evaluated a composer's lyrical poetry, as lyrics were composed first and then a suitable tune was found. The poem was then set to a tune. The group assessed and critiqued the composition, revising it as was necessary. The work was further adjusted with feedback from general audiences, more often on the tune than the text.[11] Mwelesa's hymnal *Nditsominya Yahova ne Tsinyimbu* also includes 'spirit' songs. Transcribing the lyrics of 'spirit' songs affords them a hitherto unprecedented legitimacy as works that can justifiably be used by 'educated' Quakers. Mwelesa's compilation was first published in 1988. However, booklets with the same title had been in circulation since the 1970s.[12]

Quakers use 'book' music extensively. Quakers considered themselves the most enlightened Avalogooli since they were the first to be evangelized and educated.[13] Many became teachers, administrators, politicians, and university professors. Given this reputation, the book became a precious, coveted, and prized possession. The hymn in the book assumed a similar reputation. In any case, one reason why missionaries introduced literacy was to enable Africans to read the Bible and the hymnal. The dignity associated with solemnity for ritual moments in Logooli indigenous worship resonated with the Quaker hymn practice. Except in special circumstances, few other song types were used in Quaker services. Quakers customarily sang unaccompanied except in competitions. Even here, they invoked the traditional Isigudi drum instead of the side drum (Indumba) used by other Logooli Christians. Many of Mwelesa's songs are performed at funerals attended by people from different denominations. Hand clapping and drums are included when sung in these collective gatherings and by other denominations.

Pentecostals and other denominations also use 'book' music. Their performance is also templated with hand clapping.[14] Hand clapping is absent during igwalide funeral processionals and in solemn and somber occasions like wedding services or communion rites. The performance practice of a hymn sometimes transforms its musical elements. The song leader who lines the first phrase of each stanza often sets the performance style and tempo. In this way, the leader determines the pitch, tempo, length of the piece, and the order of performing the stanzas. Chapter 5 discusses how 'book' music was accommodated into Logooli musical and cultural practice.

INDIGENOUS HYMNS AND 'SONGS OF THE SPIRIT'

Avalogooli recognize songs authored or received when the composer was 'in the spirit.' These songs are known as Tsinyimbu tsya Roho. Corbitt (1985, 39) labels this category as 'body' music, as he contends that body movements are incorporated in performing these pieces. However, Avalogooli and other Kenyans perform 'book' music with the body, depending on the occasion, congregation, or denomination. I believe a more appropriate term is 'indigenous hymns and songs of spirit.' The music was/is 'received' from or composed under the influence of the Holy Spirit as understood and defined by Pentecostal, charismatic, and Africanist groups. Logooli indigenous styles and techniques are the basis of the songs, but other traits are incorporated from and for local, national, and global forums. The body may be an intrinsic or a necessary element in the song and in its performance. Body parts are used as music instruments through clapping, shoulder or leg articulations and accentuations, and dance (when the body responds to the music made by other instruments including the voice). The body might provide the ictus or impetus for rhythmic or melodic motion and also outline the style of the song. The body sometimes regulates the mood and tempo. 'Book' music can also be treated in this manner.

Hymns by Logooli adherents were some of the first compositions by African Christians. 'Songs of the spirit' on the other hand were 'received' through dreams and visions or when people were "praying in the spirit" (Kasiera 1981, 550; Ogot and Welbourn 1966, 96–100). These songs were readily accepted during the revival that broke out in Kaimosi in the 1920s when Arthur Chilson (a Quaker missionary) embraced the doctrine of the Holy Spirit as taught from the Azusa revivals.[15] Interestingly, these songs were not automatically accepted although they legitimized the convert's Christian encounter and experience. Local congregations scrutinized songs revealed by dreams and visions for both tune and text. They were also sometimes approved or rejected relative to the composer's role or reputation in the community.

'Songs of the spirit' are especially significant in that the composers, while praying 'in the spirit,' drew on the resources that were a part of their musical socialization. Thus the earliest pieces derived musical elements from indigenous styles, while later songs incorporated missionary modes and popular ideas that had gradually been absorbed in the community. While some songs were in popular styles with a peak lifespan of three to four years, others became classics. 'Popular' songs were composed in response to a need, or they memorialized a teaching or an incident. The pieces ascribed to Logooli folk practice in that, in similar fashion, they documented events, expressed opinions, and verbalized emotions. For instance, 'spirit' songs composed during famine described the situation and referenced food. The following text exemplifies such a song.[16]

Mwigulu wa Yesu ni michele	In heaven, Jesus's abode, there is plenty of rice
Mwigulu wa Yesu, ni amaganda	In heaven, Jesus's abode, there are plenty of beans
Kulisena Setani ne ivirenge	We will stomp Satan with our feet

The first two lines affirm the abundance of food in heaven. The underlying argument in the third line (tag/refrain) is that Satan is the reason for our lack. Heaven has plenty of food, thus we will stomp on Satan (who figuratively is on earth below and we will be in heaven above him) because we will have food. Stomping is a way of claiming land and symbolically ridding a place of evil spirits or former occupants. As an expression of disdain and arrogance, stomping also signifies victory and pride. It likewise references the way a well-formed woman steps, with authority, confidence, and entitlement. It also implies stepping, as in a dance where one shows off skill, expertise, and utter control. The metaphoric imagery in this song is not lost to Avalogooli and other Abaluyia.

The song was composed during a time of a famine and poor harvest in the mid-1960s. The tune and rhythm is in *lipala*, a popular dance style of the mid-1960s to early 1970s. It is set in a major key and harmonized in parallel thirds or sixths that were characteristic of popular dance songs. The lyrics are significant in their marriage to the style when one considers that lipala footwork is like a shuffle—invoking the idea of 'rubbing it in.' Thus the lyric "Kulisena Setani ne ivirenge" while shuffling kinetically paints the text about stomping Satan with our feet. Other lipala motions include stretching out the hand as if to embrace someone. It suggests consolidation and control by gathering resources, as opposed to an open lackluster palm indicating lack, hopelessness, and uncertainty. The gesture is an apt visual representation of the text about having plenty. The piece is technically in stanza/refrain form. A stanza is made up of two or more statement lines. The leader lines each statement and the chorus affirms it definitively. In the refrain or tag, the leader prompts the chorus with the first word ("kulisena"). The chorus completes the phrase, then repeats that prompt "kulisena" in a rising sequential motif before completing the sentence. The repeated note on the phrase "Setani ne ivirenge" is a reiterative motion symbolic of the totalizing action against Satan (see music ex. 4.1.).

EXAMPLE 4.1. "Mwigulu wa Yesu"

This song is in triple meter. True to Logooli stylistics, the time signature moves from $\frac{9}{8}$ to $\frac{3}{4}$, retaining the triple feel but creating a different texture. The contrasting meter further signifies the different participants, their yearnings, their locus, and their activities. In performance, clapping and drumming are articulated in duple feel for a phrase of six counts in simple compound time coinciding with and in cross rhythm against the lyrical phrase in triple compound time for two measures. The drama is intensified by the stomping feet or lipala simple duple rhythming, coinciding with the singers' triple meter in the refrain. This example foregrounds a more extensive discussion of the characteristics of 'songs of the spirit' to be explored in chapter 6.

CHORUSES AND REFRAINS

Tsikorasi is a term that refers to both refrains and choruses. These are either the refrain extracted from a stanza/refrain piece or independent stand-alone short songs. Corbitt (1985, 140) refers to the genre as indigenous choruses. Logooli tsikorasi are drawn from a variety of sources.

The first tsikorasi taught to Avalogooli were refrains from translated hymns or independent choruses borne from the revival movement in North America and Europe from the eighteenth to early twentieth century (see examples from Rodeheaver and Ford 1941; Cayce [*The Good Old Songs*] 1913 in appendix 2). Others were Negro spirituals such as "Kumbaya." Regardless of the source, they were all called 'choruses' by missionaries. The name was translated into Lulogooli as tsikorasi (lit. many choruses, ikorasi sing.). The name suggests that the classification was new in Logooli worldview. Tsikorasi were sung in church services, at prayer meetings, and at vushuhuda as primary repertoire. They also functioned as fillers during down time, to welcome guests, to accompany a walk to the altar, to facilitate the offertory, or to dismiss a service. Ikorasi could also be raised in the middle of a sermon or prayer. Because they were easy to learn, tsikorasi were a choice song type for optimum audience participation in the absence of hymnbooks. In this discussion, I classify tsikorasi as either dependent or independent refrains.

Dependent Refrains

Dependent refrains were originally attached to a hymn or gospel song. These songs were products of the Great Awakening and other revivals of eighteenth- and nineteenth-century Europe and North America. One of the antecedents and profiteers of the revival was the Sunday school movement originally formed in the late eighteenth century in England to assist in the rehabilitation of slum and illiterate urban populations. In North America, the movement capitalized on the emerging tradition of gospel hymns partly for evangelism and otherwise to promote moral change (Rice, E. 1971).[17] Lyricists such as Fanny Cosby (1820–1915) composed repertoire to facilitate revival meetings, with singers like Ira Sankey (1840–1908) presenting the songs as 'specials' during the campaigns where he partnered with the famed evangelist Dwight Moody (1837–1899). Most songs were in stanza/refrain form. For singer/evangelist duos such as Sankey and Moody, a refrain not only facilitated congregational participation; it also condensed the thrust of the sermon. A refrain was easily remembered by audiences and was employed precisely for that purpose (Goodspeed 1876; Davis, D. 1997). Therefore, some composers began with a refrain and built stanzas around it to consolidate or exemplify a doctrine, an idea, or a concept. Other hymns acquired refrains, which eventually became intrinsic to the song.

Some refrains attained a life independent of the original songs. This practice may have begun when a whole song was performed with the refrain repeated several times. The eventual form was something like this: (A [Stanza] B [Refrain]), A B B A' B A" B B B. Some refrains gained popularity because their inherent idea applied immediately to any situation, whereas the parent verses were restricted. Others gained potency because the musical structure transformed more readily than that of the verse. Some choruses have become classics, modeling poetic and musical form. Others are suited to contexts. In order to explore some musical and cultural possibilities of a chorus among Avalogooli, I will analyze the dependent refrain "For You I Am Praying" and explore ways in which it was used, translated, transformed, and understood.

"For You I Am Praying"
(Text by S. O'Maley Cluff, Tune by Ira Sankey)

The refrain is derived from the gospel song "I Have a Savior" (see music ex. 4.2a). The original song is a call to repentance built around stanzas extolling the work of Christ. The refrain reiterates that the 'evangelist' is praying that the public turn to Christ. While the entire song can be sung in Lulogooli, the chorus was often singularly extracted. The text was a favorite among Logooli Christians as an assurance of prayer for salvation, for healing, for friendship, for traveling mercies, or as a benediction.

English: For you I am praying, I'm praying for you
Lulogooli: Ni ngusaalilanga, mulina wadiva
Translation: I pray for you, troubled (condemned/worried) friend

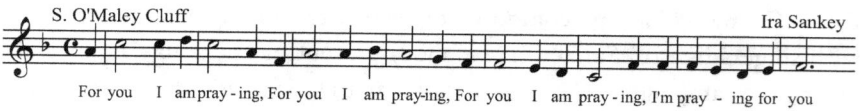

EXAMPLE 4.2a. "For You I Am Praying"

EXAMPLE 4.2b. "Ni ngusaalilanga" (PURL4.1)

The tempo of this chorus depends on the context. In solemn assembly, the piece is sung slowly and without hand clapping. Lulogooli translation also lends itself to a different interpretation, a kind of defiant statement. "Ni ngusaalilanga, mulina wadiva" can be translated as "Be aware that I am praying for you, condemned friend." Here, the person will be praying with determination for a friend in trouble. In this vein, the song is sung fast with hand clapping. The clap on every strong beat shifts the rhythm, syncopating the vocals. The resultant product is shown in music ex. 4.2b.

The general feeling of the piece is a jazz duple, rendering a possible performance in $\frac{6}{8}$. But this is the illusionary hearing, the suggested, implied oral signification, while the actual aural rendition is the notated music ex. 4.2b. Some substituted notes are added to the melody for a drone effect. Clapping provides a basis for an offbeat syncopated rhythm, effectively subverting the accentuation. But the offbeat also creates for *better* rhythmic intonation of Logooli practice, further creating lyrical tension that is resolved or upheld by the rhythmic adjustment. In speech, the strong beat should be on **Ni**, but it falls on the weaker syllable **Ngu** in this adaptation. The rest of that word is disguised by the syncopation that provides a more engaging musical reading that supersedes textual concerns. In this manner, the perceived defiant intent of the text is tempered by the whimsical rhythm.

The English language lyrics of the stanzas of "I Have a Savior" referred to a savior pleading for lost souls, mentioned a heavenly father in whom there was hope for eternal life, and even told of a resplendent robe in store for believers. The witness wished for the listeners to embrace the savior and tell others about him. While these lyrics were translated in Lulogooli, new stanzas were also composed with a rather distant relationship to the original English lyrics. The new text draws from the biblical Old Testament book of Numbers chapters 13, 14, and 22 (see music ex. 4.3). It reads:

Joswa na Kerebu lwa vali mu logendo	While Joshua and Caleb were traveling
Vatanga livola Nyasaye yavaleka	They began to say God had abandoned them
Nyasaye yavaleka mu lidiku yilyo	God abandoned them in that day
Vanyole likudza, likudza lie tsinzoka	To die a death of snakes (from snakebites)

In this new stanza, the first sentence alludes to twelve spies sent to Canaan on behalf of the Israelites. Only two men, Joshua and Caleb, provided hope despite the bad report by the other ten. The discouraged Israelites questioned God's intentions and sought to return to Egypt. They later repented and unsuccessfully attacked Canaan, this against the advice of Moses their leader. As a result of their disobedience and doubt, they wandered in the desert for forty years until that generation's adults, except Caleb and Joshua, died. While in the desert, they wished for death. God sent serpents and the bitten people began to die. They therefore prayed for deliverance. God told Moses to make a bronze serpent and set it on a pole in plain view of all. Anyone who gazed at the serpent was healed. However, in the Lulogooli narrative Joshua

EXAMPLE 4.3. "Joswa na Kerebu"

and Caleb are said to have grumbled and complained about God, so God sent snakes to bite them! The verse has no English precedent in text or tune. These lyrics are usually sung in fast tempo and as a 'song of the hands.' In this version the song shifts from a simple duple meter into $^{12}_8$ time.

The text is structured using Logooli storytelling and memory aid technique where in recounting a story, a phrase draws from the previous one, particularly when preparing for a punch line. Story songs and ballads set in this format teach language and its structure, values and social mores, genealogy, musical and other artistic ideas. The excerpt below exemplifies this technique. This particular song is usually preceded by a poem that teaches the importance of sharing and the consequences of greed. Sharing as an act of kindness initiates good relationships. Following the poem, the caller then asks, "Who is your father?" The subsequent antiphonal recitation lists ancestral names and kinships.[18] It appears these people are named according to what truly makes them vulnerable or unique. For example, Mang'ule means open wounds, Vayanza means they loved, Vagava means they shared or distributed (see music ex. 4.4).

Group 1	Group 2	English Translation
A Tonde	Tonde man'gule	He's Tonde, Tonde Mang'ule (with wounds)
A Mang'ule	Mang'ule Ngwegwe	Mang'ule of Ngwegwe (Ngwegwe's wounds)
A Ngwegwe	Ngwegwe vayanza	Ngwegwe loved
A Vayanza	Vayanza Vagava, etc.	They loved Vagava (those who shared), etc.

EXAMPLE 4.4. "A Tonde" (PURL 4.2)

The new Lulogooli verse of "For You I Am Praying" uses this manner of prompting the learner to fill in the blanks by rehearsing a previous line in order to complete the phrase. The first line, "Joswa na Kerebu," is complete in itself. It introduces the subject under discussion. The second line begins the discussion. The third line draws its beginning from the last part of the second line, then the two sections of the last line build on each other where the first section prompts the second part. In contrast to the Lulogooli model's antiphonal style, there is no call and response in the performance of "Joswa na Kerebu." Everyone prompts and everyone completes the phrase. This stanza was always performed with the syncopated and fast tempo version of "Ningusaalilanga" (For you I am praying), and always tempered by clapping.

While dependent refrains were extracted from existing songs and could be performed as independent pieces, sometimes, as in this last example, they provided a starting point or models for new compositions. The new songs could thereafter become independent pieces, or they were coupled with the refrain to create another stanza/refrain song. New songs were thus generated and added to existing repertoire.

Independent Refrains

Independent refrains are short songs with a repetitive text. These short songs were translated from English into both Kiswahili and Lulogooli from the beginning of the missionary enterprise. They were transcribed in hymnals. They are therefore part of 'book' music. Often in translation, it was more important to capture the essence of the text than to follow the poetic meter of the original song. Therefore refrains were more easily Africanized in meter and general aesthetic than hymns. Often the text and tune each became a compositional template. The derivatives were perceived as compositions, rather than arrangements or adaptations.[19]

CHOIR MUSIC

Choir music (Tsikwaya) generally has three sources: missionary hymns or hymn styles performed in four-part harmony, Makwaya Kiswahili stylistics rooted in Lutheran chorale and similar European traditions, and English anthem types. Makwaya has a history with semi-popular song and media dissemination with a range of models from European chorales to African storytelling forms. Lutheran and African Inland Church missionaries initially propagated Makwaya. Starting in the 1950s, choirs were recorded and aired on radio (Anderson, D. 1994, 227). The choirs sang in four-part harmony, SATB. Often, the melody was placed in the alto voice while the soprano harmonized up a third and the tenors down a fourth. The bass line's chord progression was structured around the tonic, subdominant, and dominant notes.

Makwaya were the first Christian story songs composed in a semi-European hymn style by Africans (Weman 1960). The texts ranged from biblical stories and direct scripture quotes to lyrics with expository evangelistic and moral content. Texts were usually in Kiswahili. Makwaya songs were initially performed a cappella but were later accompanied by three guitars: lead, rhythm, and bass in African and Afro-Latin styles (Nyman, J. 1995; Nyman, F. 1991, 2005). At first, musicians 'created' guitars and innovatively electrified them. Fred and Jan Erik Nyman and Bombay (1996) stated that when they first recorded choirs in the 1960s, musicians constructed box guitars with two to six strings in a variety of tuning systems. To electrify them, musicians appropriated a shortwave from an off-air radio station. Sometimes, announcers came on air during a recording session and effectively ended the piracy. In time, guitars were legitimized as urban instruments. They were then tuned and electrified in conventional ways. Later tambourines, shakers, and the drum set were added, before African drums were incorporated. Eventually the accompaniment resembled a jazz rhythm section, with synthesizers added, as they became part of the contemporary musicscape.

Other types of choir music were four-part hymns taught by leaders trained in solfa notation. Learning to sing in solfège was introduced when Avalogooli first learned Euro-American hymns in Kiswahili (Hole 1905, 133). Thence, teachers first taught their students the solfège and then sang the text (similar to Euro-American singing school traditions [Goff 2002, 1–60]). Teaching solfège rather than staff notation was part of a greater colonial practice that situated Africans in prebaroque space. This practice was not unique to Kenya (Shelemay 1998, 160–162); it was prevalent in South Africa (Vokwana 2006) and Anglophone West Africa (Mensah 1998, 224–225).[20] Since the average adult villager did not attend school, solfège singing was associated with the youth and with British education. At first, the songs were in English and Kiswahili, but Lulogooli and other Luluyia hymns became (and still are) standard repertoire. Of note is the influence of the 'Church of God' mission whose main adherents, Abanyore (a Luyia group), are famed for four-part singing in

Lunyore, particularly at wedding processionals. An early Lunyore hymnal (*Tsinyimbo Tsia Obwehani*) is set in solfège and staff notation.[21]

Since the 1970s, anthems in Lulogooli and other African languages have become standard in church services particularly with the Logooli urban diaspora. Here, African folk, Christian religious, and other tunes are arranged in four-part baroque harmony. This type of arrangement was propagated in educational institutions as nationalistic trends emanating from nineteenth-century Europe. African tunes were sourced and adapted to European compositional techniques. The best space to experiment was in the school system. The inevitable space for propagating these compositions to the larger public was the church. In Kenya in general, secular tunes were adapted to Christian lyrics initially in national languages and later in local languages. Among Avalogooli, 'spirit' songs were the most frequently arranged repertoire. Since the texts were already religious, the tunes were set into four-part common practice harmony.[22]

At first, a choir was formed for special celebrations such as Christmas or weddings. The choirs initially sang unaccompanied. Later, they incorporated church drums and indigenous or popular drum stylistics and idiophones like the Kayamba, a raft tray-shaped box idiophone originating from coastal Kenya. Since the mid-1980s, choirs added other indigenous instruments first as distinctive markers and later as appropriate accompaniment for the idioms. Choirs are famed for introducing new repertoire to congregations. They also broker African indigenous and global popular styles and instruments into the music life of the church. Many urban Pentecostal and Quaker church choirs perform special numbers in services and also participate in church and other music festivals. Choirs have further branched from only singing church anthems to including political and social songs.

GOSPEL MUSIC

The gospel phenomenon as a genre and commercial venture gained currency in Kenya in the mid-1980s (Kidula 1998). It is not just current to Avalogooli; it is a national, Pan-African, and global phenomenon. The term 'gospel' commonly refers to Black American religious musics that differed from earlier types, such as spirituals, in subject matter being positive, upbeat, and evangelistic. The label also applies to twentieth-century religious urban song with popular underpinnings and with evangelical and Pentecostal or Holiness association. Gospel is also a Euro-American folk and country-based genre with similar definitions, pitted against high church or Puritan hymns. Apart from religious use, 'gospel' has almost always had commercial connotations with print or audio media dissemination and management. From examining the repertoire, I observed that Avalogooli were introduced to white gospel (gospel composed by or associated with European Americans [also called country gospel] or performed in Euro-American practice) and black spirituals (folk and arranged).

Relevant to Logooli music types, 'gospel' refers to popularized or urbanized Logooli Christian repertoire or mediated Christian religious pieces for spiritual or commercial consumption. This means that any piece can be styled as gospel. The easiest route is to incorporate instruments and popular rhythms associated with the global gospel enterprises. Most performers initially sang in English and Kiswahili, but eventually, a crop of musicians targeting Luyia audiences gave rise to star personalities. Their music is commonly played at weddings or funerals.[23]

At weddings, a gospel group or recorded religious music is used in processionals or as reception mood music. Gospel recordings fill in the downtime at funerals. They may even be the only music in the evening wake. Contemporary performances in gospel styles have licensed overt dancing in churches. This is not just metronomic movement or gestures/motion intrinsic to the musical structure of the piece; it is dance. In the transfer of elements articulated by the body onto other instruments, the body is freed to dance or cross rhythm against the song and orchestration.[24]

OBSERVATIONS

With the introduction of Christianity, European and American church music was incorporated into Logooli repertoire. The most enduring music types have been hymns and choruses. Avalogooli composed songs in these styles not only as new ways of sounding music and religion but also as an elaboration of similar indigenous forms and contexts. Few European instruments were adopted. Pianos or organs were expensive. Guitars were initially considered too secular to be incorporated into the worship life of the church. African instruments were rejected as pagan and inappropriate. The side/bass drum (without snares) became the instrument of choice because of its association with the Salvation Army and with military and police bands.

Pentecostals (in experience and/or doctrine) transformed 'book' music into Logooli aesthetic and performative formats. Further, functional use was ascribed to some songs. Pentecostals were also at the forefront of creating 'African hymns' born in the 'spirit' experience, also labeled 'songs of the spirit.' Most pieces were rooted in the structural, formal, and performance practices of Avalogooli. Some musical elements—melodic, textual, or rhythmic—were transformed by Avalogooli to suit their musical preferences or as dictated by contexts. These dynamic transformations affirm the place of 'spirit' songs in Logooli historical and contemporary repertoire. The 'spirit' song phenomena occurred in congruence with the Pentecostal and Holiness movements of the late nineteenth and early twentieth centuries that solidified the gospel song.[25] Charismatics, Pentecostals, and media-savvy groups have directed the 'gospel' song phenomenon. Gospel songs are used by Logooli denominations in services and on other occasions.

Quakers have been at the forefront in composing 'book' hymns, with a better language fit than some earlier translations, and providing alternative tunes or new texts to well-loved hymns. They have encouraged the adaptation and arrangement of African hymns and tunes as choral pieces. Some pieces reflect the Quaker mode of worship by their tempo, which then precludes bodily articulation of rhythm and tempo. Contemporary Christian music therefore preserves Logooli musical structures and aesthetics, reflects the expression of religious community, creates continuity with European/American traditions and Logooli indigenous styles, and aggregates the historical and contemporary social and religious experiences of Avalogooli faithful. The accommodation of 'book' music, syncretism in 'spirit' songs, and the invocation of Logooli 'Christian' musics in academic and mediated forums are explored in subsequent chapters.

FIVE

ACCOMMODATION

Logooli Adoption and Use of 'Book' Music

Tsinyimbu tsya Ikitabu, 'book' music, refers to translated hymns, gospel songs, and choruses or refrains introduced by missionaries, and to compositions in (pseudo) missionary styles by local Christians written in hymnals or booklets. The missionary-initiated repertoire was compiled into the two most used hymnals, *Tsinyimbu tsya Nyasaye* (TTN) in Lulogooli and *Nyimbo za Injili* (NZI) in Kiswahili.[1] Missionaries came from diverse denominational backgrounds and had varied alliances;[2] songs were therefore sourced from European high churches and Protestant hymnody, from the gospel hymns of the Great Awakenings and revivals of eighteenth- and nineteenth-century North America and Europe, and from the repertoire of the Pentecostal and Holiness explosions of the late nineteenth and early twentieth century. Some sources consulted include *Redemption Songs: 1,000 Hymns and Choruses*; *Golden Bells*; *Tabernacle Hymns*; and the Kiswahili hymnbook *Nyimbo Standard*.[3]

European and other sources for hymns are listed in a front matter page of the Lulogooli and Kiswahili hymnals.[4] The hymns themselves are titled in Lulogooli or Kiswahili, with an English subtitle below the heading, including the source of the text and the tune from the appropriate hymnal.[5] For example, if a text was derived from *Redemption Songs*, the letters 'RS' and the hymn number are written after the English subtitle (e.g., RS 7).[6] However, there are some subtitles where the source is absent. Together with the subtitle is the tonic key of the original tune used (e.g., F-Doh), although the titling of the tonic is confusing (e.g., sometimes G-sol, other times G-doh, or A-sol, A-doh). Hymn titles bespeak the theologies or doctrines considered fundamental to Pentecostals and Quakers. The Luluyia title could be the general message of the song or the first line of the stanza or refrain. It is therefore difficult to find some songs in the index. The texts and musical structure reveal cultural, lyrical, and melodic sources, as well as the missionaries' musical and theological preferences. Avalogooli made room for or accommodated the repertoire introduced by missionaries in their newfound Christian religious life and in the larger musical and ethnic space. They first learned to 'sing another person's song' (Bigenho 2011) as the statement of their newfound faith.

HYMNS, GOSPEL HYMNS, AND GOSPEL SONGS
TRANSLATED TEXTS

The first hymns taught to Avalogooli were in Kiswahili.[7] From 1905, songs began to be translated into Lulogooli. Emory Rees first worked with Matolas, a non-Logooli ex-slave (African Record 1907b), and eventually with Joel Litu (Adede 1982, 9). By 1908, at least eighteen Logooli hymns were in use (Rees and Rees 1908). Hymn and chorus texts were translated to retain at least the general meaning of the English text. Translators sought to be faithful to the tune and poetic meter of the original hymn. Logooli words were fitted onto the melodies.[8] English words were assumed for concepts that did not exist in Lulogooli. Adede reports that, "In the process of translation, when Emory Rees did not find a substitute word to his satisfaction in the Luragoli language, he adopted the English word. For instance the word 'angels' was translated to 'tsingelosi'; pronounced z-angelos" (Adede 1986, 64). These new words were assimilated into the general Logooli cultural lexicon.

Translators first aimed at the general meaning of the overall hymn rather that the specifics of each line of text. Rees referred to these as free translations (Rees, E. 1910b, 544). He exemplified the process with the song "Precious Promise" translated into "our version" during the Rees's first tenure. Below is the original English text of the first stanza and refrain (Redemption Hymnal 1951 #447, text by Nathaniel Miles), Rees's "our version" (TTN 135), and Rees's retranslation into English (Rees, E. 1910b, 544).[9]

> Precious promise God hath given
> To the weary passer-by
> On the way from earth to heaven
> I will guide thee with Mine eye

> I will guide thee, I will guide thee
> I will guide thee with Mine eye
> On the way from earth to heaven
> I will guide thee with Mine eye

Lulogooli "our version" by Rees's group, Rees's free translation:

Yesu a va suuviridza	Jesus has promised
Vandu veve Vakristayo	His people on earth
Ku inzira yomwigulu	Upon your way to Heaven
Nda va himbi kumusola	I will come to your rescue
Mbeya himbi, mbeya himbi	I am near, I am near
Kali nonde inzila yosi	I have trod the whole way
Mbeye himbi, mbeye himbi	I am near, I am near
Nda va himbi kumusola[10]	I will come to your rescue

In spite of good intentions, free translations sometimes transformed the overall original idea. Below are two classic examples. The third verse of the hymn "For You I Am Praying" (TH [4] 136, text Samuel O'Maley Cluff, tune Ira Sankey) reads thus:

> I have a robe 'tis resplendent in whiteness
> Awaiting in Glory my wondering view
> Oh, when I receive it all shining in whiteness
> Dear Friend, could I see you receiving it too!

Lulogooli Translation (TTN 197)	**Retranslation from Lulogooli to English**[11]
Mbeye nengubo, ingubo indavu	I have a dress, a white dress
Mukhonyi a la mba ingubo mwigulu	The helper will give me a dress in heaven
Tsingubo tsinyikhi tsi veye mwigulu	There are many clothes in heaven
Na nyenya mu save Nyasaye tsyenetsyo	And I want to beg God for those ones

"Ingubo" in the first line translates to 'general clothing' or 'dress' depending on the context. By the end of the verse, the Lulogooli version does not carry the ideas in the English stanza. The translation focused on dress but for a reason different from that in the original. In a society where missionaries often used clothing to proselytize and identify locals, this verse implied that wearing European clothes was heavenly. The request for a full wardrobe could carry a secular intention. The Lulogooli translation appears to sidestep the evangelistic and eschatological intention of the English verse.[12]

In "Hark My Soul" (RS 565, text William Cowper), the third stanza focuses on God caring for people more or better than a mother cares for her children. In translation (TTN 159) and relative to Logooli worldviews, a different meaning emerges:

English Original	Lulogooli Hymnal	Retranslation
Can a woman's tender care	Muleri a lindanga	A babysitter takes care
Cease toward the child she bore	Umwana wa hebeywi	of the child given to her
Yea she may forgetful be	Si a la mwivirira mba	She will not forget the child
Yet will I remember thee	A la va naye hosi	She will be with her all times

Most child caretakers were usually young girls. In practice, this verse was used to instruct on the moral duty of a babysitter. The subtext differs from the English original. But it fits Logooli view that a child's nurse should be attached and committed to that child. It appears that the idioms in English could not be realized in Lulogooli within the limits of the European melodic/lyrical form.

Musically, the goal was to introduce proper repertoire for Christian worship and civilization, as the missionaries understood that music to be. Melodies of beloved hymns were borrowed and fitted new words. One example is a Holy Communion song, "Break Thou the Bread of Life" (tune by William F. Sherwin), fitted to the nativity story titled "Yesu yivulwa ndi" (This is how Jesus was born; see music ex. 5.1). (PURL 5.1) The Lulogooli text is taken from the Luke 2:1, 4, 6–11, 16–19 (TTN 35). The first stanza in the English tune reads (RS 2):

> Break thou the bread of life dear Lord to me
> As though didst break the loaves by Galilee
> Beyond the sacred page I seek thee Lord
> My spirit pants for thee oh living word

Lulogooli Version (TTN 35)	Retranslation into English
Kale mmadiku yago munwa gwa twula	In those days, a decree came
Ku Kaisari Augusto kung'odwa	From Caesar Augustus for a census
Yosefu ya ka tsia ha Bethlehemu	Joseph went to Bethlehem
Halala na Maria mukali wewe	Together with Mary, his wife

The last verse concludes with Mary pondering on the angels' words, and not with the shepherds' return as recounted in the Gospel. At first reading, this is a strange ending, but in Logooli worldview, pondering is highly valued.

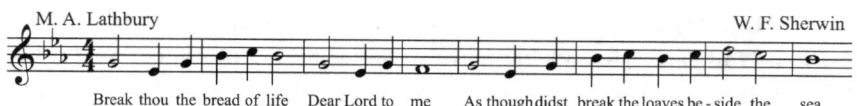

EXAMPLE 5.1. "Break Thou the Bread of Life"

As was practiced since the reformation, missionaries assigned tunes from folk, popular, and other sources to established texts. For example, the Lulogooli translation of the carol "Away in a Manger" (GB 632, text: v. 1&2 anon., v. 3 John McFarland, tune J. E. Spilman, TTN 38) is sung to Spilman's tune set to "Flow Gently, Sweet Afton" (text R. Burns, tune J. E. Spilman).[13] However, in the Lulogooli version, the rhythm is adjusted so that the body feels it in $\frac{3}{8}$ while singing in $\frac{3}{4}$. Part of the felt lilt is a consequence of the text; a tender or somber text tends to be felt in compound time even if it is conducted or sung in a simple meter.

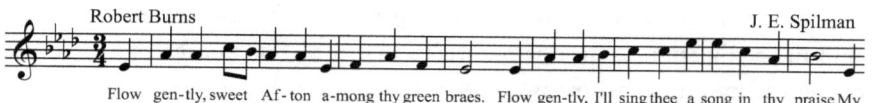

EXAMPLE 5.2a. "Flow Gently, Sweet Afton"

EXAMPLE 5.2b. "Yali ku mulinga" (1)

At Christmas services, the song is pitched at least a fourth lower than transcribed. It is sung with or without clapping depending on if it is performed as congregational song or by an ensemble as part of malago. Without clapping, it is rendered as in the English original but with the pitches as transcribed in music ex. 5.2a. With clapping, the clap is in a duple time, against the song's triple meter. Body motion is incorporated to coincide with the first beat. With

ACCOMMODATION

or without instrumentation, the piece can be performed in call and response or in antiphony.

Call	Response	Translation	
Yali ku	Mulinga	He was in	a manger
Bugira	Kitali	Without	a bed
Muyai	Muderwa	The boy	the only one
Ni Yesu	Musoli, etc.	Is Jesus	the savior

A leader 'calls' and the public/choir 'responds.' The response is deduced through logic, or fitted like pieces in a puzzle. This storytelling practice, or pedagogical tool, ensures that participants understand, learn, or absorb the style and content. It engenders a nonthreatening learning process much like play, encourages group participation, and facilitates memorization. Contrary to Logooli practice of sudden endings or ending on a rest, this song closes on a ritardando, the last note held on a fermata, a norm appropriated from European practice. The original melody is retained almost unchanged in Lulogooli rendition. The anacrusic beginning can be altered to begin the piece on the strong beat, transforming the accentuation (see music ex. 5.2c, version 2). The syllabic emphasis in the second version is a better fit in Lulogooli, but the first version is considered more engaging musically. These two versions can be performed at the same competition as different arrangements. While Christmas carols such as "Hark the Herald Angels Sing" (text Charles Wesley, tune Felix Mendelssohn) are harmonized intentionally, this carol is usually sung in unison except for a few substitute notes.

EXAMPLE 5.2c. "Yali ku mulinga" (2 versions)

Hymns also acquired new roles based on the predominant theme emerging in the translation. For example, the hymn "Rock of Ages" (TH [4] 283,

Example 5.3. "Rock of Ages"/"Yesu uveye lwanda" (PURL 5.2)

text Augustus Toplady, tune Thomas Hastings, TTN 183) is preferably sung at funerals because of the Lulogooli translation of the third and fourth verses.[14] Singing it elsewhere is considered taboo or a premonition and wish for death. It is sung in Lulogooli as in the English version (music ex. 5.3a), but it is more often sung as 5.3b, where the meter is transferred from simple to a compound time with a rest at the beginning of each phrase.

Music ex. 5.3a is performed at regular church meetings. Version b can be sung at a regular service and at funerals (at the wake, during the funeral service, or in the burial processional). It can be accompanied with clapping, with or without drums depending on the context. A cross rhythm of two against three results from the clap in $\frac{4}{4}$ against the $\frac{6}{8}$ song meter. It is sung unaccompanied during burial processionals. Here the foot articulates the rest by stepping on the strong beat, originating a march before singing the phrase. With the slow tempo, singers often breathe in the middle of a word instead of holding the dotted quarter note for its full value. The dotted quarter note in the second part of the first measure of each phrase is treated as a pickup, and a breath taken in the middle of the word as acceptable performance practice. The first eighth note in the second bar of each phrase is then weighted—a notion referred to as *kutuula* (act of placing/settling/resolving [Mulindi 1983, 250]), with the response appearing to repose, a repose that is dynamic and active rather than static and final.

Some Logooli hymnists have in recent years written new translations of old hymns. It may be that early missionaries had partial command of idiomatic Logooli expressions or Logooli translators had an inadequate command of the English language. Newer translations are a better language fit while still holding to the original hymn text and tune. On the other hand, some new translations result from Logooli musicians' familiarity with original hymn tunes and their structures. With an expanded understanding of English idioms, translators are challenged to adopt the original meaning and tune (Mwelesa 2007). Some songs are initially learned by choirs and then adopted by church congregations. Tunes are at times assigned a text other than the one in the hymnal. This practice was not unusual in the Euro-American church traditions. It was acceptable for poems in the same meter to share tunes. This exchange was rare once songs were translated to Lulogooli. New tunes are, however, composed for well-loved texts with 'difficult' tunes.

SONG LEADING AND PERFORMANCE PRACTICES

While function is the strongest variable for hymn use, the most visible distinction for Logooli Christians regarding 'book' music begins in performance practices. A new religion engendered new ways of leading and performing songs. The hymnal became a memory bank of the Eurogenic and modernizing order. Although many church members could not read, it was and still is common practice for song leaders to announce a hymn number, open the book, and sing off the page.

In church services, the song leader (*Muletelli*) or the pastor announces the hymn number from either the Kiswahili or Lulogooli hymnal, indicating the language to be used. Thereafter, the leader sets the tempo and pitch of the hymn by singing the first line of a stanza or refrain. The leader may even conduct in conventional European style. The congregation continues with the rest of the hymn. This practice was prevalent in eighteenth- and nineteenth-century Europe and the United States where lining out was practiced varyingly (Temperly 1984; Goff 2002, 19–20). Missionaries carried this convention to the field. Avalogooli appropriated, expanded, and transformed it.

The song leader sometimes anticipates a stanza by not holding a cadential long note for its full value. Instead, he or she sings the first few words of the next desired verse to cue the congregants. This turnaround through tonal/vocable/metric anticipation by the leader is rooted in Logooli indigenous song performance practice. While only one song is sung at a time, a congregant or the pastor may signal for another song to follow immediately. The song leader might acquiesce by announcing the hymn number, or he or she simply starts the song and the congregation joins in as soon as possible. This practice of appending one song to another is also rooted in indigenous practice.

There are other methods to select the hymn. In Pentecostal services, apart from calling out a hymn number, the pastor might request for a song choice. Circumstances or occasions may justify singing a particular hymn; for example, to welcome guests, or prepare for the sermon, or during offertory. Here, the pastor asks for a song to 'welcome visitors' (or whatever the need may be).

The leader faces the congregation from the front. He or she can also lead from the front row or pew. Before singing, the leader greets the congregation (usually if he or she is up for the first time). The congregation is prepared to sing when the leader recites the 'halleluiah call.' The call is intoned and rhythmed in a particular peculiar manner. The process may proceed in this way:

	Leader	**Congregation**
Greeting	Mirembe	Mirembe
	Mirembe vosi	Mirembe
	Mirembe livugana	Mirembe
	Mirembe gya Yesu	Mirembe[15]
Halleluiah call	Halleluiah	Halleluiah
Translation:		
	Peace	peace
	Peace to you all	peace
	Peace to the congregation	peace
	The peace of Jesus	peace

Drums roll during the congregational response to the halleluiah call. The call may be repeated several times. The leader then begins to clap and the congregation joins in. This clap allows the leader to determine the song pitch. The leader's clap also sets the tempo for the drums and the assembly. The leader then begins to sing. The congregation enters after the first line. A leader decides whether or not to follow the order of the stanzas in the hymnal. He or she anticipates the congregation by lining out the first phrase of the desired verse. Since most songs are memorized, the congregation joins in as soon as possible. Some members can heterophonically complement the leader by completing the first phrase with him/her. Such direction energizes a performance, indicating that members are vested in the piece. If the song extends for long, the pastor will approach the pulpit, or the congregation might respond apathetically. The song leader, always sensitive to the pastorate and the congregation, either winds down or calls the halleluiah. A 'halleluiah call' also signals the close of a singing session. Depending on the song and its performance, ecstatic manifestations might follow, indicated by rhetoric thanksgiving or 'unknown tongue' phraseology and people jumping up and down or catching their breath in prescribed 'religious behavior.'

It is customary to perform a song set. This routine emanates from traditional Logooli practice. Since tsikorasi and indigenous songs are short, a set is composed of several songs in succession. In Christian singing practice, the new song may or may not be related to the first one in subject matter. The meter might be different or the song might require a key change. A good leader convinces the audience by the way he or she segues into the next song that the pieces belong together. Without a microphone, the leader has to be loud enough to be heard above the clapping, the drums, and the crowd. In this case, the vocal timbre can either be nasalized or be approached with an open tone. Avalogooli sing with an open tone reflective of the vowels in their language. In performance, even closed vowels are sung in an open tone. Individuals recognized as having a good voice are selected or encouraged to be song leaders. The voice has to be smooth and project far. The timbre is described as *mwoyo muliduhu* (a thick textured voice, a voice with great resonance), and *mwoyo muzeleleku* (a smooth voice, with even intonation [Mulindi 1983, 67–68]).

A leader may introduce a new song if he or she senses reluctant and/or uninvolved singing. Disengagement may be due to uncertainty of the tune or text, poor pitching (too high, low), unsuitable tempo (too fast, slow), inappropriate song for the context or occasion, distraction by events such as taking offering, or just general lethargy. If the congregation appears apathetic, a good leader either changes the song or ends it. But if people appear unfulfilled, the leader either extends the song and 'climaxes' it, or he or she appends new songs. Otherwise, participants will break into spontaneous prayer or the pastor/officiant will intervene. The song leader acts as conductor, setting the tempo and pitch, guiding the course of the set/song, and ending the piece/session, turning spectators into participants to fulfill musical and religious needs.

The congregation may stand if clapping hands enhances singing, but the onus is on the leader. The clap is metronomic and may not include other instruments. Drumming, however, is always complemented with hand clapping except during special choral numbers or if the context is exhibitional or pedagogical. Metronomic clapping is also eliminated when singing during the sermon or as part of prayers. Singing during prayers serves to intensify the expression of worship and center attention. Singing during a sermon emphasizes the pastor's message or reinstates interest. The congregation remains seated at this juncture unless they are 'moved by the spirit.' Unaccompanied singing also happens at weddings, at burials, and during Holy Communion.

Words are more important than any other musical element. In fact, words energize other musical elements often beyond their religious intent. The occasion and function at which a hymn is performed are often determined by the text. Words help to generate a climax through repetition of lines and stanza or by ad-libs. Repetition is marked by more intense and emotional singing and clapping. A climax may be rendered louder than at first statement, with interpolations, in heterophony, or with expanded polyrhythms. However, the tempo once established remains steady. In the case of intense emotional singing, the congregation breaks into prayer or associated ecstatic vocables and behavior at the end. It is difficult to determine whether they are moved by the music and the direction of the performance or by the text and the 'spirit.'

The structure of a piece may render its learning and performance to be effortless or awkward. For example, in a stanza/refrain form, more enthusiasm is exhibited in the refrain. Form therefore determines the performance practice, context, and length of performance, as well as the ensemble type best suited for the song. When unsure of a text, the singing might be stopped and the correct words are taught. Alternatively, an aggressive leader will have the uncertain verse repeated several times to verify the text or rectify the mistake. The song might also be abandoned altogether and a new one substituted, or the session might be discontinued.

Most song leaders are women, who also form the bulk of church congregations. I assumed the fact was due to historical Logooli indigenous outlook on women. A man could have several wives, resulting in more adult females in a home until children were born. Thereafter the demographics were affected one way or another relative to their children's gender. I also supposed that it was due to the exodus of men in search of jobs or as they were conscripted in the army during the world wars. Wives were left in the village to manage homes. The presence of more women in the church may, however, also be due to a practice started by missionaries since the first freed slaves were housed in Mombasa in the late nineteenth century (Pavitt 2008). The convention seemed to have been practiced by various mission organizations in Kenya including Quakers and Pentecostals. In her correspondence with the PAOC Canadian headquarters in the 1920s, Mrs. Keller reiterated over and again that she focused on training women. She recounts that

> When we started work here, I remember asking God definitely what He would have me do. Very clearly, he showed me the need of the African women... God laid African women upon my heart in a special way... Dr. Aggrey, the great colored professor of the West Coast said: "Train a man, you train an individual; train a woman, you train a family." If we want the Africans to rise to a higher standard, we must begin at the foundation, the women... When I started work among the

women I got little encouragement except from above. The husbands opposed me as they did not want their women educated... their husbands thought that if they [wives] were educated, they would not work... When the Lord saved and cleaned up a few of these women it was enough advertisement of God's power. There was such a change in their lives that their husbands saw what a great transformation had taken place... Soon, others, and others, and others, began to come for teaching. Some of the men finally came and begged me to try to persuade their wives... to attend. Very soon the little round hut school-house was much too small... The girls started to come and the boys also. The mothers brought their children... The church school... was soon found too small to hold the crowds. (Keller, M. 1933, 51–53)

Thus women have always outnumbered men in the church. Mrs. Keller's decision to train women further opened a way for children to get into church. So in effect, getting women into church opened up the entire family to Christianity.

MUSICAL ELEMENTS
Pitch and Melody

For most 'book' music, the first tunes taught by missionaries became the most accepted and were therefore (considered) authentic or standard versions. Songs were usually in major keys. Most songs are pitched lower than transcribed in European hymnbooks. Rural churches rarely have a pitched instrument apart from the drum, so singers either pitch off the drum or start the song at a pitch deemed comfortable. If a song is pitched too high, the congregation might not respond, forcing the leader to stop or reconsider whether to lower the pitch or abandon the song. Alternatively, a leader might start a different song and return to the first one at a new pitch. This does not mean that Avalogooli do not sing high-pitched songs. In Christmas music festivals, older ladies encourage younger ones to sing high pitches so that they (the older women) can sing the bass part. The bass voice is really the melody an octave lower. Singers often assert that a bass voice is indicative of maturity or old age (past prime). An elderly person with a good voice is respected for her vocal type regardless of the range.

Avalogooli seem to have few problems with European intervals. When a note is too high or low, an acceptable alternate pitch will be substituted. For example, the tonic an octave higher will be replaced by a fifth, fourth, second, or a drone on the lower tonic for the notes in that high tessitura. The tonic also acts as a pedal. Surrogates also replace chromatic notes for tunes in unfamiliar modes. Singing in languages with a different timbre or tonality is often rendered in Logooli musical and tonal ethos. Most choirs learn to sing using solfège or by rote. Intonation reflects the leader's approximation of the solfège. Many choirs trained by men approach high notes in falsetto. Subsequently, soprano and alto female tone color is thick textured to imitate the male choir director.

Congregations sing in heterophony. Singers choose alternative pitches out of personal preference or comfort or for aesthetic flavor. A leader may begin by singing the melody found in the English hymnal. Subsequent alternative pitches are dictated by linguistic intonation, personal preferences, and the general mood and direction of the piece. Sometimes a leader substitutes pitches for flavor, or a singer joins the leader for contrapuntal contrast. In songs that begin on the tonic and ascend, a subsequent verse might start on the dominant or subdominant above the tonic. The practice is common if clapping and drums are added since a higher pitch is more audible over the instruments than a lower one. Personal preferences result in chord clusters when different singers choose alternative notes. This often happens at the beginning of stanzas when a leader starts on an alternative pitch but is joined by singers with the original note and others drone on the tonic or harmonize in thirds or sixths. The presence of a low-pitched drum provides a backdrop by simulating singers' choice of pitches in the harmonic series.

Rhythm, Tempo, and Meter

The occasion, function, and instrumentation determine the rhythm, tempo, meter, and general style of a song. Since the early missionaries insisted on the retention of the number of lines and syllables in translations, meter was seldom tampered with or changed when singing the learned original. However, translation sometimes altered the rhythm, which in turn affected the meter. Meter was also adjusted when appropriate Lulogooli words interfered with the syllabic meter of the English hymns. Meter was transformed when added drum or clapping patterns conflicted with or offset the original meter. Tempo was most altered in social context; for example, a hymn sung in a funeral procession was performed without clapping and/or instruments at a slower tempo than the same song in an evangelistic service accompanied by drums. There was also an aural illusion of tempo change when a song in $\frac{3}{4}$ was heard against a $\frac{2}{4}$ clap.

Mulindi (1983, 75) identifies a Lulogooli term that defines the effect of solo-response—*kuvugula*. The word literally means 'to take up.' After the song leader has sung the first line of the hymn, the congregation 'takes it up.' The moment of transfer is marked by an imperceptible delay. It could possibly be a psychological illusion, where there appears to be a delay, yet in analysis one does not 'see' it. Clapping makes this delay seem unnoticed. The delay is more 'audible' in a cappella singing. The general feeling is that of singers taking a deep breath as the leader approaches the conclusion of the 'call.' That breath, like a sigh signaling a release of tension, is exhaled as the congregation enters while still maintaining the leader's tempo. Tension is visually embodied in the steady pulse maintained by body motions (a forward-backward movement of the shoulders). The resolution is visualized in the exaggerated upward or forward chest impetus as the people 'take up' a song. This is an idiomatic Logooli aesthetic. Often, a rest formally replaces this delay so that the vocal entry is *off* the beat instead of *on* the beat with the clap. The rhythm excerpts below illustrate the point. The song "Oh Happy Day" (RS 622, text Phillip Doddridge, tune E. F. Rimbault) can be performed in two ways determined by the leader, with or without a rest. The leader sings the phrase "Oh happy day" and the congregation joins at "that fixed my choice." With clapping, it is possible, at the encouragement of the leader, to offset, anticipate, or offbeat the first note with a rest articulated by body movement or hand clap. The music is in $\frac{3}{2}$ but the clap will be in $\frac{4}{4}$, resulting in this kind of relationship seen in rhythm ex. 5.1a.

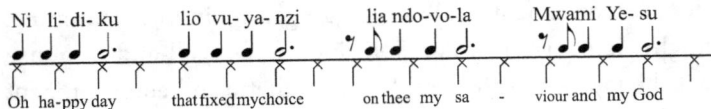

RHYTHM 5.1a. "Oh Happy Day"/"Ni lidiku"

Or the leader might effect change by beginning with a rest and clapping to result in the rhythm seen in example 5.1b.

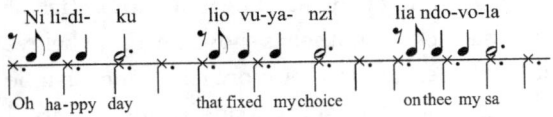

RHYTHM 5.1b. "Oh Happy Day"/"Ni lidiku"

The melody is often adjusted so that a phrase's realization optimizes on the 'best tension' by selecting appropriate alternative pitches especially during repeats. For example, the pitches for "Oh happy day" and "that fixed my choice" are the same. Therefore one or both might be varied for contrast, to create tension, or to resolve the tension. In music ex. 5.4 below, a shows the original tune, which can be sung in Lulogooli as is, or the alternatives in melodic and rhythmic choices shown in b and c. These notes are not merely substitutes; they are also harmonies since singers treat them as 'correct' notes sounded with the melody.

EXAMPLE 5.4. "Oh Happy Day"/"Ni lidiku" excerpts (PURL 5.3)

Occasion or context dictates changes in meter and rhythm, and consequently in style. Changes are dictated by whether the piece is felt in a duple or triple meter, is in simple or compound time, and whether or not it includes clapping and/or drums. For example, a song performed during Holy Communion differs from its rendition in an evangelistic procession. A solemn Holy Communion service may occasion the use of simple meter without clapping and instruments. The essence of the service is in the religious ethos more than musical interaction. With the same song, a processional may break into compound meter to accommodate walking, jogging, clapping, or drumming. The practice might transform from unison singing to a call-and-response style and impact the meter and rhythm. Here, aesthetic and entertainment principles are at play.

Instrumentation, specifically clapping, tends to affect the rhythm of a piece, which in turn might impact the meter. Beyond clapping, three of the most common instruments include *kisili* (the iron metal of the hoe), kidindi or mudindi (small drum), and indumba (large drum, pl. *tsindumba*). Drums are hung over the shoulder of the standing player and beaten with a stick or the cord is held in one hand and the stick in another as shown in fig. 5.1 below. With large crowds and in outdoor meetings, two or more tsindumba can be used. The drummers face each other instead of standing side by side as is usual in indoor services.

FIGURE 5.1. Tsindumba and kidindi.

Although the clap is metronomic, a leader can accelerate tempo before it is regularized. The most common clap rhythms are regular quarter or dotted quarter notes, an eighth note followed by a quarter note, or two eighth notes in swing time. The claps are felt in duple or triple time as is appropriate. The triple subdivision is reinforced by kisili and kidindi or mudindi. Kidindi's rhythms are intoned as a constant *di din* (short long). This rhythm is heard on and against the clap as seen in rhythm ex. 5.1c.

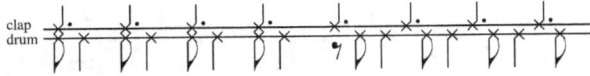

RHYTHM 5.1c. Clap drum

The larger drum, indumba, also reinforces the tempo. It further provides rhythmic and tonal variety. It maintains the same regular rhythm as the clap at a lower pitch and with tonal inflections translated mnemonically as *du ndi*. *Du* is played as an open stroke in the middle of the membrane. *Ndi* is a damped stroke stopped by the left hand on the other side of the drum. Grace notes are added by placing the left hand to damp just before striking the beat. This choreography is simulated when learning to drum. Kidindi is slung on the shoulder or held in the left hand. It is not stopped except when played by children to simulate the rhythm of indumba (bass/large drum).

The most common types of rhythm on indumba are indicated in rhythm ex. 5.1d.

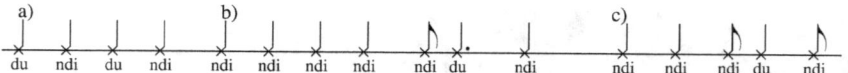

RHYTHM 5.1d. Indumba

When synchronized against kisili, kidindi, and the hand clap, one resultant effect is as seen in rhythm ex. 5.1e.

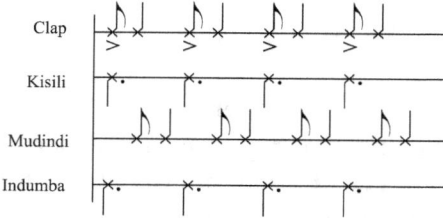

RHYTHM 5.1e. Kidindi

Structures and Use of Hymns, Gospel Hymns, and Gospel Songs

Many hymns, gospel hymns, and gospel songs taught by missionaries were structured in ways that ensured congregational participation. As this repertoire was accommodated and adopted some of these structures were adapted, syncretized, and altered. The following pieces exemplify various types of transformations applied to the missionary song that engendered the inclusion of these forms into Logooli musicking.[16]

The most common hymn structure was the stanza form. Lyrics emphasizing salvation and the cross as being *the way* were part of the theology of the late eighteenth century evinced in the works of revered European and Euro-American hymnists such as Isaac Watts. These hymns were at the core of church repertoire in Britain and the United States in the nineteenth century (and even into the twentieth century). They were transferred to the mission field. One hymn found in various European and American hymnals, "When I Survey the Wondrous Cross" (text by Isaac Watts, tune by Lowell Mason), was translated into Ludirichi (see music example 5.5a). Found in TTN, it was used by various Christian organizations in its Tiriki translation. It was sung specifically at communion services and in moments of devotional introspection. Two verses read as follows:

English (RS 573)	Ludirichi Translation (TTN 67)
When I survey the wondrous cross	Lwa inze ndola umusalaba
On which the Prince of Glory died	Ha Yesu Kristo ya khu khudzera
My richest gain I count but loss	Burhugi bwange ni vindu vutswa
And pour contempt on all my pride	Na inze ndaama burhengu bwange
Forbid it Lord that I should boast	U khonye Yesu khutsantsalikha
Save in the death of Christ my God	Mu likhudza lyo Mwami wange
All the vain things that charm me most	Ivindu vyosi ni vya nkhayerwa
I sacrifice them to his blood	Vya nda rhulidzwa mmasahi gege

The Ludirichi version appropriates the melodic and poetic meter of the English original. The translation applies the 'double-knock' technique to accommodate the essentials of the text (compare music examples 5.5a i and ii with 5.5b i and ii). However, much of the original tune and syllabic styling were retained in the translation.

This hymn, however, is rarely performed in the manner transcribed. For the four stanzas in English hymnals, the Ludirichi version has three stanzas and a refrain converted from the English second stanza. The stanzas and the

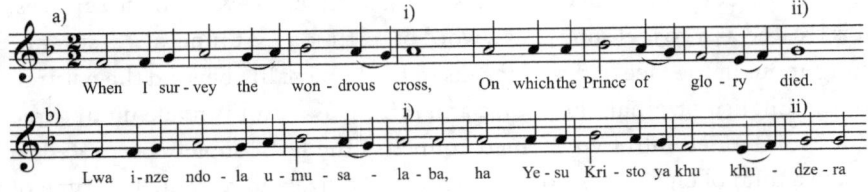

EXAMPLE 5.5a. (a & b) "When I survey"/"Lwa inze ndola" (1) (PURL 5.4)

EXAMPLE 5.5b. (c) "Lwa inze ndola" (2)

refrain are sung to the same melody. The original tune is retained except for the first three notes in the first and second phrase. The original notes are retained in the third and fourth phrases.

The duple feel of the original is retained but in $\frac{4}{4}$ rather than $\frac{2}{2}$. The rhythm, however, is adjusted to reflect Luyia aesthetics of anticipating the first strong beat with a rest rather than singing on the beat. With the creation of an offbeat, the rest of the phrase is adjusted to balance this first utterance. Four metronomic claps per beat solidify the syncopated rhythmic illusion. Drumming creates cross rhythm between singers' duple and kidindi triple subdivisions. The drumbeats entrench the compound time.

Stanza/refrain is by far the most favored form embraced by Avalogooli. Among the most popular stanza/refrain forms were those whose refrain lyrics were completely independent of the stanza, those where the refrain lyrics were carved out of the stanza, and those with an inherent refrain built into the stanza. In some songs, the stanza and refrain were made up of the same melodic material, others had different tunes for the two sections, and others derived part of the refrain melody from the stanza.

A classic example of a stanza/refrain with different melodic and textual material is Fanny Cosby's gospel hymn "Blessed Assurance" (text by Fanny Cosby, tune by Phoebe Knapp, RS 417). This hymn is sung at regular church and social gatherings, during evangelistic campaigns, and occasionally at funerals. "Blessed Assurance" is sung at any point in a regular service since the text references joy and thanks and is introspective. In evangelistic services, it is treated as a gospel song—as a word of testimony. At funerals, assurance sung about in the face of death speaks to the hope of life beyond the natural. In the English original, the stanza and refrain as a unit is made up of three lines subdivided into two rhymed couplets. The last couplet is repeated to make a total of eight lines; four each for the stanza and refrain. This type of refrain, a line of text that is repeated, is a well-employed compositional tech-

ACCOMMODATION

EXAMPLE 5.6a. "Blessed Assurance"

nique for gospel lyrics to emphasize the main thrust of the text or to facilitate congregational participation (see music ex 5.6a).

Stanza:

    Blessed assurance, Jesus is mine
    Oh what a foretaste of Glory divine
    Heir of salvation, purchase of God
    Born of his spirit, washed in his blood

Refrain:

    This is my story this is my song
    Praising my savior all the day long
    This is my story this is my song
    Praising my savior all the day long

The syllabic meter of the stanza is 9.10.9.9. The refrain is 9.9.9.9. In Lulogooli the meter becomes 9.9.9.9 for both the stanza and refrain and the rhyme is lost. The depth of the English text was not captured in Lulogooli. Instead a free translation, "Mbe no vugasu" (TTN 90), was effected, exemplified in the text of the first stanza below.

Stanza 1:

Mbe no vugasu ndi was Yesu!	I am blessed I belong to Jesus
Muhonyi wange wo bukumi	My savior of glory
Mbeye ne miandu gya Nyasaye	I have God's heritage
Kigira nyoye mwoyo muhya	Because I have found a new heart

The Lulogooli refrain conforms to the English original in repeating the first line of the couplet but alters the second part to capture the general thought

EXAMPLE 5.6b. "Mbe no vugasu"

about a song to praise the savior, and it expands the sentiment of honor to God embodied in praise singing in the fourth line. While repetition of text in the first part of the couplet is maintained—'the *story* that I am singing or living'—the English original is adjusted to focus on 'this is my *song*' as the germ idea of the text.

Refrain:

Yilu loveye lwimbu lwange	This is my song
Kwitsominya Yesu Muhonyi	To praise Jesus the savior
Yilu loveye lwimbu lwange	This is my song
Luyali ku Nyasaye wange	Honor to my God

The song is usually pitched lower than in the keys notated in English-language hymnals. The melody is structured as ABAC for stanza and EFE'C in the refrain. The Lulogooli version retains the original English melody, varying the tune for intensity of expression or using pitch substitutes indicated in music ex. 5.6b (the lower of the two notes). The compound meter in the English original is retained but felt in $\frac{12}{8}$ instead of $\frac{9}{8}$. While a leader may set the song in $\frac{9}{8}$ meter as in the English original, it will more likely be sung in the $\frac{12}{8}$ version.

A cursory analysis further exemplifies the musical readings Avalogooli choose to fit to the lyrics. The tempo is determined by the leader and influenced by the context. In a church service, the tempo is often set at a slower pace than during vushuhuda. When there is no clapping, a walk/jog and drumming may drive the tempo. The English version had an anacrusic beginning. The Lulogooli version begins on the downbeat. This is typical transformation for Euro-American hymns that begin on anacrusis. Congregations also tend to clap hands if lyrics focus on joyous sentiment. In this song, clapping and/

ACCOMMODATION

or shoulder or head movements are simulated for pulse and dance. The hand clap is in a quadruple feel on every main count of the $^{12}_{8}$ meter. Notes on strong beats are anticipated by pulsating the body or by a clap, resulting in a syncopated or offbeat entry. The clap often offsets the beginning of the song so that

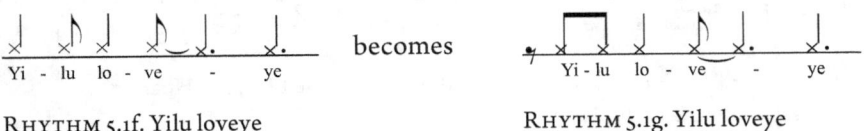

RHYTHM 5.1f. Yilu loveye   RHYTHM 5.1g. Yilu loveye

This rhythmic disjuncture intended to create tension is moderated by delivering the syllables *lo* and *ye* on the beat. The song leader signals the desired articulation of the phrase when he or she initiates or cues the refrain. Each subsequent phrase is treated that way.

The refrain ("This is my story...") is the climax of the song. The first and third lines are repeated. Singers clap increasingly louder with each successive reiteration of that text. The volume may be a function of the refrain melody that begins in the upper range—starting on three utterances of dominant, then leaping up a fourth to the tonic prime, giving a 'lift' in contrast to the stanza that just ended on the tonic. The second line stays in this upper range, seeming to anticipate a kind of downward resolution. Instead the repeated lyrics in the third line are energized by a rising melodic contour that begins on the leading tone before descending in another metaphoric reinforcement of the joyful theme of the text. The last line of the refrain is the same melody as that of the stanza. No other dynamic contrasts are observed apart from those implied by the melodic curve. The energy of the refrain may, however, be due to that fact that more people who sing the refrain may not know the stanza, as was usual before nonliterate congregants memorized the verses. I also posit that the change in meter and energy may reflect the celebratory exuberance of the refrain text contrasting the normative account in the stanzas.

An alternative treatment of stanza/refrain is presented in "There Is a Name I Love to Hear" (text Frederick Whitfield, Traditional American Melody TH [4] 288, TTN 115). The melody of the stanza is the same as that of the refrain. In the 1960s–1980s, the Logooli translation so expressed adoration for God in the revival climate of the time that congregants often became

EXAMPLE 5.7. "Oh How I Love Jesus" ("There Is a Name I Love to Hear") /"O Yesu nku yanza" (PURL 5.5)

entranced while singing. The refrain is transcribed in $^6_8$ in the English version. Avalogooli render it in this meter but often sing it with an offbeat and syncopated effect (see music ex. 5.7), and against duple meter clap.

While vocal coaches emphasize breathing through the phrase for lyrical sensibility (Hyslop 1964, 8–10), however, musical byplay can supersede textual continuity. In performance, on the first two iterations, the Lulogooli word *nkuyanza* (I'm loving you, I am enamored by you) is broken by rests: *nku* rest *ya* rest *nza*. The clap of four even eighth notes against six in the $^6_8$ also reinforces Logooli cross rhythmic preferences. That it is Logooli rather than general African idiomatic treatment is evident in that the English practice is invoked when the song is performed in Kiswahili.

In other stanza/refrain forms, the verse might be suggestive of call and response. To better learn a text or reiterate the fundamental message, a verse structure might consist of repeated alternate lines. In the song "Nothing but the Blood" (RS 99—text and tune by Robert Lowery), the message is emphasized by having the same text in line two and four and different lyrics in line one and three. A fixed text and melody is therefore embedded within the stanzas and the refrain. The result is ABCB for the stanzas in text while the melody reads ABAB. The refrain lyrics are structured DEFB while the melody is DEDB as outlined in the following transcription:

Stanza 1:

>What can wash away my sin?
>*Nothing but the blood of Jesus*
>What can make me whole again?
>*Nothing but the blood of Jesus*

Refrain:
> Oh precious is the flow
> That makes me white as snow
> No other fount I know
> *Nothing but the blood of Jesus*

The Lulogooli translation conforms to the English structure but conveys a different idea. The original text is about the work of the blood of Jesus. The translation focuses on Jesus the person, God's only begotten son, who he was, and what that means.

Lulogooli translation "Mwana wa Nyasaye" (TTN 69):

Stanza 1:

Ni wi uli musoli	Who is the deliverer
Mwana wa Nyasaye muderwa	God's only begotten son
Ni wi wayanza vosi	Who loves everyone
Mwana wa Nyasaye muderwa	God's only begotten son

Refrain:

Vulahi munono	It is all very well (this great goodness)
Vuyanzi vwa Nyasaye	The love of God / That God at His pleasure
Yahana Musoli	He provided a deliverer
Mwana wa Nyasaye muderwa[17]	God's only begotten son

Since the congregation initially only had to recall one phrase of the stanza, the song was easily learned by rote. The leader's text changed but the congregational responded on the second and fourth line with the same text and tune, resulting in a call-and-response structure. Some respondents joined the leader on the last word of the call lines. Since everybody was expected to sing the refrain, by the last verse the refrain was memorized.

Another historically popular hymn with a similar poetic structure in stanza/refrain form is "A Shelter in the Time of Storms" (GB 344, text V. J. Charlesworth, tune Ira Sankey; see music example 5.8a and b). High school students initially learned the song in English. It was popularized at youth camps, annual conferences (PAG), and Yearly Meetings (Quakers).

Kenyan Quakers produced a Lulogooli version in the 1970s (Mwelesa 1988, 108). Since text is accorded great importance in much religious music, the tune was adjusted for the much-loved text. The theme of the hymn is reiterated by three statements of the phrase "A shelter in the time of storm," twice in the stanza as an alternating line, and once at the end of the refrain.

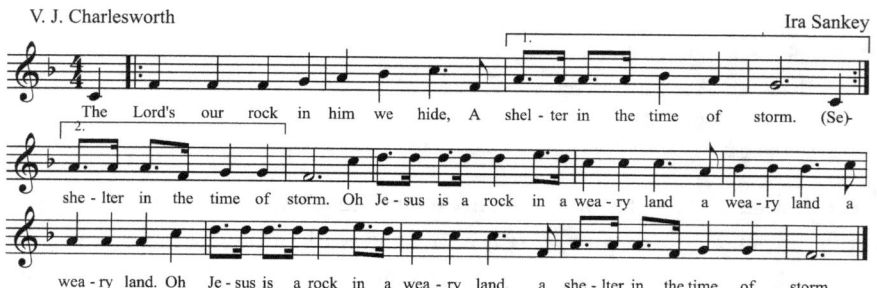

EXAMPLE 5.8a. "The Lord's Our Rock"

Stanza 1:

    The Lord's our rock in him we hide   Muhonyi niye ulwanda lwitu
    A shelter in the time of storm   Ni lilukila lie ligali
    Secure whatever ill betide   Si aleng'anywa nave kivala
    A shelter in the time of storm   Nililukila lie ligali

Refrain:

    Oh Jesus is a rock in a weary land   Oh Yesu nulwanda hano mulilova
    A weary land, a weary land   hano mulilova, hano mulilova
    Oh Jesus is a rock in a weary land   Oh Yesu nulwanda hano mulilova
    A shelter in the time of storm   Nililukila lie ligali

Translation from Lulogooli:

Stanza 1:

    The Savior is our rock
    A true shelter/refuge
    He cannot be compared to those of the world
    A true shelter/refuge

Refrain:

    Jesus is a rock here on earth
    Here on earth, here on earth
    Jesus is a rock here on earth
    A true shelter/refuge

The Lulogooli text is a fair translation of the hymn. The syllabic structure reads with comprehensive facility. Musically, the melody and its rhythm are adjusted. Of note, the dotted eighth notes followed by a sixteenth in the English are ignored in the refrain. The result is a good lyrical fit to the song's mood. This song is favored at funerals or general partings.

ACCOMMODATION 121

EXAMPLE 5.8b. "Muhonyi niye ulwanda lwitu"

Structurally, the anacrusic beginning is retained in translation. Further, the melodic reiteration of "A shelter in the time of storm" ("Nililukila lie ligali") is retained so that the first and third phrases are the same while the second and fourth begin in the same way but resolve differently. In the refrain, the first and third lines have the same text and music. The second line is built from the last part of the first line. The last line is the same as that of the stanza. Often the refrain is harmonized in parallel thirds with the melody in the lower voice, assuming a practice common in the religious and popular music of the time it was translated. In the refrain, a few people call "lwanda" after "mulilova" to energize the second line. The congregation then holds *va*, the last syllable of "mulilova" for a dotted quarter note against the callers' "lwanda."

When performed by a special group or as an anthem, the accompanying drum rhythm reflected what I call "Catholic indigenous style" common since the late 1960s, played on the Uganda drum. This 'foreign' drum with less 'pagan' associations than those ascribed to Abaluyia instruments was initially adopted at mission stations to help regulate daily activities early in the enterprise.[18] When eventually adopted as a musical instrument, the rhythm first popularized on these drums consisted of a quarter rest followed by six eighth notes per measure for a piece in duple or quadruple time. The drummer either rested on the first beat or damped/stopped the quarter note. The eighth notes were played with an open stroke. In the absence of the Uganda drum, indumba was substituted. In regular services tsindumba were played with sticks. In this case the Uganda drum or indumba was treated as a hand drum. The sound was not intended to be as loud as the regular indumba. The style relegated the drum into an accompanying rather than essential role for anthems or 'specials' during a service.[19] The anthem by its text, mood, and practice moved some hymns into coveted items at funerals or weddings. The style and instrumentation were adjusted to suit each context.

In another structurally popular 'book' hymn style, the refrain is derived from the last part of each stanza. Lulogooli translation conforms to the practice. In "Seeking for Me" (text anon., tune E. E. Hasty, RS 115), the refrain is derived from the last two lines of each stanza beginning with the last line followed by the penultimate line and a return to the last line in both text and tune. The form facilitated learning and participation if the leader sang the stanza expecting the congregation to pick up the 'refrain.' Thus the refrain is the climactic and most energetic section.

Stanza 1:

>Jesus my Savior to Bethlehem came
>Born in a manger to sorrow and shame
>Oh it was wonderful, blest be his name
>Seeking for me, for me

Derivative refrain:

>Seeking for me, for me ×2
>Oh it was wonderful blest be his name
>Seeking for me, for me

Lulogooli translation "Yesu yenyanga inze" (TTN 60):

Stanza 1:

Yesu muhonyi mu Bethlehemu	Jesus the savior in Bethlehem
Yivulwa kuli avaana vitu	Was born as our children are
Inze ng'enyanga kigira avola	I am amazed because he says
Yenyanga inze nunu	He wants me right now/today

Derivative refrain:

Yenyanga inze nunu ×2	He wants me right now ×2
Inze ng'enyanga kigira avola	I am amazed because he says
Yenyanga inze nunu	He wants me right now

The English original is 10.10.10.6, while the Lulogooli translation is 11.10.11.7 using the double-knock technique. In music ex. 5.9, the melodic structure is ABAC DD'AC. The refrain melody begins as a bridge whose second line is a variant of the first, emphasizing the message of the first line before returning to the end text of the stanza.

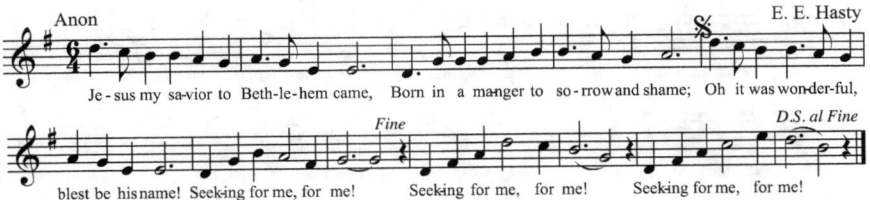

EXAMPLE 5.9a. "Seeking for Me"

The popularity of this hymn was strengthened by parts of the text that conjure familiarity with Logooli cultural practice. The second line of the first stanza, "Born in a manger to sorrow and shame," is translated as "Yivulwa kuli avana vitu" (He was born as our children are). The rest of the verse translates as "I am therefore awed because He says He wants me now." The text moved from the majesty, sorrow, and shame that set Jesus apart in the English version, to wonderment that he was born just "like our children are and is interested in us!" Subsequent verses about the death, purpose, and return of Christ that were present in the English original restored the message of the song in the Lulogooli translation. Beginning with the first stanza, each subsequent verse was sung with increasing fervor to build up the storyline.

In Lulogooli practice, the dotted rhythms were eliminated. Additionally, some substitutes were employed for high pitches as shown in music ex. 5.9b. This gospel song further exemplifies how body motion became an integral part of the musical complex. A duple time shoulder movement was applied in cross rhythm to the triple substructure of the song so that the body was in $\frac{4}{4}$ against the $\frac{6}{4}$ melody. (It is transcribed in various hymnals in $\frac{6}{4}$ or $\frac{6}{8}$.) In Logooli performance, most hymns in $\frac{6}{4}$ when sung a cappella are felt in $\frac{6}{8}$ and sung in $\frac{3}{4}$. The meter was reinforced by performers moving their chests or shoulders up and down or sideways on the strong beat of the triple subdivision. The performance became more complex when clapping in $\frac{2}{4}$ against the triple feel. The chest moved downward on the strong beat in the refrain, and singers entered on the offbeat against that impetus. The motion was contrasted by sedate elbow movements that articulated the kidindi rhythm in a kinetic reinforcement of the drum's timeline.

The discussed melodic, poetic, and metric types became compositional prototypes for Logooli hymnists. Logooli composers in missionary hymn

EXAMPLE 5.9b. "Yesu muhonyi mu Bethlehemu"

style not only adopted the stanza or stanza/refrain principle; a four-line stanza became standard. The practice of stanza/refrain is so popular that even songs that did not have a refrain have acquired one. This was not a new concept. It can be traced to the Great Awakenings.

In the Lulogooli hymnal, the title "Si gali masahi" (TTN 68, see music ex. 5.10a), translated from "Not All the Blood of Beasts" (Isaac Watts text), is assigned African origin.[20] Usually the English hymnal underscoring the Ludirichi title refers to the tune and the words. In "Si gali masahi" the English text source is not identified. I compare the English with the Ludirichi versions, after which I retransliterate from Ludirichi into English. The ethos of the text married to the African sourced tune made it a Quaker favorite. When sung a cappella, it is in a dignified slow tempo.

Original Text (RS 217)	**Ludirichi Translation (TTN 68)**	**English from Ludirichi**
Not all the blood of beasts	Si gali masahi	It is not the blood
On Jewish altars slain	Ge tsinyama tsyosi	Of any beast
Could give the guilty conscience peace	Ganyala khwogidza vwoni	That can wash sin
Or wash away its stain	No kuvurhulidza	And take it away
But Christ the heavenly Lamb	Masahi ga Yesu	The blood of Jesus
Takes all our sins away	Ganyala kwogidza	Can certainly wash
A sacrifice of nobler name	Vwoni vwange vwosi bei	All of my sin
And richer blood than they	Nokhulavidza myoyo	And cleanse the heart
My faith would lay her hand	Yesu ni shihanwa	Jesus is a gift
On that dear head of thine	Shilahi munono	A very good one
While like a penitent I stand	Shya sira ligali muno	It is way better than
And there confess my sin	Vihanwa vya avandi	The gifts of others

My soul looks back to see	Mukhonyi mulahi	A good helper
The burden thou didst bear	Ndolanga musigo	I see the burden
When hanging on the cursed tree	Gwa u gingi khu musala	You carried on the tree
And knows her guilt was there	Gwali bwoni vwange	Was my sin
Believing we rejoice	Nda suuvira ive	I will trust you
To see the curse removed	Lwa mali kweyama	Now I've owned up
We bless the Lamb with cheerful voice	Na nzeganire ubwoni	And repented of sin
And sing His bleeding love	Nda samefwa vwangu	I will be forgiven fast

Each verse is a complete idea in itself and can be sung independently. The first two verses are fair translations of corresponding English stanzas. Verse three in English is left out of the translation, but a third verse in Ludirichi is derived from ideas in the second verse. The content of verses four and five encapsulates their English counterparts. It is impossible to capture the profundity of the English lyrics by importing the structure and tune to a different language. However, the Ludirichi lyrics provide a depth to the sacrifice contained in the English original resonant in Luyia ethos. The Ludirichi text is structured as a stanza with an internal refrain. Each verse's refrain derives from repeating the last line twice, then restating the last two lines thus:

Si gali masahi	It is not the blood
Ge tsinyama tsyosi	of any beast/animal
Ganyala khwogidza vwoni	That can wash sin
No khuvurhulidza	and remove it
No khuvurhulidza	and remove it
No khuvurhulidza	and remove it
Ganyala khwogidza vwoni	That can wash sin,
No khuvurhulidza	and remove it.

The melody of the extended refrain is the same as that of the stanza. It serves to emphasize the most important activity in the stanza. The lyrical form is similar to that of "Seeking for Me" (music ex. 5.9a).

Melodic tension is suggested if a piece begins on the dominant note. To amplify rhythmic tension in slow tempo, the long notes worth two and a half beats are held for a syncopated quarter note, followed by a downward slide onto a related harmonic note before moving to the next syllable. Or one can

EXAMPLE 5.10a. "Si gali masahi" (PURL 5.6)

EXAMPLE 5.10b. "Yesu ni shihanwa"

hold out the value of the note so that the next phrase starts on a sixteenth instead of an eighth note. The piece is felt in triple or in compound triple time by applying a jazz triplet feel on the eighth notes. With clapping the general feeling is one of stretching the long note in a way that creates a rubato effect on the sixteenth notes. The third verse exemplifies these principles. In performance, the long notes in the second measure will be further ornamented with mordents and turns that are idiomatic in slow meter (see music example 5.10b).

Binary form was a favored structure, whether applied broadly as in stanza/refrain, or in other narrower duple formats. Some new songs were in Logooli folk or popular binary structures. For example, Mwelesa's Christmas song (1988, 28) "Lwa avayi vali ni valinda" is in AABb where b is altered text to the same tune (see music ex 5.11). However, the tune can be varied to accommodate the new text. For example, in the second line (beginning "Valola," measure 4) *la* is held a half note, the third line ("Vamanya ni") accommodates the syllables *nya* and *ni* scored as a dotted quarter note and an eighth note.

Stanza 1:
    Lwa avayi vaali ni valinda kyayo chavo mu vudiku ×2
    Valola uvulavu, vulavu vonene muno
    Vamanya ni vatia ligali, Engelosi yaloleka kuvo

Translation:
    While herders were watching their flock at night
    They saw a light, a very bright light (a brilliant light)
    They then became very fearful, an angel appeared to them

ACCOMMODATION

EXAMPLE 5.11. "Lwa avayi vali ni valinda" (PURL 5.7)

Although there are three rather than four lines typical of 'book' music, the first line is repeated to create four phrases. The first two full measures are sung in unison. The rest of the piece is harmonized a third above the melody line. This Christmas carol is treated as a 'special' number rather than being performed as a congregational song.

Another much used song form is AABA stanza/refrain exemplified in "Nzitsanga ha maveere" (Mwelesa 1988, 110). Both the stanza and refrain are composed of two lines, each structured as a couplet. The result is technically a four-line phrase. Both couplets of the stanza and the second couplet of the refrain are sung to the same melody. Only the first couplet of the refrain has a different tune (see music ex. 5.12).

Stanza 1 and refrain:

Mu mugela gwo liluva
Mu chiangalangwi chie kivi

Na Yesu nzambukanga
mbisangwa mu tsimbaha tsitsie

Nzitsanga ha maveere
Maguta ne waini

no vwuki vwituruka
ne milembe visunduka

Translation:

In the river where fishing occurs, I am going ashore with Jesus
In the wasteland of troubles, I hide myself in his wings

I am going where milk and honey have an overwhelming flow (is plentiful)
Oil, wine, and peace are poured out (abound)

Mwelesa ascribes the song's first performance to August 1951 at Malava. The song gained popularity in the 1970s. Since this piece was most often sung solemnly in mortuary rites, it assumed a 'special' function. "Mu mugela" was rarely sung with clapping, unlike similar-styled translated songs when performed in other contexts.

EXAMPLE 5.12. "Mu mugela gwo liluva" (PURL 5.8)

This composition is underpinned by a Logooli Christian understanding of death, a fusion of indigenous beliefs and the composer's biblical interpretation and understanding of the rite. The lyrics imply that the person is both fished out and rescued by Jesus, and that death is also a 'passing through waters.' Safe passage is possible with or escorted by Jesus to the other shore. Jesus rescues from 'absolute' death. A believer who dies arrives safely and excitedly on the other shore. The idea differs from the transition rites in indigenous society, where death was unsettling and insecure for the newly dead. The second line of the stanza establishes this kind of trauma, where one is in a desolate land of troubles. However, the composer iterates that even in that haze, one is covered by Jesus's wings. In an interesting way, the composer converges Logooli beliefs about death—the dead live on elsewhere (the living dead)—that they move on to a different space but are uncertain and unsettled during the passage. With Christianity, they have Jesus as a guide, or are hidden under his wings, and that provides confidence. Other verses describe the new land with the tree of life, a land where people do not have to move again but are at peace—again settling the anxiety of migration in Logooli worldview. The text therefore syncretizes Logooli and biblical worldviews.

INDEPENDENT REFRAINS AND CHORUSES

Choruses and independent refrains (tsikorasi) brought by missionaries (or composed in missionary style) assumed a significant position in Logooli repertoire. Some were published in hymnals; others were only orally transmitted. The most enduring refrains were translated into Lulogooli and into other Kenyan languages. This popular form of music was characterized by repetition and a stanzaic format. The style accommodated indigenous call-and-response techniques. Further, choruses acquired solo-response practice since the congregation waited on the leader to line the verses. A word or phrase could be substituted at the beginning to adjust the emphasis and create a new verse. The leader set the pitch, text, and other behavior such as accompanying physical actions. Consequently, Logooli musical aesthetics were applied from the beginning.

"Come to Jesus" (RS 105, TTN 139) was the first independent refrain/chorus translated into Lulogooli (Kasiera 1981, 179; Rees, E. 1905). The song had been popular in nineteenth-century revival meetings in the United States from whence it was transferred to the mission field.[21] The chorus has several stanzas. Each stanza is a sentence repeated, segmented, or resolved thus:

Verse 1:
> Come to Jesus (leader lines first sentence)
> Come to Jesus, come to Jesus just now
> Just now come to Jesus. Come to Jesus just now

Verse 2:
> He will save you. He will save you. He will save you just now
> Just now he will save you. He will save you just now

Verse 3:
> Call upon him. Call upon him, etc.

This chorus was sung at evangelistic services or during contemplative sections of a church service. The leader sang the first line, then the congregation took up the song. The length and text of the song depended on the leader's ability to describe within the musical phrase why one should 'come to Jesus.'[22] The English text emphasized not just coming to Jesus but also the urgency of the moment: 'just now.' Two versions are transcribed in music examples 5.13a and b, the second being the most performed.

Since the text was simple and repetitious, Logooli congregations often sang in both English and Lulogooli. In Logooli singing of the piece in English, the half note at the second "now" was shortened to a quarter note, altering the metric emphasis thereafter. With a shortened note value, the second verse started on the second rather than third beat, and the third verse began on the first beat. The dotted eighth note followed by a sixteenth in the anacrusis setup was also ignored in Logooli renditions in English.

The Lulogooli version is in $\frac{4}{4}$ while the English is in $\frac{3}{4}$. In Lulogooli, the song begins on the strong beat rather than on an anacrusis. Clapping reinforced the duple emphasis. Often in repeating "nunu" (just now) the second

Come to Je-sus. Come to Je-sus. Come to Je - sus just now Just now come to Je-sus. Come to Je-sus just now.

EXAMPLE 5.13a. "Come to Jesus" (1)

Come to Jesus. Come to Jesus. Come to Je-sus just now. Just now come to Jesus. Come to Je-sus just now

EXAMPLE 5.13b. "Come to Jesus" (2)

syllable is held for two counts the first time and for one beat the second time, creating a two-beat measure (see music example 5.13c). Kasiera (1981, 180) provided an English retranslation of the Lulogooli version in TTN (139).[23] I have expanded on it in the outline below. Only the first line of each subsequent verse was different. The other lines are the same as in the first stanza.

Yesu akulanga ×3 nunu	Jesus is calling you ×3 now
Nunu hulira ulangwa	Today listen, you are being called
Udze kuye nunu	Come to him now
Yesu akuyanza ×3 nunu	Jesus loves you now
Nunu hulira ulangwa, etc.	Today listen you are being called, etc.
Leka vwoni vuvwo ×3, etc.	Let your sins go (leave/abandon your sins)
Asulanga vwoni	He doesn't condone sin (He refuses sin)
Yenya kukusola	He wants to rescue you
Wenya kumulonda?	Do you want follow him?

In the Lulogooli translation, the essence of the call and its urgency present in the English original is retained. Of interest is the use of the word "nunu," which in Ludirichi means 'just now,' but in Lulogooli conveys the idea 'maybe'—that one can choose to respond. The meter changes as the song progresses. The syllabic structure in the translation reiterates the metric change in Lulogooli (English original 4.4.6.4.6, Lulogooli translation is 6.6.8.8.6). Repeating word "nunu" in the third line breaks the 4 into two 2s. The piece shifts to a $\frac{3}{4}$ meter for two bars before resolving into a duple time. Shifting back and forth between triple and duple or quadruple time is usual in Luyia storytell-

ACCOMMODATION

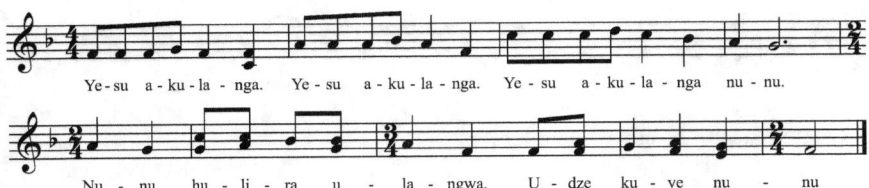

EXAMPLE 5.13c. "Yesu akulanga"

ing or ballad/epic song types. Performers of genres that reinforced cultural values and norms privileged the poetic and lyrical structure and adjusted the melody accordingly. Thus, similarly intended Christian Logooli compositions or adaptations such as "Come to Jesus" resonate with indigenous practices regarding metric and melodic manipulation.[24]

Another favorite chorus is "Oh God Is Good" (see music ex. 5.14a), also sung to text "God is so good." Of missionary origin, it was considered 'book' music although it was not transcribed in the most used hymnals. The lyrics most often sung were the two texts: "Oh God is good, He is good to me" and "God is so good, He's so good to me," with corresponding theological commutations. The most performed English version by Pentecostal youth was

Oh God is good ×3 He is good to me[25]
He loves me so ×3 He is good to me
I love him so ... etc.
He answers prayer, etc.

In Lulogooli, the piece starts on an anacrusis to provide an appropriate syllabic intonation:

Nya**sa**ye no mula**hi**
Nya**sa**ye no mula**hi**
Nya**sa**ye no mula**hi**
No mula**hi** ku **in**ze [wanje]

EXAMPLE 5.14a. "Oh God Is Good"

Nya-sa - ye no mula-hi. Nya-sa - ye no mula-hi. Nya-sa - ye no mula-hi, no mula-hi ku i - nze

EXAMPLE 5.14b. "Nyasaye no mulahi"

It is difficult to translate the essence of this text. The first line translates as "God is good" and the last line "He is good to me." The bracketed ending (preferred) changes the meaning to "God is my beloved one." The Lulogooli version adjusted several rhythmic elements to accommodate the text, but the melody was barely altered (see music ex. 5.14b).

This chorus was translated into other African languages for evangelism and to recognize diversity. A common practice was to sing the chorus in as many languages as possible. A multicultural congregation often sang in different languages at the same time—a type of 'singing in tongues.' The song was a favorite crowd pleaser and was sung often at various gatherings because it was simple, it was inclusive, and it generated maximum audience participation.

One of the most performed translations of "Oh God Is Good" by Logooli congregations was in Kiswahili (see music ex. 5.14c). Interestingly, Avalogooli readapted the Kiswahili translation to reflect a Logooli performance ethos. The song begins in Logooli up-tempo style followed by a tag that drives the piece to a climax.[26] It is structured as a verse followed by a tag that acts as a refrain and a vamp. In the tag, energy is generated through louder singing and increased body motion including stamping feet for textual density and to physically ground or emphasize the lyrics. The tag's beginning is syncopated, adding to the tension, which is resolved by reverting to the original chorus style. The Kiswahili text reads:

Mungu yu mwema ×3	God is good
Yu mwema kwangu	He is good to me (His goodness is directed to me)

Other verse possibilities include texts that state:

Ameniokoa ×3 nisipate taabu	(He has saved me so I will not be afflicted)
Ameniinua ×3 nisipate taabu	(He has lifted me up so I will not be afflicted)

Tag possibilities in call and response:

ACCOMMODATION

EXAMPLE 5.14C. "Mungu yu mwema"

Call	Response	
Tuimbe	Mungu yu mwema	Let us sing (God is good)
Tucheze	Mungu yu mwema	Let us dance...
Tusifu	Mungu yu mwema yu mwema kwangu	Let us praise...

In the tag, the leader ad-libs against the congregational response of the words of the title text ("Mungu yu mwema"). Logooli anticipatory motion is applied by resting or silence on the downbeat for the response to begin on the offbeat. The chorus holds its notes through the ad-lib then rests for an eighth note as impetus or synergy to respond. In performance, the song vacillates between the verses and the tag announced by the song leader's call. The leader signals the verse by starting on the beat or invites the tag by anticipating the response with ad-lib texts. Often, the performers move the torso or stomp their feet during the rests to visually reinforce the musical tension.

Avalogooli/Luyia are the only groups I have heard in Kenya to effect a tag to this Kiswahili translation. It is a select and deliberate choice. The dotted rhythms that accommodate syllabic rhythm of the Kiswahili lyrics are ignored in the tag. However, the tag is treated as a climax. Harmonies are intentionally added, particularly a 'bass part,' developed from the notion of *kuhola,* a vocal response suggested from the sound of a cow in heat. The term is also applied for an exuberantly impassioned cheering squad or when people announce their presence (in song) with impunity. The preferred vocal range for the sound is medium to low for women and high to middle tenor for men; a comfortable melding space where the two gender voicings can together produce a magnificent resounding. With drumming, it is set as a popular song or dance music with an idiomatic climax rather than being rhythmed in Logooli congregational drum stylings.

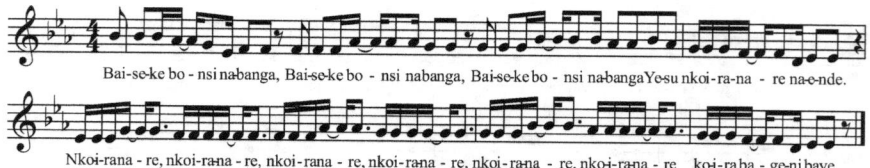

EXAMPLE 5.14d. "Baiseke bonsi nabanga"

Other texts were composed for this tune in Lulogooli and other languages, understood as new songs. The novelty referred to new texts, new styles, and alternative accompaniment. For example, Logooli Quaker, Pentecostal, and Salvation Army adherents who evangelized the Kisii culture group in the 1950s popularized the Kisii language song transcribed below (see music ex. 5.14d).[27]

Verse:
    Baiseke bonsi nabanga   (Even if all fathers dispute/challenge/contest it)
    Baiseke bonsi nabanga
    Baiseke bonsi nabanga
    Yesu nkoiranare naende   (Jesus will come back again)
Chorus:
    Nkoiranare, nkoiranare x3   (He will come back)
    Koira abageni baye   (to take his guests)[28]
Other verses:
    Banyina bonsi nabanga, etc.   Even if all mothers dispute/challenge/contest it...
    Abana bonsi nabanga, etc.   Even if all the children dispute/challenge/contest it

In stanza/refrain form, the melody is based on "Oh God Is Good" but set in Kisii language to new lyrics. This new text lends itself to a different popular music style, derived from Cuban son or mambo, appropriated to fit indigenous popular aesthetics.

Apart from being placed in hymnals, refrains were compiled into booklets such as the Pentecostal publication *Avaana vosi kwimbe* (All children, let us sing). A children's band toured, teaching the repertoire to other children. In 1962, a songbook was compiled for the Pentecostal youth movement (begun by Iris Scheel in 1958). The words-only book, *C.A. Song Book* (C.A.=Christ's Ambassadors), carried 152 entries. It was divided into three sections titled

"Hymns in English," "Hymns in Swahili," and "Choruses in English and Swahili." Most songs in the Swahili section were translations of the English section hymns respectively subtitled, as were the choruses. The text was not only the "Official Song Book of the C.A.'s in East Africa" (Scheel 1962); it was also the hymnal for all schools sponsored under the aegis of PAG.[29] Consequently, it was by default the official hymnal of the annual Pentecostal youth camp meeting held in August in Nyang'ori (relocated to Goibei in 1974). The camp, complete with tents, lasted seven days. Other camp music of new and old songs with choruses was printed in a booklet as part of the registration package. Most songs mirrored those in similar camps in Canada. A choir first learned the songs two days before camp began, then they later taught regular campers at music sessions. The choir also learned 'specials' that were presented at evening services attended by campers and participants from surrounding villages. The official music of the weeklong camp was therefore made up of selections from the CA songbook, the choir repertoire, and the camp booklet songs. The camp was also a place to share songs from elsewhere. A music competition was held featuring solos, duets, trios, quartets, and choirs. Campers learned these songs and wrote out their lyrics in exercise books. Some of the songs were so popular that they became a part of camp lore during the assembly.

Apart from the choir, the camp housed a brass band until the early 1970s (see fig. 5.2).[30] Beyond the band and choir, Iris Scheel invited ensembles playing African instruments, such as the Iteso ensemble that was showcased as the specially invited troupe in 1975. Apart from singers, the ensemble included Iteso bow-harps known as Adeudeu that were orchestrated for three- to four-part harmonies, as well as the Kayamba and other idiophones (see fig. 5.3). In this manner, Pentecostal youth of Logooli and other ethnicity were exposed to the instruments that had been appropriated for church use by other culture groups.

SPECIAL OCCASION SONGS

Several hymns and choruses were/are performed only at special occasions or functions. While some are associated with Christian rites (e.g., Easter), some 'Christian' songs were adopted in Logooli indigenous rituals and sociocultural functions. Texts determined contextual assignment. Tunes were also

FIGURE 5.2. Brass band.

FIGURE 5.3. The Iteso ensemble at the PAG annual youth camp.

ACCOMMODATION

disguised in performance style, tempo, and instrumentation to cater to these usages. The new character engendered a different connotation, or the song was considered a new composition. Occasion pieces were/are rarely sung out of context.[31] I will first exemplify a piece that was afforded 'special occasion' status due to its doctrinal significance.

"THE GREAT PHYSICIAN" (TEXT BY WILLIAM HUNTER, TUNE BY JOHN STOCKTON, TTN 56)

Pentecostals believe in supernatural healing. A sick person is always prayed for with the expectation of miraculous divine intervention. Certain medical procedures, such as surgery, invoke prayer for healing to avoid undergoing operations. Visits to patients begin and end with prayer. In Lulogooli translation, "The Great Physician" depicts Jesus as a helper leading his followers to victory (see music ex. 5.15a). Missionaries and locals were partial to this hymn themed on the healing doctrine. Beyond the belief that illness was biological or accidental, Logooli ascribed sickness to a contest between good and bad/evil powers. If a person succumbed to illness, evil powers were believed to have declared war and needed to be engaged in the supernatural. I never heard the song performed at funerals because in death, evil appeared to have won (Logooli), or it had been so willed by God (Pentecostals). The melody, in stanza/refrain, is an AA'BA" form. The English first verse and refrain state:

> The great physician now is near, the sympathizing Jesus (A)
> He speaks the drooping heart to cheer, oh, hear the voice of Jesus (A')
> Sweetest note in seraph song, sweetest name on mortal tongue (B made of b:ll)
> Sweetest carol ever sung, Jesus, blessed Jesus (A")

The notation in English is in $\frac{6}{8}$. In Logooli practice, pieces in this meter outside mortuary rites incorporate clapping. The melody is in $\frac{6}{8}$ against a clap in $\frac{4}{4}$ per measure. The rhythm is adjusted to shorten the eighth notes into sixteenth notes. The effect is one of creating tension by stretching out the

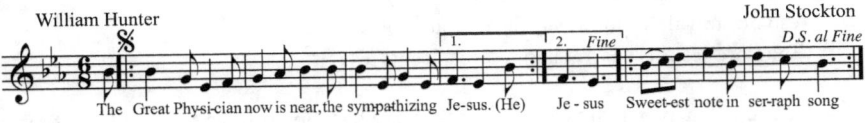

EXAMPLE 5.15a. "The Great Physician"

EXAMPLE 5.15b. "Mukonyi ali himbi nunu" (PURL 5.9)

previous note for as long as possible. It is then briefly resolved only to generate momentum to bounce again to propel the motion. This tensile technique occurs when the first moment of resolution is on a strong beat. In this example the first quarter note is extended into a moment of tension, but its anacrusic sixteenth note appears to want to resolve onto this strong beat. Instead the resolution becomes an impetuous moment that is extended in duration and by subsequent utterances. The notion resembles that of bouncing a ball. As it rebounds, the moment of contact re-energizes the ball to bounce again. The first bounce generates motion but the motion is reinvigorated for forward progress. However, the stimulus moment feigns an end point. Eventually the ball rests at the end of the phrase (measure 4). The process is repeated with a different text with some variation as if to reaffirm the musical statement. The refrain is set up as a subsequent reaction and resolution (BA). The Lulogooli first stanza whose melodic form closely follows the English original reads:

> Mukonyi ali himbi nunu vatagutwa veve (A)
> (The helper is near now, may his people not be defeated)
> Atsuuva vandu netsingulu vidzominye Yesu (A)
> (He injects people with power to praise Jesus [he empowers people to praise Jesus])

Refrain:
> Lyeta lilye lidzominywe, kwinye vosi ku mu yanze (B)
> (Let his name be praised, let us all love him)
> Yesu mwami ali himbi, Yesu, Yesu, Yesu (A')
> (The Lord Jesus is near/at hand, Jesus, Jesus, Jesus)[32]

In the refrain (music ex. 5.15b, measure 9), the singers rest on the strong beat, creating an offbeat entry, coupled with the high note, which in itself is energizing. The phrase is repeated (one note varied) before settling into the third phrase that behaves like a variation on the tidal wave that is the first phrase of the stanza. It is, however, sung without taking a breath between the second and third phrase. The momentum is finally resolved in the fourth phrase.[33] The treatment is most potent with clapping and drums.

In performance, except for the first note of the first phrase, any note starting from the dominant and higher is sung together with substitute lower pitches. The refrain employs the double-knock technique. The technique may partially be responsible for offbeating the beginning of refrain. I believe the practice eventually became stylistic, a manner of performing a long phrase/note, holding it out for as long as possible, then taking a breath at the last possible moment and either creating an offbeat or its illusion in order to begin the next phrase or note.

SONGS FOR FESTIVALS, CELEBRATIONS, AND RITUALS

Avalogooli celebrate Christian festivals such as Christmas and Easter. There is a definite body of music performed at Christmas. Other repertoire fits Easter, but it is not performed exclusively during that period. Rites such as circumcisions and burials have also acquired Christian music and practice.

"Oh Happy Day" (RS 622, Text by Philip Doddridge, Tune by E. F. Rimbault, TTN 220)

"Oh Happy Day" (see music ex. 5.16a) is sung at special Christian religious and Logooli ritual occasions such as Christmas, Easter, weddings, and prayers for significant events such as returning home after a long stay elsewhere. "Oh Happy Day" is also a staple during church services. The text accounts for its diverse assignments. The first verse of the English original, the Lulogooli translation, and the retranslation from Lulogooli to English read:

Verse 1:
    Oh happy day that fixed my choice on thee my savior and my God
    Well may this glowing heart rejoice and tell its raptures all abroad

Refrain:
    Happy day, happy day, when Jesus washed my sins away
    He taught me how to watch and pray and live rejoicing every day
    Happy day, happy day, when Jesus washed my sins away

EXAMPLE 5.16a. "Oh Happy Day" (2)

Lulogooli translation:

> Ni lidiku lyo buyanzi lwa ndovola Mwami Yesu
> Mwoyo gwidzuye buyanzi kulanditsa ling'ana lie[34]
>
> Lidiku linene lya ndivulwa mu Muhonyi
> Yegidza inze kusaala kandi kusangala kase
> Lidiku linene lya ndivulwa mu muhonyi

Retranslation:

> It was a joyful day when I chose the Lord Jesus
> My heart is full of joy to spread his word
>
> Great day when I was born in the savior
> He taught me to pray and to always rejoice
> Great day when I was born in the savior

"Oh Happy Day" is performed a cappella or accompanied by clapping and drums depending on its placement within a service or at a specific function or event. The event type is identified by the tempo. On solemn occasions (of tempered joy or contained gratitude) it is performed at a tempo of about 40 mm per dotted half note, in a slow, majestic, restrained manner instead of the exuberant excitement implied in the words. In this solemn space, the Lulogooli version takes on a $^6_4$ instead of $^3_2$ feel. The song begins on the first beat of the measure instead of the anacrusis found in the English. The dotted quarter notes in the refrain are extended into half notes starting at measure 8b. The rest is eliminated and the eighth note becomes a quarter note. The first measure of the refrain achieves a proactive impetus or declamatory stance. Because of the slow tempo, long notes are embellished by grace notes or by a pedal on the tonic. When long notes are not held for their full value, singers

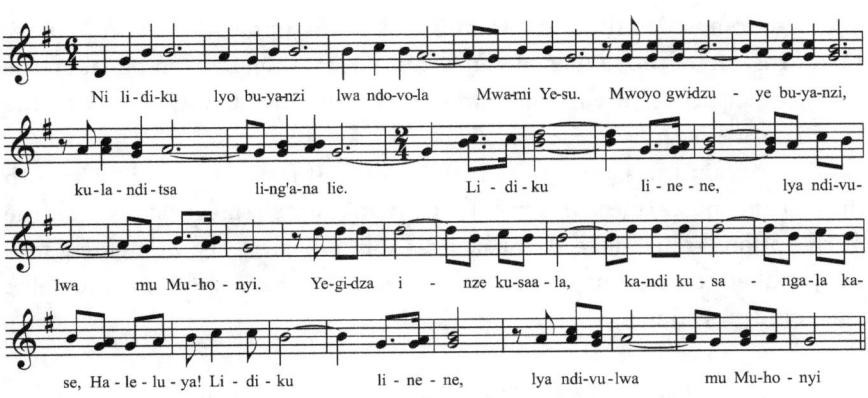

EXAMPLE 5.16b. "Ni lidiku lyo buyanzi"

execute body rhythms (such as moving the neck or head up and down in time) during the rest to signal motion into the next phrase. In my opinion, the motions are as integral a part of the music style as the notes and rests.

In a regular church gathering, the tempo is accelerated. Drums and hand clapping are incorporated. Four even claps grouped in twos create a cross rhythm against the song's three. However, there may also be a feeling of $\frac{3}{2}$ maintained throughout the song. Therefore there may be at least three different kinds of meters at the same time, with a body rhythm in 3, a clap in 4 and singing in 2 counts per measure. The clap also propels the piece so that often the rhythm is adjusted to create an eighth-note rest at the beginning of every phrase instead of the quarter-note value on the first beat.[35] The song leader lines the first two words of the verse. Syncopation begins when congregants enter and lasts until the end of the verse. With clapping, the refrain can acquire a simple meter $\frac{2}{4}$ feel. When in $\frac{2}{4}$, the quarter note is the same value as that in the $\frac{6}{4}$ meter. But the meter can also stay $\frac{6}{4}$ and be articulated as an eighth rest followed by an eighth note tied onto a double dotted quarter note, with the next syllable as a sixteenth note (at music ex. 5.16b, measure 17). Singers can opt for alternative notes to generate energy, to avoid uncomfortable pitches, or as a musical embellishment. With the ebb and flow of the stanza and its refrain due to the same cadential phrase for each line, the energy of the song stabilizes until the third line of the refrain (measure 17). The song resumes dynamic momentum until the pitches drop on "Haleluya" (measure 24) as if preparing to resolve the song (kutuula), but that interpolation forms a bridge from which the text and music of the first phrase of the refrain returns. Instead of the sequence in measures 9–12, singers often pedal on the tonic, anticipating the end (measures 25–28), and then finally resolve on the familiar cadence.

The refrain (measures 9–16) is the climax. It is declared boldly in both the text and music (measures 17–24) and then restated (measures 25–32). The pitch options transcribed in music ex. 5.16b indicate Logooli melodic motion, deliberate substitute notes, and preferred pitches, as well as acceptable harmonic procedures.

"The Solid Rock" (RS 240, Text by Edward Mote, Tune by William Bradbury, TTN 46, 279)

"The Solid Rock" (also titled "My Hope Is Built") is often performed in Lulogooli or Ludirichi and Kiswahili at funerals. It is transcribed in Ludirichi in TTN. It has become a standard because the text of the fourth stanza addresses the judgment throne, a place of final vindication in eternity. The song can also be incorporated into a regular church service in a different style from that perceived as funereal. The song is therefore a mourning dirge, a funeral processional, and a regular hymn. As a mourning dirge, it is sung unaccompanied. As a funeral processional, it is performed to the duple march of the mourners as they walk toward the grave (see music ex. 5.17b). As a regular hymn, clapping, drumming, and a shoulder shake are incorporated. The poetic structure is somehow interesting in its makeup of three rhymed couplets with the last line of the second couplet repeated like a coda. Essentially then, it has four lines per stanza and three lines of refrain. The structure was adopted in the Ludirichi translation. In simple time, the original English language tune can be sung in Lulogooli:

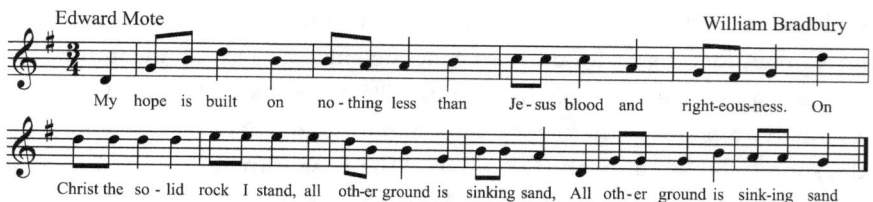

EXAMPLE 5.17a. "My Hope Is Built"

ACCOMMODATION

At funerals, the hymn is transformed into a compound duple meter in varying tempi depending on the context, whether during the wakes or at the graveside. In burial processionals, the song is felt in the duple meter inherent in the compound structure. When this compound feel is appropriated elsewhere, hand clapping is included to distance the association with death. The effect is a cross rhythm of a duple clap of $\frac{4}{4}$ against triple pulsing of $\frac{6}{8}$ in the melody. As in other instances, the dotted quarter notes in each measure are embellished by a pedal on the tonic. The pedal can either harmonize the other notes, or singers will glide onto the pedal notes.

EXAMPLE 5.17b. "Yakhudzera voni vosi" (PURL 5.10)

Performers tend to hold the dotted quarter note for a quarter and slide down onto the tonic on an eighth note. The melody of the first line can begin on the dominant above the tonic; it will be repeated, and then move through mediant to the subdominant for the long note. Therefore certain pitches are treated as harmony or as substitutes depending on whether the singers want to create or resolve tension.

It is commonplace to have alternative tunes sung to the same text if they are in the same meter. In Logooli worldview and in my experience, when a new tune was set to known text, there was usually a different function assigned to the 'new' composition. Such distanciation was also noted when texts were in languages other than Lulogooli, particularly English or Kiswahili texts. For example, "The Solid Rock" in Ludirichi is sung mainly at funerals. With Kiswahili lyrics (TTN 279), it featured anywhere, at any time. At least two other tunes exist for the Kiswahili text. They are sung without the contextual restrictions associated with the Ludirichi version. I have not heard Ludirichi lyrics sung to these other Kiswahili tunes.

Each Kiswahili version can be sung a cappella or accompanied with idiomatic church indumba style or with a rhythmic mode drawn from Swahili popular singing, derived from the Arabic mode (chifte-telli) but only using the first

EXAMPLE 5.17c. "Cha kutumaini sina" (1) (PURL 5.11)

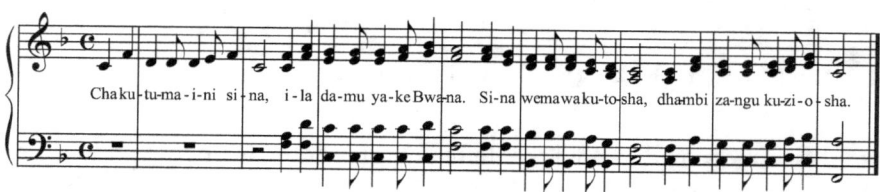

EXAMPLE 5.17d. "Cha kutumaini sina" (2)

half of it; dum—tak tak—tak tak. The Kiswahili versions are Kenyan national staples. While one version was popularized by the Machakos Town Choir in the 1970s (music ex. 5.17c), the more performed one is considered public domain (music ex. 5.17d). The Machakos Town Choir version (music ex. 5.17c) is in *Makwaya* style. Here the voices are in homophony in the stanzas. The stanza has two lines further subdivided as a couplet. Each couplet is sung to the same tune. The refrain, which is technically made up of three lines, begins with the bass line lining a call, which the upper voices then repeat lyrically. On the next line, the basses prompt the subsequent choral response or collectively reiterate significant words from a previous iteration. The whole choir then homophonically states the last line whose lyrics are a repeat of the second line.

In the more popular version (music ex. 5.17d), the stanza is set to the same melody as the refrain. The sopranos call the first line of the stanza, and then respond together with the other voice parts. They sing the melody line,

ACCOMMODATION

harmonized by the lower voices. Each stanza is repeated at least once at the discretion of the song leader or choir director. Sopranos also cue the choir for the refrain. The refrain is repeated at least once. Often a drum pattern and a shaker are implied and motioned by the singers. The song can also be accompanied by a combo of lead, solo, and bass guitar with drum set and/or bongos. Performers rarely stand still. They invoke the ubiquitous church motion of a duple pattern, stepping out with the right foot followed by the left. The movement is reversed ad infinitum. Usually the rest of the body follows the pattern of the feet with no other overt motions—not even swaying.

Music ex. 5.17d has been the most popularly performed version since the late 1980s. It has made its way into several hymnbooks such as *Global Praise* published by the World Council of Churches. Other versions have been composed or adopted in the first decade of the twenty-first century in line with current trends in popular music.

"I Am So Glad That Jesus Loves Me" (RS 671, Text and Tune by Philip Bliss, TTN 50)

"I Am So Glad" is drawn from the gospel hymn "I Am So Glad That Our Father in Heaven" (Philip P. Bliss) (see music ex 5.18a). This song was often associated with Sunday school children and adult young Christians.

EXAMPLE 5.18a. "I Am So Glad That Jesus Loves Me"

The same melody is used with two different translated texts. Although Logooli sing both versions, the first text is in Ludirichi and the second is in Lunyore, both neighboring Luyia groups. The versions use a tempo similar to the English original.

English Original

| I am so glad that Jesus loves me | Jesus loves me x2 |
| I am so glad that Jesus loves me | Jesus loves even me |

"Ludirichi" (music ex. 5.18b):
    Ntsantsalikhanga, Yesu a nyanza[36]
    Yesu a nyanza ×2
    Ntsantsalikhanga, Yesu a nyanza
    Yesu a nyanza inze

"Lunyore" (music ex. 5.18c):
    Nyanzire po, Yesu yainyaza
    Mwami Yesu wakhuyanza
    Nyanzire po Yesu yainyanza
    Yakhuyanza efwe

Retranslation from Ludirichi:
    I am so in awe/pleased, Jesus loves me
    Jesus loves me ×2
    I am so in awe/pleased, Jesus loves me
    Jesus loves particularly me

Retranslation from Lunyore:
    I am extremely glad Jesus loves me
    The Lord Jesus loves us
    I am extremely glad Jesus loves me
    He loves us in particular

The Lunyore version is a more literal translation of the English than the Ludirichi. It is considered a different song and rarely appended to the first. Both versions are felt in the meter in which they are transcribed below but they can also be treated in cross rhythm with a clap in duple time against the triple subdivision. Music ex. 5.18b is sung at regular services, at other 'happy' events, or as song leader's choice. Measures are extended for musical and textual reasons, an elaboration of the double-knock technique. The number of phrases is retained but the number of measures and the syllables are adjusted.

Music ex. 5.18c (Lunyore) is also sung by adults in church and in other 'happy' events. When felt in $\frac{3}{8}$, the number of syllables per phrase is 5 4 5 3.

EXAMPLE 5.18b. "Lero ndimbanga"

EXAMPLE 5.18c. "Nyanzire po, Yesu yainyanza"

The original rhythm is adjusted to fit the extended phrase. The double-knock technique does not adhere to the boundaries of the meter of the original tune. Another beat is added to effectively extend the meter. This is unusual but demonstrates the importance of the timeline as a unit (particularly when a clap is implied or performed) over an even number of bars. The meter accommodates the syllables of the translated text, further extending the double-knock technique. With clapping or drumming, the singers either adhere to the English rhythms or clap on the downbeat while the singers enter offbeat. Syncopation occurs at the beginning of phrases in line with instrumental and cultural preferences.

CHARACTERISTIC LOGOOLI FEATURES IN 'BOOK' MUSIC

Texts of hymns, gospel songs, and independent refrains were/are written out or printed. As such they are considered 'book' music. No difference is observed between a hymn and a gospel song, but a chorus is usually identified. Most 'book' music is performed as written. However, in instances where the first translation fell short, new words or other forms have been substituted and have acquired common usage. Songs are learned by rote. When a tune is forgotten, a transcription, musician, composer, translator, church member, or teacher is consulted. Otherwise new tunes are attached to or composed for the lyrics. Certain musical and cultural ideals brought by Euro-American missionaries have also become compositional resources for new Logooli songs. In cultures where the collective affirms, negates, and confirms compositions, the use of this repertoire outside Christian religious events signifies an accommodation of the music.

Whereas songs can be sung in the style, meter, and tune brought by missionaries, Avalogooli have transformed some pieces to reflect their cultural and musical worldview. Structural changes are evident in such elements as meter, rhythm, melody, form, instruments, and textual arrangements. Assimilation and appropriation of cultural ideas are reflected in the ways the pieces function in society. London (2005) asserts: "In specifying the tonal and rhythmic organization of a work we believe we have captured its essential structure . . . Changes in instrumentation, orchestration or dynamics (i.e., changes to the secondary parameters) are understood as different arrangements of the same musical work, whereas alterations in pitch or rhythm may result in a new, different work."

Among Avalogooli, change in 'essential' structure was not only acknowledged as innovation; a new text to a known tune could be viewed as a different melody. New uses and functions were found for Christian music. Examples include singing "Ni lidiku" to the tune of "Oh Happy Day" (music ex. 5.17a) in solemn assemblies or ritual gatherings. In slow tempo, it is performed at weddings or at certain church calendric events, such as Christmas. The text hinges on the word 'choice' (*ndovola*). At festivals such as Christmas where missionaries taught about Christ's choice to come, songs on choice regarding redemption and repentance, rather than Christmas carols, were invoked. It was appropriate to sing "Oh happy day that fixed my choice" ("Ni lidiku lyo buyanzi lwa ndovola"—It is a happy day when I make the choice) at Christmas. Christ chose to come, and people choose to follow him. In most marriage contracts, one chooses his or her partner. The mutual choice by each party makes "Oh Happy Day" an appropriate song to begin the wedding service.

Meter may probably be the most audible yet subtle adjustment to translated hymns. The changes may have been occasioned by translations where syllabic meter was adjusted. Altering syllabic meter most often led to the use of the double-knock technique. When it was not effective, the number of beats per measure was increased or reduced. The result was a metric shift, moving a song from simple to compound time or a change within a measure creating hemiola. Thus a piece in $\frac{4}{4}$ might be shifted into $\frac{12}{8}$, or a piece in $\frac{2}{4}$ or $\frac{3}{4}$ was reconstructed into a $\frac{6}{8}$ feel. More common was the presence of two meters against each other. Clapping was metronomic in duple time pitted against songs in simple triple or compound duple meter. Clapping in duple time was also felt against a compound meter shoulder movement. The resulting cross rhythms provided musical interest or instigated rhythmic adjustments.

Rhythm is the most manipulated musical element. Rhythmic alterations are perceived through actual changes in articulation, patterning, and placement. But they are also suggested or alluded to through adjustment of volume or with clapping, drumming, and body rhythms. The use of swing duplets is commonplace. Rhythmic transformation is most evident in use of duplets and triplets to accommodate texts. Cross rhythm of two against three or three against four with clapping is normal. The clap is not just a metronome; it is also a musical instrument according to the folk classification system (Mulindi 1983, 107–112). The body is treated as an instrument in its own right and interacts with other instruments. Clapping and other body motions shift the rhythmic configuration, often acting as impetus or ictus for the vocals. Therefore clapping and body rhythms are not just decorative and dispensable, they are part of the music structure.

Mulindi discusses Logooli music concepts, singling out the term *mwoyo* (heart/soul/voice) as a primary distinction between song and speech. Singing and speaking evince and validate being alive—having a voice—common to people, birds, and animals but "only humans use words . . . or speak to deliver messages . . . it is in this respect that for example musical instruments are said to 'convey messages'" (Mulindi 1983, 55). Mwoyo is further used to describe an attitude, perspective, feeling—suggestive of the idea of action or reaction toward someone or something, as used in the ditty "Spotsimani yambila mwoyo" (The cigarette brand called Sportsman has stolen my heart; I am enamored by Sportsman cigarettes). Mwoyo is also translated in music as melody, pitch, beat in regulated or unregulated rhythm, and related to the ways music is theorized and structured. "Music has rules . . . things which control it, and the most important of these are the notes and the beats" (ibid., 60). These rules nominate theoretical and structural underpinnings in Logooli musicking. Mulindi goes on to describe music as text beyond lyrical content, performed not just to communicate understandable verbal messages but appreciated for physical, spiritual, psychological, and aesthetic value. With the analysis of the properties Mulindi garnered from her collaborators' discussion of musicking in Logooli terms (ibid., 67–91), it is no surprise that composers and consumers critiqued missionary repertoire and Logooli Christian songs privately and publicly. The veneration of certain repertoire implies that the public accepted it for its musical and/or religious values by consensus but also through subtle and aggressive marketing.

In comparing Mulindi's findings with the new repertoire introduced by Euro-American missionaries, I concluded that Logooli Christians invoked indigenous practices that at times corresponded melodic movement with linguistic intonation. They also recognized that "speech unlike song had no melodic center" (Mulindi 1983, 238). Therefore melodic aesthetic considerations could supersede linguistic intonation. In Mulindi's work, the third and the fifth degree of a diatonic scale were common starting and ending pitches for songs. The sixth degree was also a tonal center for adult songs. With education and urbanization, it became common to cadence on the first degree. Thus later songs increasingly embrace the major mode. Since 'book' music is considered music of the school, these songs assumed a major mode even when another modality was implied.

Because the culture already recognized alternative notes, harmony was not a radical innovation. In both Mulindi's and my fieldwork, four-part conventional harmony was commonly applied particularly for songs in major keys. In contexts where it was not so obviously imaged as harmony, such as in congregational singing, heterophony and alternative notes were substituted deliberately as musical choices or in response to the range of a piece. The notes were also performed as pedals or in clusters. The tonic, dominant, and supertonic were deliberately used as harmony. Beyond harmony, timbral adjustments were invoked by group and context—whether function or place, indoors or outdoors. For example, the African Israel Church Nineveh practice of shutting doors so as not to let the spirit out affected the timbre in their indoor performances compared to that of their outdoor processional (Ogot and Welbourn 1966, 91–94).

Energy and tension was created not just by becoming louder and adding instruments but also by effecting rests at the beginning of a measure, anticipating the start of a phrase through syncopation, or in adjusting the syllables of the lyrics to accommodate the note values. A feeling of rubato was created either way. Tension was also created by using alternative notes, lower or higher than the original as determined by subsequent notes. Tension was released by resting just before a strong beat instead of holding the note for its longest value. It was also effected by clapping in cross rhythm—a typical Logooli practice pits two against three or three against four.[37] Lyrical tension was developed by varying the text and ad-libbing with standard words such as 'halleluiah' or using vocables intended to prolong or curtail a response or moment. Some textual intonation with inherent alternative coloration not only expanded the musical possibilities, it also energized the response.

Certain body motions are tensile and others lead to resolutions. For example, moving a foot forward will be tensile, and bringing the other foot next to it resolves that tension. The motion functions similarly for chest, hand, and head movements. The length or duration of that motion magnifies or lessens the tension. Tension is also created by the drumbeat, where an open stroke could be tensile and a stopped stroke brings resolution. But this was not always true. Certain stopped strokes used in processionals, the most common being four stopped quarter notes, were resolved by a figure containing a stopped eighth followed by an open dotted quarter and a stopped quarter followed by a rest. The idea imitates sounds played on a clay pot. It is understood to imitate a player stopping the pot for four strokes, but when each stroke is played, the air allowed in is so minimal that when the pot is finally uncovered on the open stroke, the air that was being teased inside is like someone taking a big gulp of air after successively pinching the nose several times. But it is followed by a regularization of breathing, hence the open note and the rest at the end of the figure.

Variations are melodic, rhythmic, metric, temporal, and lyrical. Melodic variation creates and resolves tension. Rhythmic tension occurs through the use of rests, syncopation, and anticipation when the body or the clap articulates the strong beat while the voice is silent. Metric tension is created by either varying or reworking the meters within or of a piece from a simple to a compound time; or combining duple, triple or quadruple meters. Changes in tempo depend on context and age group. In different times younger people have employed a faster or slower tempo than their elders. Since metronome sense is important for musical and cultural aesthetic value, tempo can reflect chronological periods and influences. Music festivals encourage youth to apprentice with seniors in order to recreate 'authentic readings.' These various techniques are summoned to invigorate Logooli music performances including 'Christian' genres.

It is conclusive that 'book' music can be performed in 'missionary' style. I believe the original intention was that the style and text, familiar to missionaries and associated with Christianity, supersede and even replace indigenous Lulogooli texts, functions, and practices. The ritual site that best reveals Logooli musical adoption and accommodation of 'book' music is the funeral. It is also the passage with the most uncertainty afterward. The notion of the living dead or translation at death to a different form was present in Logooli worldview. Naming heaven as *that place* solidified the venue where the living dead repose. Mwelesa's explanations about heaven and Logooli worldview (2007) demonstrated the variety of interpretations that have plagued Logooli Christians. Mwelesa complained that another musician had altered his text of the song "Ndilonda ku inzira ya vaguga vadzira ku" (I will walk in the way the fathers have trod [Mwelesa 1988, 63]). (PURL 5.12) Earlier, I had questioned the musician, who said he changed the text because it syncretized orthodox Christian theology with Logooli beliefs (Kidula 2005a). Mwelesa explained his inspiration when he composed the song in 1982. He stated that he based it on a Bible passage (Job 7:3–10). The passage describes Job's helplessness at the death of his children and at the loss of his health and wealth. Job knew death was inevitable but could not predict its timing. Thus he was sure to tread the path of the fathers and all humanity—the way of death. Mwelesa further invoked the Jewish heritage of Abraham, Isaac, and Jacob to reiterate that he, as a Christian birthed into God's family with a spiritual legacy located in these Judaic forefathers, would walk in the way of his new heritage (Mwelesa 2007).[38] Hence, with diverse Christian denominations layered on an equally diverse cultural heritage, it is possible to provide multiple hermeneutic readings on the same musical and religious text at a particular time. With 'book' music, it is possible that Avalogooli moved from a mere encounter in terms of musical style and religious beliefs to an experience. They henceforth became part of the imagined transcendent global Christian community through musicking in styles spread the world over by Euro-American Pentecostals, Quakers, and others.

The historical and continuing accommodation of Christian beliefs into Logooli worldview evinces multiple interpretations of biblical and denominational theology and religious doctrine. These interpretations are applied not only in the Christianity advocated by Euro-Americans and others; a place is continually afforded for different Logooli interpretations of biblical and other cultural appropriation of Christianity.

SIX
SYNCRETISM
Logooli Christian Songs of the Spirit

At the onset of the twentieth century, the Pentecostal and Holiness phenomena ignited the growth of new church musics. These musics had been fermenting in earlier revival movements in Europe and the United States. They were also rooted in the musico-cultural ethos of the peoples and denominations that embraced these events (e.g., Goff 2002, 13–32; Southern 1983, 127–130, 444–456; Synan 1987). For most of these groups, music became the primary denominational doctrinal statement. Utilizing music to bear and solidify a movement's religious canons and doctrines was not new. Martin Luther and the Reformers employed music to indoctrinate the public and to inculcate Christian morals. Music was also used during the Great Awakenings to mobilize and evangelize the public. In these cases, new converts internalized their newfound beliefs and rehearsed their experiences through song. A key source for the music was the folk and popular styles of the times. Pentecostal and other revival movements of the early twentieth century added to the layer of the repertoire, moving beyond gospel songs to 'songs of the spirit.' This catalog was drawn on to proselytize, indoctrinate, and moralize the public. Beyond Pentecostal doctrine, texts extended from biblical narrative and praise songs, to social and moral topics, and to denominational creeds. The lyrics drew on daily experiences, on social concerns, on cultural trends, and on the political dogmas of their day. The songs were exported to the mission field. The entrenchment of these musics into Logooli lifestyle was facilitated by improved communication and media systems and reinforced by the colonial powers' collaboration with missionaries.

Avalogooli embraced and developed 'songs of the spirit' ('spirit' songs). Beyond their utility by Pentecostal missionaries and evangelical Quakers, these songs were the core fare amongst the schism and secession movements that birthed Africanist Christian groups (Ogot and Welbourn 1966, 132–146). They drew from the musicking posited by missionaries and also on indigenous 'African' musics and religions, systems originally deemed incompatible with European ideals. The output evinced musical and religious syncretism. Since 'spirit' song repertoire includes music composed by Avalogooli who became a part of the 'spirit' movement, it draws from Logooli musical and poetic structures. Due to their association with 'spirit' revival meetings, these songs are referenced as 'Tsinyimbo tsya Roho' (songs of the spirit) and termed spirituals by scholars who see an analogy with American spirituals birthed in the nineteenth-century camp meetings (Otieno 1990). This section will discuss Logooli 'songs of the spirit.'

BEGINNINGS

Logooli 'spirit' songs and hymns proliferated with a revival that broke out at Kaimosi from 1926 (Kasiera 1981, 9, 324, 377). Some Quaker missionaries who had embraced Pentecostal theology encouraged and tolerated the new 'songs of the spirit.' Songs were at the heartbeat of the revival. They were acquired through dreams and visions or as spontaneous expressions when converts were 'filled with the spirit.' According to Kasiera's and his informants' reading of the 'spirit' happenings:

> Dreams, visions and spirit possession came to be the means by which even those who did not read and write and those who were "dense" and could not significantly comprehend Christian vocabulary, had access to and experienced "the Lord" or "the Holy Spirit" of Christianity ... Songs and singing ... are [were] also the media through which internalized ideas and experiences are [were] expressed. (Kasiera 1981, 366, 550)

Songs were composed or received through/from/in the 'spirit.' They were curled from the spirit, the voice, and the heart of the local people. These songs can also be read as a way for

> people who desperately need[ed] relief from the emotional strain of living between the old and the new orders ... to develop the therapeutic potential of the Pentecostal practice of public confession ... set ... in the context of traditional musical forms [in] a language far more clearly understanded [sic] of the people than a mere translation of words from one vocabulary to another. (Ogot and Welbourn 1966, 129)

Songs were vetted, scrutinized by congregations, and accepted after examining the person's character or on explaining how the song was 'received.' They were passed on orally at evangelistic gatherings and in prayer meetings. They were soon endorsed as the main repertoire of secessionist churches. Further they were adopted as staples at rites of transition and in social gatherings. Avalogooli performed these songs in the absence of missionaries, not as songs of protest, but as local expressions of Christianity.[1] This evolution signified a Logooli internalization of Christianity. Musically, it was a momentous indigenization of foreign ideas into a local idiom. The repertoire, as a musical, cultural, and religious product, attracted large crowds and a response different from that of translated hymns. It was viewed as a successful conduit for the Christian message (Ogot and Welbourn 1966).

GENERAL CHARACTERISTIC PRACTICES OF 'SPIRIT' SONGS

'Spirit' songs have become part of the musical lore of Avalogooli. These songs are generally short and in the style of independent refrains. Several songs are conjoined as a suite, an ethos locused in Logooli community musicking. Alternatively, a leader begins with a 'book' hymn and rounds off with a 'spirit' song as it 'moves people to another level.'[2] Most 'spirit' songs are in call-and-response format. The caller might line the text and the tune for the group, begin a sentence to be completed by the response, ask a question answered in the response, initiate an idea that is explicated in the response, and cue in a stanza or line by stating the first word. The caller's role can also be one where once the song begins, he or she ad-libs, interpolates, or cajoles members to continue singing, to climax, or to stop. In evangelistic campaigns and funeral wakes, drums, in addition to their timeline and polyrhythmic role, provide instrumental interludes. These interludes are the perfect space to ponder on the next song, adjust the pitch and style, repose the singers, or just jam. Often, to sustain momentum on long notes, or to generate energy, the leader anticipates the next 'call' by joining the responders on the last word, but with louder volume and at a higher pitch. Apart from boosting energy, this action signals that the leader intends to continue with the song or to extend the session.

A common practice with similar intent is for the leader to fill in the rests or the long notes with ad-libs using words like 'halleluiah,' only the whole word is never said. It is often shortened to "eluya,' as if the leader imaged the beginning of the word and voiced the rest of it, a notion similar to the Logooli musical aesthetic *kuvugula*, sort of like 'catching' the rest of the song from the air. Other interjections may relate to the subject at hand; may be names or categories of people, events, and places; or could be types of labels. The ad-lib is audible because it is pitched higher and sung louder than the sound of the congregation. The song leader therefore manages the session not only in vocals but also in attitude, body language, movement, expression of emotion through the ad-libs, energizing and being energized by the crowd, moving the congregation to new spiritual and aesthetic realms. It is Logooli practice to observe rests rather than hold out the last note. In fact it is common practice to end abruptly and leave the audience in suspense, to allow the participants—on and off stage—to resolve the tension in their own way. Therefore, songs end abruptly instead of gradually slowing down or observing a fermata unless the song is appropriated from or directly imitating European styles. After the song ends, or if there is any doubt that the song has ended, the leader intones the 'halleluiah call.'

A different type of Logooli 'spirit' song was modeled after the missionary hymn. The song was either a (re)translation of missionary hymns or new lyrics were set in missionary hymn-type poetic form. In the former case, a new tune was assigned to a translated hymn text or a new text adopted for a missionary hymn.[3] Quakers composed in the standard stanza form of Euro-American hymns or gospel songs.[4] Songs composed intentionally in missionary hymn styles were written in booklets. Further, some African Christians opposed songs in Logooli styles, since they recognized that indigenous worldview and religious ethos were intrinsic to and textured in the styles.[5] To embrace a new deity, a novel way of musicking was adopted. Before finding their voice, Avalogooli assumed the missionary style. Some songs were not in missionary style, but their authors' church denomination, reputation, and marketing techniques classified them as 'book' music. Their formal and lyrical structure, however, placed them in the Logooli 'spirit' song category. These songs were disseminated to the larger society in church services and at communal events. To justify Logooli 'ownership' of the songs as emanating from their 'spirit,' I will discuss textual features, analyze musical elements, and then provide a reading of Logooli characteristics.

TEXT AND LYRICS

For one type of 'spirit' song arising out of Logooli ethos, texts allude to 'heaven' in some form. Lyrics are concerned with what is in heaven and how

SYNCRETISM

EXAMPLE 6.1. "Mwigulu buyanzi"

to get there in anticipation of better times, a better place, better conditions, and ultimate home. Given the colonial situation, basic needs, and health concerns, it is not surprising that songs are themed on a yearning for betterment for material and emotional comforts. In the 1950s song below, the leader lines out how heaven will be, including food and things that Avalogooli imagined made for satisfaction in life:

Leader:	Mwigulu buyanzi aleluya	In heaven there is abundant joy
Chorus:	Mwigulu buyanzi aleluya ×3	
Leader:	Mwigulu maduma aleluya	In heaven there is abundance of corn
Response	Mwigulu maduma aleluya ×3	
Leader:	Mwigulu tsisuti aleluya, etc.	In heaven, suits are in abundance

The text references those things that relieve worry and stress, those that satisfy and comfort, and those that denote or signify affluence. For example, corn (maize), a staple food, will be so plentiful that there will be no hunger. Heaven will have ample and fashionable clothes such that people will be well dressed, particularly male house servants, cooks, or laborers who wore shorts and were referred to as 'boys' (*Maboyi*)[6] by colonists and others. Heaven will indeed restore the dignity of men—whose affluence and comportment will be evidenced by the suits worn. Some texts encouraged troubled Christians to have hope because heaven, the believer's final home, was a better land and was not too distant in time or place. Other songs referred to people already in heaven.

Texts about repose resonate with Kasiera's theory (1981, 598) that Avalogooli obsessed about migration. The colonial government had, however, confined them to a specific location usually referred to as *Risafu* (reserve), and redefined land rights. Owning land was a measure of wealth and belonging in Logooli worldview, with the option to relocate if the space could not support related kin. With population growth but political confinement, the promise of 'heaven' as a fertile land of abundant wealth portended real and imagined hope. Even better, the Christian message sited heaven as a spacious land owned by an omnipotent, impartial, generous God.

Other texts invited nonconverts to abandon what was considered sin, naming specific transgressions requiring penitence in order to access heaven. Guilt without repentance, given the impending apocalypse, would result in harm for the sinner, as lyricized below:

> Leader: Vahaga valalila ni va sieni ku muliru
> Response: Tsinyinga tsifweye 'luya
> Vahaga valalila ni va henzi ku muliru
> Tsinyinga tsifweye 'luya
>
> Refrain by all:
> Vatovole va Yesu
> Tsinyinga tsifweye 'luya
> Vatovole va Yesu
> Tsinyinga tsifweye 'luya
>
> Translation:
> All who are fond of stirring controversies will weep when they step on or reach the fire
> The times are coming to an end, 'luya (a shortened form of halleluiah)
> Ye, the chosen of Jesus, the times are coming to an end, halleluiah[7]

In performance, the leader lines the first phrase as an incomplete thought or a weighted comment. He or she lines in a way that melodically and rhythmically requires a response. The congregation completes the sentence, ending on a note within the tonic chord but not the tonic itself, designating closure to the text but not finality of musical idea. The congregation and leader then restate the whole sentence, resolving on the tonic note to create an AA' form. The leader and the chorus then sing the refrain together, with the same basic tune as the stanza, but alter the rhythm to accommodate the new text. The text of both the stanza and refrain contains an internal refrain ("tsinyinga tsifweye 'luya"). Repeating this phrase in both the stanza and refrain accentuates the importance of the message. For new verses, the first/third word of the stanza names a new group of sinners. The refrain text and music do not change.

SYNCRETISM

EXAMPLE 6.2. "Vahaga valalila"

One can read the stanza in various ways: that those who stir up controversies will weep when they step on the fire because the times will have come to an end; or those who stir up controversies will cry out when they step on the fire: the times have come to an end. They will cry in recognition of the truth told to them by those chosen by Jesus. Another reading is that those chosen by Jesus should note that the times are coming to an end. The weeping of those who stir up controversies is the signal.

The song is a call to penitence. Texts that call out specific sinner types to repent delineate what Logooli consider sin, not only as disobedience to God manifested in bad choices and evil behavior but also what is considered contrary to Logooli social norms (such as fruitless controversies) and those considered malicious people (like witches, adulterers, murderers, etc.). The lyrics also bring to the fore ideas about the place/role of the living in Logooli philosophy and worldview. The inherent doctrine suggests that the living must choose between a good afterlife and a troubled one. It begs the question, if one is not engaged in acts warranting hell, is entry into heaven automatic? It further suggests that humans are innocent until they opt to sin or to actively engage good. Judgment then follows. Or else one inherits a malevolent nature and becomes a carrier of that legacy. For example, thieves or witches by birthright continued to be ostracized even after converting to Christianity. In one Goibei case, a known village thief[8] became a Christian and was 'filled with the spirit.' He received a 'spirit' song. Like everyone else, the thief explained how he had received the song. The lyrics were made up of vocables (music ex. 6.3a) and text in Kiswahili (music ex. 6.3b). The church public did not identify the thief's 'vocables' with other known 'spirit possession' utterances.

Ngiri ngongo ngiri sha ×4 ngiri ngiri ngongo ngiri sha ×2, ngiri ngongo ngiri sha ×2 (vocables)

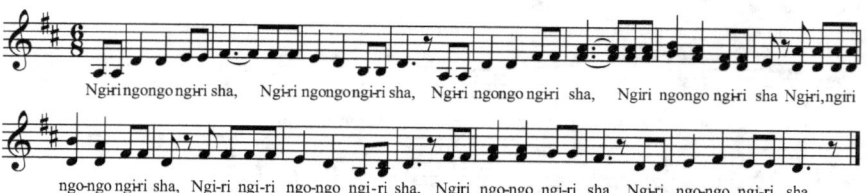

EXAMPLE 6.3a. "Ngiri ngongo ngiri sha"

The piece appears to be in $\frac{3}{4}$ because that is how it is sung. With clapping and drums, it is felt in $\frac{6}{8}$, resulting in a cross rythm between the $\frac{3}{4}$ and the $\frac{6}{8}$. The second part in Kiswahili (music ex. 6.3b) is in a different meter from the 'vocable' section. The vocable was possibly imagined in a Logooli aesthetic and the melody and meter adjusted to fit Kiswahili lyrics. Although the church accepted and adopted the song, it was always sung in Kiswahili, an interesting instance of distanciation because of the associations invoked by the composer's 'legal' profession. The Kiswahili section is clearly felt and sung in duple meter, $\frac{2}{4}$, with clapping and drumming. The contrast is more pronounced when the vocable and the text versions are adjoined.

Kiswahili lyrics:
    Nna mtafuta Yesu akae moyoni ×2
    Yesu Bwana, karibu, ingia moyoni ninataka

Translation:
    I desire that Jesus come and live in my heart
    Lord Jesus, welcome, come in. I want you in my heart

EXAMPLE 6.3b. "Nna mtafuta Yesu"

For this composer, officially the village thief, how did Avalogooli interpret indigenous views regarding birthright and the Christian notion of new birth?

The converted thief possessed a kind of nongood power that made him steal although he had converted and was 'filled with the spirit.' The thief may have experienced a new birth, but he was ostracized by his legacy.

Some Avalogooli considered themselves Christians because they did not engage in behavior categorized as hellbound. However, early missionaries considered things African as uncivilized and pagan, evil, profane, and hellish. Christianity was often embodied in a Western civilization rather than in Hebraic religion.[9] Conversion in this case meant acquiring European-style education and material possessions such as clothes, houses, jobs, and other emblems of European or American life. Logooli worldview separated the sacred from the sacrilegious or profane, the morally obligatory from what was not, and the alien from the norm. At stake was the dichotomy between the sacred and the profane, what socialized and what ostracized, and what was considered foreign and what was of Logooli essence. During the enactment of local mores, the call was often made not between being a Christian or not, but rather in acting according to Logooli essence (*mima*) or in the white man's way (*kisungu*). For the thief who became a Christian, his inherited cultural legacy precluded his entry into the village Christian community willing to warily adopt his song in light of his conversion. However, he was a known carrier of a type of nongood mystical power.[10] His tenuous position presents a convoluted reading of observations made by some scholars of Christianity in Africa that Africans were Europeanized, not Christianized, and that Christianity was accommodated and Africanized (Fashole-Luke 1978).

Song texts also recounted stories of biblical characters and their heroic or criminal acts. A common 1940s–1960s text was the story of Jonah, who initially refused to preach to the people of Nineveh. He was swallowed by a fish and after three days was dumped on the shores of Nineveh, where he fulfilled his mission. The popularity of this theme was baffling until one reads into the story and its implication—the call to preach against all odds. A faction from the Pentecostal mission, the AICN (registered officially in 1942; Barrett et al. 1973, 232), was a repository of songs on this theme. Zakayo Kivuli, who had been nurtured by Otto Keller, founded AICN. Keller had approved that prayer meetings be held at Kivuli's house. Kivuli's popularity, interpretation of scripture, and other factors led to a schism and he eventually formed the AICN (Kasiera 1981, 532–536; Ogot and Welbourn 1966, 77–83). Kivuli not only got a second chance with the Christian God as had the people of Nineveh; it was his calling to be a preacher as it had been Jonah's.[11] The practice of forgiveness and second chances was cultivated in Logooli society. The second chance could be lived out in the offender's community or elsewhere. Kivuli chose elsewhere.

The structure of one song on the story of Jonah uses call and response in a modified lining procedure. Instead of echoing the leader's line, the singers bracket it with the word 'leluya, one before and two after the phrase. Since most church members could not read, songs in this format, with a condensed storyline, served to educate the public on biblical epics and their application in life. The call-and-response setting expedited memorization (see music ex. 6.8).[12]

Another favorite story is that of Miriam, the sister of Moses. She was present when he led the Israelites out of Egypt. That Miriam led other women to celebrate in song at the crossing of the Red Sea resonated with Logooli practice where women sang and danced to celebrate major events or rituals. Miriam was also seen as an intercessor, the way a mother mediates for her place and her children in Logooli patriarchical society. Other story texts applied Old Testament stories to New Testament principles and how these lessons portended for living in the present and for eternal destiny.

Other songs recounted the Christmas story or new ideas that had been integrated into the Logooli calendar. Music ex. 6.4 demonstrates how non-Logooli words were used not just for poetic and lyrical fit; they were appropriated for novel concepts.

Text/translation:

Lwa Yesu yivulwa, haleluya malaika vimbanga no busangali: 'Milembe mwilova'
When Jesus was born, halleluiah the angels sang with gladness: 'Peace on earth'

Lwa Ye-su yi-vulwa,   ha-le-lu-ya   ma-la-i-ka vi-mba-nga   no bu-sa-nga-li: "Mi-le-mbe mwi-lo-va."

EXAMPLE 6.4. "Lwa Yesu yivulwa"

In this example, the word for 'angels' in Kiswahili, *malaika*, is substituted for the Lulogooli *tsingelosi*, an appropriation of the English word 'angels.' Stating "ingelosi [sing. an angel] yimbanga [is singing]," the *yi* recognizes the subject as a thing generally, such as a human being, a hen, and an axe. One plural form, "tsingelosi tsyimbanga" (angels are singing), qualifies angels as nonpersons by using the *tsi* prefix for angels and *tsyi* in their singing activity. New theology recognizing angels as persons rather than ghostlike beings may have engineered the substitution of malaika for tsingelosi. In "malaika vimbanga," the *vi* prefix recognizes the plural personhood of angels. The use of malaika instead of ingelosi also leads to the speculation that the adoption of a foreign but Kiswahili word—being that Kiswahili is classified a Bantu language, as is Lulogooli—underscored both the exoticism and the proximity of these beings to the Logooli world.

Some songs were social commentary with Christian mores or expounded on traits drawn from Biblical and exemplary characters or images. Betrayal is a common theme due to Logooli preoccupation with *zimbemba*, a concept embodying the effervescent properties of jealousy. Zimbemba instigates stress and worry often leading to betrayal. While community and belonging are treasured, Avalogooli covet distinctiveness or individuality. Belonging is best expressed in a term I translate as 'of us' (*Ni chyitu, Ni uwitu* [it is of us, she/he is of us: it/she/he is of our essence). Ni chyitu is invoked when debating mores, customs, or relationships; the identity bonds enacted at rites of transition. Since individuality is prized, zimbemba—real, supernatural, or imagined—are the most probable explanation for any misfortune, from simple failure, to bad luck and lack, to ill health, and to death in any form. Betrayal is therefore attributed to human inception whether mental, physical, or through supernatural aid.

The biblical narrative of Jesus's betrayal by one of his closest disciples, Judas, resonated with Avalogooli. Betrayal arises from the most unlikely people, such as bosom friends who are privy to details of a plan or idea, or are disappointed, unhappy, or greedy for gain. They, like Judas with Jesus, expose their confidants' ideas, plans, and secrets. The tendency to personify concepts led to naming traitors as 'Judases' (*myuda* [sing.], *vayuda* [pl.]). Music ex. 6.5 is a classic 'traitor' song that acts as a warning, a moan, and a witch hunt.

EXAMPLE 6.5. "Mu miganda yimu valimu"

Leader	Response
Mu miganda yimu	valimu
Mu miganda yimu	valimu, vayuda valimu
Vadzama Yesu	valimu
Vadzama Yesu	valimu vayuda valimu
Valenya kunzama	valimu
Valenya kunzama	valimu vayuda valimu

Haleloya valimu
Haleloya valimu vayuda valimu

Translation:

In this crowd	They are present (among us)
In this crowd	They are present, Judases/traitors are present
They betrayed Jesus	They are present
They betrayed Jesus	They are present. Judases are present
They are ready to betray me	They are present
They are ready to betray me	They are present, Judases are present

Halleluiah they are present
Halleluiah they are present. Judases are present

While the song invokes a biblical act of ultimate betrayal and uses Judas as an example, it has political and social overtones. It appropriates Judas, a close associate of Jesus, betraying him for monetary gain. It acknowledges the community as a nest for willing and ready grouches. The lyrics contain no resolute counsel, just a socio-political and moral statement that a close acquaintance or friend can become a traitor. Essentially it implies that no one can truly be trusted. One has to be constantly cautious, concerned, or apprehensive (*Kehenda mwoyo*).[13] This song gained prominence in the aftermath of an attempted coup against the president of Kenya in 1982. Songs with similar texts were composed in Kenya decrying the attempt.

Other songs have a cathartic effect by commenting on or documenting events. One example is a song composed during the height of famine in the mid-1960s. The song became a staple for whenever similar events occurred (see music ex. 4.1). Foods that survive drought were sung about, as were special and novelty foods that one longs for when fantasizing about being satiated. Beans, a staple food eaten cold or hot, are filling for long periods. They are able to survive drought or are eaten during a famine while waiting for harvest. Rice, on the other hand, was a novelty, a fantasy, not easily available but desired because it was associated with the elite, the rich, and the colonists. This song's lyrics were composed during famine and before harvest. Imagining these foods and affirming hope in song helped the public to psychologically deal with hunger. The text not only referenced foods that were attainable as being present in heaven but those desired, beyond the singers' budgets, were there. Access to these 'heavenly' foods effectively made the singers victors over Satan—the instigator of lack, poverty, and death.[14] The vamp/tag/refrain heightens the musical emotions and lets out frustrations by stomping, a physical expression that symbolizes a psychological and spiritual victory over the source of lack and hunger—Satan.

PITCH AND STRUCTURE

Most 'spirit' songs are pitched in medium range from about treble 'd' to 'G' below that clef.[15] Men often sing in the same range as females unless the pitch is too high, then they will drop down an octave. If a song is too low or too high, substitute pitches are at an octave, a 4th, 5th, 3rd, or 2nd above or below the note. Call and response is a preferred structure and performance practice. Whether or not the piece has stanzas, a leader provides a cue and the congregation either continues with the song or responds to the 'call.' The most prevalent types of call and response are

   a) Single phrase fixed responses.
   b) Fill-in-the-blank responses.
   c) Halleluiah responses.
   d) Lining refrains and responsorial burdens.
   e) Combination forms.

Beyond their roles in structuring a composition, it has been suggested that a composer or performer chooses a type of call and response relative to musical or lyrical objectives. Thus, single phrase fixed response style engages the audience while the leader tells a story or recounts an experience. Lining out, on the other hand, is employed in teaching new musical, linguistic, social, or religious concepts, or as an aid to memorization. Fill in the blank is used most frequently in reinforcing learned behavior or in testing a group to ensure that the work is learned or internalized. However, there is no hard and fast rule regarding when a particular brand of call and response is summoned.

Single Phrase Fixed Responses

Single phrase fixed response form is popular in story songs, in commenting on experiences, or in songs based on a vamp idea as a musical practice. The response remains unchanged regardless of the leader's lines. The leader's verbal/poetic prowess is displayed as well as his or her ability to develop the musical idea against a choral groove. In any case, the leader's ability to create and maintain the momentum yet be sensitive to a gamut of ideas makes a good or bad director. The soloist does not need to have the best voice, just outstanding musicianship. The latter is preferred in communal events.

The response is usually the punchline of the story or event. The chorus provides a stable meter, rhythm, or melody. Audiences invest in the music and emotion of the story by their ability to act, react, or recall and eventually apply the learned musical or poetic structure, the moral, or the performance behavior. Often a contrasting section is tagged on the song. By introducing a contrast or tag/refrain, the leader ensures that the audience is attentive. The space also allows the leader to regroup textually and musically. The performance resembles a wave, creating and resolving tension to structure the session. This form also explores oral storytelling and historical narrative techniques. The leader recounts the story to an attentive and participating audience. The story is paragraphed by a refrain or tag. Examples of songs in this form include "Sodoma kivala chia tenga" (music ex. 6.6):

Leader	Response
Sodoma kivala chia tenga	Gali mahing'ano genyine
Sodoma kivala chiakanga	Gali mahing'ano genyine
Lihinga liatulila ivuyuda	Gali mahing'ano genyine
Chiagila Paolo vasambwa	Gali mahing'ano genyine

Tag/refrain:

Haleloya livambwa	Haleloya livambwa, Gali mahing'ano genyine
Haleloya musalaba	Haleloya musalaba, Gali mahing'ano genyine

Translation:

In Sodom, the land was glowing	It was a matter of belligerent opposition[16]
In Sodom the land was blazing	It was a matter of belligerent opposition
Scornful behavior began in Judah	It was a matter of belligerent opposition
That's why Paul was burned	It was a matter of belligerent opposition
Halleluiah for the crucifixion	Halleluiah for the crucifixion, it was a matter of opposition
Halleluiah for the cross	Halleluiah for the cross, It was a matter of opposition

The lyrics combine text about the evil city of Sodom in the Old Testament, which was destroyed by fire (Genesis 18:16–19:29), with stories of Jewish

SYNCRETISM

EXAMPLE 6.6. "Sodoma kivala chia tenga"

leaders and Roman emperors who persecuted and killed the early Christians (Acts 5:17–40, 12:1–2). In each case, evildoers doubted the word of the righteous. In one case Sodom was set on fire, the corrupt were destroyed, and Abraham's kin were rescued. In the other, the cruel rulers who martyred Christians eventually died miserably. The piece, in stanza/refrain form, utilizes call-and-response practice. For every stanza, the leader mentions other instances in the Bible where insolence and disobedience prevailed. The text begins with the depravity of the city of Sodom and goes on to address the behavior as prevalent through biblical history and in contemporary life. The chorus completes the soloist's phrases to make up a stanza. The fixed response, "It was a matter of belligerent opposition," affirms or punctuates the caller's narrative. The leader decides when to raise the tag.

The refrain/tag is a standard text cadenced on a phrase derived from the call. To begin the tag, the caller lines out a prompt for the chorus to 'call' and then provide the punch line. This call hails the crucifixion and the cross as the antidote for insolence and disobedience. Inferred from the text is that if not for the cross, acts of insolence would continue to beget death and destruction. The piece can be brought to a close on the stanza or with the refrain/tag—a cyclic open-ended song.

The leader is always sensitive to creating and maintaining the text and conscious of the audience and their response to it. If the audience is unaware of the story, the leader educates them. The leader must be well versed in biblical stories and current events in order to convert the knowledge into song. The leader must also be cognizant of the context and the audience so as to frame the text appropriately. The leader determines when to invoke the refrain. While four lines of call are common, if the audience is truly captivated by the story, the leader can raise the refrain/tag for a breather or ignore it to build the drama. The leader therefore maintains interest at a textual and musical level. He or she determines the length of the performance. The piece can be performed alone or appended before or after another song to create a song set.

Fill-in-the-Blank Responses

Some songs require the congregation to line all or part of the leader's phrase and then complete the leader's line. Such structures test an audience's understanding of a text or their ability to recall a story. Further, the forms demonstrate the development of accounts and melodies through repetition, contrast, variation, and other principles. Singers internalize these structures through performance. The following example (music ex. 6.7) illustrates these musical and narrative structures:

Call Response

Ye - su ya-na-nga ni ngo-ni, Ye - su ya-na - nga, Ye - su ya - na - nga tsindo - lo tsia-mbi - la.

EXAMPLE 6.7. "Yesu yananga ni ngoni"

Yesu yananga ni ngoni	Yesu yananga ×2 tsindolo tsiambila.[17]
Nohenza ku mutwe gwa Yesu	Nohenza ku mutwe ×2 ingata ya mafwa.
Nohenza mikono gya Yesu	Nohenza mikono ×2 misumali gyeng'ine, etc.

Translation:

Jesus called me while I slept	Jesus called me ×2, I was in deep slumber
If you look on Jesus's head	If you look on the head ×2 [there is] a crown of thorns
If you look at Jesus's hands	If you look at the hands ×2 [there are] only nails, etc.

Each line (leader and chorus) is a complete verse. After the first line every subsequent verse describes a different part of Jesus's body on the cross. The melody is syllabically adjusted to accommodate the text. Here, the singer is cast as Jesus's disciple in the opening stanza. The analogy is drawn from the disciples who fell asleep after Jesus asked them to pray during his agonizing decision before the crucifixion. The message is clearly understood in Logooli that one who falls asleep at the darkest hour of a companion or friend has no idea of the depth of the friend's distress. The subtext is that when one is fast asleep, he or she cannot perceive the magnitude of an impending horror.[18] In the text, "When Jesus called me, I was overtaken by deep slumber," the singer was in a state of ignorance even of his or her own danger, which was why Christ called—to alert the singer to the impending threat/peril. The singer may have desired to plead ignorance but it was imperative that Jesus calls him or her to face the situation/savior. The text instructs by recounting a wrong done and how it was magnified by the context rather than focusing on what should have been done or what the singer felt about the action.

The structure compares favorably to storytelling or teaching songs in indigenous culture (see Mulindi 1983, 26–39, 43, 145–151) that ascertained audience engagement. Not only was the text important; the leader's performance and improvisation guided, and was built by, audience participation. Through this structure, musical and other cultural norms were relayed or critiqued. Appropriating the form for this text ensured that the audience became familiar with the account and the musical practice.

Halleluiah Refrains

'Halleluiah' is not a Logooli word. But it is such an identity marker for Christians that Avalogooli appropriated it in their rhetoric. In fact, it receives Lulogooli treatment. The word halleluiah is enunciated in its entirety or shortened as 'luya, 'leluya, or Halle. The treatment is as lyrical as it is musical. Most people I interviewed had no idea what the word meant.[19] However, the wider context of its use as an exclamation of joy, praise, or punctuation in song was discussed. The word and its variants functioned as parts of responses, as entire responses, or as both the call and response, or even an entire song could be made up of the word. Three music examples demonstrate some uses of the word 'halleluiah' or its abridgment. The text to music ex. 6.8 reads in Lulogooli as:

Call	Response
Isudzi yamila Jonah	'leluya, Isuzi yamila Jona, 'leluya haleluya
Yajenda naye mumadzi	'leluya, yajenda naye mumadzi, 'leluya haleluya
Yamurhudza khulujinga	'leluya, yamurhudza khulujinga, 'leluya haleluya
Va Nineve vahonyinywa	'leluya, va Nineve vahonyinywa, 'leluya haleluya

Each line is a stanza. The leader lines the text recounting the story of how a) a fish swallowed Jonah, b) traveled with him in the water, c) vomited him on shore, and d) the people of Nineveh were saved. The chorus echoes the leader's

EXAMPLE 6.8. "Isudzi yamila Jonah" (PURL 6.1)

line framed by one halleluiah before and two afterward. Initially, the whole word was sung. In order to catch a breath and for phrasing, the "ha" beginning was inhaled to provide the impetus that propelled the response. Tension was resolved by pronouncing the entire word at the end. The motion is reinforced in practice where chest movements or hand claps articulate the strong beat (inhalation) just before the chorus begins to sing. The melody ends on the mediant, sometimes heard as modal, but other times it evokes the circuitous nature of the song by not ending on the tonic but beginning with it. It ends on an offbeat syncopation, anticipating the leader's utterance on the strong beat or providing the participants with the option of a resolution in collective individual prayers.

Although metered in $^6_8$, it can be performed in $^3_4$. This practice is commensurate with Logooli musical aesthetic. When clapping in a duple pattern, the $^3_4$ meter creates a cross rhythmic effect and tension against the $^6_8$ reinforced by the body and drum. Substitute pitches accommodate linguistic tonality in subsequent verses.

Music ex. 6.9 is a personal witness in the vein of a gospel song. At evangelistic and revival meetings, gospel songs testified about conversion, the infilling with the Holy Spirit, the power of prayer, changes in a believer's life, the blessings of being a Christian, and the consequences of not converting. Each line, made up of two phrases ending at "Aleluya," is sung twice. The refrain (tag), signaled by "Aleluya," provides the leader with a place to regroup before continuing with the story. In the first iteration of this climatic tag, energy is raised through louder singing and effected by the melodic contour.

Leader	Response
Lwa ndasava	eh
ndanyola roho	aleluya
Mulilo guliho	ae
gulisamba vaheyi	aleluya
Mulilo guliho	ae
gulisamba vahaga	aleluya

SYNCRETISM

Refrain/tag:
    Aleluya   Luya, luya aleluya aleluya

Translation:
    When I asked/prayed   Yea
    I was filled with the spirit   Halleluiah
    There is a fire   Oh yeah
    That will burn adulterers   Halleluiah
    There is a fire   Oh yeah
    That will burn the hardheaded   Halleluiah

Refrain/tag:
    Halleluiah 'luia, 'luia, halleluiah, halleluiah

The tag is marked by more intense and louder clapping, as singers encourage or agree with the witness. The clap is on the two main pulses of the $\frac{6}{8}$ meter with rhythmic tension on the suspension within and over the measure.

EXAMPLE 6.9a. "Lwa ndasava" (1)

While there was an outcry about distorting meaning occasioned by translating Euro-American melodies wholesale into African tonal languages (Basil 1957; Jones 1976, 17–38), the style became a way of structuring text that was context driven for interpretation (Euba 1992). The word *ndanyola* in this context means 'I received, I found,' but the way it is intoned and rhythmed here infers removing leaves from plant stems usually in order to cook and eat the leaves. The song can also be transcribed in $\frac{2}{4}$ and adjusted thus:[20]

EXAMPLE 6.9b. "Lwa ndasava" (2)

Other songs, such as music ex. 6.10, are composed entirely of the word halleluiah. Some were born in ecstatic moments during prayer or special 'spirit' sessions. Others started as pedagogical songs where 'halleluiah' punctuated the leader's discourse and eventually acquired independent status. These halleluiah songs can now stand alone.

'Lu-ya 'le-lu-ya, 'lu-ya.   'Lu-ya 'le-lu-ya, 'lu-ya 'le-lu-ya 'lu-ya.

EXAMPLE 6.10. "'Luya 'leluya"

Call
'Luya 'leluya

Response
'luya
'Luya 'leluya
Luya 'leluya 'luya

The text is structured from mixing, removing, or adding "luya" or "leluya." The $\frac{9}{8}$ time is the general meter but the leader can anticipate the call so that the last measure is converted into a $\frac{3}{8}$. This song has acquired stanzas with other text. With the verses, the chorus repeats the leader's lines interspersed and appended with halleluiah as exemplified below:

Call
Masahi gasundukha

Response
'luya
Masahi gasundukha
'Luya 'leluya 'luya

Translation:
Blood was shed halleluiah

Lining Out Responses and Responsorial Burdens

Several types of lining exist. In one version, the congregation repeats the leader's entire text and tune. In another, the leader lines the first phrase for the chorus to develop the stanza. In other types, the response underlines the text 'called' by the leader to a different tune. One use for this form was to teach words to an initially nonliterate congregation. This structure helped to explain concepts, affirm doctrine or ideas, and also extend a piece of music. Music ex. 6.11 and 6.12 illustrate two versions. The first song is in a dance style popular from the late 1960s called lipala. The second song is in a marching style appropriated from the Salvation Army and used by Africanist churches in processionals that increased the tempo from a march to a jog.

Lulogooli text:
  Leader: Saala lisala shi, Saala lisala shi, Saala lisala shi imbeli wa Yesu
  Response: Repeats leader's line

SYNCRETISM

Leader: Soma shitabu shi, soma shitabu shi, soma shitabu shi ndukhe mwigulu
Response: Repeats leader's line

Translation:
What kind of prayer can I pray before Jesus? (How can I pray to Jesus, in what kind of way?)
What kind of book can I read in order to get to heaven?

Saa - la li-sa-la shi,   Saa - la li-sa-la shi,   Saa - la li-sa-la shi   i-mbe - li wa Ye-su.

EXAMPLE 6.11. "Saala lisala shi"

These rhetorical, probing questions do not require a response. The song can be followed by another responding to the rhetoric, or it is inserted in a sermon or evangelistic testimony. Logooli congregations prefer to sing this piece in Ludirichi.[21]

Music ex. 6.12 demonstrates that Avalogooli were not shy about singing in other languages for inclusiveness, for aesthetic reasons, or for religious purposes. Among the first Pentecostal converts were the Luo neighbors of Avalogooli. The Pentecostal mission expanded to Luo country from the beginning of the enterprise (Kasiera 1981, 229–239). Not surprisingly, Luo melodies or lyrics were incorporated in Luyia songs. In music ex. 6.12, the song's first line is in Luo and the second line is in Ludirichi.

Leader: Malo malo Jerusalemi malo
(Up there [yonder], Jerusalem is up there [yonder])
Response: Same as above
Leader: Ulinde vana yavo Petero ulinde vana yavo
(Take care of those children Peter [those already in heaven])
Response: Same as above

The meter changes from simple duple meter in Luo (a Nilotic language) to compound duple time in Ludirichi (a Bantu language). In performance the quarter note at the beginning is the same tempo as the dotted quarter note after the repeat. The leader lines the text for the chorus. The chorus (bottom alternative pitches) resolves the melody 'lined' by the solo (top line) to create an AA' form.

Ma - lo ma- lo Je-ru-sa -le - mi ma-lo(ma)   lo.   U- li-nde va - na ya-vo Pe-te - ro u - li-nde va - na ya-vo.

EXAMPLE 6.12. "Malo malo"

In another type of lining, the leader began the first line and the congregation extended the verse with the same or different lyrics to develop the melody. Music ex. 6.13 demonstrates this principle.

Call	Response
Miriamu vakhubanga vukhana	Miriamu vakhubanga vukhana
(Miriam et al. are playing zithers)	Miriamu vakhubanga vukhana dodo
	Miriamu vakhubanga vukhana

This text, as a prototype, has variants in tune and style. It builds on modified and exact sequential development of the first three lines. The fourth line begins on an ascending line but resolves like the second line. The adverb appended to the third line (**dodo** [indeed/truly]) underlines the weight of the sentence and the musical style. Perhaps without that adverb, the fourth line would have been an exact repetition of the second one. Since the melody of the third line ends on the leading tone, the fourth line was prepared to begin on the tonic.[22]

EXAMPLE 6.13. "Miriamu vakhubanga vukhana"

Expanded models from the prototype include music ex. 6.14 in *mutivo* dance style.[23] In this format consisting of two parts, the chorus completes the leader's idea first by repeating the call then concluding the thought. Often the stanza has four lines.

Call	Response
Nyasaye ulinde mwoyo	Nyasaye ulinde mwoyo
	Setani navola aladza
	Anyola roho wikaye

SYNCRETISM

Translation:

    God protect (guard) the heart   God protect the heart
                                                [so that] By the time Satan comes
                                                He will find the Spirit seated (enthroned)

Musically, the response develops the lined call through sequence, variation, and contrast.

EXAMPLE 6.14. "Nyasaye ulinde mwoyo"

The response in music ex. 6.15, on the other hand, satisfies the need raised by the call, then reiterates the whole phrase to confirm the need and its resolution. Thus the call and response in the first instance together can be considered a lining out of text. The form is also a fill in the blank with a fixed response.

Call	Response
Ingata yange ufwale	Mwoyo gwenya mwigulu
	Ingata yange ufwale
	Mwoyo gwenya mwigulu
Ndikhola ndina ndadukha	Mwoyo gwenya mwigulu
	Ndikhola ndina ndadukha
	Mwoyo gwenya mwigulu

Translation:

Crown me with my diadem	My heart longs for heaven
What will I do to get there?	My heart longs for heaven

EXAMPLE 6.15. "Ingata yange ufwale" (PURL 6.2)

This example features an internal textual refrain ("Mwoyo gwenya mwigulu"). The first line by the leader pedals around the dominant or its substitutes, creating tension through syncopation, suspension, and sustenuto. The response begins on the last note of the call, then descends. This resembles the musical notion of settling down, *kutuula*, by the response, but on touching down, the note is taken up in the third line, *kuvugula*, to prepare for a gentler repose in the last line, *koyeridza*, like a bird landing or the sun setting. Some members anticipate the response by singing the last word with the leader, energizing the call. Mulindi (1983, 72–74) describes these related concepts—kutuula, kuvugula, and koyeridza—as valuable musical resolutions that occur not only at the end of the phrase but at the beginning. These dynamics are proposed by the ebb, flow, and cyclic nature of the piece. The end of the song, the first beat, prompts the leader to raise the song literally at a high pitch. The response pretends to resolve it, only to take it up again, then settle back down. Other aesthetic choices include cadencing on the first beat rather than the last and an abrupt ending rather than a fermata, reposing in silence rather than in sound. In church, these conclusions were oftimes manifested by 'tongue' utterances, prayers, shouts, trance, prolonged bodily response, and eventually calmed by 'halleluiah calls.' Physical manifestations of the spirit such as 'tongue utterances' or ecstatic body motions were the inevitable response to the synergy of the song, or they were avenues of resolving physical, emotional, religious, and musical tensions.

Combination Forms

Combination forms are the most characteristic way of performing 'spirit' songs. While different songs are adjoined to create a song set, some single pieces are structured by combining some or all of the forms outlined above. A classic example is "Kidaho kyo mwigulu" (music ex. 6.16). The text, about the water well in heaven, is evangelistic. The text is based on the biblical story found in John 4 relating Jesus's encounter with the Samaritan woman at a well. The water Jesus promised the woman was from a heavenly well located in the new Jerusalem. The overall structure of the song is a refrain/stanza form. The piece begins with a refrain whose first line is called by a leader and completed by the responders in three phrases. A contrasting stanza follows in a different practice of the call-and-response form. The stanza is formatted like a tag that returns to the refrain. The point of that stanza text is an invitation

SYNCRETISM

EXAMPLE 6.16. "Kidaho kyo mwigulu" (PURL 6.3)

to enter the new Jerusalem. Textual and musical energy are created by the word play between the leader and chorus. In the dialogue, the leader invites the audience and the chorus reiterates the invitation. The leader then extends the parameters of the invitation, and the chorus provides its benefit. In a way, the text plays on the Logooli desire to find 'a place to feel at home,' a solution to the restless search for a place for prosperity and posterity. The response has an invariable text, prompting the leader to vary the opening word, naming different invited guest types. Hence the leader reiterates that regardless of type, profession, or intention of a person, everyone who repents is invited.

Call	Response
Refrain:	
Kidaho kyo mwigulu	kili na amadzi malahi
	Valitsia kunywa ku
	si valinyola vuluhu
Stanza/tag:	
Muloji hamba	Hamba
Hamba weganire	hamba wingire Yerulasemi imbya
Muvila hamba	Hamba
Hamba weganire	Hamba wingire Yerusalemi imbya
Translation:	
Heaven's well	has sweet/good/fresh waters
	Those who will drink of it
	will never thirst
Curser come	Do come
Come, repent	Come and enter the New Jerusalem
Sorcerer come	etc.

The refrain is invariable. The place advertised is specific and accommodates everyone. The stanza bears tensions and energies, naming the variety of sinners called to repent.[24]

PERFORMANCE DYNAMICS

'Spirit' songs have usually been performed in a manner different from the initial practice of 'book' music. It is this engaged investment in performing Logooli musics that first motivated missionaries to introduce hand clapping for 'book' music. In 'spirit' songs, a leader did not just begin the song and keep time as prescribed in 'book' music (see PAOC Archive videography), he or she began the song with the 'halleluiah call,' with exhortations, or even by recounting an appropriate experience. Whether in front of the church or during a processional, leaders moved their bodies as part of the musical process and commanded the stage as part of the drama. With a successful tenure, the leader became louder and more demonstrative, motivating the congregation to move, to clap harder/louder, walk through the aisles, jump, or pass out. All-night sings were not uncommon, neither was singing while jogging for up to twenty to thirty miles to a designated meeting place for a Christmas gathering, an evangelistic enterprise, or a ritual celebration. While instruments filled spaces between numbers, songs were conjoined, some with unrelated texts, for the energy of the musical and dramatic moment (PURL 6.4).

A good song leader was lauded for the ability to find related songs and segue in with ease or by commenting in between the songs without stopping the clapping, the drummers, or the momentum. The duple meter hand clap, as a metronome, facilitated continuity while creating rhythmic tensions or resolutions in the song set. A good leader could shift tempi, signal the congregation to stop clapping or start dancing, cue the drum in and out of the performance, and discontinue the singing altogether without stopping the drums or the clapping, just to enjoy the musical or religious moment. It was also possible to achieve a good musical act without drumming and clapping. Good managers could cue in others during long sessions and so exchange leadership in unobtrusive ways. When song was central to a service, the song leader controlled the meeting. He or she determined whether the 'spirit' was 'released' or if there were obstacles hindering a successful performance. He or she was inspired by the congregational response and in turn fired them up to inspire him or her. Song was also woven throughout a service or event as imperative to the moment or supportive of it. A service such as a prayer meeting or an event such as a funeral wake could be relayed entirely in song. Songs punctuated prayers, sermons, testimonies, and announcements. Songs signaled beginnings and were usually the penultimate item of a service. That song was this important likely accounts for the large volume and variety of repertoire.

READINGS IN MUSICAL AND CULTURAL SYNCRETISM

The fundamental ethos of 'spirit' songs is that they are either rooted in Logooli musical and social structures or musicians invoke 'book' music structures to create repertoire accepted as indigenous Logooli. The most manipulated elements here are the combinations of melody, rhythm, and text. The ubiquitous accompaniment is clapping. Clapping is metronomic in a duple feel. Drums, while mostly duple meter, are 'struck'[25] between Friday and Sunday unless a death or a special event occurs in the course of a week. If a strong triple meter drives song, singers articulate the beat with shoulders (*kusieva/kuvina mavega* [to dance shoulders]) or elbows instead of or against clapping and/or drumming. Common practice is a duple or quadruple clap/drum in a triple metered song, or a song composed of alternating measures in quadruple and triple meter.

When an overtly secular popular style is adopted from local, national, or global types, it is subverted or disguised by altering the tempo (made faster or slower than the secular counterpart). In some arrangements, instead of drums, the bass guitar articulates the indumba rhythm and the lead guitar invokes the kidindi rhythmic ostinato, or the bass guitar plays riffs based on the kidindi timeline while the solo guitar appropriates the function and styles of lute (kiriri) and lyre (*lidungu*) accompaniment. These substitutions create timbral shifts that effectively distances the song from secular or indigenous resonance.

Because of missionary influence and the notion that the new religion came with a distinctive tonality, most songs are in the major mode. Some melodies are shaped like missionary songs, starting on the tonic, ascending and then descending to the tonic. Others begin in mid-range, descend or ascend, and then eventually find their way to the tonic. Most songs fall within an octave range. They commonly end abruptly, on a rest, or the final note is not sustained. This is a characteristic Luyia musical trait; that is, to end by creating tension, not by resolving it. It is a moment of anxiety, one pregnant with expectation for something more. Therefore the leader releases the peaked unresolved tension by invoking the 'halleluiah call' accompanied by drum rolls or by 'spirit' utterances. Alternatively, a sudden ending allows each individual to find his or her own physical, textual, or emotional catharsis.

For a 'special' performance, European concert-like characteristics are observed in aspects such as deliberate part singing, shades of dynamics, structural contrasts, and ritardando or fermata at the end. On solemn occasions, songs are pitched lower than in the more exuberant services but also as is relative to song sets. A standard tempo for singing sessions in Pentecostal churches is between 120 and 132 per dotted quarter. The tempo in Quaker meetings has been slower, and that of African Israel Church Nineveh much faster. In funeral wakes or evangelistic processionals, songs are sung faster than usual not only to engage participants but also as entertainment. Some processionals are conducted like a march and others like a slow jog. A pace is determined and maintained for the duration of the procession to accommodate distance, reflect intention, or as a denominational preference. For solemn occasions, the slowed pace is consistent in all denominations. The ritual moment takes precedence over religious political identity.

Avalogooli indigenized European Christian music as early as the 1910s by translating and writing songs to service the new religion. By the 1920s, "worship was the context where community problems were church problems" because God who revealed himself through "shared experiences was involved in their individual and communal affairs" (Kasiera 1981, 552, 556). By the 1930s, the drummer and singer were among the most crucial members of the church community, which included pastors (vasaalisi) as the most venerated and prophets as essential. Kasiera notes that in the 1930s,

> people woke to the high pitched drumbeat of one of the elders, Isaya Kevelenge, who timed it with the first cock crow. He used to stand on a tall stone near his house and as he beat the drum, the sound would echo through the undulating region and was heard miles away. After drumming for about half an hour, he went back to his house to prepare to go to church. The next time the drum was heard, the directions from which its sound came was constantly changing as he was now on the way to church ... To the south of Kevelenge was an old lady Zibola who had a used up hoe but which produced a good sound. Soon the

sound of her hoe beaten to the beat of the song she would be singing joined the scattered voices of many other women, all singing as they walked to church. (Kasiera 1981, 551)

With the use of the clock, and due to government restrictions, the drummer is not as essential as, say, 1985, when we still woke up on Friday at cockcrow to the sound of the drum and people praying aloud at home or on hilltops.

The PAOC archives in Toronto houses silent movies, recorded in the late 1930s to 1948. They show singing people clapping in the manner taught by missionaries. The posture and clap type was markedly different from my experiences in the 1970s, my observations in the 1980s, and videos I recorded from the 1990s, ranging from an apologetic polite patting to cupped and slapped hands. The metronomic stance of the church clap did not change, but the body rhythm against the clap moved from a stifled European demeanor to an interactive Logooli groove present in other contexts. Imported Salvation Army side drums were replaced with versions that accommodated indigenous materials and expense and a size suited to walking long distances. A smaller drum called kidindi or mudindi was added to provide a timeline, making the ensemble similar to that of indigenous Isigudi. A hoe, iron ring, and other idiophones found in indigenous instrumental ensembles were also added.

Musical features for Christian religious song share stylistic descriptions with indigenous repertoire (Mulindi 1983, 152–254), including music as self-expression both for artistic and socio-religious purposes. More particularly, Mulindi found that much Logooli music is founded on the question-answer principle and practiced in solo-chorus medium for communal musicking. The format is not only pedagogical for social and other instruction; it is a means of inculcating Logooli musical principles. Texts can surpass religious concerns. They document social events, sentiments, and other values. The music aggregates known styles with new ideas, established on a holistic approach to performance—involving the whole person. Instead of abandoning old styles, Christian religious music is an accretive form, obligating composers and performers to explore new and different possibilities.

Christianity introduced new musical and cultural perspectives to Logooli life. Avalogooli embraced a new belief system, which was not only layered onto their established ideas; it became the filter through which they negotiated their encounter with the Kenyan nation and the global music industry.

Christianity provided access to the national and international stage, an approach to integration and difference, and a space for homogeneity and distinction. Logooli rhetoric includes things Logooli co-existing with and articulated against things 'other.' The co-existence of Logooli musical heritage juxtaposed with Euro-American Christianity in a secular Kenyan republic continues to be negotiated and evaluated in communal events and in individual choices.

SEVEN
INVOCATION

Logooli Christian Songs in Contemporary Education and Media

The negotiation of Logooli Christian musical identity since the 1970s is best analyzed through the historical dynamics of contemporary education systems and the mass media. The education system, rooted in missionary endeavor, subscribed to a European ideology advocating for music literacy as well as European compositional and performance frameworks. The media, on the other hand, sought to reach the widest audience by any means possible. While each enterprise developed its own strategies, both used and promoted the other. These institutions, however, began with choral hymn singing in English, Kiswahili, and Lulogooli. The first significant mediated Africanizing hymn style was makwaya. It was widely practiced amongst Avalogooli. Makwaya was followed by the transformation of Logooli spirit songs for the academy. The enduring heritage of the education system on Logooli musicking was most visible in the genre commonly referred to as 'adaptation and arrangement of African folk tunes.' And then came 'gospel.' While makwaya and 'adaptations' are performed by choirs, gospel music also enjoys renditions by individuals or small ensembles. All the genres invoke Logooli indigenous and Christian forms as resources and for difference.

In this chapter, I identify and describe genres in the academy and in the media. I also discuss seminal Logooli musicians, their contributions, and their idiomatic styles. I will present the genres in the chronological order in which they vitalized Logooli civic and church life.

MAKWAYA

Kwaya is a term derived from the idea of a specialized choral ensemble. The word 'choir' is spelled in Kiswahili orthography as kwaya. While the word 'makwaya' is widely used in writing, the genre terminology is *Nyimbo za kwaya* (Kiswahili for 'songs for/by choirs'—choral repertoire, repertoire by choirs). In Lulogooli, it is known as *Tsinyimbu tsie ikwaya* (songs for choirs, by choirs). Often people state "Kuziza mu tsikwaya," meaning we are going to a choir rehearsal, or to a choral competition, or to take part in a choral ensemble. An alternative statement is, "Kuziza kwimba tsikwaya" (lit. we are going to sing choirs [sic: choral music or in a choral competition]). Ikwaya is the term for a choral ensemble/group (tsikwaya pl.). The term 'makwaya' is adopted here to discuss this phenomenon that is prevalent in many parts of Christianized Africa.

The makwaya concept may be the first venue for the contemporary fusion of Logooli and Euro-American compositional styles and for the acknowledgement of composers and performers in the modernizing Logooli nation. The primary sources for choir songs were missionary hymns or gospel songs, as well as songs composed in these styles. Eventually new compositions fusing these foreign hymn types with African indigenous styles from different culture groups or with outmoded popular secular music forms became the mainstay of choral repertoire. However, early kwaya music focused on familiarizing congregations with Bible stories. In addition to missionary hymns, the songs also drew on styles rooted in Logooli narrative and instructional forms. While the songs may initially have been taught to a select group, they were soon absorbed into the corpus of congregational repertoire.

Makwaya songs are normally in stanza or stanza/refrain form with four lines per stanza/refrain. A few are structured in local metric or narrative styles. They often adopt call-and-response form. The songs, while customarily pitched lower than their European counterparts, are harmonized in three or four voice parts. Originally unaccompanied, they have now adopted the global popular music instruments of their times. Texts are based on biblical narratives with moral implication or exegete scriptures to provide practical applications. Beyond biblical instruction and evangelism, these songs propagate denominational doctrines.

The makwaya concept in Kenya was initially popularized by the radio broadcasts of the African Inland Church. The first church radio studio was started in Kijabe in 1955.[1] Pioneering AIC radio missionaries who arrived in Kenya in 1954 collected sermons and lessons by African pastors and also scouted for African choirs to sing translated repertoire in Kiswahili and Kikuyu language. The language base was later expanded to include Luo, Kalenjin, and Luyia groups. Kiswahili was favored since it was understood in Kenya, Tanzania, Zanzibar, parts of Uganda, the Congos, and in some Indian Ocean islands. Choral groups from churches and schools beyond the African Inland Mission were also broadcast. Music introduced, concluded, or was integrated in sermons and teachings. Music was also the central feature in greetings and request programs such as *Wimbo niupendao* (The song I love) or *Salamu na nyimbo* (Greetings and songs). Several programs such as *Nyimbo za Dini* (Songs of faith/religion) were made up entirely of music. These programs, hosted by a moderator, featured local church and school groups singing in Kiswahili, English, and African languages, as well as American and European choirs, solos, or small ensembles singing in English.[2]

Before its mediation from Kijabe, the kwaya concept existed amongst Avalogooli. Kwaya music was first explored in Christmas malago begun in the 1920s. A select group was required, invited, or commissioned to present the new song to educate or entertain the public. These songs were introduced as 'special' numbers in Lulogooli and Kiswahili. The initial performers were school children and young people. Churches assembled in central locations on Christmas Day, where these groups recited scriptures and sang about the life, teaching, and mission of Christ. Eventually, displays centered on the birth of Christ with groups competing to determine best presentation of the Christmas story in song, drama, and recitation.[3]

Aside from malago, makwaya music and practices were featured at annual PAG conventions and Quaker Yearly Meetings, at youth camps, and in other conferences.[4] Although songs were learned from the radio, young people brought additional repertoire from school to their village communities. These groups were even recorded and broadcast to service Christian radio programs. Makwaya paved the way for commercializing Christian music that eventuated the industrial product currently referred to as gospel.[5]

ADAPTATION AND ARRANGEMENT OF AFRICAN TUNES

The concept of the adaptation and arrangement of indigenous African tunes for religious use officially commenced in the Anglican Church. The idea was to legitimize the use of African songs in Christian worship. The practice was initiated by Anglican musician and British administrator Graham Hyslop (1910–1977). Since Kenya was a British colony, the Anglican Church was *the* de facto state church. Therefore the concept was perforce embraced country-wide. More important, the styling became a staple compositional practice in educational institutions and also in civic and other choral programs.[6] Avalogooli who attended schools run by Anglicans were introduced to the concept. The enduring impact of this development resulted from Hyslop's interaction with the premier mulogooli arranger, Arthur Kemoli (1945–2012). Kemoli interned with Graham Hyslop in the 1960s. To frame the juncture of religious song and academic music practice, I will recount some events and activities that motivated Hyslop's endeavors, roles, and ultimate influence on Kemoli and other educators, church musicians, and politicians.

GRAHAM HYSLOP AND ARTHUR KEMOLI

Graham Hyslop arrived in Kenya in 1936 as an Anglican Church layman (KNA MSS/22/1; Hyslop obituary).[7] At the outbreak of World War II, he joined the East African forces, where he oversaw an education corps unit charged with entertainment and education amongst the troops. He was responsible for his unit and also for the music performances in the army. In 1943, he was asked to consider ordination as an Anglican priest, but he declined in favor of studying to develop music for worship in the church. He studied both theology and music at Oxford University before returning to Kenya in 1953. He eventually became the colony's music and drama officer in the department of community development from 1957 to 1961. When the post was eliminated, he went to work in the same capacity at the inspectorate of the department of education. Hyslop organized workshops to document and systematize Kenya's music traditions. He was also instrumental in arranging the Kenyan national anthem. He inaugurated a diploma in music program at Kenyatta College in 1966. He moved on to the University of Dar-es-Salaam, Tanzania, in 1970. As a music educator, Hyslop was active in the development of music curricula in East Africa. He was famous not only for music arrangements but also for his plays (KNA MSS/22/1; KNA MSS/22/7).

Hyslop enjoyed choral music. He devoted much of his educational and religious endeavors in training choirmasters so that performers could attain the "standards of choirs in Britain and other countries." He encouraged African participation in the Kenya Music festival.[8] Hyslop prescribed the types of music suitable for an African choir as that "written three or four hundred years ago ... the rhythmic interest of these two periods together with the simplicity of melody are both much closer to traditional African music than the more rigid rhythms and chromatics of the 19th century" (Hyslop 1958b, 37). He also believed that "The inheritance of church music which we now enjoy is ours to enrich ... In Africa, we have an opportunity of bringing to the treasury of religious music something from the music of Africa. Man's offering of the sacrifice of praise must reflect the particular musical gifts of a people" (KNA MSS/22/32). Hyslop's examples, modeled with these mindsets, became the basis for conceptualizing arrangements rather than encouraging composition. Hyslop was not alone in debating the feasibility, use, and instruction of African music in churches and in educational institutions. He dialogued with religious leaders and educators in other colonies. The exchange was documented in letters and articles in the leading forum for discussing music in Africa: the journal *African Music* (1957, 1958, 1959, 1971, etc.).[9] However, Hyslop was critiqued by his colleagues since he seemed to be using African music as a "stepping stone to higher things" (Tracey 1964, 120) and set out to expose Africans to "European music ... to establish good taste" (Hyslop 1964, 25).

Apart from instruction for white students, music education in the 1960s was confined to training choir directors and required for elementary education teachers.[10] This situation changed with the introduction of a diploma course in music at Kenyatta University in 1966 to train lecturers for teacher training colleges and develop high school music teachers. There had previously been little music instruction for Africans at the tertiary level. However, by the late 1950s, Hyslop et al. had been pressured by Ugandans George Senoga-Zake and George Kakoma; Kenyan teachers and students Gershom Manani, Peter Kibukosya, Railton Wambugu, and Washington Omondi; and Arthur Kemoli in the 1960s to allow them to test their music skills by sitting for theory and performance exams with the British Royal Schools of Music or Trinity College.[11]

Hyslop had by then started his experiments of setting English and Kiswahili Christian texts to Kenyan tunes and arranging them in four-part harmony as British church anthems for performance at the Anglican All Saints Cathedral in Nairobi, Kenya, where he was the choirmaster. The tempo of African tunes was adjusted to fit within the understood aesthetics of both the English language and the church anthem ethos so that the Africans from whom the tune was borrowed scarcely recognized it. One reviewer indicated that although Hyslop's endeavor was important in the "resuscitation of Anglican liturgical music in its idiom and style ... [it was] indisputably foreign to anything African ... [as it] encased an African melody ... with flabby diatonic triads. The original strength and flavor of the melody [was] quickly removed."[12] Hyslop not only sought to legitimize African songs; he also held workshops to try to systematize African instrument types.[13] His attempt to temper the tunings of various Kenyan instruments was poorly received. Moreover, African instruments were rarely featured in the music that Hyslop adapted. Given the times in which Hyslop lived, it is not difficult to speculate that prevailing worldviews about African instruments' technological capability and their suitability for Christian worship may have prompted the exclusion.

Hyslop's encounter with Mulogooli and Quaker Arthur Mudogo Kemoli not only signaled the entry of the adaptation concept into Logooli repertoire; it also began the transformation of the procedure to embrace an African ethos. The two men first met in the 1960s when Kemoli was a high school student in Western Kenya (Kemoli 2001b). Kemoli's interest in music was such that Hyslop, whose offices and job were in central Kenya and Nairobi, tutored him during school vacations. The relationship continued when Kemoli joined Alliance High School (located in central Kenya) in 1965 and tried his hand at setting arrangements. His first adaptation, a Malawian tune that he set in Lulogooli for a Christmas carol service, was "Yesu alanga avaana veve" (Jesus is calling his children). The Alliance Boys and Girls Schools performed it in 1966. Later, as a university student and an intern with Hyslop at All Saints Cathedral (1967–1970), Kemoli arranged Logooli 'spirit' songs into anthems. After his doctoral studies in literature in England in 1973, Kemoli continued in this direction.[14] He affiliated himself with Kariokor Friends Choir in the 1970s to present his arrangements in the religious arena. As a lecturer at Kenyatta College (1973–1985), Kemoli directed the university choir's performance of his arrangements and those by Hyslop and other Africans.[15]

As an organizer of the Kenya Music Festival in the 1970s, Kemoli disseminated his ideas and those of other musicians into civil society through educational institutions and on government-owned radio and television broadcasts. The music not only serviced religious gatherings; it was embraced in educational, political, and social arenas. Further publicity of his style and ideas was achieved when, as the assistant director of creative activities in the government's Ministry of Education and Drama (1985–1988), Kemoli demonstrated in word and deed the idea of compositions based on local idioms with religious, social, and political content. Kemoli rejoined the academy in 1988 at the University of Nairobi. He became the director of the university choir (see fig. 7.1) in addition to the Kariokor choir. Kemoli toured locally and

FIGURE 7.1. Cover of cassette recording of Kemoli with the University of Nairobi Choir.

internationally with the Kariokor and university choirs, performing works in Lulogooli, Kiswahili, and other African languages.[16]

Kemoli's musical authority is recognized in adapting and arranging African tunes for 'high art' consumption. The primary melodic source has been Logooli folk, ritual, and Christian songs that are arranged for a staged choral presentation. The Logooli Christian community had already embraced special choral groups to exhort and entertain at religious and social gatherings such as the Christmas malago and Yearly Meetings. However, Quaker groups popularized the 'adaptation and arrangement' format. Choirs were formed and music festivals organized with denominational support as well as national government and educational institutional encouragement. The place of the choir and the modern musician was subsequently expanded but also redefined.

'Spirit' songs had been featured at civil music festivals since the 1980s as religious folk song. Before this time, any song with Christian religious lyrics was excluded from the folk song category, but it could be adapted and arranged as a choral piece.[17] Pentecostal groups balked at the idea of arrangements since 'spirit' songs were rooted in the practice of spontaneity and associated with being 'moved by the spirit' to operate beyond human control and manipulation. However, by the close of 1981, 'adaptations and arrangements' were recognized as a distinct music genre, not necessarily for worship but for elitist entertainment in civic events and music festivals.

FORM AND STRUCTURE OF ARRANGEMENTS

From the outset, it was understood by Avalogooli that an adapted tune for use in church services or Christian gatherings was to be based on an existing religious song. Melodies from 'spirit' songs and 'book' music by Logooli composers were arranged since they embodied Logooli musicking practices. Anyone familiar with the repertoire recognized the melody. Most songs were forced into a major or minor mode and set in common practice. Usually the melody was placed in the soprano line and the other parts harmonized. Homophonic syllabic block-chords or chorale-like treatments were the central organizing framework. The songs therefore sounded like 'book' music but were pitched much higher than in regular church services.

The pieces, sung by a choir, are viewed by Logooli society as different and out of character with their congregational employment in worship. Several factors account for this divorce. Because of the harmonies, the congregation is excluded from participation for fear of distorting the prescribed arrangement. This restriction deviates from Logooli practice that allows for audience involvement even in specialty contexts. Since all voice-part members have to sing the same pitches at the same time, individual preferences are eliminated. With call and response the leader can extemporize, but given time limits (music festivals and some recording formats allowed for three minutes), 'calls' are prescribed. Most arrangers adjoin at least two songs as in indigenous practice. With a broad cultural audience base, arrangers explore other musical elements more than text. Choirs often learn several versions for different audiences. To facilitate the shift, choir directors act as soloists, reading the audience and adjusting the performance to the situation.

The tempo of arrangements is either slower or faster than in indigenous practice. This procedure further distances the pieces from ecclesiastic function to academic and entertainment purposes. The interest in harmonic procedure, played out at the expense of religious sentiment, influences tempo. At first, no instruments were included. The idea was rooted in Hyslop's prescriptions and missionary reticence to African instruments. Later the Kayamba was included. The instrument lacked 'pagan' associations for Avalogooli. The Kayamba was also adopted because it was already accepted in the educational arena as an 'Africanizing' element. The instrument was played loudly enough to be heard but not detract from the European anthem or choral music festival ethos. Later, church indumba and kidindi as well as the Isigudi ensemble, bongos, and congas were incorporated. Piano and guitar were rarely featured. The guitar was associated with popular secular and gospel music. The piano was expensive, difficult to maintain, and good players were hard to find.

In indigenous contexts, performers often syncopated, anticipated, and predicated strong beats with their movements. With adaptations, choir members assumed a European concert posture, so the body impetus present in indigenous Logooli musicking was eliminated. If conductor or composer desired motion, performers reading the score with little Luyia musicking exposure often articulated or responded with their bodies in the 'wrong' place.[18]

Arthur Kemoli's Early Adaptations and Arrangements

Kemoli, as a trendsetter and primary instigator, popularized the fusion of Christian religious, African folk/pop, and European art music for general public consumption. He arranged both Logooli Christian and indigenous ritual songs for choirs. In fact, he created awareness in the larger Kenyan population of African Christian repertoire extant among Africanist, Pentecostal, and charismatic assemblies. He therefore encouraged an alternative resource for anthems beyond European sources, makwaya styles, and indigenous folk tunes. Contemporary education enthusiasts and urbanites, groups in transition, seeking to codify the process and product of modernity, contact, diversity, and change, embraced these stylings. Music became a way to systematize and bring coherence to the diverse musical intersections of multiethnic urban populations at a time of cultural anxiety in the face of national integration.

The first music degree program in Kenya was established at Kenyatta University in 1977. Experimenting with the faculty and students at the university, as well as with church groups in Nairobi (e.g., St. Stephens Choir), Kemoli and his colleagues solidified the place of African church tunes using the 'arrangement' procedure. These pieces were often recorded in studios or by broadcasting houses covering national events. Kemoli's output provides a seminal approach to the syncretism of two cultural and religious music idioms (Logooli and Euro-Christian cultural and religious systems) in a dynamic space (Logooli, Kenyan, and Christian history). He works from the position of music as sound; lyrics as literature, poetry, or drama; and the musician as a creative artist—ideas that resonate with the European 'high art.'

To discuss Kemoli's contributions and the early development of his style, I compared church congregational versions with Kemoli's adaptations and arrangements. I focused primarily on 'spirit' songs in order to underscore Kemoli's idiosyncrasies and the music's foundation in Logooli ethos. The works also illustrate the folklorization of ethnic and religious music for academic, social, and national use. I then compared Kemoli's transcriptions with recordings from the 1970s to 1990, including the Muungano National Choir's performances that propelled some of Kemoli's works to international fame.[19] I also reviewed a song's performances by different choirs, taking into account the contexts such as relaxed entertainment venues and stringently timed music festivals. I compared renditions where Kemoli conducted and soloed the pieces to when others interpreted his notation.

I will present my transcription of six signature pieces based on my reading of different performances of the same song. The selections consist of one, two, or more hymns or 'spirit' songs conjoined in indigenous performance practice or by Kemoli, with subject matter or text related by Kemoli's choice. The original melody is stated at least once with or without harmonization.[20] I begin the discussion by analyzing Kemoli's arrangement of a Lulogooli song in 'book' music style. Composed by Mwelesa, the song demonstrates the appropriation of the missionary hymn into Logooli musical psyche.

"Lwa somanga mu Lilaga Lihya"

The literal translation of the title line "Lwa somanga mu Lilaga Lihya" is "When I read in the New Testament." The title itself begs elaboration on the text. The hymn appears in Gideon Mwelesa's collection published in 1978 and in his 1988 compilation (Mwelesa 1988, 231), with its first performance dated 1975. Mwelesa states in the title subtext that the song was inspired by a Bible passage found in John 13:12, where Jesus, knowing his death was imminent, washed his disciples' feet. He then asked them if they understood the significance of his action. It was also on that occasion that Jesus acknowledged that although his was an external act of cleansing, not all of them were clean. One of them would betray him.

Mwelesa uses this conversation to initiate the act of introspection. The singer is remorseful as he or she reflects on Christ's actions. This Lulogooli composition is in stanza/refrain form, and in a mode and meter similar to missionary hymns. The stanza and the refrain, composed of four lines each, are set to the same melody. The four lines can further be condensed as two couplets. The couplets are set to the same tune in variation—A A'. In the first stanza, the narrator identifies the sources for the reflection—the Bible, the crucifixion of Christ, and the fact of Judah's betrayal. The next three stanzas concede: No amount of shedding of tears or remorse can bring salvation; It is not from works that one pleases God; There is no place to hide in order to escape temptation; The moment of contrition is a personal one. To slake his or her thirst, each person has to drink him- or herself, not use a second party. The refrain contains the human response to both God's actions and human desires. Stanzas one, three, and the refrain state:

Stanza 1:
Lwa somanga mulilaga lihya   When I read in the New Testament
Mwami wange yavambwa,   My Lord was crucified
Yuda niye wamutsama   Judas is the one who betrayed him
Mbeleranga muno.   I am filled with great sorrow

Refrain:
Mwoyo gwange gwenyanga ive   My heart wants/needs you
Mwami hamba uninde   Lord come and protect/shield me
Mbeye wovo, oveye wange   I am yours, you are mine
Hamba na uninde.   Come and protect/shield me

Stanza 3:
Nyala kukukolela ki   What can I do for you
Uyanzitswe na inze?   So that you can be pleased with me?
Nyala kwivisa haliki   Where can I hide
Mbule kogelitswa?   So that I may not be tempted/tested?

Kemoli informed me that he arranged this song for an Easter church music festival performance where he pitted the Kariokor Friends choir against the music giants of the day (late 1970s–early 1980s). In Nairobi, they included St. John's Nomiya Church directed by Sam Otieno, Our Lady of the Visitation church conducted by William Wasike, St. Stephen's Church managed by Darius Mbela, and St. Barnabas choir led by Walter Ominde.

Kemoli changes the order of stanzas as they appear in Mwelesa's book, so that the second and third stanzas are interchanged. In his arrangement (music ex. 7.1), Kemoli works with the fundamental chords commonly associated with the song's diatonic melody in a more or less block manner using basic primary and secondary chords. He differentiates the stanza/refrain melody through the harmonic procedure. The first and third verses share a harmonization different from that set for stanzas two and four. The study images each alternate verse as a different painting on the same canvas. In the first stanza, all four parts sound the tonic chord for three beats before continuing with other chords. Occasionally the tenor and alto reiterate a seminal lyric or use passing notes to generate tension that is resolved with the entry of all voices. The verse ends on a perfect cadence.

The refrain begins with a statement by the upper three voices, reinforced by the bass entry after four syllables before resolving to chord I. Tenors join basses to support the sentiment of the text, cadencing later than the two upper voices. The second line receives a treatment similar to its counterpart in the stanza. The third refrain line contrasts the stanza's third line not in chordal structure but in polyphony, while the fourth line has only two chords different from those of the stanza. In the new second verse, the melody is placed in the male voice parts with upper voices set as descant parts. Stanza three is treated like stanza one, while stanzas two and four share the same treatment. The piece therefore acquires a regular symmetry.

A Logooli factor of this piece, apart from language and solemn style, is in the dramatization of the dialogue. Kemoli attempts to portray the drama by contrasting the harmonic setting of alternate verses. However, his use of a descant for verses two and four attests to his apprenticeship with Anglican Hyslop. Further Logooli features include feeling the triple subdivision, swaying or marching in a duple compound meter, and clapping in simple duple time. When performed as an 'adaptation,' clapping, though implied, and overt motion of kind is excluded. Musicians unfamiliar with Logooli vocal aesthetics employ a lighter tone color than Logooli performers. The different performances provide fodder for discussing the author's intent, the performers' interpretation, and audience expectation.

The next five pieces demonstrate Kemoli's earliest arrangements of Logooli 'songs of the spirit.' He strictly maintains the original Logooli melody and rhythm, performed in slow Quaker tempo to avoid the lure of clapping

INVOCATION

EXAMPLE 7.1. "Lwa somanga mu Lilaga Lihya"

or movement. As a literature scholar Kemoli works with text to portray the emotion of the piece. For example, in one piece, he marries the European aesthetics of how sorrow is felt with Logooli notion of how sorrow is lived and rendered in music. Such attitudes are prevalent in rituals such as funerals, where evening wakes feature fast and cheerful music with humorous satire, in contrast to the dramatic wailing by a new arrival at the scene, who after singing solemnly in front of the corpse retires to the house to drink tea and discuss his or her excessive behavior; or weddings, where a girl is not permitted to smile or appear joyful because while she may be in love, she cannot appear too eager to leave her parents' home. Kemoli therefore marries European interpretation and mood with Logooli statements and sentiment.

In these pieces, Kemoli's idiomatic stylistic preferences are displayed. He has a predilection for solo-response or leader-chorus formats. Solo sections are 'called': by a lone person, by a lone voice part such as soprano or tenor, by individual or group duets of soprano and alto or tenor and bass in parallel thirds, or by three solo voices in parallel thirds and sixths. He rarely begins the response on a tonic chord. He has a preference for the dominant seventh chord. When performing live, he improvises texts and expects the choir to provide the correct response. In such contexts, unless it is a music competition, he will extend the length of the performance. Occasionally Kemoli includes Kiswahili words to recognize a broader national audience. In fact, when he toured other countries, like the proverbial bard, he inserted significant words in the countries' languages as was appropriate (e.g., Japanese tour recording, Kemoli collection).

When Kemoli adjoins at least two songs, he tries to retain as many 'indigenous' Logooli traits as possible. In solo-response style when one person 'calls,' he or she takes liberties with the text against a constant/groove/timeline articulated by the chorus. The leader is critical in setting the tempo and mood, in energizing, and in interpreting the piece. Kemoli's live performances and some transcriptions demonstrate these traits. He adopts musical tensions found in Logooli practices or uses indigenous tensile techniques. He includes Logooli alternative notes in his harmony, systematizing melodic liberties performers take. He also dramatizes text as happens in indigenous theatrical narratives using dynamics, silence, sudden and abrupt entries and endings, melodic variation relative to linguistic tone, and rhythmic vamps articulated in the harmony or text as a timeline. He energizes the performance by suggesting movement but not articulating it, allowing the audience to feel the multiple pulsings he seeks to portray. He exaggerates dynamics by framing them in Eurogenic postures. He employs crescendo and decrescendo in textual interpretation more deliberately than is done in indigenous culture. While such practices exist in Logooli worldview, they are not applied as conspicuously in music as they are in drama and storytelling.

"Gendi kwilwadze"

One of Kemoli's earliest arrangements, "Gendi kwilwadze," first recorded in 1979 by the Kenyatta University choir and later by the Kariokor Friends choir, was performed in religious, academic, and political contexts. Here, Kemoli embarked on experimental settings of Logooli Christian song, started to move away from Hyslop's shadow, and began to establish his own style.[21] Two songs, "Gendi kwilwadze" and "Ndali mulogi muno," are arranged to create an ABA form, beginning with "Gendi kwilwadze," contrasted by "Ndali muheyi muno" and returning to "Gendi kwilwadze." The two texts in dialogue are often sung as a set in Logooli churches. The first song states, "Let us preach in the world," while the other testifies about what happens when people respond to preaching. Through song, sin and 'sinners' are called out. In the first song, the leader lines the text and tune for the group response. The song is used as a refrain, a bridge, a breather, and a tag. In the second song, the leader calls out different 'sinner' types. The choir prefaces their reiteration of the call line with "Haleluya," then provides the appropriate antidote for the sinner. The texts of both the first and second songs are outlined below with only the first stanza of the first song later notated.

Song 1:
Gendi kwilwadze ×2 mulilova. Each phrase is sung twice, by solo and chorus.
(Let us preach on earth)
Musa yateva ×2 lisaala
(Moses asked for prayer—"Moses prayed")
Mwami yateva ×2 lisaala
(The Lord asked for prayer—"The Lord prayed")

Song 2:

Leader	Response
Ndali mulogi muno	Haleluya ndali mulogi muno, lelo ndayiganira
Ndali muheyi muno	Haleluya ndali muheyi muno, lelo ndayiganira
Ndali muvila muno	Haleluya ndali muvila muno, lelo ndayiganira

Translation:

I was such (a great) a curser/witch	Halleluiah, I was a curser, now I have repented
I was an adulterer par excellence	Halleluiah, I was an adulterer, now I've repented
I was deep into sorcery	

The first song is in two meters, similar to Logooli story songs. It employs triple and quadruple meters for each alternate measure. The second piece is in triple meter. Both are in solo-response style so designed to eliminate choral errors at metric changes. The effect with a drumbeat or clapping in duple meter is such that one actually does not conduct the pieces in two meters. In "Gendi kwilwadze" (music ex. 7.2), the leader lines the text for the chorus. Kemoli's arrangement and indigenous stylistics suggest a mobilizing call. Not only does the call-and-response format imply mobilization; the urgency of the call is entailed in the rhythmic configuration at the beginning with fast notes—three eighth notes resolving on a syncopated quarter note followed by an eighth note, a syncopated quarter note, and a rest.

The first five notes and beginning phrase "Gendi kwilwadze" (Let us preach) are repeated in a way that resembles push starting the process twice before resolving on the word "mulilova" (in the world; see music ex. 7.2). The phrase is then repeated but this time doubling the value of the first beat with a rhythmic suspension, a persuasive compulsion of those called to preach. The structure begins as a retrograde version of the first incomplete phrase that arches back to be reiterated then resolved on the tonic. Each phrase ends on a rest, literally creating a launching pad, as if preparing to dive—bouncing on the board before finally plunging in. Such offbeat phrasing is a hallmark Logooli musical structure.

A congregational caller normally employs one rhythmic figure. Thus, if the leader opts for the rhythm of the first statement of "Gendi kwilwadze" (measures 1–2), he or she will use the same figure with each subsequent utterance rather than syncopating it as in measures 2diii–4. Kemoli uses both figures in the same call. Further, Kemoli's vigorous response is to begin the harmony on a VI7 chord, itself a tensile chord, resolve it on the V7, and return to a more common progression of VI to II, cadencing with VI, V, I. He repeats the phrase beginning with the second rhythmic figure harmonized differently. The rhythmic and harmonic contrasts in the response portend for a

INVOCATION

EXAMPLE 7.2. "Gendi kwilwadze" (PURL 7.1)

crescendo at the beginning of B', compelling a reining in of the energy at the end by restating a previous cadential phrase. The structure of the first piece therefore becomes not just solo-response (AB) but solo-response-reiteration of response (ABB'). After a solo tenor calls all the verses, the entire section is repeated; but this time, the call is a duet by the soprano and alto voice parts. In this instance, the leaders sing forte, but the response (B) begins piano for the first iteration. The second iteration (B') begins with a crescendo in the first phrase, then the energy drops to piano for the second phrase (at measure

10diii). After the whole section is repeated, the second song, "Ndali mulogi muno," then follows beginning out loud. It is as though the soft ending is set up as a springboard for the loud section that follows.

"Ndali mulogi muno" is a combined stanza and call-and-response form (bars 12diii–16). The call is made by a solo male voice. The chorus punctuates with "Haleluya," repeats the call, and provides the punch line. In church services, the chorus uses the rhythm lined out by the leader. Kemoli adjusts the response rhythm in his arrangement for musical and lyrical drama. He juxtaposes two rhythmic possibilities, using one in the solo call and the other in the response on the text of "Ndali mulogi muno." In congregational singing, only one rhythmic figure is used, the one stated by the caller. Thus Kemoli plays with two rhythmic possibilities in the same sentence, similar to his treatment in "Gendi kwilwadze."

Each stanza in "Ndali mulogi muno" identifies a type of sin the singer repented of. The response sets up the agreement with "Haleluya," as is common during testimonies. They then reiterate the stated sinful act and declare the subsequent contrition. Beyond this, Kemoli uses other prefixes to the said sins—for example with the word *mulogi*, the root verb is *kuloga*, to bewitch. Mulogi is one who bewitches. Occasionally Kemoli substitutes the **mu** in mulogi with **ka** to read *kalogi*, or with **gu** to read *gulogi*. In such usage kalogi means one who practices witchcraft smalltime, while gulogi is one who has excessive bewitching power. Mulogi is therefore a normal witch. In his labeling, Kemoli acknowledges that regardless of the level and manner of malicious practice, there is need for repentance. In regular congregational singing, a sin's value is not quantified.

After "Ndali mulogi muno," Kemoli goes back to "Gendi kwiladze" to create an eventual final ABA form. But he only sings the title text of the piece. In congregational singing, the leader goes back and forth between the two pieces at will. Thus, while Kemoli tries to imitate congregational performance practice he curtails repetition in order to adhere to academic, competition, and commercial recording needs. Often Isigudi drums, a bell, and a rattle accompany the song in indumba, kidindi, and clapping styles. There is no note in the notation on accompaniment or movement. Isugudi was never used in Pentecostal congregational renditions of the piece. By using these instruments, Kemoli distanced the piece from its original worship function.

INVOCATION

These two songs are married in textual relationship and in rhythmic treatment. Kemoli combined two rhythmic configurations whose aesthetic value resonated from a vertical emphasis. Further, the pieces are wed in the hemiola effect generated by the text based on the musical relevance inherent in the original Logooli sources. The variety of meters was overridden by the consistency of the regulated duple emphasis articulated through dance motion, hand claps, or the drumbeat.[22]

"Valimu vayuda"

Arranging two contrasting songs is an idiomatic hallmark of Kemoli's early period. "Mubende yimu" and "Lobai" make up the setting "Valimu vayuda," derived from the core phrase in "Mubende yimu." Structurally, "Mubende yimu" is in stanza/refrain/tag form. Each stanza is a sentence/phrase that is completed and developed by filling in the blank. Several stanzas are stated before the refrain is raised. Thus, an uneven number of stanzas could comprise a section preceding the refrain, or the refrain is treated as a tag. The melody and rhythm of each stanza is adjusted to the text. Below are a few verses of "Mubende yimu" and their English translation.[23]

Call	Response
Mubende yimu	valimu
Mubende yimu	valimu vayuda valimu
Vadzama Yesu	valimu
Vadzama Yesu	valimu vayuda valimu
Valenya kunzama	valimu
Valenya kunzama	valimu vayuda valimu

Together/tag:
   Haleluya valimu
   Haleluya valimu vayuda valimu

Translation:
   In this Pentecostal assembly, they are present (amongst us)
   In this Pentecostal assembly, Judases/traitors are present (those with
      Judas's mindset)
   The ones who betrayed Jesus are present
   The ones who betrayed Jesus are present; Judases/traitors are present
   They are about to betray me; they are present
   They are about to betray me; they are present, Judases/traitors are present
   Halleluiah, they are present, halleluiah, Judases/traitors are present

In Kemoli's arrangement, "Mubende yimu" is first called by a solo voice with a full choral harmonized response. The chorus then repeats that call and response in harmony. In essence Kemoli sets up the piece as if the first call and response lines out the subsequent four-part reiteration of the verse. The drama of the text is built on a statement posed by the call, with a response by the chorus, and then the chorus reiterates the call and further affirms the response. The leader calls new verses, with melodic adjustment to fit the text. In church, the refrain is delayed for as long as the leader begins new verses. To climax or signal the refrain, the caller ad-libs by singing/saying "valimu" (they are present [amongst us]—measure 10) to cue the chorus to sing the tag. But the leader might as well be silent and the response group knows to come in with the refrain. The soloist thereafter becomes a commentator to the choral refrain, interjecting as desired. The caller determines when to raise new verses. Kemoli, however, raises the tag after two stanzas, moves to the next song, then returns to the first song (see music ex. 7.3).

"Lobai" (from anacrusis in measure 15b3) is in two parts. The first describes departed saints, beginning with Lobai, who will call to order the assembly of those in heaven. Those who obeyed the law will be called 'the chosen ones.' The second part of the text then explains the reward of these chosen ones. They will climb Mount Zion, a ladder.[24] The structure exemplifies how lyrical text is developed.

Call:
    Vanga Lobai valilanga   Lobai et al. will call . . . [who will they call?]

Response:
    Valilanga miganda   They will call the crowd . . . [what crowd?]
    Valiva balondi va malago   Those who have obeyed the law [what will they be called?]
    Valilangwa batovole   They will be called "the chosen ones"

Call:
    Yavo nivo   These are they

Response:
    Valinina   Who will climb/mount
    Kigulu kya Zioni ingasi ×3   The hill of Zion, a ladder
    Valilangwa batovole   They will be called "the chosen ones"

Leader:
    Vanga Debura vimbanga yo mwigulu   Deborah et al. are singing up

INVOCATION

EXAMPLE 7.3. "Valimu Vayuda" (PURL 7.2)

Response:
: Valilanga miganda — They will call the crowd ... [what crowd?]
: Valiva balondi va malago — Those who have obeyed the law [what will they be called?]
: Valilangwa batovole — They will be called "the chosen ones"
Call:
: Yavo nivo — These are they, etc.

The development of the melody in the first part affords tensions. The first phrase is tensile not just in pitch and melodic structure but also in the duration of the last note (measure 17). This sustained high pitch is held for a quarter note tied to a dotted half note, to end the phrase. Kemoli, in explaining the melodic figure of the alto line on the word "valilanga" (B♭, E♭, A♭, C), stated it was imaged like the call of a trumpet, "Kisiliva" (Kemoli 2011). Each phrase ending except the last one is sustained—signaling more to follow. The last phrase of this first part is short, one syncopated quarter note consisting of two eighth notes built by a suspension (measure 23); founded on the Logooli principle of ending off the beat so that participants can resolve tension individually. The task of the chosen ones ("Yavo nivo"—these are they) in the second section begins with an ascending motif on "valinina" (Who will climb) followed by a pseudosequential development and repetition on the words "The hill of Zion, a ladder," to resolve with the same melody and text as the first section.

In the first part of "Lobai" (measure 15b3), the two top voices 'call' in parallel thirds, and the full choir completes the statement. Here, the 'callers' cue the choir (Lobai et al. will call) to provide the action (They will call the crowd to order), then describe the character of those called (Those obedient to the law/order) and their designation (Will be called the chosen ones). As in Logooli practice, a soloist interpolates between phrases with sounds or words like "ah, aha, 'leluya, *dodo*" (truly) designed to taunt the listeners and to prompt the choral response. The fillers complement the previous and ensuing text. In essence, it is a dialogue for emphasis and drama. The text plays on ideas inherent in a 'call'—issuing a call, called to order/judgment, called out of a crowd, having a calling, designated as chosen ones. In the second section (measure 23b2), the tenor and soprano 'call' in parallel sixths, then the whole choir responds prompted by solo ad-libs.

The piece provides an interesting reading on prebaroque European notions of word painting versus Logooli imaging of action and emotion. On the word "valinina" (measure 24), which translates as "they will climb," the melody ascends, a rise as with climbing. However, the subsequent melody on the thrice-stated "kigulu kya Zioni ingasi" (the hill of Zion, a ladder or an ascent) is developed as a lowered sequence down a minor third, followed by a varied sequence down a second. Such treatment appears at variance with the text. However, the motion is suggestive of the energy expended in climbing up, the exhaustion expressed in smaller intervals and repeated notes in the sequence, as if one tires out and plateaus but plods on in order to achieve the ultimate prize. The exhaustion makes the appearance of little positive progress, so a rest or long note at the end of each phrase provides the impetus for continuing on to the final phrase in measures 31–32. Such a configuration plays into the Logooli aesthetic of *kutuula*, the process of setting down a load, the final cadence after working out. The word *ingasi* (ladder) is not merely about the tool that assists in climbing but also the effort exerted during the ascent. In Kemoli's discussion of his understanding of the text, he stated that in effect, the song's message is that one has to work hard to attain a desired goal. "Getting into heaven is not child's play. One has to persistently work to attain that goal. One must wrestle effectively in order to get to the top" (Kemoli 2011). Such metaphors as explained by Kemoli demonstrate a certain indigenization of Christianity and heaven in Logooli culture, where biblical concepts found resonance with the circumstances of Logooli life, and where play—as in the case of wrestling—had a deeper significance than just pure exercise or entertainment.[25]

"Lisuvila"

Two songs, "Lisuvila liali lya Saolo" and "Kwinye kugende ni kwilwadza," are adjoined to create one piece (music ex. 7.4). Kemoli's studies in literature are evident in his selection of two related pieces not normally performed together in church services. The progression of the idea is that 'once you acquire faith like that of the three lads Shadrach, Meshach, and Abednego [who defied King Nebuchadnezzar in the biblical narrative found in Daniel 3], go and preach with the understanding that there will be a reward/good fortune/luck.' In performance, the two songs are interchanged. Each song is complete in itself so that either of them can begin or end the set. Both songs are in stanza form and in call-and-response practice. In this arrangement, sopranos 'call' both songs. The text is as follows:

Lisuvila liali lya Aberenego	The faith of Abednego
Lienyanga kuve batovole	Requires that we be the chosen ones
Kwinye kugende ni kwilwadza	Let us journey and preach (preach as we travel)
Kulakahevwe	We will be given (we will receive)
Kwinye kugende ni kwilwadza	Let us journey and preach
Kulakahevwe ingavi	We will be given (receive) a reward/good fortune

In the first song, "Lisuvila," sopranos begin the sentence and are joined by altos in the second phrase to complete the 'call' line. The whole choir 'response' reiterates the sentence ending on a different melodic cadence and confirming the statement (AbAc). The piece, in quasipopular style with an implied 3-2 clave, is patterned like a wedding song from a female perspective in terms of musical characteristics, voice leading, and practice (the glissando from the mediant to the dominant at the beginning). It is not surprising that Kemoli scores female voices to call the song. In subsequent stanzas, the name on the call line—Aberenego (Abednego) will be substituted for Miskaha (Meshach), Sadaraka (Shadrach), and Danieli (Daniel).

Wedding songs were set in the most popular genre of their time. Kemoli appropriates the wedding song style in this arrangement. As congregational song, the stylistic essence was usually subverted by a faster speed and the superimposition of a duple meter from clapping and drums, occasioning rests and offbeat phrasing. Kemoli retains the popular wedding style tempo and eliminates clapping and drums. He imitates certain glissandi and voice leading associated with women generally and weddings in particular. Kemoli develops the wedding musical and symbolic drama with unison soprano initiating the phrase that is completed by a group duet (SA) as if the collective village women empathize with the entering female newcomer. The rest of the choir (SATB) enters from the third line to the end, as the community affirms the sentiments of the females. In this patrilineal patrilocal society, men married from outside their paternal clan. Thus most wives in a given village were 'outsiders' in one way or another. A girl left her parent's homestead and was grafted into a different clan. Her children (male and female) claimed primary descent from their father's clan. These women enabled the perpetuation of the clan and solidified inheritance by legal heirs.[26]

In his arrangement, Kemoli dramatizes the traumatic displacement of the female in song by having the highest voice part begin the song. The next

EXAMPLE 7.4. "Lisuvila" (PURL 7.3)

highest voice then joins in as if in solidarity. He then allows participation by lower voices—usually men who benefit from the incorporation of a 'foreign' adult woman into the household. Men are considered 'owners' of the home and perpetuators of the clan. However, without the work of women, sexually and otherwise, the future of the clan is jeopardized. In setting this song in the mood of a wedding, Kemoli, in the manner in which he gradually layers in different voice parts, underscores the understood interdependence of gender groups in Logooli worldview.[27] However, that consideration is convoluted by the fact that the song's lyrics are centered on 'men' of faith. The register differs from that in the previous song ("Valimu vayuda"—in the second part "Lobai") where women are named, suggesting that regarding judgment in the afterlife, in Logooli and in biblical worldviews, no one gender is privileged above the other. In the roster of "Lisuvila," males are privileged in the original song's lyrics. This position may be informed by Logooli perspective on cultural heritage in the physical and the continuing humanlike roles of the ancestors in the afterlife.

"Kwinye kugende" is styled in Tiriki male initiation mode, tempo, and melodic structure (from measure 9). Kemoli conceals the eventual modulation by beginning on the dominant of the preceding piece, which is the tonic of the new song. Because Kemoli forces tonal harmony, the modal suggestion in the first phrase is eventually abandoned. The piece evokes storytelling form with the audience incited to respond, but the phrase is abandoned mid-flight. Instead, the question is called again and this time, the audience provides the entire response. True to the syncretic practice of the time, Kemoli situates the 'call' in the female vocals, a notion that distances the tune from male initiation rites. Composers of Christian songs, whose primary musical exposure was indigenous Luyia forms, engaged such a transfer somewhat unconsciously. Because the male rite was one of the most contested rituals for missionaries and early Logooli converts, compositions in this style were performed at a faster tempo than their circumcision counterparts. The tempo change effectively disguised the adapted style, exonerating performers from the subsequent body rhythms, behaviors, and taboos associated with the ritual. In his arrangement, Kemoli reverts to the appropriate ritual tempo but disguises the form with female instead of male callers. In performance, Kemoli also adds church drum rhythms. Usually circumcision songs were performed only with sticks and no drums. Kemoli then goes back and forth between both songs in performance. It is facile to revert back to the first key when the song is repeated because the first note of the first song is an octave above the last note of the second song. The soprano callers therefore easily find the new key when they return to the first song.

When Kemoli first posited this arrangement in the late 1970s, he sang it for as long as the audience enjoyed it. The key contrast invigorated the performance. The choir rested in the lower range of each section, climaxed in the high tessitura, and relaxed at the final cadence. That Kemoli modulated into the second piece was a novelty for Kenyan arrangers, who traditionally sought contrast of style, meter, dynamics, or text rather than key. Usually, if the melody was conducive to cultural modulatory motion, the choir responded 'naturally.' But when notated in solfège, or with accidentals in the score, the choir struggled. This curious psychological response was present when members sight-read music and absent when the piece was taught by rote. Kemoli in this modulation experiment signaled novel approaches to key change in an African work.

Another reading occurs when one considers that the styles of the two pieces are invoked from rites of passage that portend adulthood and identity shifts for both genders. The ways these two styles are sonically wed could signify a coupling of disparate clans, families, individuals, or faiths. A marriage occurs in the duple feel present in the $\frac{4}{4}$ and $\frac{6}{8}$ meter of the two songs, but each meter has a different texture. Also inherent in the first song is a 3-2 clave, while the second song suggests a $\frac{6}{8}$ feeling in the first measure but $\frac{4}{4}$ in the second one—giving an underlying contrast of a triplet versus a duplet. It is these kinds of subtle readings of the text, ritual, and music that create a fascinating analysis of not just Logooli music theory and aesthetics but also Kemoli's musical, literary, and dramatic understanding, interpretation, and innovation within and beyond the collective indigenous worldview.

"Musalaba"

The arrangement "Musalaba" consists of three songs: "Kwinye kwahebwa musalaba," "Kivala kyo mwigulu," and "O Musalaba." According to his private notes, Kemoli arranged this tune to "commemorate my ancestors—Debula my Grandmother, Kemoli my father, Ndenda my grandfather" (Kemoli 2001c). More than any other, the set is arranged in a way that directly mimics a performance by a church congregation. In every recording and performance beginning as early as 1979, Kemoli used Isigudi drums in sugudi styles rather than playing church rhythms on Isigudi drums or employing the ubiquitous church drums. The melorhythms played by the Isigudi ensemble allowed for more complex polyphonic/polyrhythmic possibilities in tandem with the choral arrangement. In effect, Kemoli married the musics of European Christianity and Logooli culture in ways that were unconventional/unheard of in that time yet were musically satisfying for both worlds. I believe the practice divorced the arrangements from ecclesiastical use and enabled Kemoli to justify creating the Kariokor Nyayo choir, off of Kariokor Friends choir, with a political/social/academic agenda. Even more disconcerting was the fusion of indigenous Kenyan music with European academic styles and its performance by both a university group and a church choir, accompanied by indigenous Isigudi players who had little Western education and were possibly ostracized from Christian religious performances in their everyday living.

The first song, "Kwinye kwahebwa musalaba," was sung more or less in the way it would be treated in a church service, except for prescribing a fixed four-part harmony in the response. For the second piece, Kemoli drew from the 'spirit' song, "Kidaho kyo mwigulu (music ex. 6.16)." He substituted the first word, *Kidaho*, for the word *Kivala*, changing the emphasis from a well (kidaho) to land (kivala). Maybe non-Logooli speakers found it easier to pronounce the word 'kivala.' However, since the piece was arranged in the 1970s when the young Kenyan government was struggling to develop national cohesion from the diverse ethnic groups in its borders, 'kivala' spoke to the socio-political idea of nationhood, while 'kidaho' limited the audience to a Christian religious group with a proselytic agenda. The final piece, "O Musalaba," appears to be Kemoli's musical choice regarding the theme suggested by the word *musalaba* present in the first piece. In the late 1970s and mid-1980s, "Musalaba" in this arrangement was performed at political and social functions.

The first piece, "Kwinye kwahebwa musalaba," in stanza form, is performed in call and response (see music ex. 7.5a). The caller (tenor voice) has variable lyrics. The response consists of a phrase that is repeated three times.

Call: Vatsidzanga mwigulu mugende galaha
            Those going to heaven, walk slowly/surely/with confidence (in measured gait)
Response: Kwinye kwahebwa musalaba x3
            The cross has been given to us (we are the bearers/carriers of the cross)
Call: Noveye muheyi [ni] usale hena
            If you are an adulterer how/where will you pray?
Response: Kwinye kwahebwa musalaba x3
            The cross has been given to us (we are the bearers/carriers of the cross)

The group response is fixed in text and tune regardless of the leader's call.[28] However, the leader basically uses the two melody lines transcribed below. When referencing those "on the way to heaven," the first call melody is used; when naming different sinner types, the second call line is used. Thus, the lyrical drama and the identity of the two people groups are outlined in the appropriate melodies. The soloist or the conductor (may be the same person) decides on when to begin the second piece.

INVOCATION

EXAMPLE 7.5a. "Musalaba" (1)

The second piece, "Kivala kyo mwigulu," describes heaven as a land of sweet water where those who drink of it will not thirst. It is in two sections (see music ex. 7.5b), with the second part of the song inviting people of 'profane' or 'malevolent' character to heaven. It is these same people types that were described in the previous song as being without a prayer, unless they chose the way of the cross. In the first part, the leader (tenor solo or soprano part) cues the response by providing the first line of the refrain. The entire choir responds to the tenor 'call' for several repetitions. When sopranos take over the lead, the altos sing the countermelody transcribed in the first measure to the word "kivala," further emphasizing the idea of 'the land.'

Call:	Kivala kyo mwigulu	The land of heaven
Response:		Kili na madzi malahi
Has sweet/good/pure waters		
	Valitsya kunywa ku	Those who will drink of it
	Si valinyola vuluhu	Will not have/find thirst (will not thirst)

After several repetitions, the leaders 'call' the next section. Essentially the first section acts as a prelude, a refrain, and a postlude. The second section is a dialogue between the leader and chorus, building drama through textual manipulation. The leader invites the 'sinner'; the response reiterates the call in typical Logooli tensile manner. The leader then asks the 'sinner' to come and repent. The response then delivers the punch line—"Come and enter into the new Jerusalem."[29]

Call	Response
Mulogi hamba	Hamba
Hamba weganire	Hamba wingire Yerusalemi imbya
Sorcerer come	Come
Come and repent	Come and enter the new Jerusalem

The first word of the 'call' is changed to identify different 'sinner types,' thus *mulogi* (sorcerer) is substituted for other sorts such as *muheyi* (adulterer) or *muvira* (wizard). The leader alternates between the two sections at his or her discretion before moving on to the second song. Kemoli transcription does not indicate how long the exchange in the first song lasts. In our discussions, Kemoli referenced a theoretical framework that he called "duplicative significance" (Kemoli 2011). Repetition, he said, was an affirmation of both music and text. Further, repetition especially in live performances served to accommodate the dance—as if the dance phrases were in cyclic polyphony with the singing. The musical phrase was repeated to resolve at the moment of coincidence with the dance cycle. While such gestures were embodied in the cultural memory of Logooli practitioners, Kemoli did not acknowledge dance in his score. Thus to proceed to the next song, a savvy conductor cued the upper voices to transition into the modulation (measure 10–13) leading to the next song in measure 14.

INVOCATION

EXAMPLE 7.5b. "Musalaba" (2)

Kemoli scored for a tenor solo to begin the second section of "Kivala" (measure 4d2). The choir responded in homophony (words transcribed below bass clef). Here, the soloist named choir or audience members in the performance moment. Thus it was not just general sinner types but specific people who were 'called.' Each performance therefore became unique with rhythms altered to accommodate the names called out. The response, a stable and consistent component, became a vamp and the basis of a groove. The groove was a place to climax. Musically, the vamp was placed in the low range with a narrow melodic contour, close to speech, conversational, enchanting, a type of channeling. Additionally, it was a musical springboard for the refrain, feigning an end but really fermenting for an upsurge of energetic reprisal of the first section. The refrain was periodically called to create and resolve tension musically and lyrically.

After several 'calls' by the tenor solo, the soprano line took over the call. The altos and tenors when harmonizing with the soprano 'call' (measures 6–7) were scored to perform the heterophony congregations employ to heighten the energy of the piece, one of the few instances Kemoli deliberately included Logooli harmonic structure in his arrangements. To transition to the next song ("O Musalaba"), Kemoli inserted three and a half bars (from measure 10b2) to set up a modulation into the last piece. In regular congregational singing, there is no transition or modulation.[30]

The third song, "O Musalaba," states that the cross on which Jesus travelled/died was a ladder (music ex. 7.5b measure 14b ff, after the fermata). The ladder is invoked literally and as a metaphor. One innocent response as to why the cross was a ladder was that singers assumed that Jesus *climbed onto* the cross. He needed a ladder to get up there. Some texts actually stated that Jesus 'climbed' onto the cross. Singers recounted stories about pictures they had seen where Roman soldiers climbed up a ladder in order to nail Jesus onto the cross. There were also metaphorical and 'biblical' explanations. Based on church history, it also references the fact that a ladder has steps (*vika*), the equivalent of stations Jesus stopped at on his way to the hill, and this might well be the analogy inferred. But vika is implicit in Lulogooli as a process. Life is a process. Jesus had been prepared for death. He was processed (led) to it (PURL 7.4).

Call:	O musalaba	The cross
Response:	Yeha	Oh Yes
Call:	Yesu yatsila ku (yanina ku)	Jesus went/died on/by it (climbed on it)
Response:	Musalaba ingasi	The cross, a ladder
Tag		
Response:	Oyo yatsila ku musalaba ingasi	(He went/died) on/by it, the cross, a ladder

INVOCATION

In "O Musalaba," sopranos and altos 'call' in parallel thirds answered by the lower voices. The text of the second 'call' phrase can be altered. When there is no call, then the climax/tag occurs (measure 23b). In church sings, the tag is repeated if the caller interpolates with words such as "Halleluiah," or members add the word "dodo" (indeed) after "ingasi," signifying the cross is indeed a ladder. They can then create a vamp based on the tag. Kemoli chooses not to do that. Instead he ends the piece by slowing down, creating a European-like finalis, with the higher voices moving up an octave from measure 25 to the end, a non-Logooli type of climax.

Equally unusual is the modulation and Kemoli's preparation for it (a transition). He has the sopranos 'call' the first line of the second part in the first section "Mulogi hamba" (sorcerer come) with the other voice parts responding in agreement "Hamba" (do come). Sopranos reiterate the phrase sequentially with altos in parallel thirds answered by the lower voices. This restatement then closes in a fermata. The fermata is associated with the academy rather than indigenous practice. It appears that the piece will end here (a rather unusual cadence), but Kemoli simply pauses to prepare the audience for the next piece. The drama created in the lyrics is one of asking the said sinner to come to the cross, since the piece that follows the modulation is about Jesus work/mission on the cross. This piece is one of the earliest adaptations to deliberately modulate in European style, compared to others where indigenous modal inflections prompted the modulation.

A third area of syncretism of folk secular and folk religious elements occurs when 'callers' begin their line before response resolves its phrase in measure 18. First, the word "Yeha" in measure 15–16 is a vocable used in folk secular song, not in religious music. Some versions interjected the vocable *ha* in the narrative of the soloist, instead of "yeha" used by Kemoli. While *ha* is also a exciting punctuating exclamation, when appended to the text in the manner "O musalaba **ha** Yesu yatsila ku," the sentence reads "Oh the cross **from whence** Jesus went/processed/travelled." Here, the audience employs it to further excite the narrator. It was a way to indicate that the tale still portended more exciting and juicy details. That kind of interjection was also applied musically and lyrically in the original song.

"Yeha," on the other hand, evokes wonder in the manner of 'how exciting,' 'what a tale,' etc. In fact the lower voice parts were treated like commentators, not responders. The phrase by the upper voices then becomes "O musalaba,

Yesu yatsila ku" (Oh the cross! Jesus died [went] on it), with "yeha" as an aside. That exclamation creates a 'tender' feeling rather than the agitation evoked by "ha." The arrangement also takes away from the melodic triad created by interlocking "ha" on the tonic by the response group, followed by the mediant and dominant by the leader to create a seamless phrase. Even if the "ha" was conceptualized as an interjection, the general mood would be in the vein of shock, disbelief, intense angst. With "Yeha," Kemoli creates a pedal over which he sustains the callers' second line—evoking empathy and maybe a difference in the type of response anticipated by fundamentalist hell-and-brimstone preachers who would rather have the "ha." Avalogooli accepted the polyphony created by "yeha" by the low voices against the 'call' in the upper voices. It was an alternative resolve to musical tension different from an agitated interjection or an abrupt ending. Such polyphonic resolutions are suggested in other contexts that involve accompanying instruments such as fiddles, bells, lutes employed as a drone, pedal, or countermelody, and in the use of ululations or whistles. Although in church sings, the phrase ends on a rest on the strong beat of the next measure, Kemoli extends the syncretic reading by creating a long note on the last iteration of the final phrase—reminiscent of English anthems where a piece is likely to end on a sustained long note rather than a rest, and on the last rather than the first beat. More than any other of Kemoli's earliest arrangements, "Musalaba" interrogates the tensions inherent in Logooli drama. He also enlarges the palate of possibilities employed by Avalogooli and other Luyia to depict a variety of temperaments (PURL 7.5).

"No musalaba gogenda"

The combined set of "Nohenza mu moni mwa Yesu" and "Avamonyi ni vamonya" comprise "No musalaba gogenda," Kemoli's most famous song. Kemoli performed it on tour with the Kariokor and University of Nairobi choirs, among others, in Kenya, South Africa, Japan, and the Middle East from as early as 1985. "No musalaba gogenda" has also served as a competition set piece for educational institutions, churches, and parastatal organizations. Its global fame was secured when the Muungano National Choir not only performed it internationally but also recorded it in 1990 (see discography section in the bibliography). Kemoli revised it for different audiences and contexts. In fact, he informed me that occasionally, choir directors adjusted the piece for their particular choirs, resulting in numerous renditions, including the edition made famous by Muungano National Choir (Kemoli 2011).

INVOCATION

In this piece, Kemoli explores baroque contrapuntal stylings and techniques such as word painting more than he did in earlier songs. Further, in this arrangement a whole voice part makes the 'call,' suggesting that it was conceptualized as a choral piece from the outset. This piece is made up of two songs. "Nohenza mu moni," the first song, is discussed as music ex. 6.7. Kemoli carefully selects certain stanzas whose text and drama suited his arrangement. He retains the call-and-response format but arranges the response in SATB block harmony. As with "Gendi kwilwadze," the solo (sopranos) calls and the group (choir) responds, then the choir restates the whole line in harmony. To create new stanzas, different parts of Jesus's body are substituted in the call and taken up in the response with the appropriate resolution. Thus if you look at Jesus's face, it is calm, joyful, glad. But if you look at his feet, you will see nails. If you look at his head, there is a crown of thorns. The text of the first stanza and one other verse is transcribed below.

Solo: Nohenza mu moni mwa Yesu
Response: Nohenza mmoni, nohenza mmoni vusangali vweng'ine
(If you look at Jesus's face, [there's] only joy/gladness)
Solo: Nohenza ku mutwe gwa Yesu
Response: Nohenza ku mutwe, nohenza ku mutwe, ingata ya mafwa
(If you look on Jesus's head, [there's] a crown of thorns)

Kemoli did not transcribe the song in the order it is usually narrated by church congregations. Usually the song begins with the person saying that Jesus called me, and I was in deep slumber (see music ex. 6.7). It is when the person awoke that he or she became aware of what Jesus had experienced on the cross. The narrator looks at Jesus on the cross and describes what he or she sees. Kemoli selects particular perceptions for his stanzas. He adjusts the melody so that the same tune is sung to all the verses rather than altering the melody to fit the text, as in congregational song. In fact, he sets the beginning phrase in a hexatonic scale avoiding the subdominant note where several versions have one but no leading tone. These kinds of musical liberties are taken by arrangers. Kemoli explained that the tune was adjusted severally so that his most favored version was the most adequately performed by choirs of different ethnic and age groups.

In one of his handwritten scores (1983 for the Kenyan music festival class 27A), Kemoli meters the piece in $\frac{12}{16}$ with measure 7 in my score transcribed in $\frac{4}{4}$ time. The second section is metered in $\frac{9}{8}$ but starts on the first instead of

EXAMPLE 7.6. "No musalaba gogenda"

the second beat in my notation. I have notated the most sung melody with the lyrics focusing what the narrator saw on Jesus's head, followed by the theme of the fugue for the song "Avamonyi." In the notes for the 1983 version, Kemoli indicates that the first section is really a warmup for the second part—which he says is "the main section which is a fugue." He conceptualized the work as a prelude and fugue.

"Avamonyi," the second piece, has an ambiguous message that is part social commentary, part religious invocation. The text is in typical Logooli satirical style—"Avamonyi ni vamonya no musalalaba gogenda" (Let the back-biters continue, the cross travels triumphantly—Kemoli translation on score notes). Subsequent stanzas mention other vices; for example, "Avaheyi ni vaheyagaga no musalaba gogenda" (Let the adulterers continue, the cross travels triumphantly). The idea of the cross may have to do with religion, but it may also speak to life's process: that despite zimbemba, life goes on. It is in fugue form. Kemoli informed me that composing and analyzing fugues was required in his music training at Durham University. It is therefore no surprise that Kemoli's classic piece is a study and interpretation of fugue form. The complete fugue subject as arranged by Kemoli is notated in music ex. 7.6. In congregational singing, the leader calls the first part and the congregation responds with the "Halleluiah." Kemoli divides this treatment between male and female voices. The soprano line calls new verses with melodic and rhythmic adjustments to the text, but the response is fixed. Thus the subject is recounted several times before a statement of the fugue answer is posited. When the tenor line then states the answer a fourth above the theme, a countersubject is created for the bass. The tenor line announces both the call and its response. While the words stay the same for each successive subject entry, Kemoli manipulates the fugue form, adding more countersubjects above or below the theme. Although he informed me that he had heard the tune expressed in different modes, he scored the piece in the major tonality, effectively locating the ethos of this ambiguous lyric in Logooli Christian religious aesthetics.[31]

Kemoli began his arrangements by invoking Logooli formal structures, such as the use of combination forms (see chapter 6), but his song sets were not always aligned to those in congregational singing. As he explored text, Kemoli also sorted for melodic compatibility. He deliberately planned modulations rather than being constrained to combine songs with similar melodic range or contour. Planned modulations brought Kemoli's experiments closer to his academic training. Meanwhile, Kemoli invoked Logooli harmonies and juxtaposed styles for different contexts into one piece. The overall aesthetic was definitely a syncretism of musical ideas. Kemoli has not only arranged Logooli songs; he has also composed songs in Logooli style. While the text and tunes are Logooli, he has moved from Logooli modes and sought to fit pieces into a tonal structure with a staff-notation-friendly format. While some Logooli songs fit these structures, others are compromised.[32]

In his arrangements of Christian song, Kemoli often transformed Logooli melodies to fit Western European chorale harmonic procedures. He altered pitches or voice leading, and arranged the songs in tonal harmony even when they were modal. He rarely developed the metric permutations informed by Logooli performance practices. Other transformations include little or no audience participation. Although singers were separated from the audience, in performance, Kemoli sought crowd approval. The pieces were no longer purely for ecclesiastical or ritual function. They were entertainment and academic exercises. Kemoli directed university students of different ethnic backgrounds, but he also sought to present a Logooli reading by working with the preponderantly Logooli Kariokor Nyayo choir. Working with Kariokor freed Kemoli from detailing interpretive, timbral, and instrumental qualities that he notated for multiethnic groups. Recording the same piece with Kariokor testified to Kemoli's frustration with the university groups' rendition of Lulogooli songs. The university ensembles' sound differed from that of Kariokor, a group fully steeped in Logooli performance practices.

With recordings, Kemoli introduced ways of interpreting his scores to the broader Kenyan public. This move intimated that given proper models, notated scores of local idioms, languages, and practices could be performed with indigenous authenticity. Thus the music of Logooli Christians services more than just Avalogooli and African audiences. They transcend ethnic, denominational, linguistic, and national boundaries as religious songs. Anyone versed in staff notation can perform them. Adaptations and arrangements have expanded the expressions and broadened the consumption of Logooli music.

Other musicians imitate Kemoli's stylings. Some have developed distinctive arrangements, giving rise to a corpus of Kenyan and other artists who operate in this mode. These musicians are conceived by the Kenyan public as modern composers and conductors, emulated and vilified for their ability to read and write music, belonging to a type of elitist group. With numerous music festivals in rural and urban centers, they compose in different Kenyan languages and musical idioms and train multiethnic choral groups in the musicking of diverse nationalities.

GOSPEL MUSIC

Gospel music is a genre and a music practice. More than that, it is a media label for any recorded or mediated Christian religious music product in Kenya. As a genre, gospel music is a body of repertoire comprising different genres from chants, to hymns, to contemporary worship songs. 'Gospel' covers songs in any style with biblical lyrics, religious exhortation, denominational dogmas, spiritual encounters, or morals understood as Christian. Gospel musicking involves a cappella singing as well as music accompanied by indigenous and popular instruments conveyed by soloists or groups. The prevalence of the music is such that these recordings are ubiquitous at any event. Consequently, professional musicians have found in 'gospel' a lucrative livelihood.

I will exemplify 'gospel' from my interviews with mulogooli Francis Jumba Ilavadza (born in 1959). Ilavadza, a singer and choirmaster, branched into commercial recording when gospel music came into its own in Kenya in the late 1980s. At that time, he earned his 'serious' living doing clerical work with a trading company known as Kakuzi Shares. However, he also directed the mutiethnic Riruta Baptist Church choir that not only serviced the church; they also participated in music competitions in Nairobi. Further, the choir was recorded at the denomination's Baptist Communication Studios for evangelism and for posterity (Ilavadza 1995). Ilavadza observed that music in Logooli-based urban churches languished because few choirs compelled congregations to better musicianship. While choristers participated in festivals, choirs were not part of the weekly worshipping life of the church. The choirs organized for competitions comprised of the best singers and a conductor who were not necessarily members of local congregations. They merely assembled for the contest and performed Christian or moral songs according to festival requirements. Further, Ilavadza realized that urbanized audiences were drawn to four-part arrangements of 'spirit' songs that were a staple at competitions.

Ilavadza hypothesized that a recording would preserve the memory of festival repertoire and provide new resources for conductors and consumers. He then arranged Lulogooli hymns in the then-popular gospel stylistics for archival and commercial consumption. He produced his first Logooli Christian 'solo' cassettes in 1991.[33] Ilavadza marketed his music in the commercial vehicles that ply the route between Logooli country and Kenya's capital city, Nairobi. This audience bought the music and requested it on radio. These songs were also played at funerals in villages and at wedding receptions in cities. Soon other Luyia joined the fray as consumers and later as performers (Ilavadza 1995).

My conversations with Ilavadza in 1995 centered on the production of gospel music for commercial consumption.[34] In that period, musicians recorded in English and Kiswahili for national and other audiences. Ilavadza's Lulogooli output was therefore an anomaly from both the commercial and Luyia perspectives. The very critical Luyia audiences preferred to listen and critique music from the radio, but they were reticent buyers. They preferred to dub from the radio rather than buy personal copies. Ilavadza confirmed this opinion in the interview, stating that even if people were willing to buy, they wanted to pay the least amount possible for the pirated copies selling at the time for

Kshs. 70, instead of the original product at Kshs. 150. Ilavadza was anxious that I understand his journey to produce good music. He discussed the process of studio production and the perils of marketing, including bootlegging. Audience taste regarding technology was not sophisticated. They craved the songs regardless of the quality of the recording. In the transcribed selection of the interview, appropriated English words or sentences are italized (song titles are in boldface). Such language code switching is common in Kenya.

> FJI:[35] Ku umanye vandu vanyingi va *assuma* ndi kuli inzi lwa valola ndi, kigira nyimba, ni mwagana nu mundu akuvolela ndi, "mbe i *cassette*." Ku inze manya mbola ndi basi, ku *instead* a mbe *igita*; ngube lwimbu lwene lula. Nigava ni **Salanga ku ive Yahova** [he sings the portion], nda kuba ne *igita*, kigira i *compact* iyi, ni olola ngohe, *I have to incur some expenses on top of what I incurred. Plus the time I practice for it;* i *periodi* ila yosi ku *practisa* tsinyimbu tsila.... Tsinyimbu tsiene tsila, *after spending all that money,* kwanza kuli yengo yila, vanyala kugula mu liduka dave. Mundu mulala ni aguli, kwanza kuli, *but I'm sorry to say this, but I have to say it,* umundu mulala ni aguli ni ave kuli ni mulogooli, valogooli vosi va ku nyoola.
>
> JK: Va *duba*?
>
> FJI: Yes. Na sasa umanye lwa vakola *dubbing*, yaani va manya va *dubé*; iyi umanye *ipicha* iyi [shows me a copy] ive *colored*. Iyo sasa ajala nayo da. Alatsia vutswa kukola *photocopy black and white.* Vutswa *provided* ndi asoomi ku alole, o, yilu ku valulanga **Nimeitwa na Yesu** na yilu ni **Salanga ku ive Yahova**. Sasa lwa avika ku mu *machine* ahulila ikolela ku 'tsa ihale *itiuni* yene, ma ahulila: "Basi." A va mmbolela ndi zisilinji *70 or 80.* Sasa mundu aganaganyia avola ndi, "sasa lwa nda ve mu liduka va voye *150.* Sasa uyu avola ndi *80.*" Ku mundu agula vutswa. Na yivilila kumanya ndi tsyo mwiduka tsila *original* tsila i *quality* ni indahi sana. *To make the matter more worse,* a kolele i *dubbing* mu *machine* yengo. *A cassette, just a cassette to a cassette. It's not the commercial machine we use for dubbing.* Akolele 'tsa mu *machine* yengo ma akovolela "Basi, tsisilinji 80." Ku sasa *like those one now, we don't get even a five cents.* Kigira lwa vakolela ndio namna hi, ma unyola ndi sya vuli mundu ave ni i *cassette* yene ila. Sasa tsive mu liduka, avandu vagula da. Sasa mundu agula ku vutsa moja moja. Sasa *on your side, you go at a loss. And even it discourages you* ni wenyanji okole *imusic* yindi.

Translation:

> FJI: You know, many people assume that because I sing [produce records], when I meet with someone, s/he just tells me "Give me a cassette." My response is, in that case, just give me a guitar and I will sing the song you desire. If it is **Salanga ku ive Yahova**, I will accompany myself on a guitar because in order for me to give you a compact cassette, *I have to incur some expenses on top of what I have incurred* [to produce it], *plus the time I practice for it.* I spent a lot

of time practicing those songs.... *After spending all that money,* the folks in the village do not want to buy the cassette. If one person buys a copy *and I am sorry to say this,* if s/he is a mulogooli, then all Avalogooli now own it.

JK: So they dub it?

FJI: Yes. And when they dub—you see this cassette cover [shows me a cassette cover], it is in color. They are not concerned with that. They *photocopy black and white.* Provided s/he can read and say, this song is **Nimeitwa na Yesu** and this one is **Salanga ku ive Yahova**. So when s/he goes to his/her friend and listens to the dubbed copy and hears the song faintly, s/he feels "oh good, that's it." S/he is told to pay Shs. 70 or 80. The person reasons, "When I was in the store, I was told that it costs shs. 150. Now this seller says I can get it for 80." So s/he buys the cassette. The person has forgotten that the original cassettes in the music store are of good quality compared to those dubbed at home. *To make matters worse,* the dubbing was done on a regular home cassette player; *a cassette, just a cassette to cassette. It's not the commercial machine we use for dubbing.* The vendor dubs on a home cassette and then charges you Shs. 80 for it. Now *like those one now, we* [musicians] *don't get even a five cents.* When this happens, many people own that recording. The legal shops only sell a few items sporadically. *Now on your side, you go at a loss. And even it discourages you* from future musical endeavors.

The conversations revealed Ilavadza's cognition of the critical audience he targeted. Most telling regarding audience critique was:

FJI: Umanyi avalusha ni avandu vamanya *miuziki* sana, kandi venya *miuziki* gwavo gove ni i *quality* indahi. Yaani mpaka kwimbi *on a certain level.* Nu wimba ovyo ovyo kuli tsindi tsya vakorino yitsi, sitsikola vulahi da. Venya *miuziki* gove *very well arranged.* Venya vahulli e *message* yene ila yingila vulahi, i mioyo jila jitula vulahi.

(You need to understand that Abaluyia know/appreciate music and want their music to be of good *quality.* We have to perform *on a certain level.* If you sing such as in the manner done by the Akorino, your product will not sell well. Your music has to be *very well arranged.* They [the audience] want to hear a *message* that is well stated and that the voices are well arranged.)

Here, Ilavadza acknowledges that Avalogooli have particular standards for music excellence. He compared Logooli musicking with that of other groups—such as the Akorino, a Kikuyu-founded African independent church. Their modal style and unison singing was different from the four-part arrangements preferred by Avalogooli. Ilavadza outlined that he usually arranged for three- to four-part vocal harmonies with active lines for lead and bass guitars.

FIGURE 7.2. Cover of Ilavadza's cassette recording.

Ilavadza's recordings provide a veritable archive of songs popular in Logooli Christianity over time. He retains the melody but harmonizes and orchestrates the songs with popular instruments. In fact, he remixes old favorites with the latest technology and popular stylings. For some pieces, he adjusts the textual rhythm to accommodate the strict prescribed tempo conditioned by studio synthesizers, often to the point where the rhythm loses its swing and the text is subservient to studio demands. It appeared that Ilavadza did not have a group that vetted his work in the way Mwelesa sought feedback from his musician and church peers, or Kemoli adjusted his pieces for his performing ensembles. Since the pieces are public, Ilavadza cannot copyright the songs, according to Logooli worldview. He can, however, claim ownership of the arrangement. Nonetheless he provides a reservoir of Logooli songs for the gospel music industry. His marketing savvy is such that as soon as a body of new songs gels, he records them.

Ilavadza arranges the same song genres as Kemoli into commercial gospel styles. When he began recording, Ilavadza paid little for studio time at Baptist Communications. He mixed the tracks after hours. That way, he avoided studio fees through the kindness of his church body (Ilavadza 1995). A pool of instrumentalists from his Riruta Baptist Church choir accompanied the singers. Although the multicultural church choir members provided backup vocals, Ilavadza imported singers from the village to provide a more authentic Logooli/Luyia interpretation of the vocal tracks. Ilavadza does not employ complex chord progressions. Like other performers who straddle indigenous and urban (post) colonial cultural mélange, Ilavadza's bass and lead lines should be read as melodies in their own right, invoking Logooli indigenous and church musical styles. Thus, while chords I, IV, and V preponderate, a Logooli response to the music might generate a different musical analysis.

Ilavadza's various Logooli records are titled *Luyia No. 1*, *Luyia No. 2*, and so on (see fig. 7.2 for a cassette cover of *Luyia Vol. 9*). His repertoire depends not only on 'spirit' songs; he includes translated songs such as "Ulivolela sina Yesu" ("What Will You Do with Jesus?" Text, Albert B. Simpson; tune, Mary Stokes; see music ex 7.7). This song was a favorite at funerals and evangelistic meetings. The text and tune of the refrain is transcribed below:

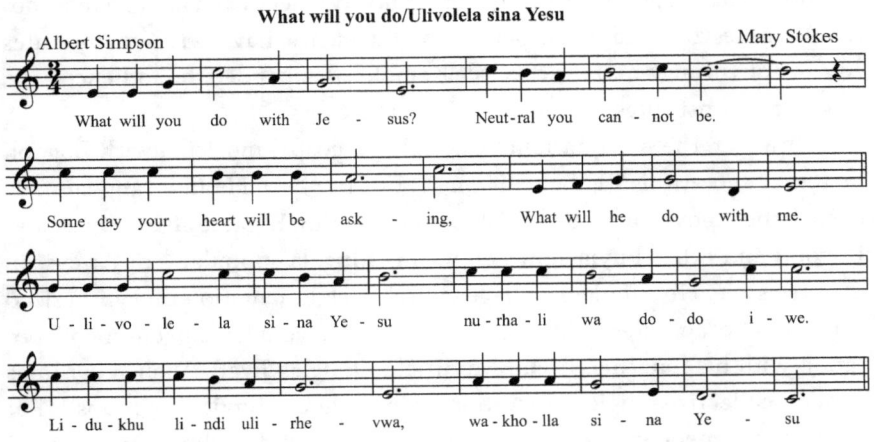

EXAMPLE 7.7. "What Will You Do with Jesus"/"Ulivolela sina Yesu" (PURL 7.6; PURL 7.7)

Original English:
>   What will you do with Jesus? Neutral you cannot be
>   Someday your heart will be asking, "What will he do with me?"

Translation:
>   Ulivolela sina Yesu, nukhali wa dodo iwe
>   Lidukhu lindi ulirhevwa, wakholela sina Yesu?

Retranslation:
>   What will you say to Jesus if you are not genuine?
>   One day you will be asked, "What have you done for Jesus?"

Ilavadza has commercially recorded songs like "Kidaho kyo mwigulu" (music ex. 6.16), and other 'spirit' songs and 'book' music. With the increased popularity of recorded music at funerals, weddings, Christmas parties, political gatherings, and other social functions, Ilavadza's output finds ready consumers in rural and urban spaces.

Like Mwelesa (discussed in chapter 4), Ilavadza invokes a traditional instrument, the one-stringed fiddle kiriri, for difference. He used to play the fiddle and transferred the techniques onto a guitar when he joined the church. His early recordings did not use the instrument, although it was posted on cassette covers. He began to include it in remixes and later recordings.[36] At the time, he was more famous for how he had fused modern instruments with Logooli 'spirit' songs. Ilavadza sings with his wife, Keren (Kerani) Imali, and some friends. While most of his output is in Lulogooli, he also performs in Kiswahili in order to reach a wider audience. At first, he scored for lead, rhythm, and bass guitar, as in old-time makwaya pieces, but later he incorporated synthesizers and studio percussion. In a sense, Ilavadza re-enculturates Avalogooli through his music. While Kemoli has expanded the audience base, Ilavadza reconstitutes the music for Luyia listeners.

However, the most nationally acclaimed gospel musician with Logooli maternal ancestry is Reuben Kigame (born in 1966). He first sang country gospel, then moved into the 'worship' music realm. Kigame also orchestrates Logooli and other Luyia songs either in "Lingala" popular[37] or American country style. He simulates village church instrumentation on synthesized drums and other effects. His best efforts in this vein have been in collaboration with his longtime friend Mudirichi Douglas Jiveti. Their recordings contain collective religious repertoire from different Luyia subgroups.[38] For their arrangements, the pair performs with contracted studio musicians with expertise in popular music stylings to provide additional instrumentation on acoustic, electric, and bass guitars; synthesized keyboard, brass, and strings; and some Kenyan instruments.

NOTES AND SUMMARIES

Logooli music by and for Christian congregations has moved beyond the purely congregational to the specialized community of the choir, gospel groups, and individual composers and arrangers. This expansion has facilitated the embrace of Logooli Christian repertoire into the larger national Kenyan civic and academic life. Kemoli moved the music into new social, political, academic, and artistic directions. In a holistic approach to the arts, it is not only melodies, harmonies, and lyrics that interest him; his music is painting, drama, history, politics, social commentary, and literature. In my view, Kemoli represents a bridging of times, places, and spaces, fusing Logooli journey from precolonial into the colonial and postcolonial, juxtaposing and blending the worlds of rural and urban folk with imported and new knowledge systems, exploring indigenous rural, Kenyan national and urban, and international sound and landscapes.

Music of contemporary Logooli Christians became a commercial product with accompanying star personalities as composers, performers, producers, and marketers. Ilavadza realized the potential of arranged hymns and 'spirit' songs for commercial purposes, for pleasurable listening, to facilitate rehearsal and improve congregational singing, to preserve contemporary repertoire, and to chronicle performative and cultural memory. This music is refurbished for new audiences; but more than that, it is innovated in time and space, moving back and forth between Western Kenya and the Avalogooli dispersion elsewhere. The market is inundated with musicians, from those who dabble solely in 'folk' religious music in Lulogooli to multilingual and multimusical persons conversant with international and global trends. This variety of musicians speaks of the diversity of palates and preferences of Logooli Christians.

EIGHT
EPILOGUE

REFLECTIONS

Beginning with the nineteenth-century encounter with Christianity, Kenyans and their musicians have processed the European or American musics introduced alongside the religion. Communities such as Avalogooli transformed the texts and forms to conform to local, acceptable, and contemporary standards. Avalogooli were introduced to Euro-American Christianity and Western hymnody from the beginning of the twentieth century.[1] Avalogooli then were described as a culture group in a specific location, guided by collective mores and associated with a particular lifestyle.[2] Avalogooli are today identified primarily as part of the Kenyan nation. However, Logooli essence (*uvulogooli*) is porous and amorphous. Uvulogooli is held together by genetic lineage and language, by a dynamic social heritage, and, to an extent, by land ownership. Of the identity rituals that bind the group, births and funerals are still definitive of uvulogooli. The transitional rites that signal adulthood and concretize gender roles (biological and socio-economic) undergo negotiation. While these rites are the definitive agglutinative markers, political, social, and economic regulators are constantly navigated. Continuity and change are evinced in the variety of musics that grace any occasion (from indigenous ritual musics to contemporary popular and academic-type arrangements) and the media through which the musics are disseminated.

While Western Kenya is the central Logooli ancestral abode (*Ivulogooli*), some members migrated, expanding the choices individuals and families make to affirm their humanity (Mundu) yet remain perseveringly Logooli. Although they were encouraged to migrate from their heavily populated lands by colonists and need (Mwelesa 2005; Kasiera 1981, 551), Avalogooli have always had a diaspora integrated into or isolated from others in dispersion. This diaspora is global and globalizing beyond Ivulogooli and Kenya. At home and abroad, Avalogooli can retain essential distinctive markers and adapt to their new environment. Therefore Uvulogooli is physically and ideologically locused in Western Kenya and in the Logooli dispersion.

The music of Logooli Christians is a local and indigenous expression, a national and mediated product, and an international and global phenomenon. The pool of musical resources that Logooli Christians draw from for religious, social, and political expression is wide. Some music introduced by missionaries is performed in a style associated with missions, while some of it has embraced Logooli styling. Other songs emanated from Logooli ethos, performance practice, and encounter with Euro-American Christianity initially legitimized in the Pentecostal movement. Other styles are Logooli musical interpretations of Christianity. These musics have been popularized in the media for local, national, and global consumption. They have undergone scholarly treatment and been disseminated. These musical expressions vitalize history and reinvigorate the community. The variety of musics packaged as Logooli Christian is composed of a body of repertoire with proximity to indigenous culture and to the practitioners' encounters within Kenya, in Africa, and in the wider world. Therefore music in Logooli Christianity has a wide incarnational range that is Logooli, Kenyan, African, and global.

POSTLUDE

In my first foray into this research (1983), I sought to provide familiar samples for my students at Kenyatta University from which to study ear training, aurals, music theory and analysis, and music history. I had been schooled to imagine these musics as European constructions based in baroque stylings. I theorized then that a pedagogical use could legitimize a notated African musical soundscape for understanding European baroque musical theory and styles. I soon discovered that the most engaging music was too difficult for my beginning students to sight-read, let alone write out in dictation. Additionally, some formal and elemental structures did not conform to European practices. Still, students easily performed the music when learned by rote because they were aurally informed beyond notation.

Meanwhile, I was convinced that African musical ideologies were not rooted in sound alone but included, at least, body motion as part of the counterpoint. This notion was arrived at during my last year as an undergraduate when my teacher Mary Oyer asked me to transcribe African musics from the Hugh Tracey collection. For some pieces, I wondered what the people were doing or wearing that seemed to suggest a different accentuation. The idea was confirmed when I watched performances of the pieces. I therefore began to look at the musics I had set out to use not as primordial European surrogates but as Kenyan compositions and performances emanating from indigenous theoretical premises. I set out to discover and describe those foundations.

For this work, I initially excluded transcribing the music and Lulogooli lyrics until I conversed with Ezekiel Kasiera (2004), who interviewed some of the founding parents of Quaker, Pentecostal, and Africanist Christianity among Avalogooli—European, North American, and Logooli. In his manuscript, Kasiera had English translations of songs but not the Lulogooli text. His research cassette tapes were dubbed over. Because Kasiera had also moved to other work and residences, some of his original notes were lost. I was therefore unable to find audiotapes and Lulogooli lyrics of a key song from the 1927 Quaker dissension, so I decided to provide transcripts of lyrics and melodies. The transcriptions have enabled a reading of resilience and transformation in text, tune, and subject matter (social, theological, musical) over time.

The decision to provide notation was also motivated by the practice of solfège singing that was part of my upbringing at home and at school. Music reading was part of the literacy effort of both the missionary and colonial educational enterprise. I wanted to reflect that dimension here. I, however, notated little of the popular music arrangements by Ilavadza because performers in this medium had moved away from missionary and academic thinking about notation. Modern developments provided alternative ways of archiving songs and performances without the notational mediator. Ilavadza and some of his colleagues have a more ambivalent relationship to notation and its association with European music and musicianship than do people of Kemoli's institutional musical education.

In a revisiting of Goibei (2004), I asked my mother and her friends to sing some old songs. (My 1983 and 1985 cassette recordings had been dubbed over with other stuff by a relative who felt the songs were so commonplace, I would find other singers.) These women included my mother, Emmy Kidula, Eside Kidake (died 2011), Rose Luganiro Mugatsia, Violet Kenyani, Jane Muhonja Likomba, Agnetta Sikina, and Jessica Kihung'ani (died 2006) (see fig 8.1). At the beginning of the session, they introduced themselves and stated that though I was interested in just songs, they considered it a church fellowship, so they narrated their faith experience. As we sang, other women passed by, joined us, or made comments. They included, among others, my mother's neighbor, Dora wa Monyi, who was about 85 years old at the time and famous in the village as a song leader, and Hannah Ivayo, another woman over 80 years old and with an infectious sense of humor and vitality that most villagers found refreshing. She was also known for her vast repertoire of songs. The core group was interested in why I wanted old songs. I responded that they were not only part of our collective heritage but they were the foundation for much of the repertoire in the church and elsewhere. They fetched various hymnbooks and selected the songs they thought best represented what they considered old repertoire. The first 'book' songs they selected had to be taught to those who had grown up elsewhere or had previously belonged to other churches. Part of the amusement of those who did not know the songs was in the ways words were fitted to tunes so they made little sense. Some veteran singers spoke out the sentences to clarify the intended meaning. These older women were accustomed to the strange linguistic tonality from years of performances (PURL 8.1).

The group first sang unaccompanied, and then they found a small drum and added it in with the kidindi timeline, completely changing the feel and aesthetic of the music. In time, they forgot that I was recording the music and got 'into the spirit' of the songs. The result was a fusion of songs, beginning with 'book' music, into older 'spirit' songs that they had written out as a set, and eventually they sang repertoire that was contemporary in their church services. Some songs were in Kiswahili. They were so engrossed in the singing that they were shocked into silence when my very simple cassette tape recorder went off. It was evident that they enjoyed the singing, that it served a communal and spiritual function. In fact, my mother had controlled the beginning by deciding on the songs and how to present them for her daughter, who was doing this important research. At the end of the session, the singing 'controlled' the women. One of them took over the lead from my mother in the middle of a set. They ended the session the way they would a church service, with a slower song, without clapping or drumming, and then they prayed before departing. We conducted the sessions for two days. On the second day, they found another drum to make closer to a church accompaniment combo and completely ignored my tape player. I then left for a week. While I was gone, the women organized themselves because I had told them I would return. Al-

Figure 8.1. The core women's group at the Singing session in Goibei.

though they tried to sing with as much freedom as before, the later gatherings were structured in such a way that some songs that had been discontinued due to either changes in theology or musical style were abandoned midsession. We finally discussed matters relating to Logooli traditions and the administration of church affairs to explain certain behaviors and worldviews (PURL 8.2).

When I returned the following year (2005), the ladies who had previously met on my mother's porch continually asked when we would have another sing. They had decided on what they thought I needed and had participants they thought should be included in the sing. They hired themselves out to my mother on the material day. After eating lunch together, we assembled at 1:30 p.m. on the veranda and they decided on a set. They even set the order; some old hymns from the books and then other songs that should have been in the books but had not been included, although they were common lore. They asked me not to record until they had 'rehearsed.' The idea of a rehearsal worked for a while but they became engrossed and forgot about me. I began to record when I realized this was no rehearsal. During a pause I asked if it was OK that I had recorded the rehearsal. They burst into laughter, as they had forgotten that they were rehearsing. As in the previous year, I requested a spirit song—one I remembered from my childhood. They tried to construct a set around it and finally decided to sing and 'let the spirit lead.' One song led to another and culminated in music sung in current gatherings. The set morphed into a session. The session turned into a religious gathering, at times breaking into prayer. I have no idea if my requests invoked certain types of spiritual or other memories. The experience became a dynamic juncture of historical and contemporary repertoire. In musicking Christian song, Goibei women had invigorated their religious beliefs; they had also inscribed, crystallized, and archived their identity.

APPENDIX ONE

ARCHIVAL AND MEDIA HOUSE RECORDS

The African Inland Church houses Christian radio broadcasts transmitted since the 1950s. The house also has selections of religious music and sermon reels dating from 1954, performed by Kenyans, other Africans, Europeans, and Americans. Recording sheets with dates when some items were recorded and aired were present. The search also yielded Bible stories in several African languages (such as Masai, Kisii, Kikuyu) recorded in the 1920s–1940s in Los Angeles and broadcast in the 1950s. I also found recordings of translated hymns such as "Blessed Quietness" in Masai or "My Faith Looks Up to Thee" in Kikamba and "Rock of Ages" in Kiswahili, produced by Gospel Recordings Incorporated—Buenas Nuevas—copyrighted 1947. There were also recordings in Hindi and Gujarati. The singers on the LPs were not acknowledged. I was permitted to search the holdings in Kijabe by the then manager of radio Mr. Stephen Kimetto in May–June 2006 and May 2007.

The British National Library in London had some recordings of Hyslop's works from the 1960s. I could only listen to the music in the library in July 2001 and July 2002.

Berlin Archives holds recordings of Gunther Wagner's research amongst Avalogooli and Bukusu in the 1930s. I had email communication with Suzanne Ziegler July–October 2008.

Earlham College, Indiana, may, to my knowledge, house the most extensive collection of Quaker work in Kenya. The archive had correspondence, reports of minutes, journals, pamphlets, microfilmed reports and board meeting minutes, private and commercially published biographies of Quaker missionaries and of prominent Logooli leaders, dissertations on Quakers and their work in Africa, readers, and hymnals in English and Lulogooli. It also contains letters of Quaker missionaries to the board. *The Africa Record*, a

Quaker journal, had reports from the field from 1905 to 1916. The Lulogooli hymnal published in 1958 seemed to be arranged in the order the songs were added when viewed alongside correspondence and reports by missionaries. The first hymn is "Yesu Akulanga." Later revisions, reprints, and publications have a different order for the hymns. The hymnal also states the source tune used relative to the translated text. Some translations were done from English and others were derived from the Kiswahili hymnal (1897). I had email correspondence with an archivist/historian from November 2007 and visited in November 2008.

Haverford College, Pennsylvania, had special collections on Quaker work. The archive had, to my knowledge, the earliest extant Lulogooli hymnal that I located published in 1920 with fifty-eight hymns. I had email communication with Anne Upton, the archivist or librarian, between December 2008 and March 2009.

Guildford College, North Carolina, had archival holdings of materials related to Quakerism in Kenya from its early beginnings to some contemporary times. There were reports on Quaker work in Kenya by missionaries, visitors, and denominational administrators. I had email communication with the librarian and archivist from March 2008. I visited the location September 2008.

Kenya National Archives holds correspondence, reports, news clippings, and other documents regarding Graham Hyslop, 1941–1977, and the Kenya music education system. It also has materials on early colonial and missionary contact with Avalogooli. I searched the archives June–August 1995, June 2001, June 2002, May–June 2003, May 2004.

PAOC Archives, Mississauga, Ontario, houses reports from missionaries in Kenya (1920s–1970) collated in "Kenya files." Included are silent movies, videos, and correspondence by and with missionaries in Kenya. In addition, the archive has minutes of board meetings in Kenya and Canada regarding the missionary work and early reports in the *Pentecostal Testimony* by missionaries and administrators. I searched the archive in March 2004.

The Swarthmore College, Pennsylvania, archives have holdings of Mrs. Deborah Rees's original correspondence from the field to her family from 1899 until she retired in the 1920s. It is labeled *African Papers RG5/329*. Some material is repeated in the journal *American Friend* in the same year or at a later time. Most of the correspondence was kept by her family until it was donated to the library through Rose Adede, the daughter of Emory Rees's African co-worker Joel Litu. The archive has Deborah Rees's original letters from the mission field in South Africa and Kenya. Also in the archive are the journal *American Friend* and *Freedman's Reports* for information about the process of translating hymns, interaction with Africans, and so forth, 1899–1926. For more information, see http://www.swarthmore.edu/library/friends/ead/5239rees.xml. Email correspondence with archivists from November 2007, visit March 2008.

APPENDIX TWO

SONG TEXT AND HYMN TUNE SOURCES

Sources have been categorized and arranged in alphabetical order by title since some do not include the editor's or compiler's name or the place and date of publication.

HYMNALS AND SONGBOOK COMPILATIONS IN ENGLISH—NON-AFRICAN PUBLICATIONS

Billy Graham Crusade Songs. Minneapolis: Billy Graham Evangelistic Association, 1960.

Choice Light and Life Songs: A Collection of the Best Loved Gospel Songs and Choruses, both Old and New for the Sunday School, Young People's Meeting, Evangelistic Service and Children's Service. Compiled by LeRoy M. Lowell [et al.]. Winona Lake, Ind.: Light and Life Press, 1950.

Come Rejoice. Edited by Michael Perry. London: Marshall Pirckering, Hope Publishing House, 1989.

Favorites: A Collection of Gospel Songs for Solo, Duet, Trio, Quartet and Group Singing. Vols. 1, 3, 4, compiled by Alfred Smith. Grand Rapids, Mich.: Zondervan Publishing House, 1943, 1951, 1956. Vol. 5, compiled by Alfred Smith and John C. Peterson, 1961. Vol. 6, 7, compiled by John C. Peterson, 1966, 1971.

Fillmores' Gospel Songs: For Young People's Meetings, Prayer Meetings, Revival Meetings and Sunday-Schools. Palmer Hartsough and J.H. Fillmore. Cincinnati: Fillmore Bros., 1898.

The Good Old Songs: The Cream of the Old Music; a Choice Collection of the Good Old Hymns and Tunes as They Were Sung by Our Fathers and Mothers. Compiled by Elder C. H. Cayce. Thornton, Ark.: Cayce Pub. Co., 1978, 1913.

Gospel Hymns and Songs: For the Church, Sunday School and Evangelistic Services. Compiled by Homer A. Rodeheaver. Chicago: Rodeheaver Company, [1920s?].

Hymns of the Christian Life. Harrisburg, Pa.: Christian Publications, 1936.

Inspiring Gospel Solos and Duets: A Collection of Special Songs for Soloists and Singing Groups. Compiled by Haldor Lillenas. Kansas City: Lillenas Pub. Co., [1943?].

Inspiring Hymns. Compiled by Alfred B. Smith. Grand Rapids, Mich.: Zondervan Publishing House, 1951.

Joyful Songs. Compiled by Cliff Barrows. Minneapolis: Billy Graham Evangelistic Association, 1977.

Living Praise: Words Edition. Basingstoke, England: Marshall Morgan and Scott, 1983.

New Songs of Inspirations Books. Vols. 2, 3, 5, 6, 7, 8, 9. Nashville: John T. Benson Publishing Company, 1952, 1958, 1963, 1965, 1967, 1970, 1973.

Old Fashioned Revival Hour Songs No. 2 Music. Compiled by Charles E. Fuller and H. Leland Green. Winona Lake, Ind.: Rodeheaver, Hall-Mack, 1955.

Pentecostal Hymns: No. 3: A Winnowed Collection for Evangelistic Services, Young People's Societies and Sunday Schools. Selected by Henry Date. Hope Publications, 1902.

Redemption Hymnal. Eastbourne, England: Victory Press, 1951.

Redemption Songs: 1000 Hymns and Choruses. Glasgow: Pickering and Inglis Ltd., 1900.

Tabernacle Hymns No. Two: Issued in Round and Shaped Notes. Chicago: Tabernacle Publishing Co., 1921.

Tabernacle Hymns, Number Four; a Choice Collection of Hymns and Songs for Every Religious Use. Chicago: Tabernacle Publishing Co., 1941.

HYMNALS AND SONGBOOK COMPILATIONS MAINLY IN ENGLISH—KENYA PUBLICATIONS

CA Song Book. Kisumu, Kenya: Evangel Press, 1962. Mostly English, some Kiswahili.

CAIM Song Book. Kisumu, Kenya: Evangel Press, [1971?]. Mostly English. A few Kiswahili.

Golden Bells. Nairobi: Scripture Union of Kenya, 1969. English.

Hymns of Faith. Nairobi: Scripture Union, 1964. English.

Nyang'ori Secondary School Chapel Song Book. n.d. English and some Kiswahili.

Songs of Life. KCC/STC, 2001. English.

Victory Songbook. Nairobi: Reginah Professional Designers, 1986. English and a few Kiswahili.

Voices Aflame: Songs from East Africa. Nairobi: Step Magazine, 1988. English and a few Kiswahili.

KENYAN LANGUAGE HYMNALS/SONGBOOKS

Avaana voosi kwimbe. Nairobi: Evangel Publishing House, 1964. Lulogooli.

Nditsominya Yahova ne Tsinyimbu. Hymn booklets self-printed by Gideon Wesley H. Mwelesa, 1978. Mostly Lulogooli, a few Kiswahili.

Nditsominya Yahova ne Tsinyimbu. Hymnbook compiled by Gideon Wesley H. Mwelesa. Eldoret, Kenya: Primus Media Service, 1988. Mostly Lulogooli, a few Kiswahili.

Nyimbo Standard. Nairobi: Uzima Press, 1974. (First published by SPCK 1897.) Kiswahili.

Nyimbo Standard Mpya. London: SPCK, 1968. Kiswahili with melody in solfège.

Nyimbo za Injili. Nairobi: Evangel Publishing House, 1959. Kiswahili.

Nyimbo za Jeshi La Wokovu. Kijabe, Kenya: Kijabe Printing Press, 1993. Kiswahili.

Nyimbo za Kikristo. Soni TZ: Vuga Press, 1984. Kiswahili.

Nyimbo za Kumsifu Mungu za Zamani na Mpya. Kimilili, Kenya: Elgon Religious Society of Friends, 1975. Kiswahili and Bukusu languages.

Nyimbo za Sifa. Mwanza, Tanzania: Inland Publishers, 1982. (First published 1964.) Kiswahili.

Nyimbo za Wokovu: Toleo la Afrika Mashariki. [Ngaramtoni, Tanzania?]: Kituo cha Maandiko habari Maalum, 1992. Kiswahili

Tenzi za Rohoni. Nairobi: Baptist Publications House, 1983. Kiswahili.

Tsinyembo tsia Obwehaani. Kisumu, Kenya: Church of God Mission, n.d. English titles, Kinyore translations, in 4 part staff notation. Lunyore.

Tsinyimbu tsya Nyasaye. East African Yearly Meeting of the Religious Society of Friends, 1966. Lulogooli and other Luyia languages

Tsinyimbu tsya Sunday School, 2nd ed. Kaimosi, Kenya: East African Yearly Meeting of Friends, 1966. Lulogooli and Kiswahili text.

Tsinyimbu tsyo Kwidzominya Nyasaye. Kaimosi, Kenya: East African Yearly Meeting of Friends, 1958. Lulogooli, mainly Luyia languages.

Tsinyimbu Tsyokwidzominya Nyasaye. Maragoli Station, Kenya: Friends Africa Mission Press, 1920. Lulogooli, mainly other Luyia languages.

Wende Injili. Nairobi: Evangel Publishing House. 1964. Luo language.

GLOSSARY OF TERMS

Abaluyia: also Valuyia, Abaluhya, Avaluhya, Valuhya, Baluhya, Abalusha, Avalusha, Valusha (sing. muluyia or mluyia). A Bantu culture and language cluster. Name of people group residing mostly in Western Kenya and consisting of at least sixteen subgroups. So called by the British since 1948 because of commonalities in linguistic and cultural history as well as political structures.

Africanist churches: also known as African independent churches, African Initiated Churches, or separatist churches. This term was mostly used to refer to Christian churches begun by African initiative and leadership from the beginning of the twentieth century until the 1970s. Originally they were perceived as being cultish. After this time, other terms are used depending on religious persuasion and location; for example, deliverance churches, nondenominational churches, and so forth.

Akorino: the Holy Ghost East Africa church commonly known as Akorino church is an Africanist church founded by Agikuyu people in the 1920s in Kenya. It was well known for its resistance to European customs and politics associated with Christianity. It sought for an African-centered and incepted Christian ethos.

Amakono: hands.

Avaana: children (sing. Mwana).

Avabukusu: also Babukusu (sing. mubukusu or mbukusu). Luyia subgroup of Bukusu heritage and descent.

Avadirichi: also Badirichi, Avatiriki (sing. Mudirichi or mdirichi). Luyia subgroup of Tiriki heritage and descent.

Avakeere: old women, or respectful term for married women.

Avalogooli: also Balogooli (sing. Mlogooli or mulogooli). Luyia subgroup of Logooli heritage and descent.

Avanyore: also Banyore (sing. munyore or mnyore). Luyia subgroup of Nyore heritage and descent.

Avasaalisi: priests (sing. musaalisi).

Avatsotso: also Batsotso, Abatsotso (sing. mutsotso). Luyia subgroup of Tsotso lineage and descent.

Avidakho: also Abidakho, Bidakho (sing. mwidakho). Luyia subgroup of Idakho lineage and descent.

Avisukha: also Visukha, Abisukha (sing. Mwisukha). Luyia subgroup of Isukha lineage and descent.

Bantu: generically means people/human beings. Most widely used as a term for more than five hundred language family groups found in Eastern, Central, and Southern Africa.

Bukusu: see Avabukusu.

Dholuo: language spoken by the Nilotic Luo people found mostly in the Western part of Kenya in Nyanza Province.

Dzimbala: blemishes, scars.

Edzinyimbu: also tsinyimbu. Songs (sing. lwimbu, ulwimbu).

Ekilili: shadow.

Elyimbu: funeral dirge songs—a derogatory, sarcastic, despicable reference to tsinyimbu.

Emungu: a reference to God.

Esai: a reference to God.

Ethnohymnody: hymnody emanating from a particular ethnic or culture group.

Gikuyu: also Kikuyu, Agikuyu. A Bantu culture and language group resident mostly in Central Kenya.

Idakho: see Avidakho. Also land where Avidakho reside.

Igwalide: a procession in file formation. Derived from Kiswahili word gwalide meaning a filed procession of soldiers.

Ikitabu: also Kitabu. Book (pl. Ivitabu/Vitabu).

Ikorasi: a chorus (pl. Tsikorasi).

Ikwaya: a choir (pl. Tsikwaya).

Imiluka: rituals, rites, customs.

Indovondovo: one-stringed earth fiddle.

Indumba: drum, usually side drum version used in church. Word derived from onomatopeic sound du-mba.

Ing'oma: drum, dance accompanied by the drum, entertainment dance.

Isahi: reference to God.

Isalasini: lit. 'of the 30th.' Indicates a meeting where different small churches assemble together at the end of the month. Also refers to tithe.

Isigudi: also Sugudi, Isugudi, Isikuti, Sikuti. Indigenous Luyia/Logooli drum ensemble made up of two to three cylindrico-conical drums. Also name of associated dance and songs.

Isilika: a women's cooperative association.

GLOSSARY OF TERMS

Isukha: see Avisukha. Also the land where Avisukha reside.
Itiru: a wooden pole. Also name for the central pole in a house/hut.
Itumbi: house/hut where circumcised initiates reside during seclusion/healing period.
Ivulogooli: land where Avalogooli reside.
Kalenjin: Southern nilotic language and culture cluster found in the Rift Valley Province of Kenya.
Kamba: also Akamba. Bantu culture group resident in Eastern Province of Kenya.
Kanzu: long gown such as that worn by Arab merchants or Muslim adherents.
Kayamba: a raft tray-shaped box idiophone made from bamboo reed and filled with seeds, originating from coastal Kenya and Tanzania.
Kebende: in the manner of Pentecostals. Also means comportment with pride and confidence.
Kehenda mwoyo: anxiety, 'worries of the heart.'
Kidindi: also called mudindi, the smallest, highest-pitched drum in Isigudi or church drum ensemble.
Kiriri: one-stringed box fiddle.
Kisii: Kisii is the name of the land where Abagusii people reside. Abagusii are Bantu language speakers found in southwest Nyanza Province in Kenya.
Kisili: a hoe. Also the name of the instrument that looks like a hoe—or when the iron hoe itself is turned into an instrument.
Kisiliva: trumpet, trumpet sound.
Kisungu: in the manner of Europeans, in an arrogant manner.
Koyeridza: the action of landing something that was in flight, for example, an airplane, a bird.. Also a musical term for a type of response to a call. Koyeridza is derived from the term Koyera, a word used to refer to a sunset or moon setting.
Kufuminya: lit. the action of enclosing as a covering. Group verbal or vocable interjections in agreement with a prayer. A musical term for a response group vamp surrounding/enclosing a soloist's improvisation.
Kugona mu maliga: lit. 'to sleep in tears.' Official phrase that means to spend the night at the bereaved person's home. To keep vigil at the bereaved person's home. Usually refers to the period before burial.
Kuhana mwoyo: to set the starting pitch. Also means to encourage.
Kuhihiza: lit. to herald or to announce, especially referring to the practice of caroling before Christmas Day or night sings before the wedding day to broadcast the event and laud the virtues of the betrothed.
Kuhola: to sing with all your heart but also related to deep-chested vocal timbre in low range.
Kuhuluka: to calm down, to unstress, to relax. Also a musical term denoting properties such as releasing tension or approaching a cadence.

Kukesha: Kiswahili word meaning to stay awake all night, usually as a vigil.
Kusaalila mwana: to pray for a child. Prayers for infant or child dedication.
Kusieva mavega: lit. to dance the shoulders. Also the name of a dance where the shoulders have the action.
Kutuula: to set down, to resolve. Musical term.
Kuva mwoyo: to be alive.
Kuvahila: to elope.
Kuvina mavega: to dance the shoulders.
Kuvugula: to take up, over, to lift. Musical term.
Kwaya: see Ikwaya.
Kwimba: to sing.
Kwitakasa: to set oneself apart. To sanctify oneself. A religious term.
Lidorondo: an aerophone made of dry bamboo stalks that are serrated.
Lidungu: a six- to eight-stringed lyre.
Lilungu: technically an 'attic' constructed in the kitchen, a little adjacent to the fireplace and over the cowshed that serves to dry and store firewood and some kitchen utensils.
Ling'ala: a pipe aerophone made from lidorondo plant to which a horn is tied with a strip of hide. Also the name for a loudspeaker.
Lingala: trade language used extensively in the Congos. Also a type of popular music emanating from the Congos. The music is also known as Soukous, Congolese, and by its various subgenres, for example, Madiaba.
Lipala: a popular music/dance begun in the late 1960s.
Liswakila: a ceremony performed for newborns.
Logooli: a root noun of Avalogooli onto which different prefixes are attached to construct meanings that denote things of, place of, people of Logooli descent or origin.
Lubukusu: language of Avabukusu.
Ludirichi: language of Avadirichi.
Luganda: language of Baganda people of Uganda.
Luhya: also Luyia, Lusha. Root noun for Abaluyia on which different prefixes are adjoined to construct meanings that denote things of, place of, people of Luyia descent or origin. Also means the clan or culture group's council of elders that typically meet around a hearth consisting of three stones where a fire was usually lit.
Lulogooli: also Luragoli. Language of Avalogooli.
Luluyia: language of Abaluyia.
Luo: Nilotic culture group resident in Nyanza Province of Kenya. Neighbor Abaluyia.
Lusimbu: a porch constructed around the house but without rails.
Lutsotso: language of Avatsotso.

GLOSSARY OF TERMS

Luyia: see Luhya.
Luvego: hair-shaving mortuary rite. Also where inheritance matters are discussed.
Lwidakho: language of Avidakho.
Lwimbu: also ulwimbu. A song (pl. tsinyimbu).
Lwisukha: language of Avisukha.
Lyaluku: the graduation ceremony for circumcised initiates.
Maboyi: sing. Liboyi. Derogatory term for house slave derived from the word 'boy.'
Makono: see amakono.
Makumbusho: commemoration/anniversary ceremony for deceased.
Makwaya: generic name for a genre of church music performed by choral groups in SATB. Derived from the word 'choir.'
Malago: lit. commandments, rules, or laws. Song and scripture recitation contest held on Christmas Day.
Maragoli: technical, outsider, Kenya/colonial government name for the land where Avalogooli reside—where their primary residential heritage is located.
Mbumbeele: a ceremonial to invoke healing for an infant. Also the name of the song used in the ceremonial.
Mfwani: the one who lights (a fire, e.g.).
Mima: mores, traditions, manners.
Mudindi: see kidindi.
Mudukilu: mature, proper, appropriate person.
Muletelli: one who leads a song or who calls a song.
Mulogooli: a person of Logooli descent or heritage (pl. Avalogooli).
Mundu: a person, a human being (pl. Avandu).
Musaalisi: a priest (pl. Avasaalisi).
Musoomi: one who reads, one who has been to school, one who embraced Christianity or the way of the book, a child who goes to school (pl. Avasoomi or Vasoomi).
Mutivo: a music/dance style popular since the late 1960s.
Mwana: a child (pl. Vaana or Avaana).
Mwifwa: consanguine relationship through maternal clan.
Mwimbaji: Kiswahili for singer. Logooli term for a gospel music performer.
Mwing'oma: in the place of Ang'oma, the primal Logooli ancestor.
Mwoyo: also Umwoyo. Heart, attitude, pitch, voice parts, and related concepts.
Mwoyo muliduhu: a heavy heart, musical term for a dense low-pitched timbre. A voice that carries because of great harmonics.
Mwoyo muzeleleku: a smooth vocal quality, well modulated, and so forth.
Ombili/omuvili: the body.
Ovwali: the altar.
Risafu: reserve, homesteads where colonists confined locals in Kenya. Also colloquial for rural home.

Sen-sen: sesame seeds.

Siguuku: Christmas Day, appropriated from Kiswahili siku kuu, meaning high day, holiday, important day.

Teso: also Iteso. Nilotic ethnic and culture group neighboring Abaluyia with some members in Uganda.

Tiriki: land of Avadirichi, also generic national name for the language and people group.

Tsikorasi: choruses (sing. Ikorasi). Appropriated from the English equivalent.

Tsikwaya: choirs (sing. Ikwaya). Appropriated from the English equivalent.

Tsingelosi: angels (sing. Ingelosi). Appropriated from the English equivalent.

Tsinyimbu: songs (sing. lwimbu, ulwimbu). Also spelled edzinyimbu.

Tsitumbi: pl. for itumbi.

Tsotso: root noun for Avatsotso—an Abaluyia subgroup.

Ulwimbu: also lwimbu. A song.

Umwoyo/mwoyo: heart, pitch, attitude, and related concepts.

Uvulogooli: that which constitutes Logooli essence.

Vabende: Pentecostals (sing Mbende or Mubende).

Vadirichi: see Avadirichi.

Vafurenzi: Quakers, Friends derived from the English word 'friends.'

Vasoomi: sing. Musoomi. Schoolchildren, those who have been to school, those who embraced the way of the book. A division of Avadirichi circumcision ritual members who embraced Christianity.

Vika: steps, stairs, procedures.

Vushuhuda: testimonies. Processional to a designated place to witness or testify about conversion. Appropriated from Swahili word ushuhuda.

Yabese: wrestling match.

Zimbemba: jealousy, covetousness, envy, resentment.

NOTES

1. PRELUDE

1. See Ogot and Welbourn (1966) for the beginnings of breakaway Africanist churches.
2. See Jones (1976), Olson (1979), Weman (1960).
3. See Carrington (1948), Kauffman (1964), Louw (1956, 1958).
4. See Corbitt (1985), King (1989, 1999).
5. See Euba (1992).
6. See Turner (1967), Martin (1975).
7. See Martin (1975), Gifford (2004).
8. See Kidula (1999a).
9. See Malm (1984), Coplan (1985), Graham (1988), May and Stapleton (1987).
10. See Erlmann (1991, 1996), Muller (1999), Askew (2002).
11. See Corbitt (1985, 1994), King (1989).
12. See Kidula (1998), Chitando (2002).
13. Also spelled Abaluhya and pronounced by Avalogooli as Avalusha.
14. A hallmark of the British colonial divide and rule axiom was to establish administrative structures "based on what came to be termed tribes, subtribes, and clans. For most of the region, the period prior to the conquest had not been characterized by the type of ethnic identity that emerged under colonial rule. Rather, fluidity marked the experience of many peoples as individuals, families, small segments of clans, and clans shifted identity and allegiance between various groups" (Maxon 2002, 101).
15. The Nandi are a Nilotic language and culture group, a part of the Kalenjin cluster found in Western and Rift Valley provinces in Kenya.
16. For example, my father's family, who immigrated to Goibei in the 1930s, are Avalogooli. My mother's family are Avanyore. However, due to her family's migration to Ivoi, a no-man's-land in precolonial times, my mother spoke Lumasaana, a Lulogooli dialect that incorporates words from Luo, Terik, Nandi, and Somali non-Bantu languages.
17. Kiswahili was adopted based on the misconception that African languages were really mutually intelligible dialects. It was also assumed that Kiswahili, as a trade language, was understood everywhere. A hymnal and Bible in Kiswahili were published in the nineteenth century.
18. For discussions of some findings, see Kidula (2005a, 2008).

2. ASSEMBLY

1. The clan is a community of extended patrilineal families tracing their lineage to the founder of the group.

2. Oral and historical information on Avalogooli is collated from Wagner (1949), Osogo (1966), Sangree (1966), Were (1967a, 1967b), Kasiera (1981), Mulindi (1983), and Kidula's research (1983–2011).

3. Kasiera (1981, 5) speculates that 'Maragoli' may be how early Arab traders referenced Avalogooli. There are other, more humorous myths regarding this misnomer (see, e.g., Ifedha 2008).

4. The word *luhya* (*lusha, luhia*) refers to the evening or morning fire hearths where elders (men) gathered to socialize, strategize, and adjudicate clan matters. The term also references where and when the council of elders meets and the process of governance, with or without a fire. *Avaluhya* (*Ava oluhya*) can further be translated to mean those governed by or identified with a particular assembly, huddle, convocation, or subgroup. The term Avaluhya likely was also adopted for an assembly that identified itself with the phrase "Ava oluhya lwa . . . ," meaning members of the community of, speakers of the dialect of, and so forth. There are terms more specific to kinship or lineage, for example, *Mwana we inyumba ya Zakayo*—a descendant of the house of Zakayo.

5. With this tripartite imaging of a human being, ideas of body, soul, and spirit, as well as the notion of a Christian triune godhead, were readily appropriated into Logooli worldviews.

6. For example, in Goibei, Daliani (Italian) was born while the father was conscripted by the British to fight against the Italians in Somalia during World War II.

7. A response to relationship queries yields such statements as *Mbeye mmaavi, mwifwa mkizungu* (I am a descendant of the house/clan of Maavi, with matrilineal lineage from the house/clan of Kizungu).

8. Names also signify whether Christianity or Islam was adopted by the parents. For example, James Mutira identifies with Christianization, while Abdul Mutira implies Islamization. Mutira is the Logooli/Luyia affiliation.

9. For the transcription, other lullabies, and further reading, see Mulindi (1983, 152–166).

10. *Mbombela* is a diminutive on the word for soothing—*Kuhombelitsa*. In the first person, one would say "Mbombelitsa." It contains the idea of pacifying, lulling, pleading, calming, persuading, and so forth.

11. Wagner's (1949) accounts were drawn from Avalogooli, some of whom lived in pre-Christian times. I compared his work to texts by Were (1967a, 1967b), Osogo (1966), Kasiera (1981), Mulindi (1983), and my own research findings (Kidula 1986). Wagner's work was further weighed against missionary and other anthropological accounts by Marian Keller (1933, 1946), Spencer (1975), Hotchkiss (1937), Stafford (1973), and Rasmussen (1995).

12. In the 1980s, Logooli politician Moses Mudavadi commissioned a document of Logooli cultural systems and religious beliefs from ethnographic and oral resources. A collated volume of the findings was never realized. It was difficult to locate and review the scattered documents after Mudavadi's death in 1989. According to Mwelesa (2007), a member of the research consortium, initial findings indicated that certain traditions are still practiced in a manner believed unchanged. Some beliefs and values have been discontinued while others have been altered or subverted.

13. Wagner (1949, 90–177) consigns religion and magic under one large heading. He discusses how each was evinced in nature, in humanity (amateur and specialist cases), and in the spiritual realm (from specialist humans, to ancestors, to supreme beings). Wako's (1954) findings reiterate the centrality of the magico-religious from mundane affairs to deeply spiritual tasks. Osogo's (1966, 26–27) discussion of kinship and naming attributes clan formation to taboos, totems, and religious practices at departure rites. Thus origins, continuity, the physical, and the metaphysical were ascribed religious determination and manifestation or coated with religious and other spiritual nuances. Amutabi's (2002, 71–83) analysis centralizes music in the cultural historiography of the Abaluyia.

14. The Logooli word for Christian God is *Nyasaye*—which is related to the words Esai or Isahi.

15. Ang'oma is tied to notions of music making: one term for a dance party and drum is *Ing'oma*. This suggests that music is intrinsic to intercession, relationship to the divine, and entertainment. Further, the Christian idea of Christ—the man who died, yet was present from creation—as a mediator or intercessor resonated with Logooli worldviews about Ang'oma and other ancestors as intermediaries between the living and the divine.

16. Christian ideas of purity of priests, public, sacrifices/sacrificial offerings, and for special places/buildings and ceremonies for collective worship resonated with the Logooli worldview.

17. Mulindi (1983, 90) asserts that Avalogooli believe that music in spiritual context "has the power to 'bring the thoughts near' (reducing one's preoccupation with negative thoughts). It is said to eliminate tension and bring happiness . . . increases one's energy, . . . is able to communicate certain verbal ideas with greater force than ordinary words."

18. Christian groups adopted this practice when they gather for a joint event or festival. It is, however, unclear if clans had identity markers such as the flags used by Christian groups.

19. In 2005, I observed Goibei women always 'accidentally' spilling food or drink while moving it from the fire. Such behavior may be a throwback to the veneration of offerings to ancestors.

20. As with Christian beliefs, Avalogooli acknowledged a Supreme Creator overseeing human affairs, spirits with good and evil intentions, and human agency and empowerment by both God and spirits in a world vaulted by heaven and hell. Additionally Kasiera (1981, 547) speculates that the Trinitarian concept was physically evinced in the structure of the cooking hearth made up of three stones. I further assert that it was symbolically encapsulated in the idea of a family understood as a father, a mother, and a child (children).

21. From discussions in 2005, if a woman has no children, it has to be established that she was 'properly' married, that is, if there had been some exchange of dowry. If she was dowered, she is buried at her husband's home. If not, her kin bury her along the fence of her parents' homestead.

22. While this report is in the past tense, Wagner's (1949) study in the 1930s, Osogo's (1966) studies in the 1950s, Mulindi's (1983) study in the early 1980s, and my fieldwork between 1983 and 2008 confirmed that basic roles of rites remained unchanged, although their expressions may have been transformed with the adoption of Christianity. Muller (1999, 162) remarks, "the myths and stories of the biblical Old Testament . . . provided a rich store of analogous socio-cultural and political contexts for the integration of African traditional beliefs with those of Western Christianity." Rites of passage are a treasure

house for examining platforms for the negotiation of identity and belonging in the encounter of belief systems of divergent roots.

23. I have elsewhere discussed the male initiation rites I observed between 1969 and 1992 in the village (Kidula 1999b) and the role and impact of the lyrics of classic circumcision songs (Kidula 2005b).

24. Wagner (1949) observed these practices in the 1930s; Mulindi (1983) saw them in the early 1980s. The women in the Goibei discussion group (2004) confirmed their presence in the twenty-first century in various forms.

25. For complete Lulogooli lyrics and translations, see Wagner (1949, 333–334) and Mulindi (1983, 160–161). Mulindi's work also contains a music transcription.

26. For more discussion of this song and alternate transcription in common time, see Kidula 2005b.

27. The word for elope, *kuvahila*, is rooted in the concept of taking a winged flight.

28. This reading of the text was derived from discussions with the Goibei women's group (2004–2005).

29. For a discussion of Logooli weddings and an analysis of "Mwana wa mberi," see Kidula 2009.

30. Author's observations and discussions with villagers (1983, 1991, 2004–2006) corroborated accounts by Wagner (1949, 159–167) and Kasiera (1981, 542–548).

31. Ezinzikuulu can translate as 'for mourning or wailing.' These were usually solo songs in free rhythm, in vocables, or with text in lament of the deceased. They had characteristic vocable texts and rhythms. For more discussion, see Mulindi (1983, 132–135).

32. The term for a song is *ulwimbu*. **Ely**imbu implies something that is despised or despicable or done because one must do it, not of free will or from a good heart but in desperation or spite. It is derogatory. Wagner (1949) transcribed several texts of these songs (462–466). He also identifies a dirge category called *edzinyimbu*—songs. This category was related to cattle drives, like a victory chant celebrating the life of a warrior. The example provided testifies to Wagner's assertion that Avalogooli, Christianized for more than thirty years by the time of his research, already had ritual songs referencing Christianity.

33. The original song had a 4 feel or was in $\frac{12}{8}$ with the last measure in $\frac{6}{8}$, but the dirge is a 2 feel in $\frac{6}{8}$ time.

34. By the 1970s, adults were buried in late morning or early afternoon. Young children were buried in the morning. Since the 1980s, most children and adults are buried late morning, early afternoon.

35. Kasiera (1981, 32) provides the reading that in death, one became a friend to all. The deceased no longer held sway over the living in the natural, neither for friends nor enemies. He analyzed a conversational piece in Wagner (1949, 294) and Sangree (1966, 37) to demonstrate the kind of dialogue the living simulated with the deceased for exoneration.

36. From my observation (1990s), older people preparing to die wanted to be 'buried well,' with dignity and be named—so as to continue to live through future progeny. Some even set aside some food supplies so if they died before a harvest, mourners would be fed. This behavior is a change from the practice in the 1960s when, as a child, I observed villagers organize meals for the bereaved family and mourners because the immediate family was too distraught to effectively manage the situation. The generosity also served to promote the reputation of the village for future marital relationship, as a place with well-bred women, or to attract girls looking for responsible and generous men.

3. ENCOUNTER

1. The beginnings of Christianity in Eastern Africa are documented in texts such as William Anderson (1977), Barrett (1986), Fashole-Luke (1978), Hastings (1979), Hildebrandt (1981), Ogot and Kieran (1967), Oliver (1965), Strayer (1978), and Were and Wilson (1971). A timeline from 1498 to 1972 is outlined by Barrett et al. (1973, 21–28).

2. Slaves were resettled in Freretown, so named after the British Sir Bartle Frere, who negotiated treaties with the Omani sultans who 'owned' Zanzibar. Frere subsequently argued for missionaries, as neutral political agents, to organize and manage slave resettlements. Slavery was officially abolished in Zanzibar in 1897.

3. The policy of comity was officially ratified in 1909 (Barrett et al. 1973, 23), but the agreement had tacitly been effected from the late 1890s with the influx of mission organizations in Kenya and the realization that ethnic groups spoke different languages. The policy not only established spheres of influence; it promoted cooperation among missions instead of isolationist claims on behalf of sending countries and organizations. For an example of the cooperative nature of the policy, see Virginia Blackburn's (1909) report on a conference where missionaries from different societies met, fellowshipped, and compared methods, results, and projects.

4. Christianity, introduced to Baganda in mid-nineteenth century, was fraught with fights between Catholics and Protestants and between Christians and Muslims. However, with British colonial interests, this situation was somewhat stabilized by the time the first Anglican missionaries to the Buganda of Uganda arrived in 1877. An Anglican diocese was formed in 1884 for the jurisdiction of Kenya, Uganda, and Tanganyika (Anderson, W. 1977, 22–39). One route into Uganda was through Luyia country, hence the presence of an Anglican outpost in Logooli country.

5. Kaimosi was until 1978 the Kenyan headquarters for Quakers (Rasmussen 1995). In 1973, Avabukusu broke off to form a separate Yearly Meeting. By the mid-1980s, Quakers from Vihiga, an early missionary settlement in Ivulogooli, decided to separate from Kaimosi. Further splits amongst Avalogooli have since followed. Most splits have occurred along Logooli dialect and clan lines (Mwavali 2005).

6. The records contain minutes of board meetings and letters to the denominational headquarters and sending churches of the missionaries. The histories are occasionally summarized in missionary reports contained in minutes or journal reports. See, for example, *Africa Record* 1912b.

7. Rees wrote the report about experiences during some of their first missionary years while on furlough in the United States.

8. Wendte was not a missionary with FAIM. He visited the mission in 1904 and was killed during a local skirmish. He kept a diary whose entries were published in several issues of the *American Friend*. During his visit, he traveled with the missionaries. In his diary, he discussed the Africans they met, the music they played, and the missionaries' work. He noted that the children

> had daily school lasting two hours after a drumbeat at 2 P.M. They are learning to read and write and arithmetic too, in Swahili... The daily life of the Friends here is thus... Breakfast at 6.30... Then one of our boys beats a Uganda drum... This is the call to service... This service... begins with a hymn from the Kiswahili hymnbook, accompanied by the tune played by Virginia Blackburn on a portable organ ... After preaching, there is another hymn... At noon the drum beats and laborers

come in to their mid-day food ... drum beats at six o'clock to call men home for the day ... On the First-day, there is no work ... We all put on better clothes to impress the natives ... There is a piece of steel rail hanging from a tree ... After breakfast, Edgar Hole whangs this with a sledge hammer to remind the natives that this is the First-day and they are expected at the meeting. Edgar Hole calls this "ringing the church bell." ... The service is very similar to the week day; perhaps one or two more hymns and always a longer preaching." (Wendte 1904, 760, 812, 813)

9. The website http://www.swarthmore.edu/library/friends/ead/5239rees.xml (accessed March 14, 2008) contains a summary of notes, correspondence, journal articles, and clippings of Emory and Deborah Rees during their tenure in South Africa and Kenya from 1899 to 1925.

10. I located uncatalogued readers and hymnals at a Library of Congress storage facility in 1986. I was permitted to search through the documents and take notes but not to photocopy nor borrow the items. According to the collection, the first readers were printed in Maragoli by Emory Rees from 1908 and revised, along with additional readers, arithmetic texts, a hymnal, some books of the Bible, and weekly scripture lessons by 1913 (also recorded by Kasiera 1981, 167; Stafford 1973, 95). The complete Lulogooli New Testament translated by Emory Rees assisted by Joel Litu was first published by the American Bible Society in 1928. The oldest hymnal I physically found was at Haverford College dated 1920. It had fifty-eight songs (FAIM 1920).

11. See Kasiera (1981); Keller, M. (1933); and PAOC Archives on the Kellers and mission work in Kenya.

12. Lit. 'of pente' [Pentecostal] heritage/descent/faith. Among its implications, the term denotes courage, mixed with confidence and a touch of defiance. It has been appropriated into Lulogooli with such phrases as *Yahenza kebende*—meaning the person displays an attitude of independence, a mixture of confidence and arrogance.

13. Kasiera (1981, 345) asserts that "spirit possession was one of the common features in dances and cattle drive parades in the wake of the death of an eminent person in a given community." Cattle drives (*elisona*) were conducted not only on behalf of well-respected men; Wagner had observed such honors for "well known and respected old women" (Wagner 1949, 453). Passing out and spirit possession at drives was condemned as of the devil by missionaries and Logooli Christians. The practices honored the spirit of the deceased and promoted beliefs that spirits of the deceased visited the living because the newly dead were unsettled, their affairs had not been properly or sufficiently addressed, or they were haunting the person visited. The host had to make proper propitiation or he or she eventually became "weak, emaciated and ultimately dies" (Wagner 1949, 164). On the other hand, interaction with the spirit world led to possessing power and gaining hidden knowledge for good or evil by human agency in healing, blessing, and cursing.

14. African Israel Church Nineveh broke away from Nyang'ori Pentecostal Mission. It was officially registered in 1942. As such, its fundamental doctrines were as Pentecostal as those of PAOC but with an African leadership informed by local and indigenous outlooks, leading to some differences in the interpretation and performance of the scriptures.

15. Footage in the PAOC Archives in Mississauga, Ontario, of silent movies included hand clapping. Africans clapped like the missionaries present. The occasion in 1948, a church-opening ceremony, was witnessed by denominational officials from Canada. Included in the footage are Christmas festivities recorded between the 1930s and 1950s. I

compared the clapping with footage from a Christmas program I filmed in 1994. The differences in clapping stance were remarkable. One was as careful and posed as the other was exuberant and deliberately metronomic.

16. Analysis of both 'book' music and indigenous Logooli hymns in later chapters illustrates this process.

17. The Salvation Army had a distinctive uniform. Their procession was in double file like a secular military or police force. They looked smart, purposeful, and unified. They carried flags. Further, they adapted the hymns to a marching band style. They were known not to use an Africanized side drum but would actually have the side/base drum. In some instances as was available, they played brass band instruments. Often they also included tambourines onto which ribbons were tied. These were rhythmed and twirled with precision by the sea of women who made up the largest portion of the file. The uniforms and flags idea was adopted by the African Israel Church Nineveh. However, the speed of AICN march was much faster—closer to a jog—than that of the Salvation Army. It also became commonplace for processionals at any burial to be arranged in double file, with participants required to wear a white dress and headscarf. Those without the appropriate dress took to the rear.

18. Hole (1911, 813) reported that four young people received as full members of the Maragoli monthly meeting had been on probation for more than two years. Probation was based on a decision made in 1905 that "as the natives are so ready to mimic and to grasp the form without the vital principle, it has been the policy of the mission to make sure a person was truly in earnest before he should be reckoned among the converts... the above statement seems to indicate that in order to please, outward effects such as wearing of clothing was readily adopted" (Hoskins 1945, 24–25).

19. Apart from the Bible, names were sourced from the British or missionaries. For example, Jean was named after a Canadian missionary who lived in Goibei at the time of her birth.

20. While some Quaker churches have retained practices introduced in the early twentieth century, others have changed. For example, a Sunday service at the Friends International Center in Nairobi on May 25, 2008, was similar to any Pentecostal and charismatic service in Nairobi. While most church members were Abaluyia, congregational songs were in English and Kiswahili. They included hymns and gospel songs and also contemporary 'praise and worship' choruses accompanied by a keyboard with simultaneous prayers and interjections by the congregation. The resident choir performed an Anglican anthem, a Negro spiritual, and an arranged Logooli 'spirit song' accompanied by the *Kayamba* and bongo drums. The order of service was similar to an Anglican or Presbyterian liturgy. The visiting preacher was from a Nairobi Pentecostal church. The preacher and the church pastor met while students at the Pan African Christian College run by Pentecostals. Such was the ecumenical exchange among churches in Nairobi.

21. For example, women's meetings, teaching sessions, or demonstrations were on topics such as nutrition and hygiene, while young adult meetings featured discussions about male/female relationships.

22. Chavakali, Vihiga, Vokoli, Lugari, East African Yearly Meeting [North], and Nairobi, http://www.fwccworld.org/find_friends/index.php (accessed October 6, 2008).

23. An assembly is an administrative unit composed of several churches. They collectively meet one Sunday a month but gather separately under an elder or pastor on other Sundays and on weekdays.

24. Kasiera's (1981, 572–574) description of *vushuhuda* concurred with my experience in the 1960s and my observations in the late 1980s. He states that "at the appointed time, a group from participating churches came from their respective directions, marching in double file and beating their various music instruments and singing at the top of their voices. As they approached the chosen spot where people bought and sold, they formed one big circle. The drummers stood in the center of the circle with one singer leading the singing. Generally they started with a session singing songs whose motifs were testimonial, convictional and invitational." The leader then stated the purpose of the gathering, followed by testimonies interspersed with group songs. The meeting climaxed with a preacher who invited onlookers to convert. The meeting concluded with singing and prayer. Thereafter, the members dispersed into the market until an appointed time. They then processed back to their villages.

25. *Kuhihiza* suggests a gradual process of gently blowing to light a spark that eventually becomes a blaze on the day of the rite or ceremony. It also carries the idea of rehearsal (*kulohiza*) and is related to the idea of hunting (*kuhiza*), where the prey is lured out of hiding and eventually captured.

26. Having the same name for the ceremony and the items is not unusual in Logooli worldview. The most popular dances/musics are called *Isigudi*, also the name of the drums and the performance context.

27. Quakers may have had some sort of gathering at Christmas, but it was not explicitly explained in the sources I found at various archives in the way that the Pentecostals described their gatherings.

28. Hymn #34 in *Tsinyimbu tsyo Kwidzominya Nyasaye*, translation of "Bells of Christmas Ring."

29. Corbitt (1994) describes *kukesha*—the prayer vigil—as a space for self-expression and identity.

30. PAG's first Bible school started in 1949 was at Nyang'ori. It was originally called Bethel Bible Institute (Kasiera 1981, 601). The Pan African Christian College (PACC) was set up in Nairobi in 1978 for an international student body. PACC was officially accredited as a private university and renamed Pan African Christian University in 2006 (http://www.pacuniversity.com, accessed July 31, 2007).

31. For example, a man may be employed as a cook in a hotel, but he will not cook in his wife's kitchen at home. His wife may be a principal of a school with male chefs. One chef may be the pastor of her church. She will defer to him in church but he is her subordinate at work.

32. Drumming for religious purpose is confined to the weekend from Friday morning to Sunday evening. But an unusual occurrence in the week, such as a funeral, is announced and recognized by drumming.

33. Following my request for this study, the women singers informed me that the songs would not be sung in a funereal manner. Some songs were omitted even though they were in the written set. In every case, the tempo was accelerated and instruments included. Immediately after a known 'funeral' song, another followed with cheerful lyrics or whose function was not connected to death. After the set, there was prayer, as if the women were absolving themselves of having participated in the song. The prayers were not just for the women but also for their families, the village, and other things such as travel portending uncertainties either due to mode of transportation (referred to as unseeing objects) or unknown circumstances on arrival.

4. CONSOLIDATION

1. Later the chief suggested 7 A.M. instead of 4 A.M. because it was too early (Kasiera 1981, 178).
2. *Ling'ala* is a pipe aerophone made from *lidorondo* plant to which a horn was tied with a strip of hide. It is also the name of a type of loudspeaker (Mulindi 1983, 101).
3. This response was typical when people heard music that suggested entertainment. The behavior was common on market days or when there was a meat slaughter. While waiting for the meat to be cut up for sale, it was common for entertainers such as drummers and dancers to put on a show for the public. Any strange music always attracted attention. People came out to see, join in, or compete against the musicians.
4. The songs were in Kiswahili, thus the song style, structure, language, and learning were foreign.
5. I am most grateful to Mellonee Burnim, who encouraged me to identify and use local classification systems during her edit of one of the versions of this manuscript.
6. The first and most nationally used Kiswahili hymnal *Nyimbo Standard*, published in 1897 by Anglicans, is comprised of translated Anglican, Presbyterian, or Lutheran hymns. *Nyimbo za Injili*, printed by PAG's Evangel Press, was first published in 1959. It drew from *Nyimbo Standard*, *Nyimbo za Kikristo* of the Seventh Day Adventists, and *Tenzi za Rohoni* of the Mennonite Mission. *Nyimbo za Injili* contains translated hymns, gospels songs, and choruses.
7. See hymnbook sources in appendix 2.
8. Mwelesa explained (2005) that his name was a nickname given to his father by itinerant traders. While haggling, they realized his father would not back down, as he did not have enough produce to barter with. Therefore they said "Ni mwele 'tsa" (He has nothing) and paid his price. The phrase became his nickname—Mwelesa. The appellation is now a family and clan name.
9. Original words and text are attributed to Jester Hairston (1956). Also titled "Mary's Boy Child," this carol was also performed by Harry Belafonte and Boney M., among others, who were popular in Kenya in the 1960s to early 1980s. I provide the Lulogooli text as it is appears in Mwelesa's hymnal (Mwelesa 1988).
10. Another Jim Reeves standard, "I'll Fly Away," translated by Mwelesa, is so associated with him that he is affectionately called *liburuka* (to fly) in Logooli Quaker communities (Lubang'a 2008).
11. Although Mwelesa acknowledges his collaborators in the preface (1988), he does not document their individual and particular contribution to any given piece.
12. In May 2007, Mwelesa said he could not finance a reproduction of his hymnal. In June 2011, he provided me with a new edition of the hymnal copyrighted 2007, although it contains glued pages of songs dated 2008. The cover page and title are unchanged.
13. The Church Missionary Society set up a mission station prior to the Quakers, but it was mainly as a stopgap for their Uganda endeavors (CMS proceedings 1906 quoted in Kasiera 1981, 187).
14. A Logooli religious song subcategory called *Lwimbu lwa amakono* (Song of hands) is identified as a performance that incorporates clapping even if a song is from the 'book.'
15. For more on the Azusa revival, see Bartleman (1980); McClung (1986); Synan (1987); and Davis, C. (1993).

16. Sourced from Goibei women's group in 1983.

17. Hymnals or songbooks of the time have instructions on how to sing these songs. The songs and their performance expectations were introduced to the mission field. See appendix 2 for examples.

18. The full text for this song is in Mulindi (1983, 180–181). For an extended discussion on Logooli children's songs, see ibid., 152–254.

19. For an extended description of independent refrains, see the discussion in chapter 5.

20. As a 5-year-old, I learned a four-part arrangement of Johannes Brahms's "Guten abend gute nacht" in an English translation titled "Slumber Song." My three oldest siblings learned the song from their teacher, Mr. Nathan Olenge, for an interschool music festival. He incidentally was also the Christ Ambassadors (CA) youth leader at the Goibei mission station (Scheel 1958). We always intoned the solfège first, and then the text. According to my sister Roselyn and her friends, they walked to music festivals, a distance of about twenty miles, singing the solfège individual parts alone and in ensemble, in a variety of dynamics, then performed the piece without the solfège, then walked back singing parodies of the song as rendered by choirs they considered inferior. My older siblings and their classmates could translate solfège into pitches on demand.

21. Unlike other Luyia hymnals that had text only, this one includes staff notation in SATB, the English title, copyright, and author information. Unfortunately it is undated, although Evangel Press printed it.

22. Both Makwaya and 'adaptations' are discussed more extensively in Logooli context in chapter 7.

23. A commercial subcategory, 'praise and worship,' is now part of Logooli rural lore. In May 2004, I observed a pastor teach a 'praise song' in English to his non-English-speaking Logooli congregation.

24. Exploration of the gospel phenomenon in Kenya is a forthcoming manuscript by the author.

25. For more information on Pentecostalism see, for example, Atter (1962); Duffield and Van Cleave (1983); McClung (1986); Synan (1987); Burgess and McGee (1988); Hollenweger (1997); Hayford and Moore (2006). On gospel music and revivals see, for example, Frankiel (1978); Cusic (1990); Rogal (1996); Boyer (2000); Goff (2002).

5. ACCOMMODATION

1. TTN carries some translated choruses in Lulogooli (248–272) and a few hymns in Kiswahili (273–287).

2. For example, Hotchkiss worked with the African Inland Mission before he joined the Quakers. He left the Quakers in 1904 and formed Lumbwa Industrial Mission among the Nandi (Hotchkiss 1937).

3. *Redemption Songs* and *Golden Bells* come in words only, staff notation with words, and solfège with words editions. The initial publication dates are not indicated—only reprint dates. All were sold in Kenya during my research period 1983–2011. See additional hymnals consulted listed in appendix 2.

4. Not all the hymn subtitles indicate the hymnal source. However, there is a partial explanation of the acronyms in the front matter of the hymnal. A few hymns have no sources or are referenced as 'African.' In examining earlier editions (FAIM 1920),

it appears Rees consulted or used Zulu resources because he ascribes some songs to Zulu sources. Rees and his wife worked in South Africa before moving to Kenya. Zulu and Luluyia are both Bantu languages, so maybe Rees found compatible relationships. He also seems to have used *Sunday School Songs* as recorded in the 1920 edition (It is unclear which particular hymnal was sourced as the definitive *Sunday School Songs* since this phrase appears in various hymnal titles that I found in the archives I visited.) However, the sources are changed in later editions. In addition, the inconsistent labeling by general theme or first line in the index makes it difficult to trace a song. Later editions and reprints contain songs in Kiswahili that were absent earlier and include the Kenyan national anthem. I bought a reprinted copy of the hymnal in June 2011. There is no change in the content. It is also still one of the most popular items sold by Evangel Press.

5. While most songs in the hymnal are in Lulogooli, a number are in other Luyia dialects such as Ludirichi (Tiriki) or Lwidakho (Idakho). The hymnal was used by other Luyia Pentecostals or Quakers or those who attended schools started or sponsored by these denominations.

6. "Mungu Mtukufu aliye Bwana" is the title of the first song in the Kiswahili hymnal. The original English source text is written under the Kiswahili title "To God Be the Glory" with the source and the hymn number RS 7. This indicates the song was obtained from *Redemption Songs* hymn number 7. The edition of *Redemption Songs* is not acknowledged or named.

7. Missionaries initially assumed Avalogooli understood Kiswahili (see Wendte 1904).

8. Euba (1992, 45–63) observes that for African proselytes, the style became a way of composing and performing Christian music. Here, songs stayed within the meter of the original songs even if an extra syllable was added to accommodate the text. This is known as the double-knock technique (Jones 1976, 20–22).

9. The 1920 edition of TTN has two texts to this tune (#10 and #11). The first text is the one provided. The other is on the resurrection of Jesus titled "Ukuvuka kwa Yesu." The 1966 edition lists these two texts as #84 and #135 sourced from SSS, a reference to *Sunday School Songs*.

10. The most used Logooli tune for this song is not the Philip Bliss version in the hymnals I examined. The second line of the refrain reads in TTN "Ndali li nondi inzira yosi," which doesn't make sense. I assume it is a misprint. The citation from Rees's report is the most commonly sung version (Rees, E. 1910b). The last line of the refrain in TTN that reads "Nda havina kukusola" also differs from Rees's reported version.

11. Unless indicated otherwise, any retranslation is the done by the author.

12. Several early missionary accounts distinguished converts from others by the fact that converts wore missionary or European-type clothes. See, for example, Marian Keller (1933, 48) and Hole (1905, 132).

13. In TTN (38), it is titled "Lwimbu lwa avaana" (A song for/by children). This Christmas carol has two other tunes in European and North American hymnals, by John Murray and by William Kirkpatrick. Avalogooli only learned the Spilman tune also set to Burns's text.

14. Texts that mention tears, heaven, or a desire for a better life are sung at funerals. Performed elsewhere, they incorporate hand clapping, as if this activity, coupled with a faster tempo, expels the agents of death.

15. *Mirembe* is the customary greeting, usually accompanied by a handshake. A greeter pronounces peace on the greeted one and their kin, as their kin, and so forth. The practice establishes a relationship and fosters a congenial frame for conversation. To greet a crowd, the right hand is raised or waved. In church, peace is bestowed on church members, on pastors, on visitors, and on children, as is appropriate to the gathering.

16. These selections were made by some church members for what they considered significant songs in 1983. They were members of Pentecostal congregations in and around Goibei in Western Kenya. In May/June 2004–2005, I asked women from Goibei PAG church for their favorite 'book' songs. They selected these songs, juxtaposed with 'spirit' songs to 'make them sweeter.'

17. Italics are the author's emphasis; they are not in the original hymnal.

18. Wendte (1904, 81) described the Uganda drum as a "block of wood hollowed into a cylinder and skin stretched over the ends." This drum was initially used to signal time and activity. It assumed musical function after Vatican II encouraged and promoted the use of vernacular music, languages, and instruments in worship.

19. A 'special' is a term used by Pentecostals to denote a select performance (mostly vocal) by a group such as a choir or an invited solo/ensemble. A 'special' has the same role as an anthem in Anglican or Presbyterian churches, therefore the term 'anthem' is sometimes appropriated.

20. Rees's reports indicated that some Logooli Christians composed songs that were sound in both musical structure and doctrinal content by 1911. He mentions convert Mango, who composed two songs that were used in daily services (Africa Record 1911a, 6). It is unclear if this is one of Mango's contributions.

21. Music ex. 5.13a was sourced in the *Revivalist* (1872, 142). Music ex. 5.13b is an undated solfège version from a hymnal with a torn cover and so source is uncertain. I reworked it into staff notation.

22. The Anthology of the American Hymn-Tune Repertory website states that the composer is unknown, but the website sourced it from William Bradbury's *The Golden Censer: A Musical Offering to the Sabbath Schools,* published in 1864. http://www.bethel.edu/~rhomar/TunePages/ComeToJesus.html (accessed August 1, 2007). RS words-only edition does not acknowledge authors of hymns or songs.

23. In the Logooli hymnal, this chorus is placed in the hymns and gospel songs section rather than with other choruses. It was the first song of the hymnal in the 1920 edition (FAIM 1920).

24. Several Logooli story songs alternate triple and quadruple time measures without assuming a seven meter. The practice is common in call-and-response forms where the leader begins the sentence and the chorus first echoes the leader's line and then completes it. This lyrical technique acts as a memory aid to impart, reinforce, and test knowledge. Stanzas will expand prior information to complete the facts or the story. The practice also exemplifies melodic extension through textual manipulation.

25. Both versions are well known. The song leader determines which version to sing by beginning one or the other. It is rare that a leader starts one version and reverts to another in the same set. The two versions are understood as different versions of the same song.

26. I use the word 'tag' cautiously. While the musical behavior is that of a vamp, it is not a true isolation of a section of the text. Neither does this necessarily indicate that the piece is about to end in true vamp fashion. The leader can use this technique merely to

energize the group before moving to other verses. The tag is also a refrain because only the words of the first verse are used in this climax.

27. In some migration accounts, Logooli are supposed to be close kin to the Kisii. It is therefore not unusual that Logooli embraced a Kisii text. However, Pentecostals and Quakers established work among the Kisii early in their endeavors (Keller, M. 1946); therefore it was not unexpected that songs in Kisii language were part of the repertoire learned by young people at youth camps and elsewhere.

28. Text correction and translation courtesy of Priscilla Araka (2007). The song is also set to Kiswahili lyrics with the same meaning, for example, "Hata wamama wapinge, Yesu atarudi tena"—Even if mothers contest it, Jesus will come back again.

29. At this time (1962), the denomination was known as Pentecostal Assemblies of East Africa, servicing not just Kenya but Uganda and Tanzania as well. The sources for the hymns were not acknowledged.

30. Information was sourced from PAOC archival reports by missionaries, camp booklets, conversations with Iris Scheel (2004) and Cathy Binayo (2007), and articles in the *Pentecostal Testimony* (1957–1965).

31. When I requested special/decontextualized performances, song styles and instrumentation were adjusted. The singers were quick to point out that the different style was dictated by the situation.

32. In congregational singing some lyrics had been adjusted. For example, in B, the second part is often sung "kwinye kwosi kulayanza"—We will all rejoice—instead of the text found in the hymnal.

33. Logooli term for eventual resolution, *koyeridza*, refers to parallel ideas such as a plane being landed, a kite being landed, the sun setting, and so forth.

34. In the different recorded versions of this song and in congregational singing amongst Pentecostals, the word *ling'ana* is used. However, the word *lyeta* (name) is transcribed in the hymnal.

35. For more details, see discussion on "Musical Elements" in this chapter, with particular attention to the section on "Rhythm, Tempo, and Meter" and the ensuing examples on excerpts from the song "Oh Happy Day."

36. In every performance I recorded or heard, the sentence was "Lero ndimbaga Yesu wainyanza." The last two words are a better translation than that printed in the hymnal. I transcribed the words I heard most often sung rather than what is written in the hymnal.

37. Cross rhythm allows individuals to feel the song in different meters and therefore move the body at different times, all of which are acceptable since they are inherent in the musical structure. It is possible to clap in one meter and feel the body or march to another.

38. Mwelesa (2007) informed me the words were not "inzira ya vaguga" (the way of the forefathers) but "inzira ya vaguta" (the path of the victors). However, his various booklets and hymnals all favor the first phrase. Of further note, TTN was meant as a literacy tool. Mwelesa's text is a record of songs. The spellings of some of Mwelesa's texts are different from the orthography posted in TTN. I adjusted a few into 'classic' spellings.

6. SYNCRETISM

1. Kasiera (1981, 548) records that a Quaker Lulogooli song was composed in 1927 to protest the forced excommunication of some members due to disagreement regarding

the nature of the 'spirit' that had been received. He only transcribed his translation into English. Kasiera had no recording of the song, nor could he recall the tune or the text in Luluyia.

2. Often the expression 'ahila ulwimbo vulahi' (he/she is taking/moving the song very well) or 'ulwimbo lwingila' (the song is jelling, satisfying, filling) signifies the impact of the song as generating deep emotion, feeling, unspeakable ethos.

3. For example, "Si gali masahi," text from Isaac Watts's "Not All the Blood of Beasts," is subtitled "African Tune," *Tsinyimbu tsya Nyasaye* #68. Other songs have English subtitles to indicate sources of tunes.

4. A favorite song by Mwelesa (1988, 210), "Inzila yo Musalaba," is in stanza/refrain form. The text on 'the way of the cross' is not derived from a European source that I could ascertain. A sizeable number of songs were about the cross and shedding blood. Logooli religion and ritual worldview embraced the concept of blood atonement. It is not surprising that 'blood' songs were popular.

5. See discussions by scholars and missionaries in 1950s–1970s *African Music* newsletters and journal.

6. *Maboyi* is a derogatory and Lulogooli corruption of the word 'boy,' a common designation of house servants. Colonists or missionaries referred to their workers not by name but called out "boy" even for grown men. Avalogooli adopted the word to mean a slave or a wimp. The prefixes **Li**boyi (sing.) and **Ma**boyi (pl.) classify these males as objects or nonhuman.

7. A version of the text is found in Mwelesa 1988, 208.

8. It was believed that he was a thief by profession and compulsion. He could even be hired to steal. This story was discussed in 2005, but the thief's conversion had occurred in the 1960s.

9. Weman (1960, 116), in assessing European church music as transplanted in Africa, comments that "there was such a strong desire to break completely with old customs and practices that native music was automatically rejected as 'heathen' . . . Folk music, its song and instruments were treated as dangerous and firmly excluded from the Christian scheme of things . . . song melodies harmonized in Western styles were introduced into Africa . . . This was the kind of music with which the missionary was familiar, and the kind *he* liked" (italics by Weman).

10. See Wagner (1949, 90–177) and Ogot and Welbourn (1966, 115–117) on the magico-religious.

11. Individual differences resulting in new churches have been a feature of Pentecostals around the world since the beginnings of the movements. Individuals either 'follow their call' or they develop a following around a doctrine, issue, or practice and then set up an institution around it.

12. See section on "Halleluiah Refrains" and music ex. 6.8 for analysis.

13. Mutongi (1999, 70) translates *kehenda mwoyo* as "worries of the heart."

14. Lulogooli translation of the word 'Satan' (Setani) was adopted from the Kiswahili word Shetani. Shetani, according to the Swahili dictionary, refers to the angel who was banished for refusing to follow the commands of the almighty God. It is also defined as someone who commits heinous acts, a deceitful person (*Kamusi ya Kiswahili Sanifu* 1981). These ideas are also present in Logooli perception, where Setani is not only an evil supernatural being; a person promoting evil deeds, deception, and disobedience can be referred to as 'Setani.' The term for evil spirits is *masetani*, from the Kiswahili *Mashetani*.

15. Transcriptions are in the treble clef to facilitate analysis.

16. The word contains the idea of rudeness, disobedience, insolence, bickering, contempt, unbelief, or scorn.

17. In some versions, the response is "Lwa Yesu yananga ×2 tsiali tsiambila" (When Jesus called, they [slumber] had overwhelmed me, I was in deep sleep).

18. Lulogooli also expresses totalizing by repeating the obvious or appending with adverbs to exclude any kind of doubt.

19. Halleluiah is frequently translated as 'praise the Lord.'

20. In replaying at slowed/half-tempo, the two eighth notes sounded like a jazz approach with the first one more relaxed than the second.

21. When I asked Goibei women why they did not translate it into Lulogooli, they stated that it "entered better" in Tiriki, which I took to denote a musical preference for the style with that text in Ludirichi.

22. The adverb 'dodo' places emphasis on the whole line—That Miriam et al. are indeed (truly) playing zithers—but can also mean, It *is* true the Miriam et al. are playing zithers.

23. Although it has religious lyrics, this song was often sung at football games, as wedding teasers, and to psych competitors for different types of contests such as music or drama festivals or political rallies.

24. I include two versions of the second section: a) and b). In version b) (2005, first version, 1983, both performed by Goibei women), once "mulogi hamba" is called, the chorus continues the phrase. It creates a synergy different from the dialogue created by the leader's interjection "hamba weganire" in version a). Previously, the soloist was joined by some chorus members on "weganire."

25. Technically instruments and stories are 'struck' or sounded. Games are 'played' and maize, beans, or millet are 'beaten' to dehusk them.

7. INVOCATION

1. Barrett et al. 1973, 26; Anderson, D. 1994, 227–233.

2. Wesonga and Ward 1972 survey is reported in Barrett et al. 1973, 85–92. More information from interviews by Nyimbo za dini announcer and Biblia Husema Studio director Christopher Mutai (2006).

3. Competing music groups at an event or a gathering were not strange to Avalogooli. Early reports indicate that whenever missionaries went to a venue with their megaphones, accordions, or records, groups of Luyia musicians also showed up to strut their stuff (Kasiera 1983, 187). In one case, Christian converts went to marketplaces to pit their music against that of indigenous male drummers with girl dancers. Kasiera (1981, 227) cites the first missionary settler in Nyang'ori—Clyde Miller—sending converts to the market to sing while a butchered cow was being sliced in order to evangelize the buyers, this against a group of indigenous drummers and dancers commissioned to publicize the event and entertain potential customers. Other music competitions occurred on days of war games (*yabese*), wrestling or bull fighting, or weddings. Opposing groups sang to cheer their candidates and belittle their opponents. At nightly funeral wakes, entertainers included lute and lyre players with dancers and singers, who entertained by recounting and dramatizing the life history of the deceased but also reported on and related concurrent social events. It was at these events that emerging musicians were discovered, encouraged, and critiqued.

4. Makwaya songs performed at such events include the new tunes to the Kiswahili hymn "Cha kutumaini sina" ("My Hope Is Built," music ex. 5.17c, 5.17d).

5. For further discussion on the beginnings of the gospel music industry, see Kidula 1998. For an example of the transformation from makwaya to gospel, see discussion on Mary Atieno (Kidula 2007).

6. For example, Ernest Waombu, the choir director of the International Friends Center Church in Nairobi, also trained the Kenyatta Hospital Staff choir and the National Social Security Fund workers choir (Waombu 2008).

7. Biographical information on Hyslop is culled from Kenya National Archives sources (see KNA in bibliography). The records contain Hyslop's communication, speeches, and reports from 1945 to 1971. A copy of Hyslop's obituary was obtained from All Saints Cathedral in Nairobi, Kenya.

8. The festival was started in 1927 as a forum for performance by colonists and taken over by the State Ministry of Education. Hyslop (1964, 6–30) provides guidelines for choir training and music festivals.

9. Weman (1960, 115–123) criticized the colonial and missionary enterprise for their emphasis on choral music, especially the restriction of music instruction to singing. He posits that the use of solfège as the basis for music education (which Hyslop advocated) "shut out the African from contact with instrumental music" (117). It was not only European instruments but African instruments that were "by and large conspicuous for their absence" (118). He felt that according to colonists and missionaries, "African music and creative ability [was] stamped as primitive" (129). Hyslop, however, described adaptation of African songs for Christian worship as a "New Song which is springing from the roots of the music of Africa" (KNA MSS/22/32).

10. McHarg's (1958, 46) discussion of a similar practice in Rhodesia (Zimbabwe) describes the end result as "UnAfrican aspects of music such as acquiring skills in reading Tonic Solfa, in singing vertical harmonies, in singing in English, in learning vernacular songs set in ridiculously twisted and inverted accents to European melodies, and in firmly resisting any yielding to spontaneous expression whatsoever."

11. Zake notes that initially they were discouraged from advanced music education, as the training was only availed to "English boys and girls and they struggle to get the licentiate in the prescribed three years" (Basudde 2006). Basil (1957), a white Catholic father, had, however, advocated for music studies for gifted African students, including bursaries for study in Europe or elsewhere.

12. See Glasser's review in *African Music* (1961, 116).

13. See Hyslop articles in *African Music* (1958a, 1959) and *African Arts* (1972) and a booklet, *Musical Instruments of East Africa* (1975).

14. For an initial discussion of Kemoli's style, see Kidula's 2008 article.

15. A popular seasonal song was Lazarus Ekwueme's "Zamiliza" (see Mensah 1998, 210–211).

16. Among Kemoli's significant accolades is the Organization of African Unity (OAU) anthem that he wrote in 1986 with input from Ethiopian poet Tesgai. The song was adopted by the African Union when OAU was renamed (Kemoli 2001a). He has also mentored arrangers and choir directors (Kemoli 1999).

17. As a student at Kenyatta University (1978–1981), I performed Kemoli's arrangements with the university choir and under his direction. In this group of mixed linguistic, religious, and ethnic heritage, Kemoli was often frustrated that most singers did not

'settle into the groove.' Kemoli therefore relied on those experienced in the parent styles to exemplify the performance aesthetics.

18. Composers did not provide notation for the drum, kayamba, or body motion.

19. Muungano National Choir was the premier Kenyan choral group of the 1980s–1990s. Its members were drawn from various choirs in Nairobi—hence the name *Muungano*, translated as United or Union.

20. This requirement has been institutionalized at music festivals. In adjudicators' workshops (1988, 1989, 1990, 2001, 2002), organizers stipulated that any group that did not clearly state the original melody at the onset violated the adaptation rule.

21. I have analyzed more aspects of this piece in a different paper (Kidula 2008).

22. In the late 1980s, Kemoli adapted the song "Gendi kwilwadze" to political lyrics in Kiswahili on rhetoric by the then-president of Kenya, Daniel Arap Moi. He adjusted the rhythm to fit the Kiswahili language.

23. The music of the first song was discussed in music ex. 6.5 with different yet related lyrics.

24. Ladder here implies that the hill will be climbed one step at a time.

25. Note that in his arrangement, Kemoli repeated the song so that the final structure was AB:llA, with A as "Mubende yimu" and B as "Lobai." He extended the B section by naming various saints. Kemoli inserts himself in that lineage. Since the piece ends with the A section, the final cadence is on an offbeat. The various recordings where Kemoli conducted or soloed also had many dynamic contrasts.

26. For additional discussion of women, weddings, and song in Logooli/Luyia culture, see Kidula 2009.

27. Incidentally, Kemoli's longest work is a wedding suite set from Logooli wedding songs. More than any other Logooli ritual, wedding music is closest to church songs in that different styled songs are performed in one set. However, in wedding sets, the accompaniment rhythms are paced in the style of the song, whereas church songs maintain clapping or drumming in a duple time regardless of other meter or style.

28. The transcriptions (music ex. 7.5a and 7.5b) were sourced from two recordings (Kenyatta University 1979 and Kariokor Friends 1985), both conducted by Kemoli. In some notations, the pickup note is an eighth note. From the recordings, it can be treated as a grace note, a sixteenth note, or a relaxed sixteenth note—coming off the last beat of a triplet eighth grouping instead of a quadruplet in sixteenth note grouping.

29. Original Lulogooli unison version is music ex. 6.16—"Kidaho kyo mwigulu."

30. The transcription does not include repeats nor does it show idiosyncratic melorhythmic substitutions from the names of choir or audience members. Also the notes of the final choral cadence are not notated.

31. For further analysis of this piece, see Kidula 2008, 122–125.

32. In various discussions with Kemoli over my reading of his treatment of modality, he always played other pieces where he stayed true to the suggested mode. However, this was not true in his arrangement of Christian religious songs. They tend to gravitate toward a major key.

33. Ilavadza's first recorded makwaya with the Riruta Baptist Church choir from 1987 (Ilavadza 1995).

34. I first encountered Ilavadza's recordings at Kesho Christian Bookstore managed by AIC in 1992.

35. FJI—Francis Jumba Ilavadza; JK—Jean Kidula.

36. At a later interview (2011), Ilavadza conceded that in his later releases (e.g., *Luyia Vol. 10* recorded in 1998 but released in 2010), kiriri was played by the son of Ingosi, a famous Tiriki fiddler.

37. Lingala is a trade language in Central Africa, particularly in the Congos. Musicians from this region were dispersed into many parts of Africa from the 1950s due to political unrest. Some of them settled in Kenya. They sang in Kiswahili but were best known for their popular songs in Lingala. Of the names of their music styles, the most generic are Congolese, Soukous, or Lingala. For an extended look at the historical development of these styles, see Mukuna 1992, 1999.

38. Kigame's Luhya output is partially discussed in Kidula 2010. I interviewed him over the years (1995–2010), analyzed and performed some of his music, and appeared as a guest on his radio programs.

8. EPILOGUE

1. Were (1967b, 155–161) discusses the establishment of formal British rule from 1894.
2. See Wagner's ethnography (1949).

BIBLIOGRAPHY

Abala, Judith Imali. 1989. "Storytelling in the Maragoli Society: A Cultural Study." Master's thesis, Ohio State University.
Abwunza, Judith M. 1997. *Women's Voices, Women's Power: Dialogues of Resistance from East Africa*. Peterborough, Ontario: Broadview Press.
Adamson, Joy. 1967. *The Peoples of Kenya*. New York: Harcourt, Brace & World.
Adede, Rose. 1982. *Joel Litu, Pioneer African Quaker*. Wallingford, Pa.: Pendell Hill.
———. 1986. "The Impact of Quaker Missionaries in Kenya: The Work of Emory and Deborah Rees." Master's thesis, Earlham School of Religion.
AFBFM (American Friends Board of Foreign Missions). 1918. *15 Years in East Africa*. Richmond, Ind.: American Friends Board of Foreign Missions.
Africa Record. 1906. Various reports. *Africa Record* 1(2): 1–8.
———. 1907a. Various reports. *Africa Record* 1(3): 1–8.
———. 1907b. Various reports. *Africa Record* 1(4): 1–8.
———. 1907c. Various reports. *Africa Record* 2(1): 1–7.
———. 1908a. Various reports. *Africa Record* 3(1): 1–5.
———. 1908b. Various reports. *Africa Record* 3(2): 1–6.
———. 1908c. Various reports. *Africa Record* 3(4): 1–7.
———. 1909a. "Quarterly Reports." *Africa Record* 4(1): 1–6.
———. 1909b. "Quarterly Reports from the Field." *Africa Record* 4(3): 1–5.
———. 1910. Various reports. *Africa Record* 5(1): 1–6.
———. 1911a. Various reports. *Africa Record* 6(1): 1–7.
———. 1911b. Various reports. *Africa Record* 6(2): 1–6.
———. 1911c. Various reports. *Africa Record* 6(3): 1–5.
———. 1911d. Various reports. *Africa Record* 6(4): 1–7.
———. 1912a. "Quarterly Report for Maragoli and Lirhanda." *Africa Record* 7(1): 4–7.
———. 1912b. "Annual Report from Maragoli and Lirhanda Stations, 1911." *Africa Record* 7(2): 3–6.
———. 1912c. Various reports. *Africa Record* 7(4): 1–6.
———. 1913. Various reports. *Africa Record* 8(1): 1–7.
———. 1914. Various articles. *Africa Record*, no. 4.
———. 1916. "Annual Report of the African Field Committee for 1915." *Africa Record* 10(2): 1–6.

Akaranga, Stephen Ifedha. 1996. "Some Aspects of Indigenous Logooli Moral Values." *Trans-African Journal of History* 25: 146–153.

Amugune, Japheth. 1971. *Yohana Amugune: A Christian Pioneer*. Nyang'ori, Kenya: Evangel Press.

Amutabi, Maurice. 2002. "Cultural History of the Abaluyia: The Role of Traditional Music." In *Historical Studies and Social Change in Western Kenya: Essays in Memory of Professor Gideon S. Were*, edited by William R. Ochieng', 71–83. Nairobi: East African Educational Publishers.

Anderson, Allan. 2004. *An Introduction to Pentecostalism: Global Charismatic Christianity*. Cambridge, England: Cambridge University Press.

Anderson, Dick. 1994. *We Felt Like Grasshoppers: The History of African Inland Church*. Nottingham, England: Crossway Books.

Anderson, William B. 1977. *The Church of East Africa*. Dodoma, Tanzania: Central Tanzania Press.

Argyrou, Vassos. 1996. *Tradition and Modernity in the Mediterranean: The Wedding as Symbolic Struggle*. New York: Cambridge University Press.

Askew, Kelly M. 2002. *Performing the Nation: Swahili Music and Cultural Politics in Tanzania*. Chicago: University of Chicago Press.

Atter, Gordon F. 1962. *The Third Force*. Peterborough, Ontario: College Press.

Barrett, David B. 1971. "Who's Who of African Independent Church Leaders." *Risk* (Geneva, W.C.C.) 7(3): 23–34.

———. 1986. *Schism and Renewal in Africa*. Nairobi: Oxford University Press.

Barrett, David B., George K. Mabo, Janice McLaughlin, and Malcolm J. McVeigh. 1973. *Kenya Churches Handbook: Development of Kenyan Christianity 1498–1973*. Kisumu, Kenya: Evangel Publishing House.

Bartleman, Frank. 1980. *Azusa Street*. South Plainfield, N.J.: Bridge Publishing House. (First ed. 1925.)

Basil, Br. 1957. "The Dilemna of Bantu Church Music." *African Music* 1(4): 36–39.

Basudde, Elvis. 2006. "Prof. Senoga-Zake Helped Arrange Kenya's Anthem." *New Vision*, February 21, http://www.newvision.co.ug/D/8/25/483097 (accessed March 10, 2010).

Bigenho, Michelle. 2011. "The Intimate Distance of Indigenous Modernities." Keynote address, biannual conference of the International Council of Traditional Music, Memorial University of Newfoundland, St. Johns, Newfoundland, Canada, July 18.

Binayo, Cathy T. 2007. Interviews with the author, September 29–30.

Blackburn, Elisha. 1908. "Quarterly Report from F.A.I. M." *American Friend* 15: 560.

Blackburn, Virginia. 1909. "Conference of Kavirondo Missionaries." *Africa Record* 4(2): 4–5.

Blacking, John. 1973. *How Musical Is Man?* Seattle: University of Washington Press.

Bohlman, Philip V., and Ronald Radano. 2000. Introduction to *Music and the Racial Imagination*, edited by Ronald Radano and Philip V. Bohlman, 1–57. Chicago: University of Chicago Press.

Bombay, Richard Calvin. 1996. Interview with the author, September

Bond, George C, Walton R. Johnson, and Sheila S. Walker. 1979. *African Christianity: Patterns of Religious Continuity*. New York: Academic Press.

Boyer, Horace C. 2000. *The Golden Age of Gospel*. Urbana: University of Illinois Press.

Burgess, Stanley M., and Gary B. McGee, eds. 1988. *Dictionary of Pentecostal and Charismatic Movements*. Grand Rapids, Mich.: Zondervan Publishing House.

Burnim, Melonee. 1990. "Culture Bearer and Tradition Bearer: An Ethnomusicologist's Research on Gospel Music." In *A Century of Ethnomusicological Thought*, edited by Kay Kaufman Shelemay, 358–373. New York: Garland.

Carrington, John F. 1948. "African Music in Christian Worship." *International Review of Missions* 37: 198–205.

Carrol, K. 1957. "Yoruba Religious Music," *African Music* 1(3): 45–47.

Chernoff, John M. 1979. *African Rhythm and African Sensibility: Aesthetics and Social Action in African Society*. Chicago: University of Chicago Press.

Chilson, Edna. 1943. *Ambassador of the King: Arthur Chilson*. Wichita, Kans.: E. H. Chilson private printing.

Chitando, Ezra. 2002. *Singing Culture: A Study of Gospel Music in Zimbabwe*. Uppsala, Sweden: Nordiska Africa Institutet.

Church, John E. 1981. *Quest for the Highest: An Autobiographical Account of the East African Revival*. Exeter, England: Paternoster Press.

Coplan, David B. 1985. *In Township Tonight! South Africa's Black City Music and Theatre*. London: Longman.

Corbitt, J. Nathan. 1985. "The History and Development of Music Used in the Baptist Churches on the Coast of Kenya: The Development of an Indigenous Church Music 1953–1984." DMA diss., South Western Baptist Theological Seminary.

———. 1994. "Dynamism in African Church Music: The Search for Identity and Self Expression." *Black Sacred Music: A Journal of Theomusicology* 8(2): 1–29.

———. 1998. *The Sound of the Harvest: Music's Mission in Church and Culture*. Grand Rapids, Mich.: Baker Books.

Cox, James L., ed. 1998. *Rites of Passage in Contemporary Africa: Interaction between Christian and African Traditional Religions*. Cardiff: Cardiff Academic Press.

Cross, Virginia Ann. 1985. "The Development of Sunday School Hymnody in the USA 1816–1869." DMA diss., New Orleans Baptist Theological Seminary.

Cusic, Don. 1990. *The Sound of Light: A History of Gospel Music*. Bowling Green, Ohio: Bowling Green State University Popular Press.

Dargie, David. 1987. *Xhosa Zionist Music: A Report for the Research Unit for the Study of New Religious Movements and Indigenous Churches of Southern Africa*. KwaDlangezwa, South Africa: University of Zululand.

Davis, Clara. 1993. *Azusa Street Revival*. Springdale, Pa.: Whitaker House.

Davis, Donald G., Jr., David M. Hovde, and John Mark Tucker. 1997. *Reading for Moral Progress: 19th Century Institutions Promoting Social Change*. Champaign: Graduate School of Library and Information Science, University of Illinois.

Duffield, Guy P., and Nathaniel M. Van Cleave. 1983. *Foundations of Pentecostal Theology*. Los Angeles: L.I.F.E. Bible College.

Egara, Kabaji Stanley. 2005. "The Construction of Gender through the Narrative Process of the African Folk Tale: A Case Study of the Maragoli Folklore." PhD diss., University of South Africa.

Ekwueme, Lazarus N. 1971. "African Music in Christian Liturgy, the Igbo Experiment." *African Music* 5(3): 12–33.

Elmer, Richard M. 1956. "Modern Evangelism in Church Music." *Hymn* 1(1): 13–17.

Emerson, Elizabeth H. 1958. *Emory J. Rees, Language Pioneer: A Biographical Sketch*. Gowanda, N.Y.: Niagara Frontier Pub. Co.

Erlmann, Veit. 1991. *African Stars: Studies in Black South African Performance*. Chicago: University of Chicago Press.

———. 1996. *Nightsong: Performance, Power, and Practice in South Africa*. Chicago: University of Chicago Press.

Eskew, Harry. 1972. "A Cultural Understanding of Hymnody." *Hymn* 23(3): 79–84.

Euba, Akin. 1992. "Yoruba Music in the Church: The Development of neo-African Art among the Yoruba of Nigeria." In *African Musicology; Current Trends*, vol. 2, Jacqueline DjeDje, 45–63. Atlanta: Crossroads Press, African Studies Association.

FAIM (Friends Africa Industrial Mission). 1920. *Tsinyimbu Tsyokwidzominya Nyasaye*. Maragoli, Kenya: Friends Africa Mission Press.

Falola, Toyin, and Christian Jennings, eds. 2002. *Africanizing Knowledge*. New Brunswick, N.J.: Transaction Publishers.

Fashole-Luke, Edward W. 1978. *Christianity in Independent Africa*. Bloomington: Indiana University Press.

Fiagbezi, Nissio. 1979. *Religious Music Traditions in Africa*. Accra: Ghana University Press.

Forde, Daryll, ed. 1999. *African Worlds: Studies in the Cosmological Ideas and Social Values of African Peoples*, 2nd ed. Hamburg: Lit.

Foucault, Michel. 1978. *The History of Sexuality: An Introduction*. New York: Pantheon.

Francis, Elizabeth, and John Hoddinott. 1993. "Migration and Differentiation in Western Kenya: A Tale of Two Sub-Locations." *Journal of Development Studies* 30(1): 115–145.

Frankiel, Tamar. 1978. *Gospel Hymns and Social Religion: The Rhetoric of Nineteenth-Century Revivalism*. Philadelphia: Temple University Press.

Friends Missionary Advocate. 1909. "Friends Africa Industrial Mission." *Friends Missionary Advocate* 25: 19–20.

———. 1913. "Items from Africa." *Friends Missionary Advocate* 29(9): 17–21.

———. 1915. "Review of This Year's Work." *Friends Missionary Advocate* 31(2): 22–27.

———. 1916. "Africa." *Friends Missionary Advocate* 32(2): 34–41.

Friesen, Albert W. "A Methodology in the Development of Indigenous Hymnody." *Missiology* 10: 83–94.

Gifford, Paul. 2004. *Ghana's New Christianity: Pentecostalism in a Globalizing African Economy*. Bloomington: Indiana University Press.

Gilpin, Clifford Wesley. 1976. "The Church and the Community: Quakers in Western Kenya, 1902–1963." PhD diss., Columbia University.

Glasser, Stanley. 1962. Reviews on *Magnificat* and *Nunc Dimitis* by Graham Hyslop. *African Music* 3(1): 116.

Goff, James R. 2002. *Close Harmony: A History of Southern Gospel*. Chapel Hill: University of North Carolina Press.

Goibei women's group. 2004. Interviews/discussions with the author.

———. 2005. Interviews/discussions with the author.

———. 2006. Interviews/discussions with the author.

Goodspeed, Edgar J. 1876. *A Full History of the Wonderful Career of Moody and Sankey in Great Britain and America*. New York: AMS Press. (Reprinted 1973.)

Graham, Ronnie. 1933. *Stern's Guide to Contemporary African Music*. London: Pluto Press.

Guthrie, Joseph Randall. 1992. "Pentecostal Hymnody: Historical, Theological and Musical Influences." DMA dissertation, SouthWestern Baptist Theological Seminary.
Hastings, Adrian. 1979. *A History of African Christianity, 1950–1975*. Cambridge, England: Cambridge University Press.
Hayford, Jack, and S. David Moore. 2006. *The Charismatic Century: The Enduring Impact of the Azusa Street Revival*. New York: Warner Faith.
Heath, Carla. 1986. "Broadcasting in Kenya: Policy and Politics, 1928–1984." PhD diss., University of Illinois.
Hildebrandt, Jonathan. 1981. *History of the Church in Africa: A Survey*. Achimota, Ghana: African Christian Press.
Hillman, Eugene. 1993. *Toward an African Christianity: Inculturation Applied*. New York: Paulist Press.
Hole, Edgar T. 1905. "Annual Report of the Friends' Africa Industrial Mission." *American Friend* 12: 132–133.
———. 1907. "Annual Report of the Friends' Africa Industrial Mission." *American Friend* 14: 364–366.
———. 1911. "Quarterly Report for Maragoli and Lirhanda Stations." *Africa Record* 6(1): 6–7.
Hollenweger, Walter J. 1997. *Pentecostalism: Origins and Developments Worldwide*. Peabody, Mass.: Hendrickson Publishers.
Hoskins, Irene E. 1945. *Friends in Africa*. Richmond, Ind.: American Friends Board of Missions.
Hotchkiss, Willis Ray. 1901. *Sketches from the Dark Continent*. Cleveland: Friends Bible Institute and Training School.
———. 1937. *Then and Now in Kenya Colony: Forty Adventurous Years in East Africa*. New York: Fleming H. Revell Co.
Hoyt, Alta. 1916. "Quarterly Report of the African Field." *Africa Record* 10(3): 2–5.
———. 1951. *Bantu Folklore Tales of Long Ago*. Wichita, Kans.: Day's Print Shop.
Hoyt, Alta, and Mabel Hawthorne. n.d. *Friends African Mission: Lessons for Youth*. n.p.: S.I. United Society of Friends Women.
Hyslop, Graham. 1958a. "African Musical Instruments in Kenya." *African Music* 2(1): 31–36.
———. 1958b. "Kenya's Colony Music and Drama Officer." *African Music* 2(1): 37–39.
———. 1959. "More Kenyan Musical Instruments." *African Music* 2(2): 24–28.
———. 1964. *Since Singing Is So Good a Thing: Handbook for Music Teachers and Choir Masters*. Nairobi: Oxford University Press.
———. 1972. "Some Musical Instruments of Kenya." *African Arts* 5(4): 48–55.
———. 1975. *Musical Instruments of East Africa*, vol. 1. *Kenya*. Nairobi: Nelson.
Ifedha, Aggrey Songora. 2008. "Mlogooli," http://andimidamu8.blogspot.com/, posted by Morris Lwenya, May 22 (accessed July 3, 2008).
Ilavadza, Francis Jumba. 1995. Interviews with the author, May–September.
———. 2011. Interviews with the author, June 10–16.
———. n.d. *Luhya No 3: Gali Mahing'ano*. Neno Productions. Audiocassette.
Jenkins, Philip. 2006. *The New Faces of Christianity: Believing the Bible in the Global South*. Oxford, England: Oxford University Press.
Jones, Allan M. 1976. *African Hymnody in Christian Worship: A Contribution to the History of Its Development*. Gwelo, Zimbabwe: Mambo Press.

Kamusi ya Kiswahili Sanifu. 1981. Nairobi: Oxford University Press.
Kasiera, Ezekiel. 1981. "The Development of Pentecostal Christianity in Western Kenya: With Special Reference to Maragoli, Nyang'ori and Tiriki 1909–1942." PhD diss., University of Aberdeen.
Kauffman, Robert A. 1964. "Impressions of African Church Music." *African Music* 3(3): 109–110.
Kawuta, S. 1967. "The Place of Music in the General Life of the African Church." *All African Church Music Association* 5(3): 3–5.
Keller, Marian. 1933. *Twenty Years in Africa, 1913–1933: Retrospect and Prospect*. Toronto: Full Gospel Publishing Company.
———. 1946. "Information Regarding the Mission Work in Kenya Colony." Paper accessed from PAOC Archives, Kenya files.
Keller, Otto, and Marian. 1926. "British East Africa." *Pentecostal Testimony*, February, 12–13.
———. 1929. "From British East Africa." *Pentecostal Testimony*, May, 12–13.
Kemoli, Arthur. 1999. Curriculum vitae and private paper titled "Arthur M. Kemoli: Background." Obtained by author from Dr. Kemoli in June 2001.
———. 2001a. Interview by Kameme 101 FM radio station as part of the series *Great Kenyans*.
———. 2001b. Interviews with author, June–July.
———. 2001c. Kemoli private notes on repertoire, author reviewed June 2001.
———. 2008. Interview with the author, June 10.
———. 2011. Interviews with the author, June 10, 13–16.
Kenworthy, Leonard S., ed. 1985. *Living in the Light: Some Quaker Pioneers of the 20th Century*, vol. 2. Kennett Square, Pa.: Friends General Conference and Quaker Publications.
Kesby, John D. 1977. *The Cultural Regions of East Africa*. London: Academic Press.
Kidula, Jean N. 1986. "The Effects of Syncretism and Adaptation on the Christian Music of the Logooli." Master's thesis, East Carolina University.
———. 1998. "*Sing and Shine*: Religious Popular Music in Kenya." PhD diss., University of California, Los Angeles.
———. 1999a. "Where Is Your Tradition? On the Problematics of an African Ethnomusicologist's Research on Christian Musics." South East Regional Seminar of African Studies, Armstrong Atlantic State University, Savannah, Georgia, Oct. 15, http://www.ecu.edu/african/sersas/programf99.htm.
———. 1999b. "Ingolole: Then We Shall See." In *Turn Up the Volume: A Celebration of African Music*, edited by J. C. Djeje, 90–97. Los Angeles: Fowler Museum.
———. 2005a. "Christian Music as Indigenous African: Appropriation and Accommodation." In *Multiple Interpretations of Dynamics and Knowledge in African Music Traditions: A Festschrift in Honor of Akin Euba*, edited by George Dor and Bode Omojola, 211–226. Point Richmond, Calif.: Music Research Institute Press.
———. 2005b. "*Nandio Kwalange*: 'Embodying' Logooli Cultural Memory in Song." *South African Journal of Musicology* 25: 1–14.
———. 2007. "Identity Dynamics in Popular and Religious Music: Mary Atieno and the International Fellowship Church Choir (IFC)." In *Music and Identity: Transformation and Negotiation*, edited by Eric Ayisi Akrofi, Maria Smit, and Stig-Magnus Thorsen, 113–130. Stellenbosch, South Africa: Sun Press.

———. 2008. "The Choral Arrangements and Performance Practice of Dr. Arthur Kemoli." *Composition in Africa and the Diaspora* 1: 109–130.

———. 2009. "Transcending Time, Empowering Space: (Re)iterating a Logooli/Luyia Kenyan Song." *World of Music* 51(2): 119–138.

———. 2010. "'There Is Power': Contemporizing Old Music Traditions for New Gospel Audiences in Kenya." *Yearbook of Traditional Music* 42: 62–80.

Kigame, Reuben. 1995, 1996, 1998, 2001, 2002, 2004, 2005, 2006, 2007, 2009, 2010. Interviews with the author, June–September, July, February, May–June, May, June, June, June, May, May–June, July–August, respectively.

King, Roberta R. 1989. "Pathways in Christian Music Communication: The Case of the Senufo of Cote d'Ivoire." PhD diss., Fuller Theological Seminary.

———. 1999. *A Time to Sing: A Manual for the African Church*. Nairobi: Evangel Publishing House.

KNA (Kenya National Archives). AB/1/82.

———. AB/1/136.
———. AB/15/58.
———. AB/17/23.
———. MSS/22/1.
———. MSS/22/7.
———. MSS/22/8.
———. MSS/22/16.
———. MSS/22/31.
———. MSS/22/32.
———. XJ/1/234.
———. XJ/4/7.
———. XJ/25/11.
———. XJ/25/12.
———. XJ/25/13.
———. XJ/27/71.

Kubik, Gerhard. 1999. *Africa and the Blues*. Jackson: University Press of Mississippi.

Lenherr, J. 1968. "Advancing Indigenous Church Music" *African Music* 4(2): 33–39.

Lipschutz, Mark, and R. Kent Rasmussen. 1986. *Dictionary of African Historical Biography*, 2nd ed. Berkeley: University of California Press.

London, Justin. 2005. "Rhythm." In *Grove Music Online*, edited by L. Macy, http://www.grovemusic.com (accessed June 27).

Lonsdale, John. 1977. "The Politics of Conquest: The British in Western Kenya 1894–1908." *Historical Journal* 20(4): 841–870.

Louw, Johan K. 1956. "The Use of African Music in the Church." *African Music* 1(3): 43–44.

———. 1958. "African Music in Christian Worship." *African Music* 2(1): 51–53.

Lubang'a, William. 2008. Interview with the author, June 8.

Lung'aho, Thomas Ganira. 1965. *Daudi Lung'aho: An African Missionary*. Nyang'ori, Kenya: Evangel Press.

Lury, E. E. 1956. "Music in East African Churches." *African Music* 1(3): 34–36.

Lynn, John, and Edna Lynn. 1995. *A Tribute to Rev. John & Edna Lynn: 59 Years of Ministry with the P.A.O.C. 1936–1995*. Private pamphlet from the PAOC Archives.

Malm, Krister, and Roger Wallis. 1984. *Big Sounds from Small Peoples: The Music Industry in Small Countries*. New York: Pendragon Press.

Martin, Marie-Louise. 1975. *Kimbangu, an African Prophet and His Church*. Oxford, England: Blackwell.
Massarelli, Lewis Gary. 1998. "A Study of the Music of the Pentecostal Assemblies of Canada and How It Changes at Times of Revival." Master's thesis, California State University.
Maxon, Robert M. 2002. "Colonial Conquest and Administration." In *Historical Studies and Social Change in Western Kenya: Essays in Memory of Professor Gideon S. Were*, edited by William R. Ochieng', 93–109. Nairobi: East African Educational Publishers.
May, Chris, and Chris Stapleton. 1987. *Africa All Stars: The Pop Music of a Continent*. London: Paladin Books.
Mbiti, John S. 1991. *Introduction to African Religion*, 2nd ed. Nairobi: East African Educational Publishers.
Mbunga, Stephen B. G. 1963. *Church Law and Bantu Music: Ecclesiastical Documents and Law on Sacred Music as Applied to Bantu Music*. Schoneck-Beckenried, Switzerland: Nouvelle Revue de Science Missionnaire.
McClung, L. Grant, ed. 1986. *Azusa Street and Beyond: Pentecostal Mission and Church Growth in the Twentieth Century*. South Plainfield, N.J.: Bridge Publishers.
McHarg, James. 1958. "African Music in Rhodesian Native Education." *African Music* 2(1): 46–50.
Mensah, Atta Annan. 1998. "Compositional Practices in African Music." In *Africa: The Garland Encyclopedia of World Music*, vol. 1, edited by Ruth Stone, 208–231. New York: Garland.
Merriam, Alan. 1967. "The Use of Music as a Technique of Reconstructing Culture History in Africa." In *Reconstructing African Culture History*, edited by Creighton Gabel and Norman R. Bennett, 83–114. Boston: Boston University Press.
Mukuna, Kazadi wa. 1992. "The Genesis of Urban Music in Zaïre." *African Music* 7(2): 72–84.
———. 1999. "Evolution of Urban Music in Democratic Republic of the Congo during the 2nd and 3rd Decades (1975–1995) of the Second Republic Zaïre." *African Music* 7(4): 73–87
Mulindi, R. L. 1983. "Music in Logooli Culture." Master's thesis, Belfast University.
———. 2000. Interviews and discussions with the author, January–March.
Mulinge, Monica. 2005. Interviews with the author, March 14–18.
Muller, Carol A. 1999. *Rituals of Fertility and the Sacrifice of Desire: Nazarite Women's Performance in South Africa*. Chicago: University of Chicago Press.
Murray, Jocelyn, ed. 1998. *Cultural Atlas of Africa*. New York: Facts on File.
Mutai, Christopher Arap. 2006. Interviews with the author, May–June.
Mutongi, Beatrice Kenda. 1999. "'Worries of the Heart': Widowed Mothers, Daughters and Masculinities in Maragoli, Western Kenya, 1940–60." *Journal of African History* 40(1): 67–86.
Mutoro, Basilida Anyona. 1997. *Women Working Wonders: Small Scale Farming and the Role of Women in Vihiga District, Kenya, A Case Study of North Maragoli*. Amsterdam: Thela Publishers.
Mwavali, Gershom. 2005. Interview with the author, May 24.
Mwelesa, Gideon W. H. 1988. *Nditsominya Yahova ne Tsinyimbu*. Hymn compilation. Eldoret Kenya: Primus Media Service.

———. 2005. Interviews with the author, May.
———. 2007. Interviews with the author, May.
Ndeda, Mildred. 2005. "Nomiya Luo Church: A Gender Analysis of an African Independent Church Among the Luo of Siaya District 1907–1999," www.codesria.org/Links/conferences/gender/NDEDA.pdf (accessed July 12, 2006).
Nketia, J. H. 1957. "Modern Trends in Ghana Music." *African Music* 4(1): 13–16.
———. 1974a. *The Music of Africa*. London: W. W. Norton.
———. 1974b. "The Musical Heritage of Africa." In *Slavery, Colonialism, and Racism: Essays*, edited by Sidney Wilfred Mintz and J. F. Ade Ajayi, 151–161. New York: W. W. Norton.
Nthamburi, Zablon. 1991. *The African Church at the Crossroads: Strategies for Indigenization*. Nairobi: Uzima Press.
Nwulia, Moses D. E. 1975. *British and Slavery in East Africa*. Washington, D.C: Three Continents Press.
Nyman, Fred. 1991. Interviews with the author, Falkoping Sweden, March–April.
———. 2005. Interviews with the author, Sweden, July 16.
Nyman, Jan Erik. 1995. Interviews with the author, Ngaramtoni, Tanzania, July.
Ochieng', William Robert. 2002. *Historical Studies and Social Change in Western Kenya: Essays in Memory of Professor Gideon S. Were*. Nairobi: East African Educational Publishers.
Ogot, Bethwell A., and J. A. Kieran, eds. 1968. *Zamani: A Survey of East African History*. Nairobi: East African Publishing House.
Ogot, Bethwell A., and Frederick Welbourn. 1966. *A Place to Feel at Home*. London: Oxford University Press.
Oliver, Roland Anthony. 1965. *The Missionary Factor in East Africa*, 2nd ed. London: Longman.
Olson, Howard. 1979. "The Growth of Ethnic Hymnody in Tanzania." *Hymn* 30: 159–166.
Osogo, John. 1966. *A History of the Baluyia*. Nairobi: Oxford University Press.
Osotsi, Ramenga Mtaali. 1995. "A Performance Analysis of the Tsing'ano of the Abanyore and Avalogooli of Western Kenya." PhD diss., Indiana University.
Otieno, Samuel A. 1990. *Luo Spirituals*. Nairobi: Acts Press, African Centre for Technology Studies. Music score.
Painter, Levinus K. 1966. *The Hill of Vision: The Story of the Quaker Movement in East Africa, 1902–1965*. n.p.: East African Yearly Meeting of Friends.
PAOC (Pentecostal Assemblies of Canada) Archives, records on Kenya missions. 1924–1976. Various documents.
Parrinder, E. G. 1956. "Music in West African Churches." *African Music* 1(3): 37–38.
Pavitt, Nigel. 2008. *Kenya: A Country in the Making 1880–1940*. New York: W. W. Norton.
Rasmussen, Ane Marie Bak. 1995. *A History of the Quaker Movement in Africa*. London: British Academic Press.
Records of Friends African Mission. 1904–1907. MF 72 Reel 1, Minute book, September 1904–September 1907. Housed at Earlham College archives.
Rees, Deborah. 1899–1925. *African Papers, RG5/239*. Friends Historical Library of Strathmore College.
Rees, Emory. J. 1905. "Kaimosi, Seventh Month 11, 1905." *American Friend* 12: 642–643.
———. 1907. "Quarterly Report for Maragoli, October 1, 1906." *Africa Record* 1(3): 3–4.
———. 1908a. "Maragoli Station: January 1–March 31." *Africa Record* 3(3): 2–3.

———. 1908b. "A Kavirondo Funeral." *Africa Record* 3(4): 5–7.
———. 1910a. "Letters from Converted Native." *Africa Record* 5(3): 7.
———. 1910b. "An African Cottage Prayer Meeting." *American Friend* 17: 544.
———. 1911. "Mudaki." *Africa Record* 6(1): 7.
———. 1918. "One Personal Glance at Maragoli." *Africa Record* 12(1): 6–7.
Rees, Emory, and Deborah G. Rees. 1908. "Maragoli Quarterly Report." *Africa Record* 3(4): 1–3.
———. 1910. "Annual Report from Maragoli." *Africa Record* 5(2): 2–3.
———. 1912. "Maragoli Station." *Africa Record* 7 (3): 3–4.
Reeve, Roxie. 1918. "Girls Work at Maragoli." *Africa Record* 12(2): 6–7.
Rhodes, Willard. 1959. "Changing Times." *African Music* 2(2): 6–10.
Rice, Edwin Wilbur. 1971. *The Sunday School Movement 1780–1917, and the American Sunday-School Union 1817–1917*. New York: Arno Press. (First published 1917.)
Rice, Timothy. 1994. *May It Fill Your Soul: Experiencing Bulgarian Music*. Chicago: University of Chicago Press.
Richardson, Paul. 1998. "Hymnody in the United States from the Mid 19th Century." In *The New Century Hymnal Companion: A Guide to the Hymns*, edited by Kristen L. Forman, 106–124. Cleveland: Pilgrim Press.
Rodeheaver, Homer, and Charles Ford Jr. 1941. *Song Leadership*. Winona Lake, Ind.: Rodeheaver Hall-Mack Co.
Rogal, Samuel J., comp. 1996. *Sing Glory and Hallelujah!: Historical and Biographical Guide to Gospel Hymns Nos. 1 to 6 Complete*. Westport, Conn.: Greenwood Press.
Rowe, John. 1958. "Kaimosi, an Essay in Missionary History." Master's thesis, University of Wisconsin.
Sallee, James. 1978. *A History of Evangelical Hymnody*. Grand Rapids, Mich.: Baker Book House.
Sangree, Walter H. 1966. *Age, Prayer and Politics in Tiriki, Kenya*. London: Oxford University Press.
———. 1980. "The 'Last Born' (Muxogosi) and Complimentary Filiation in Tiriki, Kenya." *Ethos* 9(3): 188–200.
Sankey, Ira D., James McGranaham, and Geo Stebbins. 1894. *Gospel Hymns, Nos. 1 to 6: For Use in Gospel Meetings and Other Religious Services*. New York: John Church Co.
Scheel, Iris. 1958. "Goibei Girls School . . . Kenya." From PAOC Archives report, Kenya files.
———. 1962. Foreword to *C.A. Song Book*. Nyang'ori, Kenya: Christ's Ambassadors Department of the Pentecostal Assemblies of East Afria.
Senoga-Zake, George. 1986. *Folk Music of Kenya*. Nairobi: Uzima Press.
Shaffer, Jacqueline. 1956. "Experiments in Indigenous Church Music among the Batetela." *African Music* 1(3): 39–42.
Shelemay, Kay Kaufman. 1998. "Notation and Oral Tradition." In *Africa: The Garland Encyclopedia of World Music*, vol. 1, edited by Ruth Stone, 146–163. New York: Garland.
Smuck, Harold. 1985. "Thomas Lung'aho: East African Quaker Educator, and Administrator." In *Living in the Light: Some Quaker Pioneers of the 20th Century*, vol. 2, edited by Leonard S. Kenworthy, 160–173. Kennett Square, Pa.: Friends General Conference and Quaker Publications.
Southern, Eileen. 1983. *The Music of Black Americans: A History*, 2nd ed. New York: W. W. Norton.

Spear, Thomas, and Isaria N. Kimambo, eds. 1999. *East African Expressions of Christianity*. Athens: Ohio University Press.
Spencer, Leon P. 1975. "Christian Missions and African Interests in Kenya, 1905–1924." PhD diss., Syracuse University.
Stafford, Kay. 1973. "The Southern Abaluyia, the Friends Africa Mission, and the Development of Education in Western Kenya 1902–1965." PhD diss., University of Wisconsin.
Strayer, Robert W. 1978. *The Making of Mission Communities in East Africa: Anglicans and Africans in Colonial Kenya 1875–1835*. London: Heinemann.
Sundkler, Bengt. 1976. *Zulu Zion and Some Swazi Zionists*. London: Oxford University Press.
Synan, Vinson. 1987. *The Twentieth-Century Pentecostal Explosion: The Exciting Growth of Pentecostal Churches and Charismatic Renewal Movements*. Altamonte Springs, Fla.: Creation House.
———. 1997. *The Holiness-Pentecostal Tradition: Charismatic Movements in the Twentieth Century*, 2nd ed. Grand Rapids, Mich.: W. B. Eerdmans.
Taber, William C. 1918. "A Survey of the Africa Work for 1917." *Africa Record* 12(1): 3–6.
Temperley Nicholas. 1984. "Lining Out and Psalm Singing." *Hymn* 35: 170–172.
Tracey, Hugh. 1964. "Review of Graham Hyslop's *Since Singing Is So Good a Thing*." *African Music* 3(3): 119–120.
Tsinyimbu Tsya Nyasaye. 1966 (rev. ed.). Nairobi: Evangel Publishing House.
Turner, Harold W. 1967. *History of an African Independent Church*, vol. 1. *The Church of the Lord (Aladura)*. Oxford, England: Clarendon Press.
Verma, Ritu. 2001. *Gender, Land and Livelihoods in East Africa: Through Farmers' Eyes*. Ottawa: International Development Research Centre.
Vokwana, Thembela. 2006. "Can We Sing Together? Performing Nationhood through Choral Festivals in South Africa." Paper presented at the Society for Ethnomusicology Annual Conference, Honolulu, Hawaii, November 15–19.
Wa Kinyatti, Maina. 1980. *Thunder from the Mountains: Mau Mau Patriotic Songs*. London: Zed Press.
Wachsmann, Klaus P., ed. 1971. *Essays on Music and History in Africa*. Evanston, Ill.: Northwestern University Press.
Wafula, Robert Juma. 2001. "Crossroads of Western Quakerism in Africa." *Quaker Theology* no, 5, Autumn, http://www.quaker.org/quest/issues5-4.html (accessed August 12, 2006).
Wagner, Gunther. 1936. "The Study of Culture Contact and the Determination of Policy." *Africa: The Journal of the International African Institute* 9(3): 317–331.
———. 1939. *The Changing Family among the Bantu Kavirondo*. London: Oxford University Press.
———. 1949. *The Bantu of Western Kenya: With Special Reference to the Vugusu and Logoli*. London: Oxford University Press.
Wako, Daniel. 1954. *Akabaluyia Wemumbo*. Nairobi: Eagle Press.
Walls, Andrew F. 1996. *The Missionary Movement in Christian History: Studies in the Transmission of Faith*. Maryknoll, N.Y.: Orbis Books.
Waombu, Ernest. 2008. Interviews with the author, June 2, 9–10.
Welch, David. 1985. "A Yoruba/Nagô 'Melotype' for Religious Songs in the African Diaspora: Continuity of West African Praise Song in the New World." In *More*

than Drumming: Essays on African and Afro-Latin American Music and Musicians, edited by Irene Jackson, 145–162. Westport, Conn.: Greenwood Press.
Weman, Henry. 1960. *Church Music and the Church in Africa*. Translated by Eric J. Sharpel. Uppsala, Sweden: Lundequistska Bokhandeln.
Wendte, William. 1904. "In the Africa Industrial Mission." *American Friend* 11: 678–679, 694–696, 760–761, 812–813.
Were, Gideon S. 1967a. *A History of the Abaluyia of Western Kenya*. Nairobi: East African Publishing House.
———. 1967b. *Western Kenya Historical Texts: Abaluyia, Teso, and Elgon Kalenjin*. Nairobi: East African Literature Bureau.
———. 1977. *Essays on African Religion in Western Kenya*. Nairobi: East African Literature Bureau.
Were, Gideon S., and Derek A Wilson. 1971. *East Africa through a Thousand Years: A History of the Years A.D. 1000 to the Present Day*, 2nd ed. New York: Africana Pub. Corp.
Wesonga, Moses, and John W Ward. 1973. "Religious Broadcasting in Kenya." In *Kenya Churches Handbook: The Development of Kenyan Christianity 1498–1973*, edited by David Barrett et al., 85–94. Kisumu, Kenya: Evangel Publishing House.
White, Charles. 1907. "F.A. I. M. Board Annual Meeting." *American Friend* 14: 285.
Wolf, Jan J. de. 1977. *Differentiation and Integration in Western Kenya: A Study of Religious Innovation and Social Change*. The Hague: Mouton & Co., B.V.

WEBSITES OF INTEREST

http://www.ackenya.org/history.htm.
http://www.andimi.com/history_of_mulogoli.htm.
http://www.clark.net/pub/quaker/web/archive.html.
http://www.gospelcom.net/dacb/stories/kenya/scheel_iris.html.
http://www.indianahistory.org/library/manuscripts/collection_guides/bv0401.html.
http://www.paoc.org/.
http://www.quaker.org.
http://www.religioustolerance.org/quaker.htm.
http://www.swarthmore.edu/library/friends/ead/5239rees.xml.
http://www.vihiga.com.

SELECT DISCOGRAPHY—COMMERCIAL AND PRIVATE RECORDINGS

Araka, Samuel, with Obulandi Gospel singers. *Yesu Yangula: Luhya Gospel Choruses 1*. Kassanga Music Center Productions.
Goibei women's group. 1983, 1986, 1993, 2004, 2005, 2006. Private collection by Jean Kidula.
Illavaza, Francis Jumba. *Luyia No. 1*. Neno Productions.
———. *Luhya No. 2: Ulivolela Sina Yesu*. Neno Productions.
———. *Luhya No. 3: Gali Mahingano*. Neno Productions.
———. *Luhya Vol. 9: Shila Vulahi Mudoga*. Neno Productions.
Ilavadza, Francis Jumba, and Keran Imari Jumba. *The Swahili Praise and Worship Choruses: Tunaitwa na Yesu*. Neno Productions.
Kemoli, Arthur, dir. 1979. *Gendi Kwilwadze*. Kenyatta University Choir. Single 45 rpm record.

———. 1984. *Wedding Suite*. Kariokor Friends Choir. Kemoli private collection.
———. 1985. *Nandio Kwalange, Chesaila*. Kariokor Youth Friends Choir. Kemoli private collection.
———. 1984. *Kariokor Nyayo Choir, Japan Concerts*. Kemoli private collection.
———. 2000. *Inzala and Other Melodies*. University of Nairobi Choir. Cassette tape.
Kigame, Reuben, and Douglas Jiveti. *Ari ho Yesu*. Produced at Kenya Baptist Media.
———. *Yesu Ari Mwoyo*. Recorded at Andrew Crawford Productions.
Manoah, Betty, the Manoahs. *Yerusalemi imbya*. Kassanga Music Center Productions.
———. *Yesu Yatsanga*. Kassanga Music Center Productions.
Muungano National Choir. 1990. *Missa Luba, an African Mass and 10 Kenyan Folk Melodies*. CD. Philips Classics Productions 426-836-2.
Mwauras. Released 2003. *Luyia Praise*. Cassette compilation.
Nyimbo 2&3: The Music of Robert Yaa/Kenya, Popular Christian Music/Zimbabwe. Produced by African Church Music Resource Center Nairobi, by J. Nathan Corbitt.

VIDEOGRAPHY

Kenya: Robert Eames Furlong 1963. Private holding from PAOC Archives.
Contains silent movie of this missionary's family, work, and other places of interest including Evangel Publishing House, set up in Nyang'ori, Kenya, in 1952.
Maragoli. Sandra Nichols, 1977, 1976. Film 2 reels, 59 min.: 16 mm. Berkeley: University of California Extension Media Center.
Presents viewpoints of the people of Maragoli through discussions conducted by a Logooli interviewer. Relates social and economic problems that confront the people.
PAOC Archive video.
Silent movie compilation shot between 1939 and 1948. Footage of a visit by Canadian officials hosted by Canadian missionaries, Logooli church leaders, and schoolteachers. The events include the opening of a church and singing by congregations with hand clapping and drumming conducted by an African. Includes the arrival of the officials by plane, Batwa—nomadic pygmies with indigenous houses around Nyang'ori, and dances by African troupes. It is unclear whether it was in a religious setting or a government function. Has Luo dancers in regalia walking along the road.

INDEX

MAIN INDEX

Abaluyia (Baluyia, Avaluhya), 3, 38–39, 72, 85, 121, 223, 243, 246, 248, 250–251, 255

Abaluyia subgroups: Avabukusu, 3, 43, 52, 235, 241, 243–244, 246, 253; Avadirichi, 3, 5, 7, 26, 41–43, 113, 208, 243, 246, 248, 259, 263, 266; Avalogooli, xviii, 2–5, 8, 11–15, 17, 19–21, 27, 32, 36–39, 41–46, 48–50, 54, 62, 64, 70–72, 75, 77, 82–87, 92–95, 97, 103, 105, 107, 114, 116, 118, 132–133, 139, 147–148, 152–157, 160–161, 163, 169, 173, 180–181, 183, 185, 190–191, 216, 220, 223, 226, 228–230, 235, 236, 243, 245, 246, 247, 249–253, 259, 262–263; Avanyore, 3, 45, 92, 243, 249; Avatsotso, 3, 244, 246, 248; Avidakho, 3, 42–43, 244, 247, 259; Avisukha, 3, 244, 245, 247

Abwunza, Judith, 63

academy, 2, 11, 183, 188; academic, 2, 11, 61, 76, 95, 186, 190, 197, 200, 209–210, 219, 227–228, 230

adapt, 33, 229; adaptation, 11, 89, 188, 194, 264, 265; adapted, 4, 34, 48, 93, 112, 188, 188, 190, 208, 255, 265

adaptation and arrangement, 33, 95, 117, 183, 185–220, 211

Adede, Rose, 97, 236–237

adopt, 23, 54, 102, 161, 184; adopted, 2, 9, 16, 19, 26, 33, 34, 45, 47, 48, 59, 68, 94, 97, 102, 112, 121, 124, 135, 142, 145, 155, 160, 179, 184, 191, 249, 250, 251, 255, 262, 264; adoption, 2, 12, 13, 18, 37, 50, 96, 151, 163, 251

African Independent churches (Africanist, Afrogenic), 1, 11, 44, 52, 75, 84, 154, 172, 191, 223, 230, 243. *See also* denominations

All Saints Cathedral, 188, 264

Alliance High School, 188

ancestors, 19–21, 23, 26, 28, 32, 48, 70, 208, 209, 247, 251

ancestral name, 23, 90; grove, 28; rite, 23; spirit, 20

Ang'oma, 19–21, 251

aporia, 8, 9–10, 12

appropriate, 17, 24, 39, 52, 73, 84, 93, 96, 108, 110–111, 131, 148, 178, 196–197, 208, 210, 217, 247, 255, 260appropriated, 2, 9–10, 12, 52–53, 71, 77, 101, 103, 134–135, 143, 156, 169, 172, 222, 248, 250, 260; appropriation, 1, 10, 76, 147, 152, 162

arranged (music), 10–11, 79, 93–94, 188–191, 193, 197, 209–210, 219, 221, 223, 227, 236; arrangement, 64, 91, 93, 95, 101, 147, 179, 186–188, 190, 192, 194, 197–198, 200, 202, 205–206, 208–210, 214, 216–217, 219–221, 223, 225–226, 228, 230, 258, 265

assembly (gathering), 10, 53, 55, 88, 104, 135, 201, 250, 255

attitude, 10, 16, 23, 43, 149, 156, 196, 247, 248, 254

Avaana vosi kwimbe, 134

Avalogooli (singular—mulogooli). *See* Abaluyia subgroups

Avasaalisi, 21, 243, 247

baptism, water, 49–50, 49, 61; 'Baptism in the Holy Spirit,' 44, 46, 61
Blackburn, Elisha and Virginia, 42, 253
body motion, 76, 100, 109, 123, 132, 148, 150, 176, 229, 265
Bombay, Richard C., 92
'book' music (songs of the book), 76–83, 91, 96, 131, 151, 156, 190, 226, 231, 257, 260; Logooli features, 147–152; musical elements, 107–112, 192; structure and use, 112–128, 179; song leading and performance practices, 103–107, 155, 178. *See also* chorus(es); hymn; refrain
booklet(s), 77, 80, 81, 83, 96, 134–135, 156, 240, 261, 264

C. A. Song Book, 135
call and response, 51, 55–56, 62, 91, 101, 110, 118–119, 128, 132, 155, 162, 165, 167, 169, 175–176, 184, 190, 198, 200, 202, 205, 210, 217, 260
call and response, types: combination forms, 176–178; Fill-in-the-blank responses, 168–169; Halleluiah refrains, 169–172; lining out, 103–104, 144, 155, 162, 165, 168, 172–176, 197, 260; lining refrains and responsorial burdens, 172–176; single phrase fixed responses, 165–168
camp, 40, 119, 135, 136, 154, 185, 261
Canada, xviii, 8, 44, 45, 74, 106, 135, 236, 254, 255
ceremony, 14, 20, 21, 23, 24, 25, 26, 27, 31, 32, 35, 60, 65, 66, 67, 68, 70
Chavakali, 255
Chilson, Arthur, 41, 46, 72, 84
choir, 7, 12, 59, 63, 76, 78, 91–93, 102, 108, 135, 144, 183–186, 189–192, 216–217, 221, 228, 258, 265; conductor, 56, 105, 191, 210, 212, 221; director, 108, 145, 187, 190, 216; music, 55, 76, 91–93. *See also* makwaya; Tsikwaya
choirs / choral groups: Kariokor Friends Choir, 188, 193, 197, 209, 265; Kariokor Nyayo Choir, 209, 220; Kenyatta University Choir, 197; Machakos Town Choir, 144; Muungano National Choir, 192, 216, 265; Nairobi Pentecostal Church Choir, 11; Riruta Baptist Church Choir, 221, 225, 265; University of Nairobi Choir, 189, 216
chorus(es) (Tsikorasi), 10, 75–77, 86–91, 94, 96–97, 104, 128–135, 147, 239–240, 244, 248, 255, 257–258, 260. *See also* refrain
Christian Endeavor, 52
Christian villages, 8
Christmas, 15, 58–60, 76, 82, 93, 100–101, 107, 127, 139, 148, 162, 178, 188–189, 226, 254–256, 259; Day (Siguuku), 54–55, 57, 185, 245, 247–248. *See also* malago
Christ's Ambassadors, 52, 134, 258
code switching, 222
colonial, 2, 3, 7, 8 10, 12, 14, 18, 20, 38, 42, 43, 45, 46, 50, 64, 75, 79, 80, 92, 153, 157, 225, 227, 230, 236, 247, 249, 253, 264; colonialism, 3, 5, 36, 62
comity, policy of, 39, 45, 49, 253
contemporary, 2, 3, 11, 12, 33, 68, 70, 78, 81, 92, 95, 167, 183–184, 191, 220, 227–228, 231, 233, 236, 255
conversion, 40, 44, 50, 161, 170, 248, 262
Corbitt, J. Nathan, 76–77, 83, 86, 249, 256
council of elders, 14, 64, 246, 250; luhya, 14, 22, 246, 250

dance, 31, 56, 73, 84–85, 94, 117, 201, 212; lipala, 85–86, 172, 246; mavega, 179, 246, mutivo, 174, 247; song and, 28, 65, 68, 133; styles, 26
denominations, 5, 8, 11, 49, 66, 75, 83, 95, 152–153, 180; African Divine Church (ADC), xxiii, 53–54, 54; African Inland Church (AIC), xix, 8, 92, 184, 235, 265; African Israeli Church Nineveh (AICN), xxiii, 6, 46, 53, 75, 150, 161, 180, 254, 255; Akorino, 223, 243; Anglican, 8, 76, 185, 186, 187, 253, 255, 257, 260; Dini ya Roho, 46; Lutheran, 37, 91–92, 257; Pentecostal(s), xviii, xix, xxiii, 5–8, 10–12, 44–47, 49–54, 57, 61, 68, 73–75, 77–78, 83–84, 93, 95–96, 103, 106, 131, 134–135, 137, 152–154, 161, 173, 180, 190, 200–202, 229–230, 254–255, 260–261; Pentecostal Assemblies of God (PAG), xix, xxiii, 77, 119, 135, 136, 185, 256, 257, 260; Presbyte-

rian, 255, 257, 260; Quaker(s) (Friends), xvii–xix, 5–6, 8, 10, 12, 39–46, 49–53, 71–72, 75, 78–79, 81–84, 93, 95–96, 106, 119, 124, 134, 152–154, 180, 185, 188–189, 194, 230, 235, 236, 253, 255, 257, 261, 264; Roman Catholic, 5; Salvation Army, 5, 7, 8, 47, 48, 53, 94, 134, 172, 181, 255; United Methodist, 37

diversity, 4, 5, 8, 10, 132, 191, 227

drama, 31, 55, 57–58, 64, 68, 86, 167, 178, 185–186, 192, 194, 196, 197, 200, 202, 204, 206, 209–210, 212, 215–217, 227

drum, 21, 25, 69, 72, 74, 83, 92–94, 107–108, 110–112, 121, 123, 133, 145, 170, 178–181, 208, 231 (see also instruments); drumming, 35, 44, 59, 69, 75, 86, 110, 133, 142, 147, 148, 160, 178, 179, 180, 231

'duplicative significance,' 212

Easter, 54, 60, 135, 139, 193

education, 5, 6–9, 11, 29, 38, 41–43, 49, 62–65, 76, 92, 149, 161, 183, 186–187, 191, 210, 230, 236, 264

Egara, Kabaji Stanley, 19

ethnic groups, 1–3, 5–7, 9, 22, 26, 39, 44–45, 61, 192, 210, 217, 220, 244, 248, 253. See also languages and peoples

Euba, Akin, 12, 171, 249, 259

Euro-American, 1–2, 7, 12, 37, 47, 62, 68, 71, 75, 92, 94, 103, 113, 116, 147, 149, 152, 156, 171, 182, 184, 228, 229

Eurogenic, 2, 103, 197

European, 1–2, 6–7, 36–39, 41, 45–46, 49, 64, 73, 75, 77, 91, 93–96, 98–99, 101, 103, 107, 113, 154, 156, 161, 180–181, 183–185, 187, 191–192, 196, 204, 209–210, 215, 219, 228–230, 243, 259, 262, 264

evangelical, 40–41, 44–45, 47, 93, 153; Evangelical Quakers, 47, 153

evangelism, 33, 41, 43, 55, 61, 64, 87, 132, 184, 221; evangelize, 2, 41, 44–45, 83, 134, 153, 263

festivals: music, 11, 55, 64, 93, 107, 151, 189, 190, 192, 193, 220, 221, 258, 263, 264, 265; religious, 54, 58, 66, 139, 148. See also Kenya Music Festival

form and structure, 47, 80, 87, 90, 94, 97, 106, 112, 114, 122, 125–126, 128, 138, 143, 147–149, 156, 158, 162, 165–178, 190–191, 198, 201, 208, 257, 260, 261; AABA, 127, 137; ABA, 197–200; binary, 126; call-and-response, 165–178; fugue, 218–219; lyrical, 99, 125, 131, 156; stanza, 112, 156, 184, 200, 210; stanza/refrain, 77, 85, 87, 91, 106, 114, 118–119, 126, 134, 167, 176, 184, 193, 201, 262

Fox, George, 39

Friends. See denominations

global, 3, 10, 12, 77, 84, 93, 94, 152, 179, 181, 184, 216, 227, 229

Goibei, xvii, xviii, 5–10, 6, 56, 74, 135, 159, 230, 232, 233, 249, 250, 252, 255, 260; women, 232, 233, 251, 252, 258, 263

gospel, 2, 40, 43, 73, 78, 220; hymns and songs, 10, 55, 74, 77–78, 87–88, 95, 96–128, 145, 147, 153–154, 156, 170, 184, 225, 260; musical elements, 107–112; structures and use, 112–128. See also 'book' music

gospel music, 77–79, 93–94, 96, 183, 191, 220–227, 258, 264; performers, 11, 79, 221–226. See also Ilavadza, Francis Jumba; Kigame, Reuben

Great Awakening, 75, 78, 87, 96, 124, 153

groove, 166, 181, 196, 214, 265

gwalide (igwalide), 69, 76, 83, 244

'halleluiah call,' 104, 156, 176, 178, 180

hand clap, 10, 44, 47, 51, 59, 75–76, 83–84, 86, 88–89, 91, 100, 102, 105–106, 108–112, 114, 116–117, 123, 126–127, 129, 137, 139–143, 146–148, 150–151, 160, 170–171, 178–179, 181, 194, 198, 200–201, 206, 231, 254–255, 257, 259, 261, 265

harmony, 55, 64, 77, 91–93, 108, 143, 150, 187, 196, 198, 202, 208, 210, 217, 219; heterophony, 80, 106, 108, 150, 214; homophony, 144, 190, 213; polyphony, 194, 209, 212, 216

historical, 1, 2, 3, 9–10, 12, 13, 14, 31, 95, 106, 152, 166, 183, 233, 250, 266

Hole, Edgar T., 41, 43, 49, 72–73, 92, 254, 255, 259
Holy Spirit, 46–47, 61, 76, 84, 154, 170
Hotchkiss, Willis, 41–43, 250, 258
hymn, 1–2, 7, 10–11, 27, 40–44, 46–47, 51, 55, 58, 59, 66, 68–69, 71–84, 86–87, 91–92, 94–99, 101–103, 105, 108–109, 112–114, 116, 119–120, 122–123, 135, 137, 142–143, 145, 147–148, 154–156, 183–184, 192–193, 220–221, 227, 232, 235–237, 253–255, 257–261, 264; how introduced, 71–75; missionary hymn style, 75, 77, 156. *See also* 'book' music; gospel
hymnal, xvii, xxi, 44, 61, 76–81, 83, 91, 93, 96–97, 103–104, 108, 113, 116, 123–124, 128, 131, 134–135, 235, 236, 254, 257–261
hymnbook, 42–43, 87, 96, 107, 145, 231
Hyslop, Graham, 64, 118, 185–188, 191, 194, 197, 235, 236, 264

Ikwaya, 77, 184, 244, 246, 248. *See also* Tsikwaya
Ilavadza, Francis Jumba, 221–227, 224, 230, 265, 266
Imali, Keren Jumba, 224, 226
indigenous, 1–2, 5–7, 10–13, 15, 17, 19, 26, 36, 46, 50, 60, 62, 65–66, 68–70, 72–73, 75–77, 80, 83–84, 86, 93–95, 103–104, 106, 121, 128, 131, 134–135, 149, 151, 154, 156, 160, 179, 181, 183–185, 190–192, 196–198, 208–210, 215, 220, 225, 227–230, 244, 254, 255, 263; indigenization, 2, 205
indigenous hymns, 77. *See also* 'spirit' songs; Tsinyimbu: tsya Roho
ing'oma. *See* dance; instruments
"Inner Light," 40, 51
instruments, 51, 80, 94, 107, 121, 148, 188, 191, 226; Accordion, 72; Clay pot, 150; indumba (drum), 69, 83, 110, *111*, 112, 121, 143, 179, 191, 200, 244, ing'oma (drum), 21, 251, isigudi (drum), 83, 181, 191, 200, 209–210, 244, 245, 256; kidindi (mudindi) (drum), 25, 110, *111*, 112, 114, 123, 179, 181, 191, 200, 231, 245, 247; Indovondovo, 65, 244; Kayamba, 93, 135, 191, 245, 255, 265; Kilili (kiriri), 80, 179, 226, 245, 266; Kisili, 245; Lidorondo, 246, 257; Lidungu, 179; Ling'ala, 72, 257. *See also* hand clap
Isahi (Esahi), 19, 21, 244, 259
Isigudi. *See* dance; instruments
Isilika, 62–63, 244
itiru, 22–23, 245
Ivayo, Hannah, xviii, 231
Ivulogooli, 3, 14, 39, 228, 229, 245, 253

Jiveti, Douglas, 226

Kaimosi, 41–42, 44, 46, 72, 77, 82, 84, 154, 253
Kakoma, George, 187
Kasiera, Ezekiel, 40–41, 44, 65–66, 71–73, 80, 129, 154, 157, 180–181, 230, 250, 251, 252, 254, 256, 261, 262, 263
kebende, 10, 245, 254
kehenda mwoyo, 164, 245, 262
Keller, Marian and Otto, 45–47, 49, 50, 55, 57–58, 73–75, 106–107, 161, 250, 254, 259, 261
Kemoli, Arthur, xvii–xix, 10–12, 186–189, *189*, 191–194, 196–198, 200–202, 204–210, 212–220, 224–227, 230, 264, 265
Kenya Music Festival, 186, 188, 217, 264. *See also* festivals
Kenyatta University, xvii–xviii, 11, 191, 229; Kenyatta College, 186–188
Kibukosya, Peter, 187
Kidula, Emmy, xix, 230
Kigame, Reuben, xvii, 226, 266
Kijabe, 184–185, 235
Kitoshi, 43
Kitts, Sophia, 64
Kivuli, Zakayo, 161–162
Krapf, John Ludwig, 37
kufuminya, 51, 245
kuhihiza, 55, 245, 256
kuhola, 133, 245
kukesha, 60, 246, 256
kusaalila mwana, 66, 246
kutuula, 102, 141, 176, 205, 246
kuvugula, 109, 156, 176, 246

kwaya, 55, 82, 183–185, 246. *See also* makwaya
kwitakasa, 51, 246

languages and peoples, 4, 26, 31, 45, 55, 76, 78, 93, 108, 128, 132, 134, 143, 171, 173, 185, 196, 220, 235, 241, 249, 253, 259, 260; Bantu, 3, 5, 45, 163, 173, 243, 245, 249, 259 (*see also* Abaluyia); Kalenjin, 3, 254, 249; Kikuyu, 223, 235, 244; Kisii, 61, 134, 235, 245, 261; Kiswahili, 5, 8, 43, 53–56, 66, 68–69, 71–72, 75, 78, 82, 91–92, 94, 96–97, 103, 118, 132–133, 142–144, 159–160, 162–163, 183–185, 189, 196, 221, 226, 231, 235–236, 240–241, 244, 246–249, 253, 255, 257–259, 261–262, 264–266; Luo, 3, 5, 45, 61, 173, 184, 241, 244, 246, 250, 279; Maasai, 3, 38, 235; Nandi, 5, 41, 43, 45, 249, 258; Nilotes, 45, 173, 244, 245, 246, 248, 250; Somali, 38, 45, 249; Terik, 45, 249; Teso, 3, 135, 136, 248; Zulu, 259 (*see also* Lulogooli)
Lirhanda, 41, 43
liswakila, 23–24, 65. *See also* Rite(s): birth
Litu, Joel, 97, 236, 254
local, 3, 10, 19, 48, 80, 82, 84, 155, 188, 220, 228–229, 254
Logooli, xvii–xx, 3–19, 4, 15, 21–22, 26–27, 32–33, 35–37, 39, 41–48, 50, 53, 60, 65, 68, 70–71, 73, 75–84, 86, 88–90, 93–97, 99, 101–104, 106, 108–109, 112, 117–118, 123, 126, 128–129, 131–135, 137, 139, 142–143, 145, 147, 149–157, 159–163, 168–170, 173, 177–179, 181–184, 188–192, 194, 196–198, 201, 204–205, 207–210, 212, 214–216, 218–221, 223–230, 232, 235, 243, 246, 250, 252, 258, 260, 261, 262, 265; aesthetic, 108–110, 156, 160, 170, 173, 176, 201, 205, 219; beliefs, xix, 4, 6, 19–22, 24, 48, 70, 128, 137, 151, 152–153, 181, 233, 250, 251, 252, 254; clan, 8–9, 13, 14–16, 20–29, 31, 36, 38, 50, 61–62, 64, 66–69, 206–207, 209, 246, 247, 249, 250, 251, 253; clan name, 14, 16, 23–24, 50, 66, 257; composer, 10, 18, 79–84, 123, 128, 147, 149, 160, 165, 184, 191, 208, 227 (*see also* Kemoli, Arthur; Kigame, Reuben; Mwelesa, Gideon Wesley S.); composition, 12, 26, 32, 47, 65, 77, 79, 81–84, 93, 123, 128, 131, 137, 143, 147, 165, 184, 188, 193, 208; essence, 16, 130, 161, 163, 206, 228, 248; features in 'book' music, 147–152; language, *see* Lulogooli; modes, 35, 84, 108, 219; morals, 18, 26, 99, 164, 166, 222; mores, 90, 161, 163, 228, 232, 247, 250; music types (Christian), 77–78; practice, 10–12, 18, 19–36, 42, 44, 46, 47, 50–51, 65–70, 73, 80, 84, 99, 101, 103–104, 123, 131, 149, 150–151, 156, 161–162, 170, 190, 196, 197, 200, 204, 219, 220, 229, 245, 251, 252, 254; religion, 4, 12, 19–22, 36, 50, 251, 262; religious practices (new), 65–70; repertoire, 4, 7, 11–12, 18, 28, 31, 32, 35, 68, 71–72, 97, 128, 154, 155, 179, 181, 188, 190, 191, 227, 229, 231, 233; social education, 7, 18, 26, 29, 61–62, 64–65, 90, 181; values, 18–19, 22, 26, 29, 32, 36, 48, 65, 90, 131, 149, 181, 250; worldview, 4, 33, 47, 60, 70, 80, 86, 96, 128, 143, 147, 151–152, 154, 156–157, 159, 161, 197, 207–208, 224, 232, 250–251, 256, 262
Lulogooli, xviii, xx, xxi, 3, 26, 41–43, 46, 55–56, 68–69, 71–73, 75–76, 78, 82, 86, 88–89, 91–93, 96–103, 108–110, 115–116, 118–120, 122–124, 128–132, 134, 137–140, 142–143, 151, 162–163, 169, 183–185, 188–189, 192–193, 214, 221, 226–227, 230, 235–236, 240–241, 246, 249, 252, 254, 257–265
Luyia (Luhya), 3–5, 8–10, 14, 26, 31, 38–39, 43, 61, 71–72, 75, 85, 92, 94, 114, 121, 125, 130, 133, 145, 173, 180, 185, 191, 208, 216, 221, 223, 225–226, 241, 243–244, 246, 247, 248, 250, 251, 253, 255, 258–259, 263, 265–266, 268, 271, 273, 275, 277, 278, 279; identity, 10; nation, 9

makwaya, 91–94, 144, 183–185, 191, 226, 247, 258, 264, 265
malago, 55–60, 57, 59, 76, 82, 100, 185, 189, 247. *See also* Christmas
Manani, Gershom, 187

Maragoli (place), xvii–xviii, 14, 27, 41–43, 254, 255; South, 71
marriage, xix, 4, 22, 28, 61, 67, 85, 148. *See also* Rite(s): of passage
Mbale, 71
Mbela, Darius, 193
meeting, 5, 14, 40, 42, 46, 49, 51–54, 102, 110, 178, 236, 253, 254, 255; evangelistic, 54, 71, 170, 225, 256 (*see also* vushuhuda); monthly, 40, 42, 52, 244, 255; prayer, 42, 47, 52,75, 86, 155, 161, 179; Quaker, 40, 79, 82, 180; quarterly, 40, 42; revival, 40, 78, 87, 129, 135, 154, 170; yearly, 40, 52–53, 119, 185, 189, 241, 253, 255
melody, 80, 89, 92, 101, 107–108, 110, 114, 116–118, 120–123, 125, 127, 131–132, 134, 137, 143–145, 147–149, 160, 166, 168, 170, 173–174, 179, 186–188, 190, 192–194, 201, 204–205, 209–210, 217–218, 224, 265
meter, 34, 86, 90, 100, 102–103, 108–112, 115–118, 123, 126, 130, 137, 141, 143, 146–148, 160, 166, 170–173, 178–179, 193–194, 198, 206, 209, 259, 260, 261, 265; poetic meter, 91, 97, 113
metronome, 148, 151, 178; metronomic, 51, 94, 105, 111, 148, 179, 181, 255
migration, 4, 7, 8, 15, 80, 128, 157, 249, 261
Miller, Clyde, 45, 263
mission, 8, 27, 37, 39–46, 63, 71–73, 75, 77, 92, 106, 113, 121, 129, 153, 156, 161, 173, 185, 215; mission station, 8, 27, 37, 41–43, 45–46, 71–73, 75, 77, 121, 257, 258; Pentecostal, 8, 45–46, 161, 173 (*see also* Goibei); Quaker, 41–44 (*see also* Kaimosi; Kitoshi; Lirhanda; Maragoli; Mbale; Vihiga)
missionary, xviii, 2, 6, 8, 18, 26, 27, 37–39, 41–47, 50, 64, 79, 80, 179, 183, 191, 230, 236, 250, 253, 255, 259, 262, 263, 264; Apostolic Faith Mission, 45; Church Missionary Society (CMS), xxiii, 37, 39, 41, 43, 45, 257; education (Western), xix, 6, 38, 41, 43, 49, 62, 63–65, 92, 149, 161, 183, 186, 191, 210; Friends African Mission (FAM), xxiii, 39, 42; Friends Industrial African Mission (FIAM), xxiii, 39, 44; hymns/songs, 55, 60, 71–72, 75, 77, 81, 84, 91, 112, 123, 128, 151, 156, 179, 184, 192, 193 (*see also* 'book' music; chorus[es]); Nilotic Interior Mission, 45; organizations, 39, 45–46, 106, 253; Pentecostal Assemblies of Canada (PAOC), xviii, xxiii, 45–47, 49–50, 55, 57, 64, 75, 106, 178, 181, 236, 254, 261; Pentecostal missionary, xxiii, 45, 47, 77, 236, 255, 259 (*see also* Bombay, Richard C.; Keller, Marian and Otto; Kitts, Sophia; Miller, Clyde; Scheel, Iris); Quaker missionary, 39, 41–42, 73, 84, 236 (*see also* Blackburn, Elisha and Virginia; Chilson, Arthur; Hole, Edgar T.; Hotchkiss, Willis; Rees, Deborah); South African Compound and Interior Mission, 39
Monyi, Dora wa, xxiii, 231
Mulindi, Luzili, 17, 18, 102, 109, 149–150, 169, 176, 181, 250, 251, 252, 258
Mulogooli (progenitor), 14, 19
Mundu, 15, 16, 22, 228, 247
musical: aesthetic, 47, 51, 91, 95, 108–110, 149, 151, 156, 160, 170, 173, 176, 201, 205, 219, 231; characteristic(s), 13, 16, 85, 86, 156, 176, 180, 206; elements, 83–84, 95, 105, 107–128, 156, 165–178, 190 (*see also* form and structure; harmony; melody; meter; pitch; rhythm; texts); feature(s), ii, 10, 12, 35, 44, 51, 75–76, 156, 176, 181, 185, 194, 196; song style, 17, 31, 75, 81, 206
musicking, 10, 12, 21, 112, 149, 152, 154, 155, 156, 181, 190, 191, 220, 223, 233
musoomi, 78, 247, 248. *See also* Rite(s): circumcision
Mwelesa, Gideon Wesley S., xvii–xix, 10, 11, 36, 64, 79–83, 119, 126–128, 151, 152, 192–194, 224, 226, 228, 250, 257, 261, 262
mwing'oma, 20, 59, 247
mwoyo, 16, 105, 149, 164, 245, 246, 247, 248, 262

Nairobi, xvii, 54, 79, 187, 188, 191, 193, 221, 255, 256, 264, 265
national, 1, 3, 8–10, 12, 14, 19, 60, 61, 66, 82, 84, 93, 144, 179, 182, 189, 191–192, 196, 210, 220–221, 227, 229; nationalism, 2, 5, 15
Nditsominya Yahova ne Tsinyimbu, 79, 80, 81, 83

INDEX

North Kavirondo Native Reserve, 14
Nyimbo Standard, 96, 257
Nyimbo za Injili, xxiii, 78–79, 96, 257
Nyman, Fred and Jan Erik, 92

Ominde, Walter, 193
Omondi, Washington, 187
orthography, xvii, 43, 183, 261
Osogo, John, 4, 38, 250, 251
Otieno, Sam, 154, 193
Ovwali, 21, 247
Oyer, Mary, xiii, 230

Pan-African, 3, 5, 93
patrilineal, 5, 9, 15, 62, 206, 250
Pentecostals, *see* denominations; Pentecostalism, 39, 46
performance practice, 47, 76, 77, 83, 102, 103–107, 165, 178–179, 192, 200, 229
pitch, 16, 56, 83, 103–105, 107–108, 111, 116, 129, 142, 147, 149, 155, 165, 176, 204, 245, 247, 248
"praying in the spirit," 84
process, 1–3, 5, 7, 8, 10, 12, 14, 16, 38, 191, 214, 228; incarnational, 1, 10
procession, 35, 48, 53–54, 55, 57, 67–69, 76, 83, 93, 102, 108, 110, 142, 143, 150, 172, 178, 180, 244, 248, 255, 256. *See also* gwalide
proselytize, 8, 39, 46, 53, 98, 153
public confession, 49, 154

Quakers. *See* denominations

Rasmussen, Ane Marie Bak, 39–40, 46, 64, 250, 253
readers, 42–43, 71, 235, 254
Rees, Deborah, xiv, 31, 50, 72–73, 233, 237, 254
Rees, Emory, 8, 19, 35–36, 41–44, 71–73, 97–98, 129, 253, 254, 259, 260
refrain, 24, 47, 56, 77, 82, 85–88, 91, 96–97, 103, 106, 113–127, 132, 134, 137–142, 144–145, 158, 165–167, 170, 178, 193–194, 197, 201–202, 211–212, 214, 225, 258, 259, 261; dependent, 87–91; independent, 77, 86–87, 91, 114, 128–134, 147, 155, 258; internal, 125, 158, 176

repertoire, xiii, 2, 4, 7, 11–12, 18, 28, 31, 32, 35, 47, 55, 59, 61, 68, 71–72, 78–79, 86–87, 91–97, 99, 113, 128, 134–135, 139, 147, 149, 153–155, 179, 181, 184–185, 188, 190, 220–221, 225, 226, 227, 229, 231, 233, 261
revival, 40, 46, 77–78, 84, 86–87, 96, 117, 129, 153–154, 170, 257, 258
rhythm, 34, 62, 69, 74, 84, 85, 88–89, 92, 94, 95, 100, 102, 108–112, 114, 121, 123, 133, 137, 141, 143, 147–151, 166, 179, 181, 191, 200, 224, 226, 252, 261, 265; cross rhythm, 86, 94, 102, 114, 118, 123, 141, 143, 146, 148, 150, 170; polyrhythm, 47, 106, 155, 209
Rite(s), xv, xvi, 4, 7, 10, 13, 18, 21–22, 42, 48, 50, 54, 59, 62, 65–66, 73, 83, 128, 135, 163, 241, 244; birth, 16, 23–24, 50, 60, 66; Christianity and rites of passage, 65–70, 139; circumcision (initiation), 7, 18, 22, 23, 24–28, 65, 66, 139, 208, 248, 252; dirge, 33, 142, 244, 252; funeral, 18, 32–35, 62, 68–70, 76, 83, 102, 108, 137, 142, 151, 155, 179, 180, 251; itumbi, 25–26, 31, 245, 248; makumbusho, 69, 247; marriage, 28–32; of passage, 7, 21, 22–35, 155, 163, 209, 228, 251, 269; Vadirichi, 26–27, 248; Vasoomi, 26, 247–248; wedding, 18–19, 23, 28, 31, 59, 62, 65, 67–68, 83, 93–94, 105, 122, 139, 148, 196, 206–207, 221, 226, 245, 252, 263, 265
ritual, 10, 17, 20–21, 22, 23, 24, 31–32, 35, 47, 54, 65, 81, 83, 139, 148, 151, 178, 180, 189, 191, 208, 209, 219, 228, 248, 252, 262, 265

sacrifice, 19–23, 26, 28, 32, 59, 66, 125, 251
Sankey, Ira, 78, 87, 88, 98, 119
Scheel, Iris, 8, 134–135, 258, 261, 276
school, xix, 7–8, 9, 29, 44, 45–47, 55, 61, 63–64, 65, 66, 74, 78, 92, 93, 135, 149, 185, 186, 188, 229, 230, 247, 248, 253, 256, 258, 259
Senoga-Zake, George, 187
Serem, 5
service, 11, 40, 42, 46, 53, 54, 61, 66, 67, 76, 81, 86, 93, 102–103, 114, 116, 121, 122, 129, 139, 140, 142, 156, 190, 205, 210, 231, 253–254, 260; Christmas, 60, 100; Easter, 60; Evangelistic, 108, 129; Holy Com-

munion, 110, 113; New Year's Day, 60; Quaker, 83; Pentecostal, 68, 75; Sunday, 42, 50–52, 72–73
Society of Friends, 40, 52
solfège, 7, 72, 92–93, 108, 209, 230, 258, 260, 264
song: categories, Logooli Christian, 75–78; leader, 18, 51, 53–54, 56–57, 83, 85, 92, 101, 103–109, 111, 116–117, 119, 122, 129, 133, 141, 145–146, 155–158, 162, 165–174, 176–178, 180, 190, 196–200, 202, 210–212, 216, 219, 231, 256, 260, 263; lullaby, 17–18, 65; mock-abuse, 31, 68; play, 7, 17–18, 26, 65; popular, 7, 26, 31, 65, 82, 266; ritual, 26, 31, 191; social, 7, 26, 66; special occasion songs 135–159; story, 7, 17–18; types, 58, 75–78, 83, 91–94, 131, 184, 186; work, 31, 73. *See also* 'book' music; choir; gospel; hymn; 'spirit' songs
spirit possession, 46, 154, 159, 254
'spirit' songs (songs of the spirit), xiv, 2–3, 10, 44, 75–78, 81, 83–84, 86, 93, 95, 153–182, 184, 188, 189, 190, 192, 194, 220, 221, 225, 226, 227, 231, 233, 255, 260; characteristics of, 155–179
spirituals, black/negro, 86, 93–94, 154
Stafford, Kay, 39, 40–41, 61, 250, 254
Stanley, Henry M., 38
story, 5, 7, 50, 58, 63, 65, 92, 161–162, 165, 166–168, 169–170, 176, 184, 214, 235, 263
style, 1, 4, 6, 9–11, 17, 26, 31, 34–35, 39, 44, 47, 50, 53, 55, 64–65, 67, 69–71, 73, 75–78, 81, 83–85, 91–96, 101, 103, 108, 110, 121–122, 124, 128, 132, 134, 137, 141–144, 147, 151–153, 155–156, 161, 165, 171–172, 174, 179, 181, 183–184, 187–188, 191–192, 194, 196–198, 200, 206, 208–210, 215, 218–220, 223, 225–226, 229, 232, 261, 262, 265, 266
Supreme Being, 19–21, 48, 70, 251
syncretic, 6, 208, 216; syncretism, ix, 95, 153–154, 179, 192, 215, 219

Tag, 85, 132–133, 165–167, 170–171, 176, 197, 201–202, 215, 260, 261
tempo, 47, 51, 53, 56, 69, 83–84, 95, 102–106, 108–109, 111, 116, 125, 137, 140–141, 151, 172, 179–180, 187, 190–191, 194, 196, 206, 208, 224, 256, 259, 263
tension, 89, 109–110, 117, 125, 133, 137–138, 143, 150–151, 156, 166, 170, 176, 180, 194, 204, 214, 216, 245, 251
texts, translated, 97–103
timbre, 16, 105, 108, 150, 245, 247
timeline, 51, 123, 147, 155, 179, 181, 196, 231
transcribe, xiii, 11, 217, 230, 252, 261; transcription, xvi, 147, 192, 196, 212, 230, 250, 252, 263, 265
transform, 1, 9, 12, 48, 65, 76, 78, 83, 87, 95, 96, 103, 108, 143, 147, 148, 219, 251; transformation, 12, 17, 36, 40, 112, 116, 183, 188, 230, 264
translation, xvi, 18, 32, 36, 43, 55, 72–73, 75, 76–79, 81, 82, 91, 95, 97, 99, 100, 101, 102, 108, 113, 117, 119, 120, 121, 122, 123, 125, 128, 130, 132, 133, 135, 139, 142, 145, 147, 148, 151, 154, 156, 184, 192, 218, 230, 235–236, 252, 254, 256, 257, 258, 259, 261, 262; free translation, 72–73, 98, 115
Tsikorasi. *See* choir: music; chorus(es); refrain
Tsikwaya, 77, 91. *See also* choir: music; makwaya
Tsinyimbu: tsia avaana, 17, 76, 134, 243; tsie ikwaya, 76–77, 91–93, 183–185 (*see also* Tsikwaya); tsya amakono, 10, 76, 243, 257; tsya Ikitabu, 76–78, 96 (*see also* 'book' music); tsya Roho, 76–77, 84 (*see also* spirit songs). *See also* song
Tsinyimbu tsyo Kwidzominya Nyasaye, 44, 78, 81, 256; *Tsinyimbu Tsya Nyasaye* (TTN), xix, 78, 96
tune, ix, xvi, 33–34, 56, 72, 82–85, 90–91, 96–97, 102, 105, 116, 119, 124–126, 134, 143, 147–148, 155–156, 158, 172, 174, 187–188, 190, 193, 197, 208–210, 217, 219, 230, 236, 259, 262

Uvulogooli, 228–229, 248

Vafurenzi, 46, 248
vamp, 132, 165, 196, 214–215, 245, 260; tag, 85, 132, 153, 165–167, 170–171, 176, 197, 201–202, 214–215, 260–261

INDEX

variation, xvi, 138–139, 151, 168, 175, 193, 196
Vihiga, 41, 253, 255, 274, 278
vocables, 32, 35, 103, 106, 150, 159–160, 215
vushuhuda, 53–54, 60, 86, 116, 248, 256

Wagner, Gunther, 19–21, 23–26, 36, 43, 235, 250, 251, 252, 254, 262, 266, 277
Wambugu, Railton, 187
Wasike, William, 193
Weman, Henry, 262, 264, 278
Western Kenya, xiii, 5, 38, 188, 227–229, 243, 260, 268, 272–273, 277–278
witness, 53, 89, 170–171, 249. *See also* vushuhuda

zimbemba, 163, 218, 248

SONG INDEX
"A tonde," 90
"Avamonyi ni vamonya," 216, 218–219
"Away in a Manger," 100. *See also* "Flow Gently Sweet Afton"

"Baiseke bonsi," 134. *See also* "Oh God Is Good"
"Blessed Assurance," 114–117
"Break Thou the Bread of Life," 99–100

"Cha kutumaini," 144–145, 264. *See also* "The Solid Rock"
"Come to Jesus," 72–73, 129–131

"Elori," 67–68

"Flow Gently Sweet Afton," 100
"For You I Am Praying," 87–88, 91, 98

"Gendi kwilwadze," 197–201, 217, 265
"Great Physician, The," 137–138

"Hark My Soul," 99

"I Am So Glad That Jesus Loves Me," ("I Am So Glad That Our Father in Heaven"), 145–147

"Ingata yange ufwale," 175–176
"Isudzi yamila Jonah," 169–170

"Joswa na Kerebu," 89–91

"Kidaho kyo mwigulu," 176–178, 210, 226, 265
"Kivala kyo mwigulu," 209–214. *See also* "Kidaho kyo mwigulu"
"Kwinye kugende ni kwilwadza," 205–206, 208–209. *See also* "Lisuvila liali lya Saolo"
"Kwinye kwahebwa musalaba," 209–211. *See also* "Musalaba"

"Lelo kunyoye idimbidi," 30–31
"Lisuvila liali lya Saolo," 205–208
"Lobai," 201–205, 208, 265. *See also* "Valimu vayuda"
"Lord's Our Rock, The" ("A Shelter in The Time of Storms"), 119–120
"Lufweye kulanga," 33
"'Luya 'Leluya," 171–172
"Lwa avayi vali ni valinda," 126–127
"Lwa inze ndola," 113–114. *See also* "When I Survey"
"Lwa ndasava," 170–171
"Lwa somanga mu Lilaga Lihya," 192–195
"Lwa Yesu yivulwa," 162–163

"Malo malo," 173–174
"Mbe no vugasu," 115–117. *See also* "Blessed Assurance"
"Mbumbelee," 24
"Mihiga tsimilioni javita," 81–82
"Miriamu vakhubanga vukhana," 174
"Mu miganda yimu," 163–164; "Mubende yimu," 201–202, 265. *See also* "Valimu vayuda"
"Mu mugera gwo liluva," 127–128
"Muhonyi niye ulwanda," 120–123. *See also* "The Lord's Our Rock"
"Mukonyi ali himbi," 138–139. *See also* "The Great Physician"
"Mungu yu mwema," 132–133. *See also* "Oh God Is Good"
"Musalaba," 209–216, 218

"Mwana wa Nyasaye," 119. *See also* "Nothing but the Blood"
"Mwigulu buyanzi," 156–157
"Mwigulu wa Yesu," 85–86
"Mwilwadze kuli Petero," 33–34

"Nandio Kwalange," 26, 28
"Ndali mulogi muno," 197, 200–201. *See also* "Gendi Kwilwadze"
"Ndolo," 17
"Ngiri ngongo," 159–161
"Ni isiguku," 58–59
"Ni lidiku lyo buyanzi," 109–110, 140–141, 148. *See also* "Oh Happy Day"
"Ni ngusaalilanga," 88–91
"Nnamtafuta Yesu," 160–161
"No musalaba gogenda," 216–218
"Nohenza mu moni," 216–217. *See also* "No musalaba gogenda"; "Yesu yananga ni ngoni"
"Nothing but the Blood," 118–119
"Nyanzire po," 146–147. *See also* "I Am So Glad That Jesus Loves Me"
"Nyasaye no mulahi," 131–132. *See also* "Oh God Is Good"
"Nyasaye ulinde mwoyo," 174–175
"Nzitsanga ha maveere," 127–128

"O Musalaba," 209–210, 214–216. *See also* "Musalaba"
"O Yesu nku yanza," 118. *See also* "Oh How I Love Jesus"
"Oh God Is Good" ("God Is so good"), 131–134
"Oh Happy Day," 68, 109–110, 139–142, 148, 261
"Oh How I Love Jesus," 117–118

"Precious Promise," 97–98. *See also* "Yesu a va suuviridza"

"Rock of Ages," 101–102, 235

"Saala lisala shi," 172–173
"Seeking for Me," 122–123, 125
"Si gali masahi," 124–126, 262
"Si walinda ndeya," 28–29
"Sisi wa Goibei," 56
"Sodoma kivala chia tenga," 166–168
"Solid Rock, The," 142–145

"Ulivolela sina Yesu," 225–226, 278. *See also* "What Will You Do With Jesus?"

"Vahaga valalila," 158–159
"Valimu vayuda," 163–164, 201–203, 208

"What Will You Do With Jesus?," 225–226
"When I Survey," 113–114

"Yakhudzera voni vosi," 142–143. *See also* "The Solid Rock"
"Yali ku mulinga," 100–101. *See also* "Away in a Manger"
"Yesu a va suuviridza," 98
"Yesu akulanga," 130–131, 236. *See also* "Come to Jesus"
"Yesu uveye lwanda," 101–102. *See also* "Rock of Ages"
"Yesu yananga ni ngoni," 168–169
"Yesu yenyanga inze," 122–123. *See also* "Seeking for Me"
"Yesu yivulwa ndi," 99. *See also* "Break Thou the Bread of Life"

JEAN NGOYA KIDULA is Associate Professor of Music with an emphasis on Ethnomusicology at the Hugh Hodgson School of Music, University of Georgia. She is co-author of *Music in the Life of the African Church*.

www.ingramcontent.com/pod-product-compliance
Lightning Source LLC
Chambersburg PA
CBHW070753230426
43665CB00017B/2337